BARE FEET

AND

BANDOLIERS

BARE FEET
AND
BANDOLIERS

WINGATE, SANDFORD, THE PATRIOTS
AND THE PART THEY PLAYED
IN THE LIBERATION OF ETHIOPIA

by
DAVID SHIRREFF

Pen & Sword
MILITARY

First published by The Radcliffe Press in 1995

Republished in this format in 2009 by
Pen & Sword Military
An imprint of
Pen & Sword Books Ltd
47 Church Street
Barnsley
South Yorkshire
S70 2AS

ISBN 978 184884 029 4

A CIP catalogue record for this book is
available from the British Library

Printed and bound in England
By CPI

Pen & Sword Books Ltd incorporates the Imprints of Pen & Sword Aviation,
Pen & Sword Family History, Pen & Sword Maritime, Pen & Sword Military,
Wharncliffe Local History,
Pen & Sword Select, Pen & Sword Military Classics, Leo Cooper,
Remember When, Seaforth Publishing and Frontline Publishing

For a complete list of Pen & Sword titles please contact
PEN & SWORD BOOKS LIMITED
47 Church Street, Barnsley, South Yorkshire, S70 2AS, England
E-mail: enquiries@pen-and-sword.co.uk
Website: www.pen-and-sword.co.uk

TO THE ASKARI, THE AFRICAN SOLDIER
— UNDER WHICHEVER FLAG HE SERVED —
WHOSE LOYALTY, COURAGE AND CHEERFULNESS REMAIN
A HEARTENING MEMORY

The story of the Ethiopian Patriots, of Mission 101 and Gideon Force who fought with them against the Italians, and of the return of the Emperor Haile Selassie to the throne of Ethiopia in the 1941 Ethiopian campaign. The story of a wrong righted.

Until Ethiopia was liberated the major wrong which brought in its train the present war had not been righted and success for our arms could not be expected.

Colonel O. C. Wingate DSO
Toast to HIM Haile Selassie I
Debra Markos, 19 April 1941

Contents

Maps and Sketches

Photographs

Acronyms and Abbreviations

ADC	Assistant District Commissioner, Aide-de-Camp
AOI	*Africa Orientale Italiana* (Italian East Africa)
C-in-C	Commander-in-Chief
CB	Companion of the Order of the Bath
CBE	Commander of the Order of the British Empire
CCNN	*Camicie Nere* (blackshirt militia)
CCRR	*Carabinieri Reali* (military police) (native ranks were *Zaptie*)
CIGS	Chief of the Imperial General Staff
CO	Commanding Officer
CQMS	Company Quartermaster Sergeant
CRA	Commander of the Royal Artillery. Officer commanding royal artillery units in a division
CSM	Company Sergeant Major
DAA&QMG	Deputy Assistant Adjutant and Quartermaster General (officer dealing with supply and administration)
DC	District Commissioner
DCM	Distinguished Conduct Medal
DO	District Officer
DSO	Distinguished Service Order
GCMG	Knight Grand Cross of the Order of St Michael and St George
GHQ	General Headquarters
GOC	General Officer Commanding
GSO1	General Staff Officer Grade 1

GSO2	General Staff Officer Grade 2
HIM	His Imperial Majesty (Haile Selassie)
HMG	His Majesty's Government
HQ	Headquarters
KAR	King's African Rifles
KCB	Knight Commander of the Order of the Bath
KCVO	Knight Commander of the Royal Victorian Order
LMG	light machine gun
LRDG	Long Range Desert Group
MBE	Member of the Order of the British Empire
MC	Military Cross
MG	machine gun
MM	Military Medal
NCO	Non-Commissioned Officer
OBE	Officer of the Order of the British Empire
OC	Officer Commanding
OETA	Occupied Enemy Territories Administration
RMC	Royal Military College
SDF	Sudan Defence Force
SOE	Special Operations Executive
TD	Territorial Decoration
UNUCI	Unione Nazionale Ufficiali in Congedo d'Italia (Italian discharged officers' association)
VC	Victoria Cross
VM	*Valor Militare*
WO	War Office, Warrant Officer

Glossary of Terms and Titles

Ethiopian Military and Other Titles

abuna	archbishop
ato	mister, esquire
azaz or *azaj*	commander
balabat	landowner, lord of the manor
balambaras	commander of the fort
banda	irregular units
bitwoded	counsellor
dejasmatch	commander of the threshold
echege	patriarch of the Coptic Church
fitaurari	commander of the advanced guard
gerazmatch	commander of the left wing
imperial fitaurari	chief of staff in emperor's army
kenyasmatch	commander of the right wing
lij	nobleman's son ('the Honourable')
negus	king
negus negusti	king of kings, emperor, also known as *janhoi*
ras	commander of an army
shalaka	major
shambul	captain

Egyptian/Sudanese Ranks (adopted from the old Turkish ranks)

ansar or *askari*	soldier (KAR soldiers were also *askari* and Italian colonial soldiers *ascari*)
bash shawish	warrant officer C1 II (sergeant major)
bey	courtesy title of colonels and seconds-in-command

bimbashi	major or company officer (British)
effendi	courtesy title of Sudanese officers
kaid	general officer commanding Sudan
kaimaquan	second-in-command of regiment
lewa	chief of staff (Sudan)
miralai	colonel commanding regiment
mulazim	lieutenant
mulazim tani	second lieutenant
onbashi or *ombashi*	corporal
pasha	courtesy title of brigadiers and above
shawish	sergeant
sirdar	commander-in-chief (Egypt)
sol hakindar	warrant officer C1 I
yuzbashi	captain (Sudanese)

Italian Ranks

Ranks of Italian officers and non-commissioned officers (*sottufficiali*) in the regular and colonial army similar to the British army, see below, with the following additions:

maresciallo	warrant officer
brigadiere	sergeant in the *carabinieri* (military police)

In the colonial army the only ranks open to non-Italians after Mussolini introduced the colour bar in 1938 were the following former Turkish ranks:

bulucbasci	equivalent to sergeant, commanded a *buluc* of 25–28 men
graduati	(sing. *graduato*) see *muntaz*
muntaz	equivalent to corporal. Known generally as *graduati*
sciumbasci	equivalent to warrant officer

Officer ranks in the blackshirt militia (CCNN) were:

capitano	captain
capo manipolo	lieutenant

centurione	captain
colonello	colonel
console	colonel
console generale	brigadier
maggiore	major
primo seniore	lieutenant colonel
seniore	major
sergente	sergeant
sergente maggiore	sergeant major
sotto capo manipolo	second lieutenant
sotto tenente	second lieutenant
tenente	lieutenant
tenente colonello	lieutenant colonel

Civilian administrative ranks, often held by soldiers, were:

commissario	provincial commissioner or governor
residente	district commissioner

Italian Decorations and Awards

Crocia al VM
Medaglia d'Argento al VM
Medaglia d'Oro al VM (highest award, equivalent to the VC)
Medaglia di Bronzo al VM

Size of Units

Readers unfamiliar with military terminology may wish to know the size of units. In the British and colonial army a *battalion*, commanded by a lieutenant colonel was 800–1000 men, and consisted of four *rifle companies*, commanded by a major or captain and a headquarters company, the rifle companies each about 120 men with (in 1941) four *platoons* of about 30, commanded by a subaltern or sergeant divided into three sections of six to eight men under a corporal or lance corporal. A *brigade*, commanded by a brigadier usually consisted of three battalions with artillery and engineers (3000 to 5000 men) and a *division* under a major general of three brigades (15,000 to 18,000 men).

Italian units were similar except that the companies were larger

(240–250 men), as were the SDF companies, and brigades often had four battalions and were commanded by colonels.

Banda (plural *Bande*) was an Italian irregular colonial unit.

Italian colonial battalions and brigades were numbered in Roman numerals but for the convenience of English readers Arabic numerals have been used.

Other Terms

amba	flat-topped mountain
Amhara	ruling ethnic group under the Empire
Amharic/Amharinya	language of the Amhara, derives from Ge'ez
awaj	decree
Dergue	ruling committee under the dictator Mengistu in revolutionary Ethiopia
emma (Arabic)	turban
Galla	now known as *Oromo*, the largest ethnic group, subjected to the *Amhara* in imperial times, mainly Muslim, speaking *Gallinya* or *Oromo*
Ge'ez	classical language of *Axum*, from which *Amharic*, *Tigrinya* and *Tigray* derive
Ghibbi	Imperial Palace
Habash	Abyssinian. Term used for Ethiopians by their Arab and African neighbours. Origin obscure
hamla (Arabic)	caravan. *Shid* is a march
injera	unleavened bread, the staple Ethiopian food, eaten with *wat*. Made of *tef* flour
Janhoi	Emperor
Kantiba	Mayor
khor or *wadi*	river bed
Maskal	feast of the finding of the true cross, celebrated at the end of September
sangar	stone breastwork
shamma	light Ethiopian robe, worn by both sexes
shifta or *fannu*	bandit
tef	small millet-like grain from which *injera* is made. *Tef* hay is used for bedding

tej	fermented honey-wine, mead, the national drink
Tigray	language of the Coptic people of the Eritrean Highlands
Tigrinya	language of the people of Tigre
tukul	hut
wat	spiced meat stew, eaten with *injera*

Acknowledgements

Publication of this history has only been possible because of the generosity of my correspondents who have not only provided documents and oral recollections, but in many cases money. To all these I am deeply grateful. Because of the richness of the material, and my inexperience, the original draft was over twice as long as the present book and to make this viable for publication a great deal has had to be sacrificed. I hope those whose contributions are affected will forgive me. There are many whom I must thank personally.

I wish to thank Veronica Pawluk for the Tutton papers and photographs, particularly for her brother Michael Tutton's diary which started off this work; to acknowledge the great help given by the late Brigadier Maurice Lush and members of the Sandford family (Philippa Langdon and Eleanor Casbon in England and Stephen and Pippa Sandford in Addis Ababa) for access to the Sandford papers; to thank Brigadier Michael Biggs for the Gondar papers, Mervyn Bell for his Sudan papers, Maurice De Bunsen and Bridget Buxton for the De Bunsen papers, Diana Spencer for the translations of Kabada Tesemma's book, Lawrence Keen for his photographic expertise, the Reverend Paul Kelly for the use of his Africana library, David Rooney for allowing me to read the draft of his chapter on Wingate in Ethiopia in his new biography, Julian Lush for his father's photographs, Major General John Stanyer for explaining Fuse 101, the secretaries of regimental and ex-service associations in Great Britain, Australia and New Zealand and the many correspondents listed in the bibliography who have helped with information. I have had great help from the directors and staff of the Public Record Office, the Imperial War Museum, the National Army Museum, the keeper of the Sudan Archives at Durham University, the keeper of the KAR records at Rhodes House, Oxford, and the staff of the British Library.

For access to Italian records I wish to thank Colonel Ficuciello, then military attaché at the Italian Embassy in London, General Spadea, editor of UNUCI, General Bertinaria and the staff of the Ufficio Storico in Rome, Professoressa Rita Dinale for the papers of her father Captain Silvi, Dr Vanni Maraventano for documents and photographs of his father General Maraventano, Professor Luigi Goglia, General Bastiani, General Braca, General Gonella-Pacchiotti, Gastone Rossini, and Salvatore Raho for photographs and documents, and the Italian correspondents listed in the bibliography among them several surviving officers of the Maraventano column for whose hospitality and interest at their reunion at Pesaro in 1989 my wife and I are deeply grateful. For the Italian language I must also thank Alice Eastaugh, Vanessa Nicholson and Father Olindo Cramaro for their help and instruction.

For my visits to Ethiopia I owe special thanks to Ian and Antonia McPherson who put me in touch with their friends the Walkers, and an enormous debt to Sir Harold Walker, then ambassador, and his wife Jane, not only for their hospitality in 1989, but also for introducing me to many interesting people, to Stephen and Pippa Sandford for organizing transport and efficient escorts, Getachew and Ayana Bire, for a safari to Gojjam and for their hositality in 1991, to Kegnasmatch Ibbsa Beri, chairman of the Patriots Association, who introduced me to the old soldiers listed in the bibliography, to Professor Richard Pankhurst, Dr Taddese Beyene and Professor Taddese Tamrat of the Institute for Ethiopian Studies, and Bruce Nightingale of the British Council.

I am deeply grateful to Gordon Lee who read and advised on the original rather muddled draft and to whom the credit is due for whatever merit there is in the present version, to Luigi Goglia for his most helpful comments, for correcting my Italian errors, and for going to a lot of trouble trying to find a publisher in Italy, to my agents Mike Shaw and then John Welch for their help and encouragement and much hard work in the search for a publisher in England. I would like to thank that publisher, Lester Crook, and Selina Cohen for their help and advice and Professor Christopher Clapham for his helpful comments and for writing the Foreword. My grateful thanks also to the ladies who helped with the typing, Anne Pickard, Christine Vernetti, June Attwood and Marion Elvin, to the Tuck Shop at Walberswick and Jarrolds of Lowestoft for office services, and finally I owe a great debt to my wife, Dione, my son Richard for his help over military matters, and all my family for the love and support they have given me for years over the 'bally book'.

David Shirreff
Walberswick 1995

General Foreword
to the Series

Anthony Kirk-Greene MBE
Emeritus Fellow of St Antony's College, Oxford University, and
formerly of the Colonial Administrative Service, Nigeria

A whole generation has passed, nearer two in the case of the Asian sub-continent, since Britain's colonial territories in South-East Asia, Africa and the Caribbean achieved independence. In the Pacific the transfer of power came about a decade later. There was little interest in recording the official or the personal experience of empire either in the inter-war years — viewed by some, often among those personally involved, as the apogee of the British Empire — or in the immediate aftermath of empire. And in this latter period attitudes were largely critical, largely condemnatory and even positively hostile. This is not surprising: such a reaction is usual at the end of a remarkable period of history.

With the passing of time and with longer historical perspective it was possible to see events in a better and more objective light and the trend was gradually reversed. In due course there came about a more sympathetic interest in the colonial period, both in Britain and in the countries of the former empire, among those who were intrigued to know how colonial government operated — in local, everyday practice, as well as at the policy level of the Colonial

Office and Government House. Furthermore, those who had themselves been an integral part of the process wanted to record the experience before, in the nature of things, it was too late. Here was a potentially rich vein of knowledge and personal experience for specialist academic historians as well as the general reader.

Leaving aside the extensive academic analysis of the end of empire, the revival of interest in the colonial period in this country may be said to have been stimulated by creative literature. In the late 1960s there were novels, films and radio and TV programmes, now and again tinged with a touch of nineteenth-century romance and with just a whiff of nostalgia to soften the sharp realism of the colonial encounter. The focus was primarily on India and the post-1947 imagery of the 'Raj': there were outstanding novels by Paul Scott — surely destined to be one of the greatest twentieth-century novelists — J. G. Farrell and John Masters; epic films like *A Passage to India* and *Gandhi*, the charming and moving vignette of *Staying On*, and, for Africa, *Out of Africa* and *Mister Johnson*.

In the second half of the 1970s there emerged a highly successful genre of collective 'colonial' memoirs in the *Tales of...* format: Charles Allen's splendid trilogy *Plain Tales from the Raj* (1975), *Tales from the Dark Continent* (1979) and *Tales from the South China Seas* (1983), followed by others like *Tales of Paradise: Memories of the British in the South Pacific* (1986), all good history and good reading.

Throughout the period from India's independence until that of the last crown colony there had, of course, been those splendid works which combined both academic history and creative literature: for example, Philip Woodruff's *Men who Ruled India: The Founders* (1953) and *The Guardians* (1954); and Jan Morris's *Heaven's Command*, *Pax Britannica* and *Farewell the Trumpets* (1973–8).

Finally, as the 1970s gave way to the 1980s, those voices which had remained largely silent since the end of empire now wanted to be heard. The one-time colonial officials, be they district officers, agriculturists, veterinary, medical or forestry officers, policemen or magistrates, and just as often their wives, began to write about their experiences. They wrote with relish and enthusiasm, with a touch of adventure and few personal regrets. There was a common feeling of a practical and useful task well done, although some thought that more could have been achieved had independence come about more slowly.

These memoirs often began as little more than a private record for the family, children and grandchildren, some of whom had never seen a colonial governor in full fig, shaken hands with an emir or paramount chief, discussed plans with a peasant or local politician, or known at first hand the difference between an *askari* and an *alkali*, an *amah* and an *ayah*. By 1990, the colonial memoir had begun to establish itself as a literary genre in its own right.

The initiative of the Radcliffe Press in harnessing and promoting this talent, primarily autobiographical but also biographical, promises to be a positive addition to both the historical and the literary scenes. Here are voices from the last Colonial Service generation, relating from personal experience the lives and careers involved in the exercise of latter-day empire. They were part of what was arguably the most influential and far-reaching international event of the second half of the twentieth century, namely the end of empire and the consequent emergence of the independent nations of the Third World. It could also perhaps be argued that this is part of an even greater process — de-colonization 'writ large', a sea-change in world affairs affecting greater and lesser powers into the late twentieth century.

It may well be that by 2066, the centenary of the closing down of the Colonial Office, great-great-grandchildren will find the most telling image of Britain's third and final empire in these authentic memoirs and biographical studies, rather than in the weightier imperial archives at the Public Record Office at Kew or in Rhodes House Library, Oxford.

Foreword

The campaign that started in the Gojjam region of Ethiopia in the second half of 1940, and culminated a year later in the surrender of the last Italian forces in Ethiopia at Gondar, has gained a legendary status both in Ethiopia and in Britain. For Ethiopians, it played a key role in the liberation of their country from Italian occupation; during Haile Selassie's reign, the role of the emperor received the greatest attention, and helped to erase the shame of his defeat and flight in 1936; but even when the reputation of that great and remarkable man was at its lowest, after the revolution that overthrew him in 1974, the Gojjam campaign still showed the importance of the Patriot or Ethiopian resistance forces, and enabled Ethiopians justifiably to feel that they were liberated, not merely by foreign arms, but by the courage of their own people. For the British, it launched the extraordinary career of the brilliant, inspiring and sometimes quite insufferable soldier, Orde Wingate, that was to lead to fame and eventual death in Burma. For that reason alone, it merits more than a footnote in the history of guerrilla warfare. Two other participants, the Englishman Wilfred Thesiger and the South African Laurens van der Post, were later to inspire many people with their love of the wild places of Africa and the Middle East. This was unconventional war, fought by unconventional men.

Though the outlines of the campaign are familiar from many works, written from both British and Ethiopian viewpoints, none approach the care and detail with which David Shirreff has examined its military features. Drawing on a mass of unpublished material, including original diaries never previously used, and on interviews with surviving British, Ethiopian and Italian participants, he sheds a fresh light on the campaign and retrieves much valuable information that would otherwise have been lost. Writing largely from an Anglo-Ethiopian viewpoint, he nonetheless recognizes the skill and courage of their Italian opponents who, because they were defeated, have never received the recognition that was their due. And while most accounts close with Haile Selassie's entry into Addis Ababa in May 1941, David Shirreff rightly reminds us how much more fighting remained before the end of the campaign more than six months later. It is good to see proper recognition given to the role of that devoted servant of Ethiopia, Daniel Sandford.

On a personal note, my wife's uncle, Michael Tutton, fought through the campaign with the second Ethiopian battalion, and died in the final fighting at Gondar. I would have liked to have known him.

Christopher Clapham
Lancaster University
December 1994

Introduction

This book tells the story of three men who served Ethiopia[1] in different ways and had an influence on Ethiopian history, the Emperor Haile Selassie I, whose country had been conquered by the Italians in 1936 and who returned in 1941 with British help, and two Englishmen, Orde Wingate and Daniel Sandford, who both played considerable parts in that return, and also of the Ethiopian Patriots who had kept the flame of revolt burning.

In 1940 the patriotic revolt was encouraged by a British military mission, Mission 101, led by Brigadier Daniel Sandford DSO Royal Artillery, which entered the Gojjam province of Ethiopia from the Sudan shortly after Italy declared war, and the contribution made by the Patriots to the defeat of the Italians in the 1941 campaign was considerable.

In 1941 British and Commonwealth forces from the Sudan and Kenya advanced into Italian East Africa and defeated the main Italian armies. At the same time the emperor also entered from the Sudan with a small force, Gideon Force, under Colonel Orde Wingate DSO Royal Artillery, which accompanied him to Addis Ababa.

The part played by Mission 101 and Gideon Force was small in relation to the campaign as a whole, but significant both politically and militarily. Its political significance was that the emperor was seen to accompany and command forces which contributed to the defeat of the Italians and this helped to establish his authority. The military achievement was that Wingate, 'that odd creature' (Wavell's description), later one of the most successful unconventional commanders of the Second World War, although not achieving all that has been claimed for him, by his bold and effective command of his small force eventually forced the surrender of a considerable part of the Italian forces in Gojjam. He was able to operate freely because of the rebellion being sustained by the patriot chiefs, armed and encouraged by Mission 101, which confined the Italian garrisons largely to the roads and forts.

Of these three men Wingate's name is today the most honoured in Ethiopia; Sandford, for reasons which will appear in the narrative, is not remembered with the respect and affection his record merits, but it is hoped that the evidence in this book will restore him to the distinguished place he deserves in Ethiopia's history. Haile Selassie, the ageing emperor deposed in 1974 by the Marxist dictator Mengistu, was only referred to during the rule of Mengistu as the last representative of an outdated oppressive regime. Now that Mengistu has departed there is an opportunity for Ethiopians to realize that Haile Selassie's long and on the whole (to Ethiopia) beneficial career is a part of Ethiopia's history that cannot be ignored.

The campaign was against the Italians, portrayed by British propaganda at the time as both cowardly and incompetent. This was both untrue and unfair to the British and Commonwealth troops and Patriots who had to fight them. Many examples will be found in this story of the gallantry of Italian troops, both national and colonial. The contest between two traditionally friendly nations was gentlemanly, so far as operations permitted, and there are few villains, perhaps only one, and he a fairly engaging one, Ras Hailu, the renegade Prince of Gojjam.

Before embarking on the story, a brief account will be given of Ethiopian history, the Italian war and Ethiopian resistance since then.

Note
1. Ethiopia — always Ethiopia to the Ethiopians, generally known as Abyssinia to the Western world in 1941.

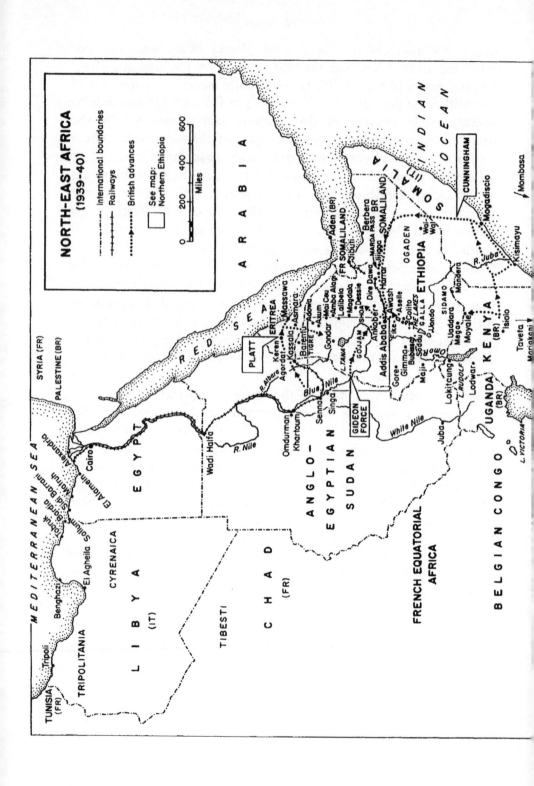

NORTH-EAST AFRICA
(1939–40)

International boundaries
Railways
British advances

See map:
Northern Ethiopia

Miles
0   200   400   600

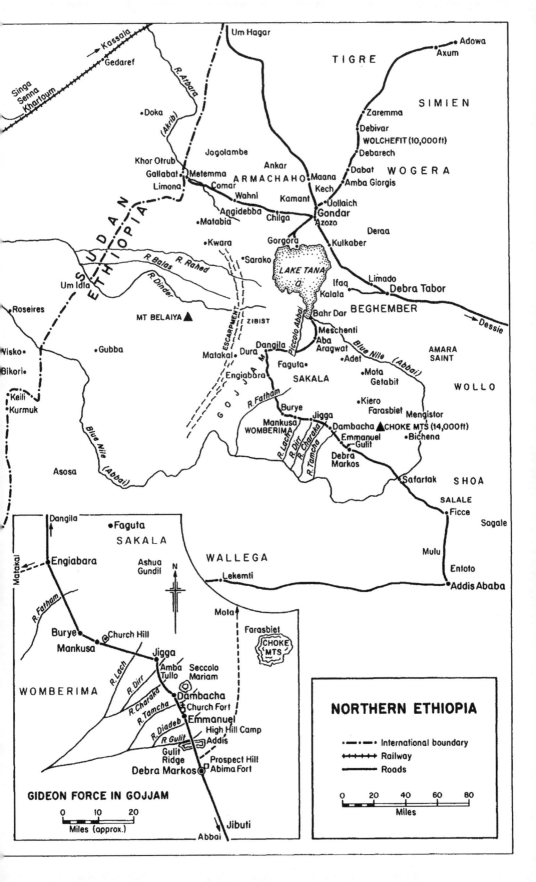

NORTHERN ETHIOPIA

- · — · · — International boundary
- ++++++ Railway
- —————— Roads

0   20   40   60   80
Miles

GIDEON FORCE IN GOJJAM

0   10   20
Miles (approx.)

1

Historical Background*

T here is a continuous history of a Coptic Christian Kingdom of Ethiopia stretching back to AD 300 at the time of the Kingdom of Axum, and linking up with the Greek Orthodox Church of the Byzantine Empire. From the seventh century, the rise of Islam cut Ethiopia off from the outside world, but the kingdom survived, with difficulty and in increasing isolation. In the fourteenth century there emerged the Solomonian legend whereby the royal line of Ethiopian kings claimed descent from the union between King Solomon and the Queen of Sheba, a legend of great importance so long as the empire survived. During the nineteenth century there were three rulers of importance in Ethiopia, the Emperors Theodore or Tewodros (1855–67), Johannes or John (1871–89), and Menelik II (1889–1913). Theodore enlarged his empire by conquest and died by his own hand after being defeated at Magdala by a British expedition under General Napier, sent to release the British consul and some Swiss-German missionaries whom Theodore had imprisoned. His successor, Johannes, the first Tigrean Emperor, died in battle at Gallabat in 1889 against an invading Dervish army of the khalifa (successor to the Mahdi) who ruled the neighbouring Sudan from 1885 (the death of Gordon) to 1898 when he was defeated by an Anglo-Egyptian army under General Kitchener at the battle of Omdurman.

Menelik II, greatest of the three and of the royal line, succeeded when Negus of Shoa, built his new capital at Addis Ababa (the

---

* See General Maps 1 and 2.

'New Flower'), and extended the rule of the Christian Amhara of Shoa over the whole of what is now Ethiopia. During his reign there was no conflict with the Sudan, after 1898 under Anglo-Egyptian administration, though there was suspicion of British colonial motives, and the Russian envoy at Menelik's court reported with alarm to St Petersburg an alleged plan by the British to extend the railway from Khartoum to Mombasa through the Ogaden. There was conflict with Italy, which had established a colony in Eritrea in 1882. This led to war, culminating in the battle of Adowa in 1896, which put an end to Italian expansion. Here an Italian force of 16,000 Italian and Eritrean troops was defeated by Menelik's armies. The defeat was no disgrace since the Italians were greatly outnumbered and fought bravely, but it was a total defeat and the Italians never forgot it. It was to avenge Adowa (among other motives) that Mussolini went to war against Ethiopia in 1935. In Ethiopia today Tewodros and Menelik are the two great historical heroes because both resisted imperialistic aggression.

Menelik was succeeded by his grandson, Lij Yasu, son of his elder daughter and Negus Mikael of Wollo, who was never crowned and was deposed in 1916 because he showed leanings towards Islam and flirted with Ethiopia's Muslim enemies. This was unacceptable to the Shoan nobles and to the ministers of the Allied powers, then engaged in the Great War against Germany and Turkey. Menelik's other daughter, Zauditu, was appointed empress, and Dejasmatch Tafari Makonnen became crown prince and regent with the rank of *ras*. Lij Yasu escaped and raised a rebellion with Negus Mikael, and a decisive battle took place at Sagale between Negus Mikael's army and the forces of Shoa under Ras Tafari and his elder cousin Ras Kassa in which the Shoans were victorious. This crucial battle settled the fate of Ethiopia and henceforward Ras Tafari, later the Emperor Haile Selassie I, was the country's effective ruler. During the crisis Tafari's family were sheltered in the British Legation by the minister, the Hon. W. G. Thesiger DSO, whose son, Wilfred, then aged six, later an officer in Mission 101, watched with awe the victory march past. Ras Tafari remained always grateful to the Thesigers, father and son.

Ras Tafari was the son of Ras Makonnen, Menelik's cousin and therefore of the royal line, his best general and governor of Harrar since 1879. Tafari was physically small, not a warrior prince like his father, but nevertheless courageous and a fine horseman. In character he was serious, deeply religious, at times simple to the point of naivety, and very much on his dignity. He had succeeded his father as governor of Harrar in 1910, and after his appointment as regent in 1916 worked hard to bring Ethiopia into the twentieth century, subject to the constraint of having to deal with a very conservative nobility. He introduced many reforms, visited several European countries, including Great Britain, France and Italy, and pressed for recognition of Ethiopia's position in the world, and in particular for membership of the League of Nations, which was achieved in 1923. In 1928 Tafari was crowned *negus*, and in 1930 *negus negusti* or Emperor on the death of Zauditu, taking the title of Haile Selassie I. The next few years are a story of mounting conflict with Italy, not sought by Ethiopia, and Italian complaints of border incidents, culminating in an incident at the Wal-Wal water holes in the Ogaden on 5 December 1934 when heavy fighting broke out between Eritrean troops under Italian command and Ethiopian troops escorting the Anglo-Ethiopian boundary commission. Italy insisted that the incident happened in Italian territory and demanded a grovelling apology with compensation. Ethiopia appealed to the League of Nations, which appointed a Commission for Arbitration. This sat for months and eventually decided that it had no jurisdiction.

Among the Italian accusations against Ethiopia, which they used to justify their interference in Ethiopian affairs, was that of slavery and slave-raiding on the borders, and Haile Selassie turned for help over this to Daniel Sandford, a retired British Army lieutenant colonel, aged 53, who was then farming at Mulu, 35 miles north of Addis Ababa, and who had become a good friend and counsellor over many years. Sandford's previous career, including his very distinguished record in the First World War, is described in the biographical index, but as he is one of the principal characters in this book a short personal description is appropriate. He was a big burly man, balding and bespectacled. CSM Grey thought he looked more like a farmer (which he had been for the last 15 years) than a soldier and all his colleagues and subordinates describe him as a 'very nice man', characterized by great energy, cheerfulness and supreme optimism. The title of his daughter Eleanor's biography of her parents, *The Incurable Optimists*, is particularly apt. From January 1935 Sandford was frequently called in to advise on the growing difficulties with Italy, and in July 1935 he was appointed adviser to the newly appointed governor of Maji in southwest Ethiopia (the province where most of the slave-raiding was alleged to take place) with the double task of countering the Italian propaganda and creating a model province. The fact that he held this office under the Emperor was to cause difficulties with one Ethiopian colleague when Sandford commanded Mission 101 in 1940.

War with Italy

In 1934 Benito Mussolini, *Il Duce*, the dictator who ruled Italy was 51. He had been in power for 13 years and his power was supreme. He wanted to add Ethiopia to the Italian Empire and plans to invade started to be made in 1932 when he sent his Minister of the Colonies, Marshal Emilio De Bono, to Eritrea to report on what needed to be done to prepare the colony as a base for invasion. As a result roads, airfields and water supplies were built, and the eight Eritrean colonial battalions were increased to 30, mostly with Eritreans but a considerable number of Ethiopians also enlisted. The Wal-Wal incident provided Mussolini with an excuse to intensify preparations. In January 1935 De Bono arrived in Eritrea to take command, and from then on troops and military equipment (including 680 tons of mustard gas or Yperite[1]) flooded into Massawa, and also into Mogadiscio for Somalia, where similar preparations were being made. Mussolini promised De Bono ten divisions by the end of September, five Royal and five Blackshirt, in addition to his colonial battalions, and told him to be prepared to take the initiative, 'should the Negus have no intention of attacking us'.

The *negus* had no such intention. Haile Selassie was relying on the covenant of the League to stop the aggressor, as were Daniel Sandford and his wife, Christine, in Addis Ababa, who heard of the Italian preparations with foreboding. In the event neither the League, nor Britain and France, the two major powers, had the

will to stop Mussolini, though Britain alone could have put an end
to the war with ease by closing the Suez Canal, as the Labour
Party would have done had it won the election due in November
1935, according to its deputy leader, Clement Attlee, speaking in
the House of Commons in July 1935. Without declaration of war
Mussolini's armies invaded Ethiopia on 3 October 1935 from two
directions, Marshal De Bono from Eritrea in the north and
Marshal Graziani from Somalia in the south. Sandford had sent his
family to Cairo for safety and himself went to take up his post at
Maji. De Bono's advance was extremely dilatory and Mussolini
acquiesced in this until after the British general election in November. Had Labour won, he could still have pulled back. When the
Conservatives won he instructed De Bono to go ahead and when
he did not move fast enough replaced him with Marshal Badoglio.
Adolf Hitler, chancellor of Germany, learned from Mussolini that
the Western democracies were committed to appeasement, and it is
arguable that the wrongful invasion of Ethiopia 'brought in its
train' the Second World War.

Almost all Ethiopian leaders rallied to Haile Selassie. Only one,
Dejasmatch Haile Selassie Gugsa, son of the Ras Gugsa[2] who had
rebelled against Haile Selassie with Lij Yasu in 1932, defected to
the Italians with 1200 men. Dejasmatch Ayelewu Birru, governor
of Gondar, who commanded 17,000 men including 1000 cavalry,
corresponded with the Italians but never actually defected. He put
up a show of fighting and submitted as soon as Addis Ababa was
taken. Despite their great bravery and several early successes, both
northern and southern Ethiopian armies were defeated. The
Italians had better weapons and complete air superiority. The
decisive and horrific weapon used was mustard gas, which broke
the morale of the bare-legged and thinly-clad Ethiopian soldiers.
Their only protection, as one old soldier, Shalaka Alemaiyu Hailu,
recalls, was to urinate into their handkerchiefs and hold these to
their faces. By the end of March 1936 the Italians from the north
had taken Amba Alagi and reached Mai Ceu. It had taken them
five months to reach this point, illustrating the strength of Ethiopian resistance. Haile Selassie took his Imperial Guard and the
remnants of the northern armies and led them personally against
the entrenched Italian (Eritrean) troops. After a fierce two-day

battle with many casualties on both sides the Ethiopian attack failed and Haile Selassie's generals insisted on withdrawal. The retreating Ethiopians were bombed and gassed by Italian aircraft and attacked by Azebu and Yeju and Yeju Galla tribesmen in Italian pay now coming out openly on the winning side. His army disintegrating, Haile Selassie, who had behaved with great personal bravery, made his way to Addis Ababa, arriving on 30 April, after stopping for two days 'at the holy place of Lalibela' to pray.

At first his intention was to continue the fight himself, but the majority of his Council was against this, preferring the advice of Ras Kassa that the Emperor should go to Europe and appeal to the League of Nations, leaving Ras Imru in the north and Ras Desta in the south to continue the war under Bitwoded Walda Tsadaq as regent at Gore. This was a controversial decision, a gift to Italian propagandists at the time, fiercely disapproved of by some, and held to Haile Selassie's discredit in Ethiopia today. Never before had an Ethiopian Emperor left the country in the face of the enemy. Blatta Tekele, police chief of Addis Ababa, one of three Council members who opposed the decision, presented Haile Selassie with a loaded revolver and invited him to use it as Emperor Theodore had done. Haile Selassie defends his decision in his autobiography, and his actions then, and afterwards, were entirely consistent with his faith in the League of Nations and his belief that they would right the wrong. Unfortunately it took a world war to do this.

Haile Selassie left Addis Ababa on 1 May by train for Jibuti and arrived in England on 30 May, having spent a short time in Palestine, then a British mandated territory, from where he wrote to the secretary general of the League of Nations requesting that the League should honour the covenant. He travelled in a British cruiser as far as Gibraltar (to prevent any Italian kidnap attempts) and then in a civilian liner to show that his arrival was not made under official auspices. No British government representative met him at Victoria station in London, although 'the British public gave us a great welcome', and Anthony Eden, the foreign secretary, called on him at his hotel.

Among those who left Addis Ababa with the Emperor were Ras

Kassa, Lorenzo Taezaz, Birru Wolde Gabriel, the imperial *fitau-rari*, and Azaj Kabada Tesemma, his court chamberlain, with his handcuffed prisoner Ras Hailu, held in 'close confinement' in Addis Ababa since his involvement in the 1932 rebellion. Ras Hailu was sent back from Dire Dawa, probably because the British declined to accept a political prisoner, and soon made his submission to the Italians, as did Ayelewu Birru and the two northern *rases*, Ras Seyum of Tigre, grandson of Emperor Johannes and always a possible rival to a Shoan Emperor, and Ras Getachew. Ras Kassa and Lorenzo accompanied the Emperor to England. Kabada, Birru and a number of other refugees remained in Palestine.

Sandford succeeded in escaping from Maji to Lokitaung in northern Kenya and from there contemplated trying to join Ras Imru in Gore, but when the Foreign Office made it clear that they did not want British nationals involved in the war against the Italians, he made his way to his family in Cairo and from there to England where the family settled in Ewhurst in Surrey.

Still relying on the League of Nations, Haile Selassie travelled to Geneva on 26 June to attend a meeting of the League called to discuss the dispute between Italy and Ethiopia, accompanied by Ras Kassa and Lorenzo. He there spoke (in Amharic) with great feeling and fervour, his speech interrupted initially by catcalls from Italian journalists until they were expelled from the Assembly. He could legitimately ask for help from the League because both the aggression and the resistance to it were continuing. The only answer he got was that on 6 July 1936 the League voted to suspend all sanctions against Italy, and some European countries — Germany, Austria, Hungary, and later Switzerland — recognized the Italian conquest. Great Britain did not do so, but then Ethiopia's fate became embroiled with international politics and the appeasement policy of the British government under their prime minister, Neville Chamberlain. In March 1938 Hitler brought about the Anschluss between Germany and Austria and was already threatening the Czechs. In the hope of removing Mussolini's irritation at Britain's refusal to recognize his conquest and to induce him not to throw in his lot with Hitler, Chamberlain promised to recognize the Italian conquest and to do his best to persuade other League members to do so. In May 1938 at a meeting of the League Council the British foreign secretary, Lord Halifax, undertook to recognize Italy's *de facto* sovereignty over Ethiopia once Italian troops were withdrawn from Spain, where they were supporting General Franco. His predecessor, Anthony Eden, with his deputy, Lord Cranborne, had resigned honourably over this issue in February 1938, refusing to negotiate with Italy while their troops remained in Spain.

Haile Selassie attended the meeting of the Council and made a moving plea against recognition, but nine out of twelve members supported Lord Halifax, and only two spoke against, New Zealand and the Soviet Union. In the succeeding months most countries, including Great Britain, recognized the Italian conquest. Only the USA, the Soviet Union, Mexico, New Zealand and China never did so. Discouraged and depressed, but still believing that ultimately the cause of justice would prevail, Haile Selassie returned to Bath where he was living with his family in a house called Fairfields, keeping regal state but making friends with the local people. He kept in touch with the Sandfords at Ewhurst and also with affairs in Ethiopia by correspondence via Khartoum, receiving and sending many letters in Amharic and hearing about the state of the country from the many chiefs and leaders still loyal to him. He never allowed the issue of his country's independence to die, attending meetings and receptions where, in the words of Christine Sandford, his 'quiet dignity and graciousness won the approval of all', and maintaining a correspondence with the League.

Ethiopian Resistance

The first phase of Ethiopian resistance was simply a continuation of the war. On the occupation of Addis Ababa Marshal Badoglio had been appointed viceroy of Italian East Africa (AOI), but he soon returned to Italy and was replaced by Marshal Graziani. Fighting continued in the west under Ras Imru and the sons of Ras Kassa, in the south under Ras Desta, the Emperor's son-in-law, who had commanded in that sector, and in Ankober under Ras Ababa Aregai. Mussolini's instructions to the viceroy were brutal and clear. Rebels should be shot, gas used to 'finish off the war', and (in a telegram of 8 July 1936) 'Your Excellency is authorized to begin conducting systematically the policy of terror and extermination against the rebels and the accomplice populations. Without the law of tenfold retaliation the wound will not heal quickly enough.' Ras Imru was surrounded and captured in December 1936, exiled to Italy, and not released until the Italian armistice in 1943. He was held on the island of Ponza, and by a quirk of fate Mussolini was imprisoned in the same house after his fall in 1943. Of Ras Kassa's four sons, Dejasmatch Wandwassen was killed and Aberra Kassa and Asfaw Wossen were persuaded to surrender after lengthy correspondence with the Italian commander General Tracchia and a personal assurance from Graziani 'that nothing will happen to you'. Their respective fathers-in-law, Ras Hailu and Ras Seyum, also wrote advising them to surrender. One factor which induced Aberra to consider surrender was that they were still waiting to hear the result of the Emperor's appeal to the League, 'and the League's decision is not arriving as soon as we expected it'. The brothers were taken to Ficce, the main town of their father's fief of Salale, shot in the market square and beheaded. Only the fourth son, Asrate Kassa, survived. General Tracchia and Ras Hailu also wrote to Ababa Aregai inviting him to surrender. Graziani made considerable use of Ras Hailu in trying to persuade rebel chiefs to submit, writing to Mussolini that Ras Hailu was the only chief whom he could trust and without him he was 'paralysed'. Ras Hailu failed with Ababa Aregai, who had more sense than to surrender to be shot, and who never submitted. Starting with only ten followers he built up his army, his resistance being encouraged by his correspondence with the Emperor; 'the letters of His Majesty were hope and nourishment to his people'. When Haile Selassie returned to his capital on 5 May 1941, Ababa Aregai's army of 7000 Patriots lined the streets of Addis Ababa to welcome him.

The last government chief to continue resistance was Ras Desta who in February 1937 was captured and shot. After his death government resistance disintegrated. Then an event occurred which led to the revival of resistance. On 17 February 1937 two Eritreans attempted to assassinate the viceroy, Marshal Graziani, in Addis Ababa with a grenade attack. The marshal was badly wounded and several Italian officers were killed. Savage reprisals followed and in Addis Ababa alone it is believed that between 6000 and 9000 Ethiopian civilians were slaughtered, mainly by Blackshirt militia. Persecution continued during the remainder of the Graziani regime, which lasted another nine months; however, this persecution did not cow the national spirit but rather revived it. Many chiefs who had submitted dug up buried rifles and joined the rebellion, but where resistance revived it was no longer led by government leaders or the nobility, who had been largely liquidated, but was a resistance of the people led by leaders of their choice, in separate pockets and encouraged by correspondence with Haile Selassie in England. From 1937 onwards there are two parallel developments, the continuing resistance and the spread of Italian rule, backed by impressive road development.

During the persecution that followed the attack on Graziani, many Ethiopians left the country, some with their families, and either crossed into French or British Somaliland or into Kenya across the Northern Frontier District (of Kenya). Those who reached Kenya joined the many others who had escaped in 1936 at the refugee camp established for them at Isiolo. In the initial exodus 8000 refugees left Ethiopia and 6000 reached Isiolo, where the Kenya administration built a camp for them (in fact 'round them', as Sir Richard Turnbull, then district officer at Isiolo, describes it). Most were soldiers of Haile Selassie's army and had their arms, including an Oerlikon anti-aircraft gun, which they had managed to carry across the Northern Frontier District and which caused much interest, nothing like it having been seen in Kenya at that time. After the outbreak of war with Italy, the refugees were moved to a camp at Taveta in southern Kenya. From these men were recruited the Ethiopian battalions and irregular units that took part in the 1941 campaign. There was some feeling later between those who stayed to fight and those who left the country, but in the end they were all Patriots, fighting for the same cause.

Who Were the Patriots?

The death of Ras Desta marked the end of Ethiopian government resistance to Italy's war of aggression and, very soon afterwards, Ethiopia's struggle for liberation began. The revolt, however, only affected a limited area of the empire. The three constituent parts of AOI were the old colonies of Eritrea and Somalia (colonized, like Eritrea, in the 1880s) and newly conquered Ethiopia. Despite the attempt on Graziani's life having been made by two disgruntled Eritreans, neither in Eritrea nor in Somalia was there any resistance to Italian rule, under which the populations were quite content. In the Galla areas in the west, southwest and southeast of Ethiopia, conquered by Menelik in the nineteenth century, the replacement of the ruling Amhara governors and soldiery by the Italians was not entirely unwelcome and the Italian administration was extended without much opposition, although there was resistance in some areas, and guerrillas emerged to accompany the Commonwealth forces when they invaded Ethiopia in 1941. The chief resistance was in the mainly Amhara provinces of Gojjam, Beghemder, and Shoa, and to a lesser extent in Gondar and Tigre. In the last two provinces the submission of Dejasmatch Ayelewu Birru and Ras Seyum deprived any resistance movement of its natural leaders.

By tradition every Ethiopian male was a soldier, whether Amhara or Galla, ready to fight at the call of his chief like a Highland clansman. His weapons were shield, spear and sword, but many had rifles also, of varying degrees of efficiency. Menelik's army, which defeated the Italians, included 70,000 riflemen. Haile Selassie's army consisted of his Imperial Guard of about 5000 and his personal troops from Harrar, about 10,000. The rest were the armies of the *rases*, who in time of war owed a duty to produce troops for the *negus negusti*. No Ethiopian army could stay in the field for more than two or three months. They lived off the country and no region could stand the voracious soldiery for too long and, in any event, the men had to go home to cultivate and harvest their crops. Ethiopian titles were all military. Below the *ras* was the *dejasmatch*, and further down the scale the *fitaurari*, the battalion commander, who led the men in fighting.

When resistance started up again in 1937 the men who fought had all been soldiers and they chose their own leaders, who, with a few exceptions, were all men of rank. The men had their own rifles and acquired more, and machine guns, in conflict with the Italians or from deserters from the Italian colonial forces. The Patriots generally fought as guerrillas, ambushing convoys and cutting off stragglers, though by the beginning of 1940, some patriot forces, for example those of Dejasmatch Mangasha in Gojjam, were strong enough to tackle a colonial brigade. We shall look at the position in Gojjam in rather more detail in a later paragraph. Despite the Italian belief that the 'rebels' were encouraged by subversive propaganda from London the Patriots neither received nor expected any outside help save for the letters of encouragement from 'His Majesty'. Their goal was the freedom of their country, the liberation of the Amhara, the 'free people' who had never been conquered, from the Italian yoke. Many swore not to cut their hair until their country was liberated and British officers in the 1941 campaign often commented on the wild-looking, long-haired 'rebels'. They predicted the outbreak of a European war involving Italy and that this would contribute to their country's independence, but did not look beyond this. 'No one planned for Ethiopia's future. They wanted independence and the return of Haile Selassie.'

These then were the Patriots, although not named as such by the outside world until 1940. To the Italians they were *ribelli* or *shifta* and to the British up to 1940 they were the same, rebels or *shifta*. To themselves they were Patriots or *arbenya*, and in 1940 first Sandford and then Wingate insisted that the British should call them Patriots. Before we take the story any further let us look at some principles of guerrilla warfare and the differing views of Sandford and Wingate.

The Principles of Guerrilla Warfare

The term 'guerrilla' or irregular fighter derives from the Spanish word *guerrilla*, a diminutive of *guerra*, war. In the Peninsular War of 1808–14 Spanish guerrillas were of major assistance to Wellington's army, ambushing French convoys and cutting off stragglers, forcing the French to use many troops to protect their lines of communication. Another important use of guerrillas was in the First World War when T. E. Lawrence raised Arab irregulars to fight against the Turks, starting with attacks on Turkish road and rail communications, and finishing with a major sweep by his Arab forces on the right flank of Allenby's advance to Jerusalem and

Damascus. Lawrence had some British machine-gunners and armoured cars, and in his final advance had 300 regular camel corps in support, but he refused the offer of a Franco-British brigade. All he asked for was guns and gold. Regular troops would have diverted attention from the true object of the Arab revolt, which was to secure the freedom of the Arab people, and given the French and the British a greater stake in the postwar settlement. Sadly for Lawrence, his promises to the Arabs were not honoured by the British and French governments. Lawrence refused promotion and honours and died Private Shaw of the Royal Air Force.

Whether there was any family relationship between Lawrence and Orde Wingate is doubtful, but there was certainly an interesting family connection. Lawrence's commander, until he came under Allenby's command, was General Sir Reginald Wingate, *sirdar* of Egypt, and before that the first governor-general of the Sudan after Kitchener. This was Orde Wingate's 'Cousin Rex', his father's first cousin, to whom appeal was often made in Orde Wingate's military career when he came up against obstruction. Initially General Wingate distrusted the Arab revolt, but later saw its value and was helpful to Lawrence. Both Lawrence and Orde Wingate had strong supporters in their commanders-in-chief, Lawrence in Allenby, Orde Wingate in Wavell. In the Ethiopian campaign Wingate got on reasonably with the *kaid*, General Platt, less well with General Cunningham. Inevitably the two unconventional soldiers have been compared. In recommending Wingate to Wavell, L. S. Amery, then Secretary of State for India, described him as 'a much more virile and solidly based Lawrence, but with much the same power of inspiring others'. There was a sadder point of similarity too. Lawrence felt that he had let down the Arabs and refused all honours. Wingate attempted suicide because, as he wrote himself afterwards, he felt that he had let down the Ethiopians. This is arguable and will be looked at later.

In considering the effectiveness of the Ethiopian Patriots some useful comparisons can be made with the Spanish guerrillas and the Arab irregulars. Of relevance also is the fact that Wingate's ideas on how guerrillas should be used differed from those of Lawrence, and of Sandford. The Spanish guerrillas operated best independently of the regular forces. So did the Patriots, and attempts to coordinate their attacks with the regulars were usually unsuccessful, with the proviso that the most effective patriot forces were those which had a hard core of regulars. Both Spanish and patriot guerrillas had their greatest success in disrupting communications, forcing the occupying power to employ many troops on internal security. In the Arab revolt Lawrence's Arab forces also operated independently, but their attacks were coordinated with the regulars as part of the general plan. Allenby, a great man, gave Lawrence what he wanted, relied on his diversion and profited by it with outstanding success. Cunningham, a lesser man, ignored Wingate and got rid of him as soon as he could.

Sandford's policy was to increase the issue of arms to the Patriots, bring forward the Emperor as their leader, and use them to the full in rounding up the Italians in Gojjam. He always envisaged a British task force in support. He never had a chance to implement this policy because Wingate took command and his policy was different. In his dispatch written after the campaign Wingate sets out the right and wrong methods of raising a revolt; 'to raise a real fighting revolt you must send in a *corps d'élite* to do exploits and not pedlars of war material and cash. Given a population favourable to penetration, a thousand resolute and well-armed men can paralyse for an indefinite period the operations of a hundred thousand.' By inference Sandford and Lawrence were pedlars of war material and cash. Wingate's *corps d'élite* was Gideon Force and whether his policy succeeded as he intended we shall see from the narrative which follows.

The Arrival of the Duke of Aosta

In November 1937 Graziani was replaced as viceroy of AOI by Amedeo di Savoia, Duke of Aosta, cousin of the King of Italy, Victor Emmanuel. Fighter pilot and air force general 'the tall young man' was described[3] as having 'an extraordinary quality ... his humanity caused him to be interested in everything and everyone.' He was certainly greatly loved by those serving under him. Aosta instituted a policy of reconciliation instead of repression. Feelers were sent to Haile Selassie in England, suggesting that he should return, which he rejected, and General Guglielmo Nasi, an experienced regular soldier who had commanded the Libyan division in Graziani's advance from Somalia in 1935/6, and was at the time governor of Harrar, was moved to the capital as Aosta's deputy to establish a conciliatory administration. This policy had some effect in reducing the strength of Ethiopian resistance, but this nevertheless continued, particularly in Gojjam. The change in policy, and the extension of Italian administration, led to an improvement in border relations with the British administrations in the Sudan and Kenya, a development which caused the exiled Emperor much concern.

Then Mussolini dealt another blow to rebel movements by persuading Britain and France to sign the Bon-Voisinage Agreement on 16 April 1938 whereby the three countries agreed not to carry out any intelligence activity or support rebel movements in the others' territories. The British Foreign Office, whose main concern was to do nothing to encourage Mussolini to throw in his lot with Hitler, was scrupulous in observing the agreement, as were the governments of the Sudan and Kenya. The result was that apart from border contacts, not much was known of what went on in Ethiopia, nor was any encouragement given to rebel movements save by Haile Selassie's correspondence, three visits to Gojjam by Lorenzo Taezaz, and some activity by the French, who were less scrupulous. The French sent in two agents in 1939 and 1940, Paul Langrois and Paul Monnier, to contact the Patriots, and their visits, together with those of Lorenzo, gave the Patriots much encouragement. The gist of the agents' reports was that Haile Selassie's return in the event of war with Italy would be supported, certainly in Amhara and Shoa, and the revolt would intensify and would immobilize the Italians.

The Gojjam Patriots

The Gojjami people had an undistinguished record in the Italian war, mainly for dynastic reasons. The province was ruled by the Negus Tekle-Haimanot until 1907 and then by his son, Ras Hailu Tekle-Haimanot, until 1932. Ras Hailu kept great, if primitive, state and pursued an almost independent foreign policy of friendliness towards the Italians, inviting an Italian doctor and consul to his capital, Debra Markos, and visiting Rome. This displeased Haile Selassie, and when in 1932 Ras Hailu was implicated in the rebellion of Ras Gugsa and the escape from custody of Lij Yasu, Haile Selassie removed him from the governorship, kept him in close confinement in Addis Ababa, and replaced him with Ras Imru, his cousin and a Shoan. Ras Imru was never accepted by the Gojjami people and when the Italian war broke out and he went off to the northern front with his Shoan troops, a grandson of Negus Tekle-Haimanot, Gassasse Belao, raised a revolt in Gojjam and later handed over the province without a fight to the advancing Italian commander, General Achille Starace. It is said that all Gojjami chiefs then submitted to the Italians, with one exception, Belai Zelleka, who never submitted.

Then in February 1937 came the Graziani assassination attempt, followed by the general revival of resistance, sparked off more particularly in Gojjam by the brutality of the Italian *residente* in Bahr Dar, Captain Corvo. It is reported that this officer summoned a number of chiefs who had formerly supported Ras Imru and who had then submitted, ostensibly in order that they should go to Gondar to make their submission to the governor. He took them out in a boat on Lake Tana and threw them into the lake, their bodies weighted with heavy stones. The Gojjami people rose in revolt and attacked the Italians and invited Dejasmatch Mangasha Jemberie and Dejasmatch Nagash Bezahbu to be their leaders. Both were connected with the ruling Tekle-Haimanot family and both hereditary *balabat*s. Mangasha was Ras Hailu's son-in-law and Nagash his nephew. Mangasha set up his headquarters in Sakala in western Gojjam, and Nagash in central Gojjam near Burye. Further east there were two other leaders of importance, Lij Hailu Belao, a grandson of Negus Tekle-Haimanot, at Mota, and Belai Zelleka at Bichena. Belai Zelleka was a fine fighter when he chose to fight, but 'a nobody, of peasant origin, illiterate and a believer in magic'.[4]

From 1937 onwards these four leaders maintained a continual war against the Italians, but it was maintained in separate pockets with no cooperation with each other. Mangasha squabbled with Nagash, and Hailu Belao and Belai Zelleka hated each other. Although they knew the Italians were the common enemy the Gojjam Patriots never moved out of their own territory to fight them, even to other parts of Gojjam, and the same was largely true of patriot groups in other parts of Ethiopia. Even against such divided opposition the Italians had a hard struggle to pacify Gojjam, but they set about it methodically by the building of an all-weather road from Addis Ababa to the Blue Nile crossing at Safartak and thence to Debra Markos and linked by a series of forts. In a telegram to General Terusci of the Ministero Africa in Rome dated 28 June 1939 General Frusci, commander Northern Sector, reported that in the 400-kilometre stretch between Debra Markos and Bahr Dar he had established garrisons at Bahr Dar, Meschenti, Dangila, Engiabara, Burye, Dambacha, Baremma (Emmanuel) and Debra Markos, that his troop strength was '2 CCNN bns, 8 colonial bns, 3 artillery groups, 6 sections pack artillery, and the workers are all armed and incorporated into military formations'. All these forts will figure in Gideon Force's operations in February/ March 1941 and it is noteworthy that they had only just been established in June 1939.

The road workers were all Italian nationals, armed and trained to shoot, and they built excellent roads and bridges. While the Blackshirt (CCNN) battalions provided the garrisons, the main fighting against the guerrillas was done by the expanded colonial battalions and the *banda* (irregular units), the majority of whose *ascari* were now Ethiopian. The fighting was exceedingly bitter, taking on all the characteristics of a civil war. The Patriots did not distinguish between the colonial battalions and the *banda*; to them anyone in Italian uniform was '*banda*'. The nature of the fighting had one advantage for the Patriots in that they acquired a considerable number of weapons from *ascari* who deserted to them. Others they acquired in battle.

It is evident from Italian colonial unit records and battle honours that fighting against the Gojjam Patriots was continuous between 1937 and 1940. Patriot memories recall two major actions, the first in November 1939 at Idbi near Adip (possibly the modern Adet between Bahr Dar and Mota), where tradition has it that the Patriots severely mauled Colonel Natale's brigade. This action cannot be confirmed from Italian sources. The second is remembered as the battle of the Piccolo Abbai ford and took place on 14 March 1940 and can be identified precisely from Italian records. A column consisting of three colonial battalions (one the 69th) and a cavalry group from Lieutenant Colonel Torelli's 22nd Colonial Brigade, after carrying out the evacuation of the garrison of Faguta, was ambushed at the Piccolo Abbai crossing by Patriots under the command of Mangasha. Fighting was severe and lasted all day. Torelli, not for the first or last time, led a counterattack to recover the dead of the 69th Colonial Battalion and succeeded in forcing his way across the ford with all his vehicles, suffering one officer and 18 *ascari* killed, three officers, including himself, and 35 *ascari* wounded. The Patriots made considerable use of automatic weapons, acquired in previous engagements. In recommending Torelli for the *Medaglia d'Oro al VM* (the highest military award), General Frusci commented that 'the combat was sharp, particularly by the rebels, who presented themselves in a robust formation — a brilliant fight, worthy of the quality of a commander of the calibre of Colonel Torelli.'

This action is significant for a number of reasons. First, it took place in March 1940, after the Second World War started, but before the Italians came in, and although Sandford had since September 1939 been corresponding with rebel leaders, no help had yet reached them. Secondly, Mangasha's men were strong enough to tackle a colonial brigade of about 5000 men, and thirdly it happened in the course of the *withdrawal* of the garrison from Faguta, which was not replaced because it was too isolated and too vulnerable. The Patriots won a considerable local victory here and Sandford was able to use Faguta later as his headquarters. It is clear that the resistance, although in isolated pockets and not coordinated, was certainly not ineffective, and equally that the Italian counter insurgency effort was robust and well led. But humanity did occasionally shine through the conflict. Take this example.

Medical Orderly Spriglio, stationed at Debra Markos, liked to go shooting guinea fowl and francolin, and one day while out with his shotgun alone on foot some distance from Debra Markos he was stopped by an Ethiopian who asked him to go and see a sick man in a nearby village. He found a badly wounded Patriot and treated him. He continued to visit and treat the wounded man secretly from Debra Markos until one day he was warned by Ethiopians that the Fascist police had heard what he was doing

18

and were about to arrest him. He defected to the Patriots and served with the band as their 'doctor' until the British arrived in 1941. After the Emperor's return he set up his practice as a 'doctor' in Debra Markos, married an Ethiopian wife and had numerous children and eventually died there, much lamented.

The Opposing Forces in 1940

On 3 September 1939, as a result of the German invasion of Poland, Great Britain and France declared war on Germany. Britain's declaration was followed very soon by similar declarations by Australia, Canada, New Zealand and South Africa. Italy was then allied to Germany by the Rome-Berlin Axis, but the Italian dictator, Mussolini, did not then enter the war, biding his time. The situation in North and East Africa was then as follows. The garrison of AOI, comprising the three colonial territories of Eritrea, Ethiopia and Somalia, consisted of 280,000 troops, increased to 330,000 on 10 June 1940 by the call up of reserves on the outbreak of war. The forces consisted of 16 National battalions, two armoured-car companies, two squadrons light and medium tanks (all European troops), ten artillery groups (mixed European and colonial), 100 colonial battalions and 23 *banda* groups, eight colonial cavalry groups and two groups pack artillery (colonial). The European infantry were mainly Blackshirt militia, but there were some troops of the Royal Army, notably a regiment of the Savoia Grenadiers. The armoured car and tank crews, the heavy gunners, and the officers and NCOs of the colonial units were all from the Royal Army, regulars or from the reserve.

The 100 colonial battalions had been expanded from the 30 Eritrean battalions that took part in the Italian war by a massive recruitment of Ethiopians, despite Mussolini's promise to the League of Nations that he would not do this. A typical colonial battalion had 12 to 16 Italian officers, a few senior NCOs, Eritrean *graduati* (native NCOs), and Amhara or Tigrean *ascari*. Even the famous 'Eritrean Brigade' of General Lorenzini which fought at Keren had a large admixture of Amhara.

The 23 *banda* groups were either *bande regolari*, officered and equipped to much the same standard as a colonial battalion, or *irregolari*, irregular units, often locally raised, commanded by a single officer, a senior NCO, or sometimes an Ethiopian leader collaborating with the Italians. Some groups were irregular cavalry.

The colonial battalions were armed with Mannlicher rifles, Breda light machine guns and two Schwartloze heavy machine guns per company. The men were trained to shoot and were tremendous marchers, capable of 50 to 60 kilometres a day. The pack artillery, which formed part of the colonial brigades, had 65-millimetre guns and 81-millimetre mortars, carried on mules.

The Italian air force, the Regia Aeronautica, had 325 aircraft and sufficient petrol and supplies to mount an offensive. The bombers were mainly old, slow, Caproni CA133s and Savoia S81s, but there were two squadrons of the modern and powerful Savoia S79s. The fighters were Fiat CR33s, the veteran fighter of the Spanish Civil War, and two squadrons of Fiat CR42s, a biplane, but faster than the British Gloster Gladiator and more manouevrable than the Hawker Hurricane.

There was a naval base at Massawa with a number of old destroyers and submarines and one modern light cruiser, *Eritrea*, which had an adventurous career after the British occupied Massawa. She escaped and reached Japan, joined in with the Japanese navy in escorting convoys when Japan entered the war, and on the Italian armistice in 1943 escaped again and gave herself up to the Allied fleet in Ceylon.

To the west of AOI lay the Anglo-Egyptian Sudan, under British administration, where the British forces on the outbreak of war consisted of three British battalions, the 2nd West Yorks, 1st Essex, and 1st Worcesters, and 4500 men of the Sudan Defence Force (SDF). The SDF was divided into five corps or battalions, commanded by regular British officers on secondment and Sudanese officers. They were fine troops who consistently did well, but were restricted to the defence of Egypt and the Sudan, though they were allowed to go into Ethiopia.

The air component in the Sudan consisted of three squadrons of elderly Vickers Wellesley bombers, seven Vincent bombers, and nine Gloster Gladiator fighters, all Royal Air Force. Commanding in the Sudan was the *kaid*, Major General William Platt, with Air Commodore Slattery in charge of the air forces.

West of the Sudan was the French territory of Chad, which

declared for de Gaulle after the fall of France. The troops there were not a factor in the Ethiopian situation, although Free French contingents later served at Keren and Gondar. Further south was the Belgian Congo which remained loyal to the Allies after the fall of Belgium. Belgian African troops took part in the advance into southwest Ethiopia, Belgian officers served with the Patriots, and a Belgian field corps ambulance served with East African forces up to the end of the war, accompanying them to Burma.

South of AOI was the British Colony and Protectorate of Kenya whose forces consisted of six battalions of the King's African Rifles (KAR), one Indian Mountain Battery (3.7 howitzers), and one squadron of Hawker Harts of the South African Air Force, later increased by four other squadrons. The KAR was, like the SDF, officered by regular British officers on secondment and they soon proved themselves excellent infantry though slowed up a little by the decision of the War Office to put them into boots for fear of mustard gas attacks by the Italians. Until then in their sandals they could have matched any Italian colonial battalion in marching.

East of AOI was British Somaliland, with its capital and port Berbera, where there was the 1st Battalion of the Northern Rhodesia Regiment (similar to a KAR battalion) and the Somali-land Camel Corps, and across the Gulf of Aden the naval base at Aden with a garrison and naval and air forces. To the north was French Somaliland with its capital and port Jibuti, terminus of the railway to Addis Ababa. Here there were 5000 good Foreign Legion troops under General Legentilhomme on whom the British had been relying in any attack on AOI.

To the north of the Sudan lay Egypt where there were 36,000 British ground troops, supported by air forces and a naval base at Alexandria, and the headquarters of Middle East Command at Cairo under the commander-in-chief, General Sir Archibald Wavell, who had taken over in July 1939 and who commanded all British forces in North and East Africa. West of Egypt and the Sudan lay Libya, comprising the Italian colonies of Cyrenaica and Tripolitania, where there were 250,000 Italian troops, supported by air forces, commanded at first by the governor-general, Air Marshal Italo Balbo, and after his death in an air crash on 28 June 1940, by Marshal Graziani, the former viceroy of AOI.

On 10 June 1940 Italy declared war on Britain and France and Mussolini's divisions invaded the south of France, their leader hoping to establish his claim to a share in the spoil. On 22 June 1940 the Franco-German armistice was signed and on 24 June the Franco-Italian armistice. The evacuation of British and some French troops from Europe through Dunkirk and other ports had been completed by 10 June 1940. By the end of June 1940 France had surrendered, Britain and the Commonwealth were alone, and Germany, now allied to Italy, controlled most of western Europe.

In 1940 Italy appeared to have great strength in Africa. Her forces in Libya and AOI were numerically superior to the British forces in the neighbouring territories, and those in AOI were experienced and battle hardened, having been fighting the Ethiopian guerrillas since 1937. The surrender of France and the neutralization of the French forces in North Africa and Somaliland meant that the British in Egypt faced attack from Libya while the territories adjoining AOI could all expect attack from what was believed to be a formidable enemy, British Somaliland being particularly vulnerable because of the loss of the French force in Jibuti.

In the long term there were factors that would favour the British. The Italian forces were isolated and could not be reinforced except to a limited extent by air, and a considerable part of the garrison was committed to fighting the Ethiopian Patriots, who were to prove important allies in the forthcoming invasion of AOI. British forces were not strong enough to invade until reinforced and it may be asked why Britain did not simply blockade AOI and leave the Patriots to finish off the Italians. This option was not viable for several reasons. While the Italian forces remained intact they were still a danger, particularly to the Sudan; without the support of regular forces the Patriots could not succeed and might well be defeated piecemeal; Britain's prestige in the area demanded that she should not simply sit on the defensive; finally, and of the greatest importance, Britain was committed to the restoration of Ethiopia's independence.

The Origins of Mission 101

The title, Mission 101, was imaginatively chosen and suitable for

22

the gunner colonel who was to command the mission, Daniel Sandford. Fuse 101 was a percussion/graze fuse used widely by the Royal Artillery in many calibres of guns before and during the Second World War. Mission 101 was the fuse that would ignite the Ethiopian revolt. Up to the time of Italy's entry into the war British foreign policy had been to do all they could to keep Italy out of the war, and, conversely, to do nothing Italy might interpret as a *casus belli*. Fortunately for the Ethiopians and their Emperor in exile, the War Office took a more realistic view, as did General Wavell in Cairo, who strongly disagreed with Foreign Office policy. In March 1939 Hitler had invaded and occupied Czechoslovakia, and it was evident that war with Germany would break out before long with the likelihood that Italy would join in on the side of Germany. The War Office warned the *kaid* in Khartoum that he must be prepared for war with Italy, when 'propaganda to encourage rebel movements must be accompanied by the support of troops'.

In August 1939 Wavell sent for Daniel Sandford from England. Since his escape from Maji in 1936 he had been living with his family in Ewhurst in Surrey as a half-pay lieutenant colonel, strongly disapproving of what he regarded as the supine Foreign Office policy towards Ethiopia, keeping in touch with Haile Selassie in Bath, and occupying himself as secretary of the Guildford Cathedral Appeal Fund, a job he performed with his usual enthusiasm and, according to his brother-in-law Maurice Lush, he was known in Surrey as 'Public Enemy No 1'! Sandford, now 57, arrived in Cairo on 1 September 1939, was given the rank of colonel and put in charge of the Ethiopian Section in Middle East intelligence. His brief from Wavell was to prepare immediate undercover plans for rebellion in Ethiopia in the event of war with Italy. Wavell told him, 'You are my expert on Ethiopia. I will leave you to get on with it until it comes my way.' Sandford immediately started a correspondence with rebel leaders in Ethiopia and visited Khartoum at the end of September to tackle the most difficult task of persuading the authorities in the Sudan to back the Emperor and the revolt. He went with Brigadier Clayton of Middle East intelligence and Colonel Elphinstone from the War Office. In Khartoum they met the *kaid*, General Platt, his head of intelligence, Colonel Penney, and the governor-general, Sir Stewart Symes. They found that 'all was clouded by friendly relations with the Italians and the Duke of Aosta ... who had given a false impression that they were doing a good job among a lot of savages'. Platt disagreed with Sandford on two issues affecting Ethiopia. He was not convinced, as Sandford was, that Haile Selassie had universal support, or indeed sufficient support to make his return the focus of a national cause. Secondly, Platt did not agree that encouragement of the rebels alone would be sufficient to defeat the Italians, even with the support of British mobile columns. His view was that they would have to be defeated by British imperial forces in substantial numbers. If supplied with arms the rebel leaders would be as likely to use them against each other as against the Italians, and Haile Selassie would be incapable of welding such resistance together.

Events were to prove that Sandford was right about Haile Selassie, and Platt was right about the need for imperial forces to defeat the Italians, but he underestimated the influence of Haile Selassie and the effect of his return to Ethiopia. The discussions in Khartoum did result in some useful decisions, the setting up of arms depots on the frontier for the supply of arms to patriot chiefs as soon as war with Italy was declared, the formation of a new unit of the Sudan Defence Force, the Frontier Battalion, with five patrol companies, to escort arms to the Patriots, and the establishment of an intelligence bureau in Khartoum to collect information about Ethiopian refugees and leaders in effective revolt. To run the bureau a former British consul at Dangila in Gojjam, Robert Cheesman, was summoned from England. Writing later to his wife Sandford referred to, 'Old Cheesman, the man who has a kind of halo round his head as the man who knows' (Sandford was then 58, Cheesman 61!). Cheesman was an ornithologist and botanist who sent over 2000 specimens home to Lord Rothschild; in his seven years of wandering round Dangila he had acquired a deep knowledge of the country and its personalities, which was of great value.

On his return to Cairo Sandford carried on with his work of contacting rebel leaders, seeing his duty clearly as the encouragement of the revolt and believing that the return of the Emperor to lead it was of paramount importance. The British government's policy of appeasement towards Italy made this a frustrating time for him and for his chief, General Wavell. Wavell told Sandford in December 1939, after a visit to London and Paris, where he had found 'only Weygand a valuable ally in the face of strategic and tactical supineness', that officially he must stop what he was doing. 'I was told to send no agents into Italian territory, though all our territories were full of Italian agents, to do nothing to get in touch with Abyssinian rebels, and so on.' (Weygand was then French commander-in-chief.)

Privately Wavell told Sandford, 'Go with what you are doing,' and Sandford did so, planning a tour in January 1940 of the colonial capitals bordering AOI to assess the attitude of the authorities to the Ethiopian revolt. Before he left Cairo he met Lorenzo Taezaz, who was on his way back to England to see the Emperor after a visit to Gojjam, and 'brought useful and comprehensive reports'. He was pleased to hear that a Gojjam Patriots committee had been formed under Getahun Tesemma, with a printing press producing a newsletter with 'news of events in the outside world and the possibility of coming help'. He was anxious that Lorenzo should urge the Emperor to be ready to move out as soon as the time was right, writing to Christine on 16 January 1940, 'I hope you have seen Lorenzo and got all his and my news. ... Time is short and if Strong havers, he'll miss the boat. Hope does *not* spring eternal in the savage mind.'

This is important contemporary evidence that Sandford was urging the Emperor (Strong), against all official thinking, to be ready to move out (to the Sudan) as soon as the time was right, that is as soon as the Italians came into the war, which Sandford anticipated would be at any time. He also appreciated that without encouragement the revolt might falter.

On his tour of colonial capitals in various RAF planes at the end of January 1940, on which he reported regularly in letters to Christine, Sandford had a mixed reception. In Khartoum he found much the same reception as on his previous visit, in Jibuti 'much friendly cooperation and a *dîner d'honneur* with General Legentilhomme and his lady', in British Somaliland the governor 'entirely unsympathetic to the idea of encouraging the Ethiopian revolt', but he enjoyed seeing old friends, 'who trotted in from the bush to see me. This afternoon I spent three or four happy hours with the exiles from the land we love.' (These were Ethiopian refugees.) In Kenya he found the authorities 'encouraging and interested' and set up an intelligence bureau through an Ethiopian shopkeeper in the Northern Frontier District (of Kenya). On his return from Kenya Sandford stopped at Juba in the southern Sudan to see an old friend, Major Whalley, who had been British consul at Maji, and discuss with him plans for helping the Patriots. He wrote to Christine, 'I have been able to do a good deal of piecing together of "the young men over the way" during my visit ... and it's interesting and they are interesting, and, given a leader, could accomplish much.' Whalley was able to tell Sandford about any rebel activity in southwest Ethiopia and later was himself an effective leader of irregulars.

What Sandford learned during his tour about the Patriots, 'the young men over the way', convinced him that, given the right leadership, namely the return of the Emperor, the rebel movement had great potential strength. On his return to Cairo he drew up a plan in a lengthy document entitled 'Scheme "A" – Notes on the Abyssinian rising to be brought about in the event of war with Italy'. The objectives were the prevention of attacks on British and French territories and the eventual defeat of the Italian armed forces in AOI, the British role to be the supply of arms, the training and equipment of Ethiopian refugees willing to fight, and the provision of technical advice and assistance and a military task force. Immediate practical steps were to be the formation of seven arms supply depots on the frontier (already agreed with Platt), the supply of six mobile wireless stations, and the dispatch of a military mission as soon as war broke out to make contact with rebel leaders and coordinate their efforts.

Herein lay the genesis of Mission 101. Scheme 'A' was submitted to the British Cabinet through Wavell and approved, as was Scheme 'B', also drawn up by Sandford, on the propaganda methods to be adopted. Despite the Foreign Office's formal adherence to the Bon-Voisinage Agreement, behind the scenes the British government was actively preparing for war with Italy. Sandford had already raised the question of wireless equipment in correspondence with the War Office, and we now have a good example both of War Office efficiency and of the thoroughly professional way in which a regular British NCO tackled the job he was given.

On 17 January 1940 Staff Sergeant George Grey, Royal Corps of Signals, then serving in Northern Ireland, was ordered to report to the War Office, sent to the Services communications centre at Waddon Hall, and told to prepare six pack wireless stations, modified for mule transport, for a mission to be formed to assist rebel forces in Ethiopia. The sets he prepared were suitcase sets, smaller and lighter than the standard unit No 11 set but with similar range, adapted for three mule loads, the set and equipment on one, the two batteries on the second, and the battery charger on the third.

While at Waddon Hall Grey was assigned for duty behind the lines in the Norwegian campaign, but when Norway was evacuated he was told that he was back with the 'fuzzy-wuzzies',[5] and in May 1940 he left England for Cairo with the six sets, comprising half a ton of equipment, in his sole charge. He arrived in Alexandria by sea on 23 May, having had a difficult journey across France by rail to Marseilles with the Germans already in the Netherlands, and reported to Sandford in Cairo. There he was given 13 Ethiopian refugees to train as signallers. Three had French signal training and were excellent, of whom two, Gabre Maskal and Mavid Mangasha, accompanied the mission.

Following Cabinet approval of Scheme 'A', Sandford selected the personnel to accompany him on Mission 101. They were Captain R. A. Critchley, 13th/18th Hussars (GSO3); Acting Major D. H. Nott MC, Worcesters (DAA&QMG); Acting Captain T. M. Foley, Royal Engineers; Acting Captain C. B. Drew, Royal Army Medical Corps; and Staff Sergeant G. S. Grey, Royal Corps of Signals (CSM). Later additions were Major Count A. W. D. Bentinck, Coldstream Guards (GSO2); Second Lieutenant Arnold Wienholt DSO MC (intelligence); Staff Sergeant D. S. Rees, Cheshire Yeomanry (administrative sergeant); and Corporal Frost and Signaller Whitmore, Royal Corps of Signals. The formal appointments were not made until Italy entered the war.

The CIGS sanctioned the formation of the Frontier Battalion in March 1940, and in April and May recruitment and training of the five patrol companies was under way in the five corps depots of the SDF. Lieutenant Colonel Hugh Boustead OBE MC was selected as battalion commander.

Also in March 1940 Cheesman arrived in Khartoum to set up the intelligence bureau. Of the refugees whom he listed many were later recruited as muleteers and *askari* for Mission 101 and for the operational centres which would accompany Gideon Force. He selected 11 patriot leaders who would be contacted immediately on the outbreak of war with Italy, seven in the area northwest of Gondar, three in Gojjam, Mangasha, Nagash and Belai Zelleka, and three in Beghemder. Letters in Amharic signed by the *kaid* were left in the DC's office in Gedaref for dispatch to them by messenger as soon as war broke out. Ababa Aregai was not selected as he was too far away, but he was contacted later by Sandford when he entered Gojjam. So far as was possible all steps were taken so that moves to help the Patriots would go ahead as soon as war broke out.

Notes
1. Yperite — so named because first used at Ypres in 1915.
2. Ras Gugsa, husband of the Empress Zauditu, rebelled against Haile Selassie in 1932, and was joined by Lij Yasu who escaped from custody. Ras Hailu, governor of Gojjam, was implicated and dismissed from the governorship.
3. Alberto Denti, Duke of Piranho, in *A Cure for Serpents*.
4. Ato Yohannes Berhane, 'A Review of the Gojjam Patriots'.
5. 'Fuzzy-wuzzies' — the Dervish soldiers of the Mahdi and khalifa who 'broke the British square' and for whom the British Army had a great respect, not a term of opprobrium. To Western eyes the long-haired Ethiopian Patriots looked like them.

2

Mission 101*

W hen Italy declared war on 10 June 1940 Sandford's comment in a letter to Christine was that a more robust attitude 'instead of the weak-kneed and apologetic attempts at appeasement' would certainly not have increased the danger of war and might have lessened it. Middle East Command went into action immediately and issued an operational instruction dated 10 June 1940 to the commanders in all adjoining territories, headed 'Rebel activity in Italian East Africa'. This listed the method by which the revolt would be fostered by the supply of arms and provision of advisers, stated the intention which was to spread the revolt and 'so harass the Italians as to make them expend their resources on internal security', and made it clear that 'the Allies have no intention of acquiring any land in Italian East Africa for themselves, their wish being to see the Italians driven out and Ethiopia happy and free'. The Allies were then still Britain and France, but France was soon to surrender, leaving Britain and the Commonwealth alone, and this declaration, that Britain had no territorial ambitions in Ethiopia, could not have been clearer. The directive was, however, silent as to the position of Haile Selassie.

Wavell told Sandford to go ahead and the formal appointments to Mission 101 were made. During the next few weeks Sandford had to work hard to persuade the authorities in the Sudan to accept Haile Selassie as the force behind the revolt and the future

---

* See General Maps 1 and 2.

leader of his country, while the logistic burden of getting the mission ready fell mainly on Nott. Nott and Critchley left Cairo for Khartoum on 12 June by rail and steamer, arriving on 17 June, and immediately set about getting to know the local staff officers, collecting stores and transport, and engaging muleteers. Sandford arrived by air the same day, having secured some rifles but no mortars or light machine guns, commenting to Christine, 'One's labours have been greatly lightened by hearing that Haile Selassie may be on his way out.' News of the capture by the Royal Navy of two ships carrying munitions to AOI was also heartening.

On 18 June, his fifty-eighth birthday, he wrote in praise of his three chief officers, '58 . . . and ticking over quite steadily. I've got three awfully nice lads working with me, Donald Nott, Ronnie Critchley, and the doctor, Pansy Drew.' Each was to perform sterling service for the mission. On 19 June Drew went off to Gedaref by train with 'A' Echelon, taking two assistant surgeons, a medical orderly and 40 mules with food stores for two months, evidence of fast work by Nott. By 20 June the mission was complete except for Bentinck, Wienholt having arrived by air direct from Aden with his servant, Achine, nephew of Ababa Aregai.

The letters signed by Platt and held in the District Commissioner's office at Gedaref had been sent off on the outbreak of war to the selected chiefs inviting them to come in for arms, and on 21 June Platt issued a directive to Sandford ordering 'the entry into Abyssinia of British Mission No 101 under Colonel Sandford who will coordinate the actions of the Abyssinians under my general direction'. The mission was to be established in Ethiopia before 1 August, the peak of the rains, and was given two priority tasks, 'the coordination of rebel activity so as to prevent enemy troop movements *north* from Gondar and *south and east* from Dangila in Gojjam'. Sandford himself tackled the latter task with Mission 101 and sent off Bentinck and Foley to carry out the former with Mission 101 North. This directive not only confirms that Platt took the mission seriously, but an examination of the objectives shows that British plans, even at this early stage, contemplated advances from the Sudan into Eritrea in the north and from Kenya into Ethiopia in the south, the mission's tasks being to prevent the movement of reinforcements from Gondar to the Eritrean front in the north, and from Gojjam towards Addis Ababa against any advance in the south. In other words, Platt regarded Mission 101 and the patriot forces as a diversionary, and hence subsidiary, operation, but relevant to the operations as a whole.

Sandford went off with Critchley on 22 June to Gedaref and from there to Gallabat to interview chiefs and prepare for the mission's entry, and signalled Nott that the mission should leave Khartoum on 2 July. Meanwhile Nott had sent off a second party to Gedaref on 26 June under Foley, recording an interesting piece of English social history. He had bought valises, camp beds and mackintosh capes for the British NCOs; 'Pop Browne [a staff major with old-fashioned ideas] was furious, saying that they should sleep hard-arse in the rains!' Nott, the good officer, was even more furious and 'told him I was going to look after my men's health or they would be down and dead in no time'.

On 27 June Sandford returned to Khartoum, ready to leave with the mission by special train on 2 July. On the same day they heard that Haile Selassie had arrived in the Sudan and was at Wadi Halfa.

While preparations for the mission were going on in the Sudan, the first recruitment of Ethiopian refugees had taken place in Kenya. Some 500 men were enlisted in Taveta camp, formed into the 1st Ethiopian Battalion, and moved to Lodwar in Turkana District. There they were given a few days' training under Captain Ted Boyle, and sent off with 14 days' rations under their own officers led by Dejasmatch Wolde Mariam Bedada to contact guerrillas in the Maji area. They had to pass through the territory of the Merille, a warlike Nilotic tribe well armed by the Italians, who later shot down four South African Air Force planes with rifle fire and wiped out a platoon of 2nd/4th KAR. Not surprisingly after 14 days they were back in Turkana, having failed to make any progress or obtain any food from hostile, pro-Italian tribesmen. This episode gave the Ethiopian refugees a bad name with the staff, but it was utterly irresponsible to have sent off an untrained unit without proper leadership or logistic support into hostile territory in this manner.

The Arrival of Haile Selassie

Haile Selassie had remained at Bath, seeing in the likely entry of Italy into the war hope for the liberation of his country. When Italy declared war moves started both in Cairo and in London for his return to the Sudan. The Foreign Office did not oppose his move, but seems to have had dubious faith in him as a future ruler of Ethiopia. The Sudan government was totally opposed to Haile Selassie's return, and some Frontier officers reported on his unpopularity in many areas, a view much encouraged by Italian propaganda. According to Lush it was Wavell, on Sandford's instigation, who persuaded Churchill to overcome Foreign Office negative feeling. Sandford himself does not claim the credit, attributing this to the War Office, who, on advice from Brigadier Clayton in Cairo, appreciated Haile Selassie's military value.

There had been concurrent moves in London, made by Haile Selassie's friends, Philip Noel Baker MP and Sir Sidney Barton, former ambassador in Addis Ababa, who arranged a meeting with R. A. Butler, then Under-Secretary of State for Foreign Affairs. As a result of this, and on the advice of the War Office, Haile Selassie's departure was approved. He left Southampton in great secrecy by flying boat on 24 June, accompanied by Lorenzo Taezaz, Wolde Giorgis and George Steer. He was seen off by Butler, who, when writing his memoirs later as Lord Butler of Saffron Walden, did not mention the incident, either because he overlooked it or considered it of minor importance!

By then the Germans had overrun France and the flying boat flew high over Bordeaux and Marseilles to Alexandria via Malta. To ensure secrecy there was complete radio silence and no advance warning was given to Cairo until the flying boat was approaching Alexandria. There Haile Selassie was met by Brigadier Clayton and Andrew Chapman-Andrews, first secretary at the British Embassy in Cairo, and after a night in the Italian Boat Club, was flown on to Wadi Halfa in the Sudan next day. Maurice Lush, whom he had known when Lush was vice-consul in Addis Ababa in 1919/20, was then governor of the Ed Damer Province in which Wadi Halfa lay and seeing a familiar face must have lifted his spirits a little, as there was not much enthusiasm about the rest of his reception.

In Khartoum, 'the *Kaid* and Governor-General sent for Dan and told him to go to Wadi Halfa and tell the Emperor to go back to England again'. So wrote Christine Sandford, but this being hardly possible Sandford flew to Wadi Halfa, was greeted as an old friend, and at a meeting with the Emperor, his councillors, and Chapman-Andrews and Steer, explained with great confidence and his usual optimism the situation in Ethiopia, his plans for Mission 101 and for the supply of arms to the Patriots. At the same time, 'I had to disabuse His Imperial Majesty ... of the belief that a large force was waiting for him with tanks and guns with which to enter his kingdom.'

Sandford returned to Khartoum on 29 June, Nott noting that it had been a difficult conference 'as Symes does not want HS in the Sudan and refuses to recognize his presence'. Then Wavell stepped in, asking the Foreign Office to put pressure on Symes to provide proper accommodation for the Emperor, and in a few days he was moved to the 'Pink Palace' on the banks of the Nile near Khartoum where he set up his court with Chapman-Andrews as political officer and Steer as staff officer, and was joined from Palestine by Ras Kassa, the *echege* (the Coptic patriarch) and the imperial *fitaurari*, Birru Wolde Gabriel.

We can sympathize with the reaction of Symes and Platt to the unheralded arrival of Haile Selassie. They had a war to fight against a greatly superior enemy, there was a real danger of an Italian invasion of the Sudan, and his arrival added a security burden which they did not want. However, they quickly accepted the situation, and on 1 July congratulated Sandford on 'a difficult task, admirably performed', as he wrote to Christine. Sandford was also heartened to receive from the RAF commander, Air Commodore Slattery, a promise of air support for Mission 101, the 'sign from the skies', which would show the Patriots that the British would be effective allies.

There was no plan to delay the mission because of Haile Selassie's arrival. Nott had left for Gedaref with the remaining men and animals on 3 July, and Sandford followed on 7 July after seeing Haile Selassie in Khartoum, and further talks with Platt and Symes. In a letter to Christine of 6 July Sandford gives a remarkable picture of Haile Selassie, arriving very tired and disappointed at his reception, but 'he has recovered and takes a very sane view.

He is a wonderful little man. He handled the generals today perfectly.' (The generals were Platt and Brigadier Scobie, his Chief of Staff.) He was the same throughout the months ahead, holding to his objective, the freedom of his country, and accepting delays and frustrations as unimportant. Until Mission 101 left he was involved in the planning, but after Sandford entered Gojjam his patience must have been severely tried until the Eden conference in late October and the arrival of Orde Wingate in early November stimulated action.

While the discussions over the Emperor's arrival were taking place, events had occurred on the frontier which postponed the departure of the mission, but before describing these let us first consider the position of Haile Selassie. One misconception current in Ethiopia today (a Wingate myth) is that Orde Wingate brought the Emperor Haile Selassie out to Khartoum and later insisted that he went in to Addis Ababa to take his place as the rightful ruler, against the wishes of the British establishment, including Sandford, who wanted to use him as a military pawn to help defeat the Italians and return him to London once Addis Ababa was reached. The devious British, it is said, would have annexed Ethiopia, but Wingate stopped this. The evidence which follows will show that this is no more than a myth with some grains of truth. It is true, as will be seen later, that there were some moves towards a protectorate which were quickly squashed. It is true also that Wingate did bring Haile Selassie into Ethiopia in January 1941, but it was Sandford who, almost alone, insisted from the beginning that Haile Selassie must return to lead the revolt and take his place as rightful ruler. Whatever Ethiopians think about Haile Selassie today, in 1940 the war of liberation without him would have been impossible. Churchill and Eden knew this and Wavell appreciated Haile Selassie's military value and backed Sandford. At a more local level in July 1940, as Sandford wrote, 'Platt and Symes still look on the little man in the light of a beastly nuisance, at the most as a rather useless pawn.' Lush comments that neither Platt nor Symes were convinced of the value of Haile Selassie to the military operations. 'Only Sandford had faith in the presence of the Emperor as a magnet for the Ethiopian tribes.' Later both Platt and Cunningham came to recognize Haile Selassie's military value

but it was Sandford who from the beginning envisaged him returning as the ruling Emperor, and Wingate, after he arrived in
Khartoum in November, held identical views. By January 1941,
when Haile Selassie entered Gojjam, his future role as the ruler of
Ethiopia was universally accepted.

Events on the Sudan Frontier

The Duke of Aosta, as a sensible soldier, had wanted to take the
offensive immediately by an advance into the Sudan before British
reinforcements arrived, but this was vetoed by Marshal Badoglio,
Minister of Defence in Rome. Aosta was told to remain on the
defensive. There was to be no offensive without the approval of
Rome. Denied his offensive Aosta proposed withdrawing to the
Ethiopian Highlands and holding out to the end of the war. This
was refused as politically unacceptable. The Italians confined
themselves to limited advances on the frontiers where there was a
British post close to their own, apparently with the object of giving
some exercise to the aggressive spirit of their colonial troops and
eliminating an enemy post which was close enough to be a
nuisance. Thus on the Sudan frontier first Gallabat (4 July), then
Kassala (5 July) and then Kurmuk (7 July) were attacked and
captured.

The loss of Gallabat, where the Italian post of Metemma was
only 500 metres away, affected Sandford's plans, as he had intended to cross the frontier close to that post, and Drew, with 'A'
Echelon, was already at Khor Otrub, seven miles from Gallabat.
Gallabat and Kassala had been garrisoned by detachments of the
SDF, which withdrew after offering resistance and causing casualties. A number of frontier posts, including Kurmuk, were held by
Sudan police who had volunteered for active service, commanded
by assistant district commissioners (ADCs) who had been given
governor-general's commissions in the SDF with the rank of
bimbashi. Kurmuk was commanded by Bimbashi Mervyn Bell,
ADC at Roseires, with three British auxiliaries and 51 police
armed with .303 rifles under a *sol hakindar* (warrant officer),
Abdel Rahman Abdullah. Bell, himself a first-class rifle shot, had
trained his riflemen well, and when, after an aerial bombardment,
the post was attacked on 7 July by a colonial battalion and 100

banda supported by machine guns and artillery, they put up a sturdy resistance until Bell withdrew his men in good order. British casualties were one killed and two wounded, including an American missionary who happened to be staying that night; Italian casualties were reported as four Italians and 40 *ascari* killed, including the battalion commander, Major Christini.

Bell left the *sol* and eight men to observe and report, who succeeded in recovering under fire the cash left in the office (E£ 1100) and handed it over proudly at the next government post, Wisko. Bell and his men received the congratulations of the *kaid*. This incident illustrates the part played by the Sudan Political Service and police in holding the frontier, and a police battalion was formed under Bimbashi Davies until the army took over. At that time the Frontier Battalion was still under training and the regular British and SDF units were fully stretched garrisoning the main centres and frontier posts.

The *kaid* decided to assess the situation on the frontier himself and travelled to Gedaref by train on 7 July with Sandford, Boustead, commanding officer of the Frontier Battalion, and a company of West Yorks to reinforce the SDF garrison, it being assumed that the Italian advance would continue. After conferences on 9 and 10 July it was decided to postpone the entry of the mission because of the Italian advances. Nott recalled his advance echelons, repacked E£ 640,000 worth of Maria Theresa dollars, which he had broken down into donkey loads, and on the evening of 10 July boarded the train for Khartoum with Platt, Sandford and Boustead, leaving the rest of the mission at Gedaref. More conferences followed in Khartoum with Platt and Symes in which the Emperor took part, and we can guess they discussed when the mission should go in, the route, and whether the Emperor should go with it. He was very keen to go, but even Sandford felt that this was premature and persuaded him to be patient. It was agreed though that the Emperor's representative and Ethiopian officers should be added to the mission. Sandford wrote confidently to Christine on 16 July that things were smoother with the Sudan authorities, 'I am almost the blue-eyed boy and the future is bright.'

Wavell passed through Khartoum on 14 July and called on Haile Selassie, commenting, 'the Emperor is an attractive personality though not always easy to deal with'. Wavell also had to explain, like Sandford before, why he had no large force ready to go in with him. 'I could never discover who the moron at the Foreign Office was who had led the Emperor to believe this.' Haile Selassie had a mind of his own and could be 'difficult' when he did not agree with what was proposed for the future administration of his country, as senior political officers found later.

On 16 July Major Count Bentinck and Sergeant D. S. Rees reported for duty with the mission, and on 18 July, after Nott had selected 39 volunteers from among the Ethiopian refugees for the colonel's party, he was taken by Sandford to be introduced to the Emperor, whom he found in his bungalow on the bank of the Nile with one Sudanese policeman on guard. Nott records, 'The Emperor was in white silk shirt, and white tie and trousers. He is very small, about 5' 6". Fine face, black beard and shrewd brown eyes. He spoke to me in English as I told him I could not speak French well. . . . On the table before him were a pair of field glasses and a book, *Gordon at Khartoum*.' Nott excused himself after a few minutes, bowing himself out backwards to the door, and noticing 'those calculating brown eyes which . . . gave me the impression that they had spent many a long hour patiently waiting'. Nott and Haile Selassie had much to do with each other over the next nine months and they got on well. It had been decided that the mission should go ahead as soon as the Emperor had chosen his representative. The Italians had made no attempt to advance any further into the Sudan, though on the Kenya frontier they captured Moyale on 14 July and Mandera was occupied at the same time. Sandford took the train to Gedaref on 20 July, leaving Nott to follow with the Emperor's representative, his departure not as quiet as he has hoped, as Nott records, 'handshakes all round . . . and a large Abyssinian flag waved from the carriage window'. This must have given Italian agents something to think about. As Sandford left he received a bundle of letters from his wife and replied to her in the train, writing that he had Platt's promise of support, 'The little man [Haile Selassie] is happier and is prepared to fall in with their [the generals'] plans. Symes admitted that he had been obstructive but thought his reasons for doing so had been adequate.' Sandford goes on, showing his characteristic confidence and optimism, with some pertinent comments on what the war against the Fascist dictators was all about, contrasting their 'swift devastating power, the devil to defeat', with 'our own little family and hundreds of other little families ... and the power behind these simple things is much more tremendous and permanent as time will show. You and I have not the slightest reason or excuse for doubt as to the outcome of the struggle.'

Sandford had chosen Gojjam as his area of operations after consultation with the *kaid*, the Emperor and Lorenzo Taezaz, because it was the most accessible area where effective resistance was continuing, and his plan was to concentrate at Doka, cross the frontier south of Metemma, and pass between that fort and Kwara into the territory of Fitaurari Ayellu Makonnen. He was not to know that Captain Giovanni Braca, an experienced and energetic officer commanding the 1st Gruppo Bande di Confine, was stationed at Metemma with orders to intercept arms convoys to the rebels. The mission had to wait for a few days for 'Strong's man' (the Emperor's representative). Then on 31 July Bentinck and Wienholt arrived from Khartoum, followed on 1 August by Nott with Lorenzo and Azaj Kabada Tesemma, former court chamberlain, chosen by Haile Selassie as his representative on the mission, with two other Ethiopian officers, Ato Getahun Tesemma and Ato Asegaiheu, both members of the Gojjam Patriots committee.

On 4 August Nott took the mission to Doka while Sandford remained to have further talks with Lorenzo, who was returning to report to the Emperor, to type out detailed orders for Bentinck on the portable typewriter which he carried everywhere with him, and to write to Christine, commenting to her on the date, 4 August (the outbreak of the First World War) 'To think back 26 years! We have brought it all on ourselves.' Of Kabada he said, 'Azaj Kabada is a very worthy old thing. He is quite young really but has a weighty look about him. I see no reason why we should not get on well together,' ending with his usual optimism, 'It's going to be a muddy business but otherwise I don't anticipate any difficulties.' On the surface Sandford and Kabada did work well together and achieved much. Below the surface, after a time and unknown to Sandford, Kabada harboured bitter resentment at what he regarded as his subordinate position.

Sandford caught the mission up by lorry late on 5 August after a difficult journey in mud and rain, sending a final note to Christine with love to her and the children, 'I go in high hopes', the end of their correspondence until he reached Addis Ababa. This was the last use they made of motor transport. From now on they were on foot with mules and donkeys. After a day of preparation and sorting out loads they marched out of Doka for the frontier on 6 August, Nott recording that they moved off at 16.10 hours after 'the Colonel and Kabada had addressed the parade, and sheaves of bills ... had been thrust into my hands. The camp was exceedingly quiet when the captains and the kings had departed.' Nott was left behind with Sergeant Rees to keep the mission supplied and to organize and dispatch the echelons of Wienholt and Bentinck.

The party consisted of Colonel Sandford, Captains Critchley and Drew, CSM Grey and Corporal Whitmore (British), and Azaj Kabada, Ato Getahun, Ato Asegaiheu, Mavid Mangasha, Gabre Maskal, ten signallers, and 50 bodyguards and muleteers (Ethiopian). They had 54 mules and 36 donkeys, carried the six wireless sets which Grey had brought out from England, and their armament consisted of 13 .303 rifles, three revolvers, and 30 antiquated rifles. In addition to stores and ammunition they carried several donkey loads of Maria Theresa dollars and 14 days' rations. When these ran out they would live on the country. The weather was not propitious. It was still raining and, apart from the discomfort of wet weather, it was likely that the rivers would be swollen and difficult to ford. Altogether, enemy activity apart, it was an arduous physical journey for the party to undertake, particularly for their 58-year-old leader.

The mission reached the frontier on 12 August, escorted by a troop of mounted infantry of the Western Arab Corps, and crossed into Ethiopia at Limona, 12 miles south of Metemma, the rendez-vous arranged with Fitaurari Werku of Kwara, whose men were ambushed on their way to the frontier by one of Braca's patrols. This news caused consternation at Gedaref as it was feared that Sandford would also be ambushed, and it was evident that there had been a leak, Nott recording, 'Apparently Azaj Kabada had blown the gaff and Abyssinians were talking openly of the meeting place — Limona.' Wilfred Thesiger, then serving with the Eastern

Arab Corps near Gallabat, caught Sandford up on horseback and warned him, and the party got through the border area safely, zig-zagging and avoiding tracks and villages, although the Italians were active both in the air and on the ground. Grey records that they saw Italian planes every day, and were once spotted and had to scatter into the bush; they crossed the tracks of Italian patrols. The route of the mission lay to the southeast, leaving Lake Tana on their left, passing through low bush for about 50 miles, and then climbing the 3000-foot escarpment onto the Gojjam plateau, which lay at an altitude of 6500 to 8000 feet. The march was arduous, as Grey records, 'Going up the escarpment we did a forced march of 28 hours from 6.00 a.m. one day until 10.00 a.m. next day. . . . We lost 12 mules and I lost one wireless set in a river crossing.' On the plateau, which was open grassland with culti-vated fields and patches of acacia forest which provided good cover, they would meet the Amhara Gojjami people who had in the main been supporting a resistance movement against the Italians since 1937, and on whose help and cooperation the mis-sion would rely.

The situation of the Italian forces in Gojjam was that the border area was actively patrolled by Braca's *banda* group at Metemma, with detachments at Kwara and Matabia, a new post where they were assisted by armed Gumz tribesmen. On the plateau there were 13 colonial and three CCNN battalions, with supporting artillery, cavalry and armoured cars, disposed mainly in brigade strength at Dangila, Burye and Debra Markos, with detachments at the other forts on the all-weather road from the Abbai to Bahr Dar — altogether 15,000 regulars with 10,000 irregular *banda* in support. Overall commander and *commissario* was Colonel Natale at Burye, his deputy was Colonel Maraventano at Debra Markos, and Colonel Torelli commanded at Dangila. The three senior com-manders were officers of great experience, the colonial units were well officered by officers of the Royal Army with mainly Eritrean *graduati* and Tigrean or Amhara *ascari*. These were good, battle-hardened units, with high morale, capable of taking casualties and tremendous marchers. These forces were capable of maintaining the status quo, controlling the countryside within a few miles of the main roads and forts, but beyond that range the Patriots were in control, although the Italians did make raids in strength away from the main garrisons. The central area of Sakala was now quite empty of Italian forces since the withdrawal of the garrison of Faguta in March 1940. Sandford was aware of this, and it was for this area, the headquarters of Dejasmatch Mangasha, that he was heading.

Meanwhile on 2 August the Italians had launched an attack on British Somaliland with two divisions under General Nasi, authorized by Mussolini in the belief that Britain was finished so that he would have one success to his credit at the postwar conference table. The British forces, of about six battalions, conducted a fighting withdrawal to Berbera where they were evacuated by the Royal Navy on 15 August. Captain E. C. T. Wilson, East Surrey Regiment serving with the Somaliland Camel Corps, was awarded the Victoria Cross, the first of two such awards to East African forces in the Second World War. This reverse had an effect for a time on the morale of the Somali tribesmen of Kenya's Northern Frontier District but was too remote to be of any consequence to Mission 101. Also while Mission 101 was advancing, the second unit to be raised from the Ethiopian refugees at the Taveta camp in Kenya, the 2nd Ethiopian Battalion, was being formed and trained at Gotani camp near Mariakani in Kenya. Captain Ted Boyle, who had been concerned with the brief training of the 1st Ethiopian Battalion, was appointed to command with the rank of major. This unit later formed part of Gideon Force.

Sandford's plans were to increase supplies of arms to the Patriots, select a base for Haile Selassie, and reconcile the main patriot leaders and coordinate their efforts, in particular Mangasha and Nagash. Possible sites for the base were Belaiya, an isolated mountain mass between the frontier and the escarpment, and Kwara, where there was an Italian garrison. The mission reached Sarako on 20 August, where Sandford and Kabada saw local chiefs and read out the Emperor's proclamation. Since the wording of this may have contributed to the misunderstanding by Kabada of his position *vis-à-vis* Sandford, it is quoted here in full:

To the elders and patriots of the Ethiopian people. How have you kept? We, by the grace of God, are well. Our hopes have been realized and we are returning to our country. We have entered into a covenant with the British Government of military co-operation to restore freedom to Ethiopia. Azaj Kabada Tesemma has been ordered by us to proceed to Ethiopia and tell you the good news and he brings with him English commanders under orders from the British Government to help the Patriots. Therefore we tell you to receive him and those English officers and their followers who are with him with every possible assistance, to see they encounter no difficulties, and to help them speedily on their way.

Hamle 20 1932 [20 August 1940]

The Emperor also gave Kabada a detailed 'Memo of Orders' setting out the steps he must take, 'in consultation with Colonel Sandford', to prepare Gojjam for the Emperor's return, and 'to explain that England has no territorial designs on Ethiopia and that the Emperor is returning to restore liberty to the people and country'. To this end he must get the leaders to collaborate, and attack the enemy wherever possible.

Kabada responded with extreme humility to these orders — 'To His Majesty, my master Haile Selassie, Emperor of Ethiopia, I kiss the ground at your feet, saying, "May the Saviour of the World give you long life and health"' — and suggested that Haile Selassie should send him letters for dispatch to those patriot leaders with whom, for reasons of geography, Sandford had not yet been in touch, in particular Ababa Aregai in Shoa and Gurassu Duke in Galla-Sidamo. Kabada's correspondence with the Emperor, and Sandford's regular typed dispatches to the *kaid*, were sent by the traditional method, a runner with a cleft stick, and nearly all got through, saying much for the loyalty of the population. Grey did not open up wireless communication until later in September.

The Emperor's proclamation and orders could be interpreted as giving Kabada equal status with Sandford, and that is what, according to his own account, Kabada believed. When therefore Sandford made it clear to Kabada that he was in command of the mission, responsible to the commander-in-chief and the *kaid*, and Kabada and his officers were there to assist him, Kabada resented it deeply, although his resentment was not apparent until he spilled it out in his book, *Recollections of History*, published in Amharic in 1969. He describes how Sandford explained that he was no longer an adviser working for the Emperor as he had been at Maji,

> but in this business was answerable to the British Army Commanders. . . . The plan of operation that we should be travelling together as equal companions came to an end; consciousness of rank, of superiors and inferiors, took over . . . every idea proposed by this Englishman . . . seemed to increase the discord so that most of the time we were in opposition.

Kabada's reference to Sandford as 'this Englishman' shows that the anger was still there nearly 40 years later. Sandford was not aware of this, nor were other officers of Mission 101 such as Nott and Thesiger. Sandford in fact was often complimentary about Kabada in his dispatches as an energetic and courageous subordinate. It was the subordination which Kabada resented, but Sandford had to make it clear that he was in command. Kabada's feelings are important for this story because many Ethiopians have read his book and their views on Sandford, and on the British, have been coloured by it.

On 24 August Critchley, remembered to this day as a strong man and great walker who never rode a mule, went off with two *askari* to reconnoitre Kwara, an isolated mountain massif, 7000 to 8000 feet high, birthplace of the Emperor Theodore, as a possible base for the Emperor. He returned on 27 August having covered 90 miles on foot, reporting that Kwara was held by a *banda* garrison under Tenente Parodi, who was also *residente*. (In fact the number one *banda* of Braca's group, 250 strong, plus auxiliaries.) He brought back a sketch plan and description of the fort and of the best method of attack, and reported that Fitaurari Werku was highly regarded, that there was ample grain and meat on the plateau, but no suitable ground for a landing strip. Sandford sent on Critchley's report to the *kaid*, properly commended as a first-class reconnaisance.

On 29 August Sandford split his party, going on to Zibist with

43

the remaining 24 mules, and taking Critchley, Kabada, Getahun, Asegaiheu, Gabre Maskal, some of the men and one wireless set. Drew and Grey and the rest of the party were left to give support to Werku. The reason was simply lack of mules, but Kabada interpreted the fact that he now had to share his aide-de-camp, Getahun, with Sandford as another slight, an example of the ideas 'proposed by this Englishman' that increased the discord.

After a week's difficult march, with two flooded rivers to cross, the Rahed and the Dinder, Sandford's party arrived at Zibist on 9 September with 11 mules remaining out of the 54 with which they had crossed the frontier. There they were met by Fitaurari Ayellu Makonnen, the loyal chief of the area. Sandford praised Kabada's conduct on the march, not only for 'taking his share of the physical exertions of the road, ... but as an able and sensible adviser'. At Zibist they also met the enemy, a strong patrol of 500 colonial troops from Torelli's brigade at Dangila, supported by two guns and a low-flying aircraft, who appeared at noon on 10 September. Ayellu deployed some of his men to hold them up while others drove the cattle into a ravine, and advised Sandford to move his party to a cave at the bottom of an 800-foot escarpment. They were seen and fired on as they scrambled down but not hit. Torelli's troops burnt and looted Ayellu's village but found no cattle, although they seized 250 head of cattle from nearby villages. They then retreated, covered by the guns and pursued by Ayellu's men who inflicted several casualties, while Sandford and his party returned to their camp. Sandford believed that Torelli tried to 'put him in the bag', and General Nasi claimed afterwards that they nearly caught Sandford, but it seems more likely that this was a typical Torelli raid to punish *ribelli* and seize cattle, with a typical patriot reaction, and the presence of the mission was quite fortuitous. From Zibist word was sent to Mangasha, Ayellu's overlord, for an escort, and on 16 September Sandford's party left for Faguta escorted by Ayellu and 1500 of Mangasha's men, less Critchley whom Sandford had sent off on another reconnaisance, this time of Mount Belaiya.

Wienholt and Bentinck
In the Sudan meanwhile Nott had been preparing and sending off

the echelons of Wienholt and Bentinck. Wienholt, delayed by lack of transport animals, left Khor Otrub on 31 August with three men and eight donkeys, intending to join Sandford but taking a different route, passing south of Matabia and heading for Kwara. Between Matabia and Kwara he was attacked by armed Gumz tribesmen from the Matabia post as he was loading at dawn. His men left their rifles and ran and he was last seen running into the bush holding his side. His body was never recovered, but, as Nott records, his '"1814" topi and bits of his clothing and kit were found at a later date' by a British patrol. This was a sad end for the Australian cattle rancher and philanthropist whose adventurous career covered the Boer War, the war in German East Africa, and the war against the Italians in Ethiopia, and whose name should be added to those for whom the defeat of the Italians and the return of the Emperor was a crusade.

Bentinck's orders from Sandford were to report to the *kaid* on conditions in Armachaho, contact chiefs and foster the revolt, disrupt communications north and west of Gondar, and try and win over the strongly pro-Italian Kamant tribe west of Gondar. Foley was to go with him to carry out demolition work on roads and bridges. His route required that he should cross the river Atbara at Akrib, a formidable obstacle in the rainy season, and Foley built a raft to ferry the equipment across. This activity attracted the attention of the Italians at Metemma who made several bombing raids and sent a ground patrol who blew up Foley's explosives dump. Bentinck and his party crossed the Atbara on 11 September, helped by two veterinary officers, John Jack and Ian Gillespie. Nott records, 'We had to swim the horses across. ... We tried all methods of getting the mules across, but found holding their heads under the gunwale the best.' Bentinck headed for Jogolambe, taking Wolde Giorgis as the Emperor's representative, Inspector Mohamed Effendi, an Amharic-speaking officer of the Sudan police, 46 men and 61 animals. Foley stayed behind to collect more explosives and follow later.

The Meeting between Mangasha and Nagash
On 18 September, after crossing the intervening plateau by night, Sandford and his party arrived at the Piccolo Abbai ford, the scene

of the ambush of Torelli's column by Mangasha's men on 14 March 1940. There they were met by Mangasha and 700 Patriots who fired a *feu de joie* from captured machine guns in greeting, Mangasha, a tall, dignified figure, welcoming the 'wet and shivering mission', as Sandford described himself, the red tabbed colonel, his uniform soaked from fording the river. Mangasha's men escorted Sandford to Faguta, a journey made quite openly through central Gojjam and without fear of interference from Torelli's strong forces at Dangila, an indication of the strength of the resistance and of Mangasha's authority in the area he controlled. There Sandford established his headquarters and the mission's principal task was to persuade the patriot leaders to cooperate with each other, particularly Mangasha and Nagash. Sandford and Kabada set about trying to arrange a meeting between the two men. Nagash had less authority than Mangasha and his difficulties had increased with the arrival at Burye of Dejasmatch Mamu Mikael, like Nagash a nephew of Ras Hailu and his equal in hereditary status, but, in Sandford's words, 'being a more dashing fellow he had a certain fascination for the people', and was able to recruit an Italian-paid *banda* to fight for the Italians.

On 23 September Critchley returned from his reconnaissance of Belaiya and reported that it was suitable as a base. He had met the loyal Fitaurari Teffere Zelleka, who had asked for a 'sign from the skies', a visible demonstration of RAF strength to convince the people that Haile Selassie was being supported by a stronger power than the Italians. As a result of Critchley's reports GHQ Khartoum decided that Belaiya was the most suitable base for the Emperor, but not before November because of malaria and horse sickness in the rainy season. This timing suited the *kaid*'s plans for an advance. The idea of Kwara as a base was abandoned, but Sandford was now considering another and much bolder proposal — Womberima, south of Burye. For these difficult and dangerous reconnaissances Critchley was awarded an immediate MC.

Under the persuasion of Sandford and Kabada, Mangasha and Nagash met at Ashua Gundil on 24 October and, standing under the green, yellow and red flag of Ethiopia in the presence of the mission and a crowd of Patriots, set their seals to a pact, agreeing not to interfere in each other's territory, not to accept deserting

Patriots (*arbenya*) from each other's force, and to cooperate in the fight against the common enemy. Lush comments that this agreement between the two leaders was one of the finest political achievements of Mission 101.

Italian Countermoves

By the end of September 1940 news had reached the Italian HQ at Debra Markos of British officers meeting Werku at Sarako, and in the same month General Nasi was moved to Debra Markos from Harrar, where he had been commanding the British Somaliland operations. Nasi took command of Gojjam from 11 October 1940 with orders to report on the possibility of containing the rebellion. Writing later Nasi attributed the spread of the rebellion to the 'Sandford British Mission' and the arrival of the *negus* in Khartoum and even if he overpaints the picture to emphasize his own achievements in Gojjam, it is clear that the Italian High Command blamed Mission 101 for intensifying the revolt and sent their best general to deal with it.

After touring his command by air in a Caproni CA133 'because it was too dangerous to use the roads without a strong escort', Nasi concluded that to defeat the rebels, whom he estimated had 40,000 rifles, would require a force of 30,000 men. He could raise 10,000 men for a police operation from the forces then in Gojjam, but this was not enough and he decided that a political solution must be found and his thoughts turned to Ras Hailu, then living in state in Addis Ababa. We shall see later how the return of Ras Hailu affected the situation in Gojjam, but in the meantime Nasi claims to have brought about some improvement 'by concentrating his forces in the forts and securing the loyalty of the chiefs and *ascari* by rewards and payments'.

Further south, and independently of any operations in Gojjam, in mid-October the Italians carried out a probing attack towards Roseires through Kurmuk, which could have had very serious consequences, not only for the defence of the Sudan, but also for the success of Mission 101. The raiding force was a *banda* group, the Banda Rolle, commanded by Lieutenant Colonel Rolle, a veteran of the Libyan and Ethiopian campaigns, and consisted of about 20 Italian officers and NCOs and 1800 *ascari*, mostly Shoan with Eritrean and Somali *graduati*. The plan was for the *banda* group to capture Roseires and a colonial brigade then at Asosa would pass through and capture Singa and Senna on the railway line to Khartoum, cutting communications in the Sudan.

The frontier posts were still manned by the thin blue line of the Sudan police, among them Bimbashi Bell's police, formerly at Kurmuk, although the first troops of No 2 Patrol Company, Frontier Battalion, had arrived at Roseires on 5 October to support the police under Major Jock Maxwell, second in command of the battalion. The Banda Rolle, advancing from Kurmuk, occupied the posts of Keili and Wisko on 18 and 20 October, from which Bell's police fell back, and reached a point within 16 miles of Roseires. Maxwell sent out a strong patrol, which made contact but withdrew under fire, while one auxiliary police constable, Abdullah Marhun, put up a remarkably brave performance, running ahead of the *banda* to warn villagers to evacuate and finally sacrificing himself for their sake. As Bell describes in a report to the governor, 'He was with a group of villagers when the enemy arrived . . . and was shot at by the enemy. He separated himself from the villagers, . . . took cover alone and killed four of the enemy before being shot by an Italian with a LMG. . . . Later the villagers found and buried him. He had three bullets in his chest.'

Meanwhile the rest of the Frontier Battalion had been rushed to Roseires in hired traders' lorries (Boustead travelling in his own box-body Ford), and on 26 October a patrol by Bell confirmed that the Italians were withdrawing. They were pursued by Frontier Battalion patrols on 27 and 28 October who took prisoners, and a party of them were intercepted by Bimbashi Charles De Bunsen, like Bell an ADC in the Sudan Political Service, who had been in charge of the frontier post at Bikori. He had withdrawn on orders with his police with much regret, leaving his loyal tribesmen to the mercy of the Banda Rolle, but had the satisfaction of shooting up the *banda* as they were watering their mules in a river, causing a number of casualties.

Rolle's raid failed, defeated by the country and the hostility of the Sudani tribesmen. His men were Shoan highlanders, used to living off the land in their own country, but quite out of their element in the hot, waterless semi-desert of the Sudan border.

Apart from the Watawit, a border tribe who favoured the Italians, the tribesmen gave the Italians no help and even refused to show them the water holes away from the river. One man who escaped from the *banda* told Bell that another had been hanged for refusing to help. It is fair to say that both colonial powers were equally ruthless in dealing with tribesmen who helped the enemy. De Bunsen records that two Watawit were shot as spies after being caught putting up Italian propaganda leaflets in Roseires market. Although generally the Italians received no help, tribal support is fickle, and if Rolle had won a victory, the position might have been different.

This was the last advance made by the Italians. By the end of October 1940 the Frontier Battalion was concentrated at Roseires, and two Indian brigades had arrived in the Sudan. These, with the three British battalions already there, now formed the 5th Indian Division, a formation which would have a distinguished record in Africa and Burma. In Kenya two regular Royal West African Frontier Force brigades had arrived, the 23rd Nigerian and the 24th Gold Coast, and the 1st South African Brigade, to be followed by the 2nd and 5th South African Brigades. Recruitment for both the SDF and the KAR was going ahead steadily, and in Kenya two new formations, the 25th and 26th East African Brigades, were formed to join the two regular KAR brigades, the 21st and 22nd. There had also been substantial reinforcement of the air forces.

The Eden Conference
In October 1940 Anthony Eden, then Secretary of State for War in Churchill's Cabinet, was visiting Middle East Command, and, as a result of complaints from Haile Selassie of lack of action and lack of recognition, a conference was held in Khartoum on 28 October attended by Generals Wavell, Platt and Cunningham (the new general officer commanding East Africa) and Generals Smuts and van Rynevelt from South Africa. This conference had far-reaching consequences for the campaign in AOI and stands greatly to Eden's credit. The most important decisions were to mount an offensive in which the Patriots would play a major role, with initial limited advances to Gallabat from the Sudan and to Kisimayu from Kenya, to appoint two staff officers to GHQ Khartoum to

assist with the training and use of irregular forces in support of the Emperor's return, to bring the 2nd Ethiopian Battalion from Kenya to Khartoum, and to recruit operational centres to assist Mission 101. The staff officers, notably one Orde Wingate, the 2nd Ethiopian Battalion, and the operational centres were all to have important roles in this story. The latter were each to consist of one officer and four sergeants, recruited from volunteers in Middle East Command and trained in the use of explosives, who would provide foci for patriot activity.

The conference dealt with the immediate and practical problems of the war against AOI. It did not address itself to the future political role of Haile Selassie about which the British government was as yet unwilling to commit itself. This was reasonable in view of the extreme danger in which Britain stood in the summer and autumn of 1940. Haile Selassie did not attend the conference but saw both Eden and Wavell and was clearly satisfied with the results, writing to Sandford on 18 November, expressing the hope 'that I would have the pleasure of meeting with you in the heart of Ethiopia. I had a lengthy talk with Mr Anthony Aden (*sic*), who, as you know, has always been very sympathetic to Ethiopia ... and promised every possible help to conduct the war.' He expressed pleasure at the appointment of the two staff officers, which had been carried out immediately after the conference. The officers appointed were Major Orde Wingate DSO Royal Artillery (GSO2) and Major R. E. L. Tuckey of the Worcestershire Regiment (DAA&QMG). Their brief was a limited one, but the fact that they had been appointed at all was an important advance and the fact that one of those officers happened to be Wingate and he was given the operational job as GSO2 was crucial.

There was another reason why 28 October was an important date. On that day Mussolini presented Greece with an ultimatum and Italian troops from Albania, which Mussolini had occupied in 1939, invaded Greece. Eden asked Wavell to send help to Greece. Wavell had been secretly planning his attack on Graziani's army in Libya. He had not informed Churchill of his plans, and was only forced to tell Eden in Cairo because of the demand to help Greece and the need to retain the bulk of his forces for his own offensive. Wavell did send some help, and later, when the Germans invaded

Greece in April 1941, sent considerable forces, denuding his Western Desert Army. The result was that the German commander Rommel was able to recover the ground lost by the Italians in North Africa and the Italian forces still holding out in Gondar in northwest Ethiopia were encouraged to prolong their resistance in the hopes that the Axis forces would come to their assistance.

The Arrival of Wingate

Wingate's previous career had included a tour of duty in the Sudan with the Eastern Arab Corps SDF mainly on border duties against Ethiopian ivory poachers and slave raiders, and a spell in Palestine from 1936 to 1938 when he had successfully formed and commanded the Jewish-British night squads against Arab guerrillas, winning his first DSO and being wounded in action. He had there come to the favourable notice of General Wavell, then general officer commanding Palestine, but left Palestine under something of a cloud with a bad report by Wavell's successor, General Haining, as being too pro-Zionist and politically unreliable.

When Amery suggested to Wavell in September 1940 that Wingate, then on anti-aircraft duties in England, was a suitable person to lead guerrillas in Ethiopia, Wavell welcomed the proposal and Wingate arrived in Cairo on 17 October, and in Khartoum, as one of the staff officers appointed after the Eden conference, on 6 November. These dates are important. There is another Wingate myth current in Ethiopia that nothing was done to help the Emperor or the Patriots until Wingate arrived. In fact by the time Wingate arrived on the scene Mission 101 had already been in Gojjam for three months, Haile Selassie in Khartoum for four months, and the Eden conference had got things moving. Wingate's arrival stimulated action and he achieved a great deal but not quite all that has been credited to him.

What sort of a man was this gunner officer whose name still lives in Ethiopia and who achieved greater fame later in Burma? His substantive rank was still major after 17 years commissioned service and he had not been to Staff College, in spite of representations to 'Cousin Rex' (General Wingate). He had commanded an SDF company and, more recently, guerrilla groups in Palestine, but he had not yet commanded any considerable body of troops. In person most of his surviving pictures show him wearing a scrappy beard, a battered old solar topi and khaki slacks and sweater, and this is the image that has survived. In contrast the photograph which appeared with Wingate's obituary notice by General Slim in 1944 shows him as a smart, good-looking man wearing major general's field service uniform with two medal ribbons, the DSO with two bars and the Palestine General Service Medal. (He used to say that he did not wear the latter with pride as he disagreed with British policy.) He was a man of medium height, very active and strong, and a clue to his character is given by the fact that after leaving Woolwich he took to fox-hunting enthusiastically while stationed on Salisbury Plain. There are three types of fox-hunters, those who avoid obstacles, those who follow a leader over obstacles with reasonable safety, and those who strike across country and take their own line. Wingate was in the third category, always taking his own line and the most difficult line at that. Professionally he was the same, never accepting conventional wisdom, working out his own ideas on how to deal with a situation, putting all his immense energy and drive into the solution regardless of obstacles, and brooking no opposition. We shall see what impact this man made on the Ethiopian campaign.

The Second Battle of Gallabat

On 6 November 1940, in accordance with one of the decisions taken at the Eden conference, the 10th Indian Brigade of the 5th Indian Division, consisting of the 1st Essex, the 4th/10th Baluch Regiment, and the 3rd/18th Royal Garhwal Rifles and commanded by Brigadier W. J. Slim, attacked the old British fort of Gallabat which the Italians had occupied on 4 July, intending to go on and take the Italian fort of Metemma, 500 metres away. These forts were defended by the 27th Colonial Battalion and Captain Braca's 1st Gruppo Bande di Confine, about 1600 mixed Ethiopian and Eritrean infantry with heavy and light machine guns but no anti-tank weapons save for mines.

The attacking brigade was supported by 12 tanks and 26 air-craft. The Garhwalis captured Gallabat against stiff opposition, the Essex formed up to attack Metemma, but then most of the tanks were knocked out by mines or damaged their tracks on rocks and the supporting Gladiator fighters, who arrived in pairs, were shot out of the sky by the Italian CR42s of 412 squadron, leaving a clear run to the Italian bombers who made the small rocky hill of Gallabat untenable. Some of the Essex in the rear companies retreated in disorder, the battalions were withdrawn and the attack abandoned. The Italian colonial troops, in number about half the attacking British, behaved with great gallantry and suffered severe casualties, including several officers. Thesiger remembers watching the attack by British medium tanks on Metemma and seeing *ascari* lying down and firing at the tanks with light machine guns, the tanks passing though their lines and sometimes over their bodies, but not one running away.

This was a serious British reverse, not only, in Slim's words, because 'British troops behaved even worse than the Italians', but because it had important consequences well appreciated by the Italians. Had the British attack succeeded, the Italians would have had to retreat 120 kilometres to Chilga, the next defensible position and only 40 kilometres from Gondar. Gondar would have been threatened, the Italians would not have been able to reinforce Keren, and the whole position on the Eritrean front radically altered in favour of the British. The effect on patriot morale would have been significant and the move of the Emperor into Gojjam could have taken place earlier, though the decisive factor on this move was the state of readiness of his bodyguard. Fortunately for the British Army the reverse was not held against the commander, Brigadier Slim, who, like Wellington after Sultan Pettah, rose from this debacle to command the Fourteenth Army in Burma, and was unquestionably the finest British commander in the Second World War; the 1st Essex also redeemed themselves under Slim's command in the Fourteenth Army.

Sandford and Kabada

In Mission 101's camp at Faguta Sandford and Kabada had daily meetings with chiefs from near and far while messengers came in and left with letters in the Emperor's name to leaders in all parts of the country. Sandford pressed Khartoum for the early return of the Emperor and for air support. Despite a serious setback for the RAF on 16 October when 412 squadron's CR42s destroyed eight

Wellesleys and two Vincents on the ground at Gedaref, the RAF bombed Bahr Dar, Dangila and Engiabara on 21 and 22 October, raids which probably did little damage but were a boost to patriot morale. An old soldier of Mission 101, Ayana Bire, describes how they pitched their tents in the open and could rely on the loyalty of the local population: 'The majority of the peasants were loyal. Some *fannu* (bandits) joined the *banda*. We often saw Italian aircraft and once a plane from Bahr Dar dropped a bomb but it did not explode.' The mission was never betrayed to the Italians, but it remains a mystery why the Italian air force did not try harder to destroy their camp.

Sandford and Kabada took some time to settle down to a satisfactory working relationship, at least according to Kabada's account. He recalls that at a staff meeting when duties were allocated he was given the job of propaganda, which he clearly resented, complaining that he had no money.

> As I said this he [the colonel] realized that his ploy had been seen through because he became embarrassed and flustered, ... 'I have arranged for $50,000 to be allocated specially for you,' he went on in a garrulous way. I could have quarrelled with him ... but I remembered ... the great responsibility which His Majesty had cast on me and so I ignored the matter.

Kabada's resentment, of which Sandford was quite unaware, is shown by the language he used, saying that Sandford was 'embarrassed and flustered' and spoke 'in a garrulous way'. For several days after this Kabada corresponded with patriot leaders without showing the letters to Sandford, who solved the problem by walking over to Kabada's tent with a bunch of signals received from the *kaid* and suggesting that it would be sensible if they saw each other's correspondence. Kabada concedes that, 'after this we came to a *rapprochement*, but it was only a superficial political *rapprochement*. Any meeting of hearts had been severed at the time of the first speech.'

The 'first speech' was when Sandford told Kabada he was no longer an adviser under the Emperor, but responsible to the British commander-in-chief. Among misconceptions current in Ethiopia today is the belief that Sandford played a double game, pretending to favour Ethiopian independence, but in fact furthering British interests. Wingate, in contrast, was the single-minded champion of Ethiopian freedom. No one would quarrel with this view of Wingate. The view on Sandford probably stems from the 'first speech'. Kabada and other Ethiopians who have read his book failed to understand how Sandford, who had lived in Ethiopia for many years and learned its secrets, could now be working for the British. It was as if he had changed sides and betrayed Ethiopia's trust. How wrong the belief about Sandford was can be deduced from the evidence so far and to follow.

The Visit to East Gojjam

On the surface Sandford and Kabada continued to work well together and both were concerned with the situation in east Gojjam. The Italians appeared to be strengthening their defences by moving troops from Addis Ababa to Debra Markos, and the 3rd Colonial Brigade from Debra Markos to Burye. Leaving Critchley in charge at Faguta, Sandford and Kabada marched east on 2 November to stimulate patriot activity in east Gojjam, skirting the northern edge of the Choke mountains, and arriving at Getabit on 5 November. There they met Lij Hailu Belao, who signed an agreement in writing not to supply the Italians with food, to invest the forts of Mota and Kiero, and to keep in touch with Mission 101 headquarters by mounted messenger. Hailu Belao invested Mota and Kabada opened communications with the garrison hoping that this would lead to surrender. Hailu Belao's activities were a serious worry to the Italians, at least until Ras Hailu returned to Gojjam.

On 6 November Sandford and Kabada moved to Mengistor, 50 miles to the southeast, where they concluded a similar agreement with Belai Zelleka, who undertook to invest Bichena but was afraid of being stabbed in the back by Hailu Belao. Sandford recorded of Belai Zelleka prophetically, 'We can make use of him ... but there is no place for him in the future of Gojjam.' Sandford then returned to Faguta, having received a message that Wingate was flying in to see him, arriving on 16 November, after another 120-mile mule-back journey across mountainous country. Kabada remained to try to bring about a working arrangement between the two patriot leaders; Kabada, the Shoan aristocrat, commented on Belleka, 'After the Colonel left I remained . . . to talk to and try and tame this peasant wild animal patriot.'

The visit to east Gojjam had positive results, at least for a time. The people now believed that Haile Selassie was in the Sudan and would soon be returning to his country, the forts of Mota and Bichena were besieged, and some pressure was taken off west Gojjam by the removal of one colonial battalon from Burye to Debra Markos. Messages sent by Kabada to Ababa Aregai and the Shoan leaders gave them encouragement.

Wingate in Khartoum

Wingate lost no time in turning his staff appointment into a command, in the words of his Israeli clerk, Abram Akavia, 'as he always did'. He saw the Emperor and pledged his loyalty to him and by all accounts made a deep impression on him, and made plans to fly in to Gojjam to meet Sandford. The meeting took place at Faguta on 20 November, Wingate flying in in a Vincent bomber piloted by a courageous volunteer, Flight Lieutenant Collis, who landed on a temporary airstrip prepared by Sandford's men with patriot help. Wingate told Sandford of the results of the Eden conference, which was all good news to him, particularly the decision to take the offensive and to recruit operational centres, an idea Sandford had himself floated in Cairo. Both men agreed that as soon as his bodyguard was ready the Emperor should enter Gojjam. This was agreed by GHQ Khartoum provided that it coincided with other operational plans, but not yet approved by the British government. The Emperor's force would need to climb the escarpment, preferably using mules, but it was clear that insufficient could be obtained from the Patriots so it was agreed that Wingate would collect camels in the Sudan.

Wingate flew back to Khartoum on 22 November, the takeoff being even more hazardous than the landing, and a few days later the RAF bombed Burye and Dangila, and these raids, together with Wingate's flight, were a good boost to patriot morale. The two men had got on well at their first meeting; later their relations were not so happy. Wavell wished he could have been at the meeting and his description of the contrasting characters is graphic: 'Few people looked more like a fiery leader of partisans than Wingate, few people looked less like one than Sandford — solid, bespectacled, benevolent — who in his way was as bold and as active as Wingate.' The courageous Collis was awarded the Distinguished Flying Cross for his skilful piloting.

Wingate sent for two men to join him, Major A. C. (Tony) Simonds MBE, Royal Berkshire Regiment, from Cairo, whom he had known in Palestine, to be his GSO2, and Abram Akavia, who had been his interpreter in Palestine, to be his clerk. Simonds recalls receiving a signal from Wingate asking if he was prepared to parachute into Ethiopia. He replied that he was willing to walk and received another signal, 'Walk'. Before he left Cairo he received another Wingate signal, 'On encountering Lt Col. Brocklehurst you will shoot him.' Brocklehurst,[1] a retired game warden, had an ill-conceived plan to incite the Galla against their Amhara overlords and against the Italians, which Wingate and Haile Selassie managed to put a stop to. The story, however, gave rise to a rumour, still believed by some in Ethiopia today, that the devious British planned a colony of Greater Somalia, embracing all the Somali and Galla peoples. Akavia had no military rank. He had taught himself shorthand and typing and 'was happy to serve under Wingate in any capacity'.

It was still then envisaged that the Frontier Battalion would carry out its intended role of escorting arms convoys to the Patriots. Nott had been sending off small convoys both to Sandford and Bentinck but the first large convoy left Roseires on 27 November escorted by No 4 patrol company under Bimbashi Peter Acland. This was a sizable force, nearly 300 men, 220 camels and 40 horses, including 11 pack ponies carrying Lewis guns. In addition to their own stores and water the camels carried 100 rifles with ammunition for the Patriots and a large supply of dollars. Bimbashi Charles De Bunsen accompanied Acland as one of his officers. The destination was Belaiya and the original plan was to deliver arms and establish a base against future operations leaving one platoon there, which would clear a landing strip where a fighter plane would be stationed to ambush Italian bombers. The rest of the company would then return.

The journey was a hard 14-day slog through the bush, uneventful, but a useful trail blazer for Wingate's Gideon Force, which later followed the same route. De Bunsen recorded a meeting on the way with 'a ragged figure with bare legs and an old khaki topi, who addressed us in English'. This was Critchley, on his way to Roseires to have treatment for his eyes. Critchley's replacement in Mission 101 was Thesiger, who from the beginning had wanted to join Mission 101 but had been told by Platt to learn some soldiering first. He now had his wish fulfilled.

Nott met Wingate for the first time on 8 December in Khartoum, when Wingate made it clear that he did not think much of Sandford's plans: 'Wingate's plan ... seems to leave out Dan and nearly leaves out Arthur [Bentinck].' Wingate explained this plan at a conference on 9 December, Nott describing it as 'bold and refreshing', and on 10 December Nott was told he was going in: 'Hurrah! The *Kaid* has moved at last.' Wingate's plan was for a striking force consisting of the Frontier Battalion and the 2nd Ethiopian Battalion, which had arrived from Kenya on 8 December, to assemble at Roseires and march to Belaiya and from there into Gojjam to be followed by the Emperor and his bodyguard. The escort role of the Frontier Battalion would cease and a message explaining this was dropped by air on Acland at Belaiya, who was told to remain there with his company and develop a forward base for the striking force and the Emperor.

Much to his disappointment De Bunsen was sent back to Roseires escorting the camels with a platoon, and from there was ordered to return to civilian duty. With five of their officers in the force, the Sudan government possibly felt that they were risking enough already. On his way back De Bunsen met Thesiger riding a camel on his way to join Mission 101, who was nearly shot by a sentry, 'but shouted at him in the worst Arabic he could think of to put down his gun, which the man did — recognizing that no one but a *bimbashi* could be so rude.' De Bunsen tells the first of several stories about Thesiger, who was admired for his toughness, but had his leg pulled when he boasted about 'living on the country'. 'He had nothing but a few dates in his saddle bags and started by saying that he was completely indifferent to food, but was glad to share our meal off a broken down camel.' De Bunsen reached

Roseires with a very hungry platoon — they were on short rations, having taken longer than anticipated on the journey out — where they were personally congratulated by the *kaid*, and then went back to his district, but he did return to Ethiopia later as Political Officer Tigre.

Bentinck's Mission

While Acland consolidated the base at Belaiya, and Sandford went on with his work at Faguta, ignorant as yet of the effect Wingate's arrival would have on his plans, Bentinck was beyond Wingate's control and continued with the orders given to him by Sandford. By December 1940 he had established his headquarters at Jogolambe, and Foley and Mohamed Effendi had had some success with mining operations on the roads Chilga–Metemma to the west and Gondar–Asmara to the north, causing casualties to troops and vehicles. The Italian High Command at Gondar reported 'organized sabotage by rebels assisted by white emissaries' and warned all convoys to take precautions. Foley was awarded the MC for these operations. Despite these successes Bentinck, who kept a daily log, felt despondent about the failure of the main object of his mission which was to encourage a full-scale revolt. He lamented his lack of soldiers, the continual disappearance of chiefs to Khartoum to see the Emperor who always returned with malaria so that they were useless when they came back, and the casual attitude of the Patriots who when issued with new rifles sold the old ones to the Italians.

The picture one gets of Bentinck's mission is very different from that of Sandford's. Wolde Giorgis was ineffective as Haile Selassie's representative; there was no leader of authority on whom he could rely, and the revolt was not a popular rebellion as in Gojjam, but more in the nature of bandit activity in an area where Haile Selassie's writ had not run strongly before the Italian war, and where news of his likely return had less effect. Some tribes, such as the Kamant, were still actively supporting the Italians, and Bentinck himself did not have the experience or confidence of Sandford. Only a minority of chiefs were taking direct action against the Italians, although reports of interminable conferences of chiefs threatening action did reach the Italians and, indirectly, so Cheesman believed, deterred them from invading the Sudan; no Italian evidence in support of this belief has been found.

Drew Rejoins Mission 101

In September 1940, when they were left at Sarako by Sandford, Drew and his party had moved to within three miles of Kwara to support Werku and his men in the siege of the fort. Grey opened wireless communication with Khartoum on 17 September, and heard on that day of the shooting down of 185 German planes in the Battle of Britain (as then reported); they kept listening to BBC bulletins after that, thinking that Britain would be invaded. Evidently the investment of the fort was effective in denying the garrison food supplies as a number of *ascari* were reported to be suffering from scurvy. Even so Grey succeeded in obtaining some much needed sugar and tea from Kwara by sending in local Ethiopians. Grey also describes how late in November Drew sent in a letter signed by himself, Grey and Whitmore demanding that the garrison surrender to 'the British forces (all three of us!), but all they did was to lock up our messenger'.

On 1 December Werku attacked and reduced the post of Matabia, dispersing the garrison. Unfortunately on returning to his camp he was ambushed and shot and died of his wounds. He had been a fine leader, much feared by the Italians, and the loss was serious, though the siege continued under his successor, Lij Belaya, until the garrison was relieved by a bold stroke by Captain Braca, which will be mentioned in the next chapter. Werku's death was successfully concealed from the Italians who continued to believe that he was in command.

Drew and his party left Kwara on 10 December and rejoined Sandford at Faguta on 20 December, Drew being praised by Sandford for his 'admirable handling of his detachment'. Sandford was disappointed with the apparent lack of action from Khartoum after Wingate's visit and exercised his right as Wavell's staff officer to appeal direct to Wavell. His signal was not sent on by Platt who told him firmly but kindly to fall into line: 'You will render greater assistance ... by complying with instructions from my HQ, which are designed to coordinate activities from Kenya, the Sudan and on your part.' Platt and Cunningham were planning a three-pronged attack on AOI, from the northern Sudan through Kassala into Eritrea, from Kenya into Somalia and southern Ethiopia, and, numerically on a far lesser scale, but politically of great importance, Wingate's advance with the Emperor into Gojjam. It obviously made strategic sense to coordinate the Emperor's return with the two major advances, now planned for January 1941.

Ras Hailu Returns to Gojjam

General Nasi proposed his political solution for the Gojjam revolt — bringing back its former ruler, Ras Hailu — in a letter to the viceroy of 25 November, mentioning two conditions that would make the position acceptable to the *ras*, a title which would give him precedence over the other nobility, and a liberal allowance. The proposal was approved by the viceroy and Ras Hailu arrived at Debra Markos on 8 December, his arrival described by Nasi as 'a veritable apotheosis ... many thousands flooded in from the heart of Gojjam to render him homage'. An allowance of 100,000 lire a month was granted, and sufficient weapons to form a *banda*, initially 1500 strong and later increased to 4000. The question of title proved difficult, Nasi proposing either *Mesfin* (Prince) or *Padrone* (Lord) of Gojjam. Neither was acceptable to the government in Rome who finally proposed '"Viceroy's representative in Gojjam", but this was not communicated to the *Ras* for fear that he might not be satisfied.'

Sandford heard of Ras Hailu's arrival and signalled Haile Selassie who replied on 13 December enclosing a letter to be sent on to the *ras*. Ras Hailu did not reply to the Emperor's letter. On 20 December Sandford received a report from one of his Ethiopian officers that Ras Seyum had accompanied Ras Hailu to Debra Markos but had not stayed, that Ras Hailu was proposing to visit Bichena to arrange for the marriage of his granddaughter Alau Sahau to Belai Zelleka (as a bait to win him over), that he promised to clear all opposition from Gojjam if the Italians made him *negus*, and that he was here in fulfilment of a prophecy that Hailu in his old age would rule all Ethiopia as representative of a foreign power, his power likened to that of the moon rather than the sun. Sandford also wrote to Ras Hailu, begging him, 'for the sake of our old friendship', to be reconciled to the Emperor, informing him of British advances in North Africa and that the Emperor was expected to enter Gojjam soon. Ras Hailu refused to respond to this letter also, and a copy of Sandford's letter and a record of Hailu's refusal was sent by Nasi to the Director General of Political Affairs in Addis Ababa.

According to Nasi, Ras Hailu 'secured the submission of many chiefs and subchiefs', and wrote to all the main patriot leaders of whom only one, Fitaurari Haile Yusus of Dambacha, replied saying that he would join the *ras* as soon as he reached Dambacha. Hailu set off for Bichena, a march of 120 kilometres, on 9 January 1941, accompanied by an Italian political officer, Dr Sarubbi, and an impressive show of armed men to boost his prestige: 'The festive population ran to meet him. . . . The old Lord of Gojjam, who had been away for 10 years, was received triumphally everywhere.' At Bichena Ras Hailu invited the local chiefs to submit. Belai Zelleka did not then 'rise to the bait' until pressure was put on him by Ras Hailu's *banda* and the large *banda* of Colonel Anderson, *commissario* of Amara Saint. This, together with the bait of the *ras*'s granddaughter, apparently persuaded Belai Zelleka to submit. In any event, on 30 January 1941 Nasi signalled to Addis Ababa; 'Dr Sarubbi reports that Belai Zelleka today submitted to Ras Hailu.' So at any rate Nasi reported, although, from Belai Zelleka's subsequent dealings with Mission 101 and Gideon Force, it seems he still kept his options open.

Before returning to Debra Markos Ras Hailu and his *banda* relieved the garrison at Mota, which had been under pressure from Hailu Belao's Patriots since the visit of Sandford and Kabada to east Gojjam. On 4 February Nasi left Gojjam to take up a new post as commander of the Western Sector and governor of the Gondar region, leaving with regret his political offensive in Gojjam for which he claimed considerable success.

The Achievements of Mission 101

In western and northern Gojjam Ras Hailu's arrival had little impact and both patriot and RAF activity increased. By the end of December 1940 GHQ Khartoum had decided on Belaiya as the base for the Emperor, but it seems that the Foreign Office was still doubtful about allowing the Emperor into Ethiopia, and we have here a Churchillian intervention, made in response to a direct appeal to the prime minister from Haile Selassie through Chapman-Andrews:

(Action this day) 30.12.40 Prime Minister to Foreign Secretary [now Anthony Eden]. It would seem that every effort should be made to meet the Emperor of Abyssinia's wishes. ... I am strongly in favour of Haile Selassie entering Abyssinia. ... I should be glad if a favourable answer could be drafted for me to send to the Emperor.

When the Foreign Office demurred on the grounds of the risks Churchill minuted on 31 December 1940, 'One would think the Emperor would be the best judge of when to risk his life for his throne,' noting that the Foreign Office was giving attention 'to the question of what pledges we give to the Emperor about his restoration'. To Sandford and Wingate it was beyond doubt that Haile Selassie was returning as the country's ruler, and Platt concurred, with the proviso that his return must coincide with the other advances.

Sandford had an alternative and extremely bold plan for a base, at Womberima south of Burye. This came to nothing but illustrates how Sandford's mind was working. His strategy was to bring the Emperor right forward as a focus for the revolt and achieve a concentration of patriot forces in sufficient strength to defeat the Italians. In pursuit of this strategy Sandford sent Grey to clear a landing ground, and appointed Ato Makonnen Desta, an Ethiopian officer who had joined the mission, to command the advance base and 'threaten Burye in cooperation with Nagash's forces and Brown's centre'. This was No 1 Operational Centre, which was expected soon.

Grey returned very pleased with himself, as a signals' warrant officer, for having cleared a 500-yard strip and was indignant when Sandford said, 'That's a pretty poor effort,' until he realized that Sandford was referring to his beard. Sandford was overruled about Womberima by GHQ Khartoum, which had accepted Wingate's plan and decided on Belaiya as a base. On 21 January he received a signal from the *kaid* ordering him to hand over Mission

101 temporarily to Thesiger and proceed 'by quickest route to Belaiya where Emperor awaits you'. Sandford went immediately to Belaiya, arriving on 27 January, and there he waited for the Emperor. Wingate was dismissive about Mission 101 in his dispatch:

> The Mission, although its efforts were of great value as an indispensable reconnaissance, was too inconsiderable and unsupported to do more than raise a query in the minds of the population in its immediate neighbourhood. ... While the effect of its presence on the patriots was mildly encouraging, that on Ethiopians who adhered to the Italian Government was nil.

The Italian view was quite different. General Martini, Nasi's predecessor and then deputy in the Western Sector, wrote about 'the rebellion in Gojjam, which the Sandford mission had succeeded in reviving and maintaining at powerful level'. Certainly in Gojjam Sandford had executed Platt's orders, stopping troop movements south and east from Dangila by increased patriot activity having reconciled the main patriot leaders, particularly Mangasha and Nagash. Bentinck's northern mission had disrupted, but not stopped, troop movement north and west from Gondar.

Mission 101 was more than a 'reconnaissance', as described by Wingate. Its greatest achievement was that, because of the patriot activity it stimulated, the force Wingate was now assembling to enter Gojjam with the Emperor was able to move freely away from the main forts without fear of interference from the strong Italian forces. Furthermore, Mission 101, soon to be reinforced by No 1 Operational Centre, initiated under Sandford quite successful aggressive action against the Italian forts until Wingate's Gideon Force took over. These developments, and the entry of Gideon Force, will be described in the next chapter.

Note
1. There was an element of truth in the Greater Somalia story. This was actually proposed by Ernest Bevin in 1946! Brocklehurst and Bentinck both refused to serve under Wingate when he was sent by Wavell in 1942 to organize guerrilla resistance in Burma against the Japanese. Brocklehurst was killed in the retreat.

3

Gideon Force:
'A Sword of Rare Metal'

Wingate called his small force Gideon Force after his command was confirmed at Belaiya. The choosing of this name is illustrative of Wingate's character and biblical knowledge. Gideon, in Judges 7:7, 'chose the 300 men that lapped', surrounded the Midianites so that they panicked, and 'the Lord delivered them into his hand'. Wingate surrounded the Italian garrison at Burye and induced their commander, Colonel Natale, to believe that he was surrounded by a large force, so that he panicked and retreated. Wingate knew exactly what he wanted to do and chose a biblical reference to fit it.

Wingate arrived at Roseires on 24 December to find half his force assembled there, the Frontier Battalion, the Ethiopian mortar platoon, and No 1 Operational Centre. These units must be briefly described.

The Frontier Battalion was a formidable unit of five patrol companies, each recruited from one of the five SDF corps areas, and each about 250 strong so the total strength was about 1250, with 14 British officers. The men were mainly Muslim Arab Sudanese, with Nubas in No 5 patrol company and some Nubas in No 1, the majority new recruits with some re-enlisted soldiers, under experienced regular NCOs and warrant officers, all soldiers of high quality with a long tradition of service. Of the British officers, four were regulars, the others from the Political Service, the Plantation Syndicate[1] or commercial companies, all Arabic-speaking with long experience of the Sudan and able to communicate (and joke) directly with the men. Each company also had experienced Sudanese officers. This was a highly efficient disciplined unit, which nearly always performed with distinction, equipped with modern infantry weapons and trained by Boustead to shoot straight and conserve ammunition. Dick Luyt, a sergeant in the 2nd Ethiopian Battalion, described the Sudanese as a 'rock in the whole campaign', and to Wingate 'the sight of an *emma* [turban] on a hillside was worth a hundred men'. In the words of W. E. D. Allen, later their animal transport officer, 'a sword of rare metal has been cast out of a dozen Englishmen and a few hundred Africans'.

The Ethiopian mortar platoon consisted of one officer and 50 men, all Ethiopians, who had been recruited at Gedaref by Nott from the Patriots of Shalaka Mesfin and trained by Sergeant West of the 2nd West Yorks. They were equipped with four three-inch mortars made in the railway workshops in Khartoum, which were carried on mules with the ammunition. This unit arrived with Nott and rear HQ Mission 101, also with Mesfin, who wanted to go in with them but was refused permission by Haile Selassie. The mortar platoon were Wingate's only artillery and performed well throughout the campaign, including the Gondar operations, suffering 50 per cent casualties.

No 1 Operational Centre was the first to arrive of ten such centres recruited from volunteers in Middle East Command. It consisted of one officer and four sergeants from 2nd/1st Field Regiment of the 6th Australian Division, then stationed in Palestine, and 240 Ethiopian *askari* recruited from the refugees in Khartoum. Its history was different from that of the other centres in that the officer, Lieutenant Alan Brown, volunteered for sabotage work in Ethiopia after talking to an Ethiopian Coptic priest in Jerusalem before the Eden conference, persuaded the four sergeants to go with him, and they were undergoing commando training in Egypt when the call for volunteers went out.

Wingate's other infantry battalion, the 2nd Ethiopians, did not arrive at Roseires until 5 and 6 January but will be introduced here. Recruited from the Ethiopian refugees at Taveta, the unit consisted of six British officers, four sergeants and 600 Ethiopians, including 24 officers. None of the British officers were regulars, not even the commanding officer, Major Ted Boyle; Michael Tutton, a DO from Tanganyika, was the only native Englishman, the others were 'colonials'. All the Ethiopians were former soldiers of Haile Selassie's army, the officers selected because of the rank they held under the Emperor, the other ranks for their physical fitness. The battalion had had four months' basic training, three in Kenya and one at Soba camp near Khartoum. They were equipped with 1870 French Labella single-shot rifles, and a few Lewis and Vickers machine guns and Boyes anti-tank rifles, which they had picked up in Uganda during the month-long journey by rail and river steamer from Mariakani to Khartoum. This was very much a scratch unit, the men natural soldiers but with little formal training, the officers immensely keen but inexperienced, and there was a weakness in command. Communication between officers and men was in basic Swahili, which the men had picked up in Taveta camp. The unit's performance in the campaign was patchy, fighting with great gallantry at the Charaka river action on 6 March, after that suffering some lapses but finishing strongly at Gondar. There was nothing wrong with the spirit of the men. Dick Luyt recalls that at Gotani camp in Kenya they forswore drink and women until the Emperor was restored to his throne, a pledge they did not always honour. After retreat each evening they held their own ceremony, praying for the success of the campaign and the freedom of their country. Luyt found these ceremonies moving.

To get this force to Belaiya and thence into Gojjam required an enormous number of baggage animals, and these could only be camels hired from the Sudanese since mules could not be obtained in sufficient numbers from the Patriots. The camels were obtained and got to the assembly area through the help of district commissioners and veterinary officers and pressure from Wingate on the Sudan government — 25,000 according to Wingate, 18,000 according to Allen, with 5000 camel drivers. Particular credit must go to two veterinary officers, John Jack and Ian Gillespie, who examined the animals and passed them fit for the journey, the same two officers who had helped Bentinck with the crossing of the Atbara river. Very few of the camels survived the journey but they were a necessary sacrifice.

On Christmas Day 1940, at a conference at Roseires, Wingate gave out his orders for the entry of his task force, his *corps d'élite*, into Gojjam in front of the Emperor. No one questioned Major Wingate's right to give orders to Lieutenant Colonel Boustead and others. Nott was impressed, commenting in his diary, 'What a brain!' Wingate's plan was for a motor road to be pushed forward to Um Idla on the frontier. From there camel convoys would take the force to Belaiya, which would be the forward base. The 2nd Ethiopians would go straight to Um Idla to prepare an airstrip so that the Emperor could fly in on 20 January. From Belaiya the force would enter Gojjam, choosing a route up the escarpment suitable for camels, and in advance of the force the operational centres would go straight into Gojjam to join Mission 101 and start sabotage operations. The first of these, the Australian No 1 Centre, left for Belaiya immediately after the conference. To protect his right flank Wingate sent off No 5 patrol company under Bimbashi Guy Campbell to neutralize the Italian garrison at Gubba. They joined Lieutenant Colonel Gifford's Composite Battalion SDF, became involved in operations at Asosa and later at Chilga and never formed part of Gideon Force, though we shall meet them later at Chilga in the Gondar operations.

Wingate had ideas, dismissed correctly as impossible by Boustead, of bringing the Emperor to Belaiya by car, and sent off Major Simonds, who had arrived in response to his summons, with Bimbashi le Blanc, transport officer of the Frontier Battalion, and Douglas Dodds-Parker, staff captain at GHQ Khartoum, to reconnoitre a route to the mountain. They found the motor journey impossible and Dodds-Parker and le Blanc returned while Simonds joined up with the Australian convoy and completed the journey on foot.

The March to Belaiya and the Arrival of the Emperor*

The force that left Um Idla for Belaiya under Wingate consisted of his two battalions, Mission 101 HQ with wireless, the mortar platoon, camel transport, and, as he put it, 'no aircraft and no artillery'. In addition to the *hamla*s (camel convoys) of his force

---

* See General Map 2 and Sketch 1.

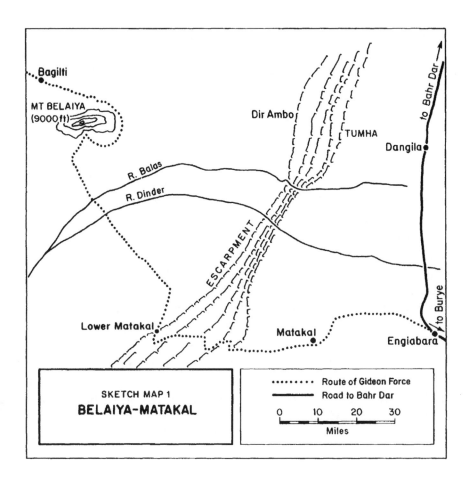

Bagilti

MT BELAIYA
(9000 ft)

Dir Ambo

TUMHA

Dangila

to Bahr Dar

R. Balas

R. Dinder

ESCARPMENT

Lower Matakal

Matakal

Engiabara

to Burye

SKETCH MAP 1
BELAIYA-MATAKAL

· · · · · · · · Route of Gideon Force
―――――― Road to Bahr Dar

0   10   20   30
Miles

numerous separate *hamla*s of the operational centres followed and the bush between Um Idla and Belaiya would be criss-crossed by the tracks of different *hamla*s and littered with the corpses of dead camels, the convoys leaving at intervals so that there would not be overcrowding at the water holes. It is recorded that only the *hamla* of Captain Laurens van der Post of No 5 Operational Centre lost no camels on the march. The journey to Belaiya was about 150 miles and took 12 to 14 days. Boustead did it in four-and-a-half days with horses when ordered forward by Wingate to take charge of the base. A further 50 miles on was the 3000-foot escarpment they would have to climb in order to enter Gojjam. The nearest occupied Italian positions were Engiabara and Dangila, about 15 miles from the escarpment, which was itself easily defensible.

Nott followed the Australians with Mission 101 HQ and the mortar platoon, joining forces with John Jack, who was going in to buy mules for the Emperor. They left Um Idla on 7 January, learned to travel with full water carriers and frequently had to use them, and shot game for meat whenever possible, recording eland, waterbuck, roan and sable. They caught fish in the rivers, including 'one gigantic eel with a freshly caught fish still alive in its mouth', and arrived at Belaiya on 21 January having lost 28 camels, three mules and one donkey. They found there Acland and No 4 patrol company — 'He has a hell of a beard, looks like a Pathan' — Simonds and the Australians, and No 3 patrol company under Bimbashi Alec Jarvis, who had gone ahead of them.

Nott set about organizing the base, pacifying the local Patriots who had been upset by peremptory demands for mules — 'talked to Mangasha and Nagash's representatives about mule question over tea. Parted amicably with promise of maximum mules' — and got to know the Australians, Lieutenant Brown and Sergeants Wood, Howell, Burke and Body, 'all gunners — very good type of chaps — Burke was the Waratah[2] fullback and the one man the All Blacks couldn't hurt.' The mules were for Brown's centre and turned up next day. Nott found his interpreter, Johannes Abdu, very helpful over the negotiations.

Bimbashi 'Henry' Johnson's No 1 patrol company and Bimbashi Bill Harris's No 2 Patrol Company left after Nott, the latter leaving Um Idla on 11 January. Harris has left us a detailed account of the journey. The SDF companies were trained and equipped to march with animal transport, so for them the journey was nothing new. Only the terrain, the lack of water, and the frequent deep sand river beds where crossings had to be made for the camels, made the march difficult. They carried a month's rations, three days water at half a gallon a man per day, and grain for the horses. They were dependent on finding water for the horses every 24 hours; the camels could go for four to five days without water and did not require extra food provided there was enough browsing of the right type (acacia thorn), and time to browse. The heaviest mortality occurred among the camels after they had climbed the escarpment and were out of the thorn bush country, which provided them with their natural food. On the way to Belaiya there was a waterless stretch of 70 miles, which they had to cross by marching at night — 'the camels always went their best at night, striding along with an almost ghostly tread.'

Harris arrived at Belaiya on 25 January after losing seven camels, a low average, and was sent on by Boustead to take up a defensive position on the Balas river facing the escarpment. On the way he passed Jarvis and his No 3 company working on the landing ground. Harris had raised and trained this company, and the NCOs came up to shake his hand, 'grins spreading over their faces', while his own men 'took no part in these salutations beyond ... ribald remarks to the effect that while they were moving towards the enemy No 3 looked like doing a labourer's job until the end of the war'. There was great rivalry between the Sudanese companies, and great loyalty towards individual officers who had served with them. No 3 company had been bombed by two Capronis while working on the landing ground, with no casualties to men, but several camels had been killed, 'the men delighted at seeing so much meat delivered to the door'.

The 2nd Ethiopian Battalion had been re-equipped on arriving at Roseires with .300 Springfield rifles, the standard American rifle of the First World War with a peep sight and holding five rounds in the magazine. These were part of a consignment intended for the Polish brigade in Palestine but diverted to the Emperor's force by the Eden conference. They were less handy than the British .303 Lee Enfield, but good rifles and the men were delighted with them.

A, B and C companies followed the camel route to Belaiya leaving D company, with Boyle and Wingate, to await the Emperor. D company was commanded by Second Lieutenant Michael Tutton, an Eton and Oxford educated Tanganyika DO, whose second in command was Sergeant Dick Luyt, a South African from Cape Town, Oxford Rhodes scholar and rugby football blue, also destined for the colonial service. Both men kept diaries, now valuable sources. D company's task was to prepare a landing ground and provide the guard of honour for the Emperor on his arrival.

While waiting for the Emperor Tutton put his men through a firing practice with the new rifles, recording that 134 men fired a course at 110 yards, 'including Major Boyle and J. Anderson Esq, Reuter correspondent', who accompanied them to Belaiya. He also took the opportunity to have things out with Boyle, who was 'unreasonably intolerant', overdid fines on the men for petty offences and also was 'at daggers drawn with Wingate'. On one occasion Tutton himself clashed with Wingate, who showed remarkable forbearance in dealing with a mildly insubordinate young amateur soldier. Tutton had just sat down to breakfast at 10.00 a.m., having been working on the landing ground since early morning, when he was called by Wingate to inspect the ground. Tutton declined, saying he had a kit inspection. 'He [Wingate] stared a bit and then pushed off without a word. Like most bullies, he seems to be best met with a rough tongue.' Matters between Wingate and Boyle did not improve, and Wingate's low opinion of Boyle did not make for the cohesion of the force.

How Tutton dealt with a promotion in his No 16 platoon illustrates the importance of rank in Ethiopian society. Platoons were commanded by Ethiopian lieutenants with a corporal second in command. The officers in 16 platoon had been taken for the Emperor's bodyguard and needed replacing. Tutton took counsel with his senior Ethiopian officer, Fitarauri Garadou. Both would have liked to promote the company quartermaster sergeant, Ayella, but he was a 'nobody' and the men would not have him. Tutton suggested Kenyasmatch Kumsa, then serving as a rifleman, as lieutenant, and Wodaju Abijaz as corporal, and Garadou agreed. The men were delighted to be commanded by a *kenyasmatch*, the appointments were made, and both men did well in action. Tutton had experience of dealing with men as a DO in Tanganyika, but no military training apart from the Eton officers' training corps, but he had a wise head on him and his company always did well. Both he and Luyt believed in consultation provided that discipline was maintained. 'The essential thing is to retain the affection of the men if we are to make them a good fighting unit.' Tutton did retain his men's affection and, like C company's commander, Ken Rowe, is remembered by old soldiers to this day. Boyle and his adjutant, Allen Smith, unfortunately did not, and herein lay the seeds of future trouble.

Haile Selassie arrived by plane at Um Idla on 20 January escorted by two South African Air Force Hurricanes. His party consisted of his two sons, Ras Kassa, Lorenzo, the *echege*, his staff and counsellors, Chapman-Andrews, who would accompany him into Gojjam, and Dodds-Parker. He was greeted by Wingate with a speech of welcome and a guard of honour of D company, Tutton recording, 'as he crossed an imaginary line representing the border up went the Imperial Standard on the flagstaff and we gave the Royal Salute and Present Arms. The bugler really surpassed himself and blew the General Salute without a single mistake.'

Despite Simonds's failure to reach Belaiya by car and Boustead's advice, Wingate had decided to take the Emperor there in a convoy of lorries, starting on a motorable track, which had been cut for 30 miles from Um Idla, and then on a compass bearing through the bush. The convoy of eight trucks and one staff car started on 21 January, the princes returning to Khartoum with Dodds-Parker. In those days vehicles did not have four-wheel drive, and after grinding through in great heat and discomfort covering a few miles each day the Emperor's party gave up the struggle 50 miles short of Belaiya and continued the journey on horseback. Tutton with his camels had been escorting the Emperor and watched the little procession go by, 'First Wingate, then the Emperor (on horseback), then if you please the High Priest, with his venerable beard, gallantly padding along on foot through the African bush with his black robes flapping and his prayer book in his hand.'

Tutton and his company reached Belaiya on 8 February after covering the 150 miles in 12 days' marching, losing 13 camels out of 48. Near Belaiya they passed 'a huge chasm full of the rotting corpses of camels — vultures hovered in the air and flapped down into the ravine to gorge themselves.' The officers of the Frontier Battalion were mounted but in the 2nd Ethiopians the officers marched with the men except when prevented by some physical reason. Luyt put his knee out and had to ride for a time (an injury which was to cause him much trouble), and Tutton suffered from the unpleasant complaint known as 'Wajir clap', blood in the urine induced by particles of mica in the water, and at the urging of his Ethiopian officers rode a camel for half a day.

The march was a useful exercise for the force and both battalions did well, but there were serious deficiencies. Neither battalion had a medical officer, nor signalling equipment. The only wireless telegraphy was with Wingate; otherwise communication was by runner. Wingate had no staff save for Akavia, nor second in command. He tried to persuade Acland to act as his staff officer, but Acland preferred to remain with Boustead. There was very little cooperation between the two battalions, who went their way separately, and Wingate did not get on particularly well with either Boustead or Boyle. He had to respect Boustead for his seniority and experience, but he was openly critical of Boyle. One big advantage they had over the Italians was that the Italian codes had been broken and their signals were being read by Middle East signals.

While the camel convoys of Wingate's small force were plodding towards Belaiya, momentous events had been taking place elsewhere. In North Africa, after his spectacular victory over the Italians at Sidi Barrani on 11 December 1940, Wavell had captured Bardia on 1 January 1941, Tobruk on 12 January and Benghazi on 1 February. After the victory of Sidi Barrani the 4th Indian Division was switched from Cyrenaica to reinforce Platt's army in the Sudan, arriving during January 1941, and he thus had two divisions, the 4th and 5th Indian, for the advance he was planning into Eritrea. This advance started by the capture of Kassala on 20 January, and of Agordat and Barentu on 31 January and 2 February. Then Platt's force came up against the massif of Keren, and strong opposition, and the first, inconclusive, battle of Keren took place from 3 to 14 February. Nasi, in Gondar, sent considerable reinforcements to Keren, according to General Martini 11 battalions and eight batteries, including two battalions of Savoia Grenadiers, a movement the sabotage activities of Bentinck's mission sometimes disrupted but did not stop. On the southern front the two divisions of East, West and South African troops under General Cunningham (11th and 12th African) started their advance into Somalia and southern Ethiopia on 23 January, occupying Kisimayu, an Indian Ocean port, on 14 February, and Mega on 15 February.

The Relief of Kwara

The Patriots under Werku's successor, Lij Belaya, had continued to invest Kwara after Drew and his party left, and early in February news reached Fitaurari Teffere Zelleka, the patriot leader at Belaiya, that the garrison was closely besieged and could not escape. This information was passed to Boustead, then in charge, and as a result Regimental Sergeant-Major Shaw of B company of the 2nd Ethiopian Battalion with No 7 platoon under Lieutenant Tagany Maisha was sent to assist the Patriots. Tutton and the other officers of the battalion were very envious of Shaw having the first chance of action, as they thought, but in fact Shaw arrived at Kwara too late to help after a very daring rescue operation of the garrison had been carried out by Captain Braca. Braca with his *banda* group was then at Comar, southeast of Metemma, the headquarters of General Martini, then sector commander at Gondar. To conform with the retreat from Kassala in the north in the face of Platt's advance, the Italian forces at Metemma withdrew back to Chilga (a move that would have been forced on them if the second battle at Gallabat had succeeded in November 1940). Braca sought and obtained Martini's permission to try to relieve his *banda* at Kwara in the course of the withdrawal and rejoin Martini at Angidebba on the way to Chilga. He left Comar on 23 January with a force of 12 officers and 1020 *ascari* from his *banda* group and the 57th Colonial Battalion, with 265 horses and mules. He had heavy and light machine guns but no mortars or artillery. After a march of 133 kilometres over mountainous country, his force fought its way into Kwara against fierce resistance by the Patriots on 27 January, suffering in two actions 23 *ascari* killed and two officers and 72 *ascari* wounded.

75

On 29 January, with the close support of a Caproni aircraft sent from Gondar, they fought their way out again, the column now augmented by the Kwara garrison and the sick and wounded and non-combatants. These latter amounted to 300, including 130 sick and wounded of whom 73 were stretcher cases and the rest *ascaris'* wives and children. Many of the sick were scurvy cases from the garrison, confirming the reports that had reached Grey earlier. The column had to fight two more severe actions against the Patriots while negotiating the precipitous paths, encumbered by the non-combatants and stretcher cases. In the second of these actions Tenente Alessandrii, who had already distinguished himself by scaling a cliff and outflanking a patriot position on the march in, held off the attackers with a heavy machine gun to enable the column to get through until he was himself killed while serving his gun.

The column rejoined Martini at Angidebba on 5 February, having marched 339 kilometres in 14 days, fought four actions against the *ribelli*, and suffered altogether casualties of one officer killed and four wounded and 129 *ascari* killed and 222 wounded (about 35 per cent of the force). This was a high price to pay for the relief of the garrison, but one the Italian commanders and their troops were prepared to pay, believing that if the relief failed the result would be a massacre. Braca, a world-war veteran aged 41, stood up to the gruelling march as well as the younger men, marching always on foot to show an example. His report to his superior officer, dated 28 February 1941, is still extant in the Ufficio Storico in Rome and describes the operation in detail, together with an excellent map as one would expect from a cartographer.

Tenente Alessandrii was awarded the *Medaglia d'Oro al VM* posthumously for his gallantry, and some days after the column returned the Duke of Aosta flew up to Gondar to confirm the award and to distribute other medals, including the *Medaglia d'Argento al VM* to Braca (his second, the first was won in the First World War). Braca described the viceroy, 'flying up alone in his personal aircraft and defying the English fighters. The high significance of this gesture remains alive in our memories.'

There are two points of significance arising from this operation from which the British could have profited. First there were two medical officers with the column and all the wounded survived. Secondly the ground to air close cooperation was excellent, Braca indicating targets to the Caproni by firing rockets, which then strafed them, and this reduced casualties on leaving the fort. The operation is peripheral to the story of Gideon Force, but deserves mention because of the intensity of the fighting and the gallantry of both sides, the colonial troops taking very high casualties to achieve their object and the Patriots equally brave and self-sacrificing in trying to prevent the relief. We do not know their numbers or their casualties. Braca estimated their numbers as 1000 on approaching the fort and 4000 when leaving, and their casualties as 1000. Despite Braca's belief that he heard Bren-gun fire and detected the *'mano inglese'* because of the rebels' efficient tactics, it is certain that Shaw and his platoon did not arrive in time to join in the fighting. These were Patriots fighting on their own without any British or indeed imperial support, and fighting very hard. An interesting sidelight is the visit by the Duke of Aosta, piloting his own aircraft and alone, to congratulate the unit and distribute medals. Wingate would have done the same if he had been a pilot but the more conventional British commanders flew escorted.

Wingate Appointed to Command

Haile Selassie arrived at Belaiya on 6 February 1941, with Wingate, Chapman-Andrews, Ras Kassa, and his staff, and was met by an SDF guard of honour, Boustead, Nott and Sandford. He settled in to the grass-roofed 'palace' built for him by Nott and started to receive the many people who came in to see him. The arrival at Belaiya was important as it gave the Emperor his first base in his own country from which he could, and did, issue proclamations.

Sandford then had no inkling that any change of command was contemplated; he expected to remain in charge of operations as head of Mission 101 and that Wingate would serve under him. On his way to Belaiya he had met Sergeant Body marching towards Gojjam, and Body recalls that Sandford, 'a very nice man, not at all the military type', asked him if he knew where his 'staff officer, Major Wingate, was' — a description Wingate would not have much liked. Sandford had made plans for attacks on Dangila and Engiabara, had left Simonds in charge of Mission 101 with orders to carry these out, and was intending to fly to Khartoum as soon as the Emperor arrived to discuss these plans with Platt.

Then on 8 February came the bombshell in the form of a signal dated 6 February from Khartoum with orders that Wingate was to be commander of British and Ethiopian forces in the field and Sandford military adviser to the Emperor with Chapman-Andrews as his assistant. Nott records, 'Dan is awfully cut up about it and the whole situation is strained.' Sandford and Wingate were summoned to Khartoum to discuss their respective responsibilities with Platt and were picked up by the RAF on 11 February. To quote Nott again, 'about time as the tension in the camp was very tense. They were jumping at each other for God's sake.'

At Khartoum their responsibilities were defined at a conference on 12 February attended by the *kaid*, Brigadier Lush, and Lieutenant Colonel Airey, GSO1. Orders on military operations would henceforth go direct to Wingate with copies to Sandford. Wingate was to inform Sandford of the role to be played by the Patriots, and Sandford, after consulting the Emperor, would arrange for orders to be sent to patriot chiefs in the Emperor's name. Wingate would then carry out the plans. It was a cumbersome arrangement, which worked after a fashion, but which was often ignored by Wingate who got on with the operations, using Thesiger as liaison with the Patriots. Nott, as principal staff officer, had a difficult time trying to serve two masters until the matter was finally resolved at the end of March and he became responsible to Wingate alone.

Wingate, promoted lieutenant colonel, flew back to Belaiya on 14 February and on 15 February left to take command of his force, henceforth called Gideon Force, which had moved towards the escarpment. Nott records Wingate's promotion to 'Colonel commanding Mission 101', which is the rank he held until he left Ethiopia, though for a time he still signed as 'Lt Col.' We will leave Wingate and Gideon Force for a time and describe what happened at Belaiya when Sandford returned. Sandford, promoted brigadier, flew from Khartoum to Cairo to see Wavell and returned to Belaiya on 19 February with Brigadier Lush, Nott recording, 'Dan has been made a Brigadier and are we pleased!' All the evidence is that Sandford, an entirely reasonable man, once he had got over his initial disappointment, accepted the decision on the command and let Wingate get on with the fighting. Wingate never really accepted the 'Brigadier with the roving commission', as he described Sandford later in his dispatch, and at times complained bitterly about interference.

The reason given for the change of command was political and is explained in a letter from Wavell to Haile Selassie dated 15 February and brought by Brigadier Lush, whose role was also explained in the letter. Wavell quoted the statement made by the British foreign secretary, Anthony Eden, in Parliament on 4 February 1941. 'HMG would welcome the reappearance of an independent Ethiopian State and will recognize the claim of the Emperor Haile Selassie to the throne ... HMG reaffirm that they have themselves no territorial ambitions in Abyssinia.' He went on to say that he had set up an administration for the territories conquered from the Italians to be known as the Occupied Enemy Territories Administration (OETA) under Major General Sir Philip Mitchell as chief political officer, Middle East Command, with Brigadier Maurice Lush 'with whom I believe you are acquainted' as his deputy in Ethiopia, and that he had given orders that the administrative measures were to be carried out 'in full consultation with Your Majesty'. To facilitate that consultation he had appointed Brigadier D. A. Sandford to be 'Your Majesty's principal personal adviser on military and political matters and to be the liaison officer between Your Majesty and myself and Lt Generals Platt and Cunningham. Major Wingate will replace Brigadier Sandford as Head of the Military Mission. ... Major Chapman-Andrews ... will assist Brigadier Sandford in political matters.'

Wavell concluded by saying that he had sent Brigadiers Sandford and Lush to Belaiya 'to consult Your Majesty on the preliminary administrative measures to be taken'. This the two brigadiers proceeded to do with the Emperor over the next three days with Chapman-Andrews taking notes. Lush had a difficult row to hoe in trying to persuade the Emperor to accept Wavell's policy of insisting on British control of those areas where operations were continuing. Effectively this meant British political officers in the liberated areas, a concept the Emperor never accepted except as a temporary measure. He wanted to make it clear that he was a sovereign ruler returning to claim his kingdom and not a pawn of the English. Any move that might be construed as derogating from his authority, even for good operational reasons, would be resisted, and in this he would be supported by Sandford and Chapman-Andrews. Discussions were, however, amicable at this stage and Lush flew back to Khartoum on 22 February bearing Haile Selassie's reply to Wavell. In this he welcomed the appointments of Lush, Sandford, Wingate and Chapman-Andrews, 'who are known to me', expressed confidence that HMG would bring the administrative measures to an end 'as soon as the situation permits', but insisted that he must issue proclamations and appoint judicial officers. On the day of Lush's departure Sandford wired Khartoum for approval of the Emperor's move into Gojjam and received the reply, 'HIM could proceed if Wingate thinks the road clear'. We will see soon what Wingate has been doing, but first let us look at the Italian position and the military operations of Mission 101.

The Operations of Mission 101

As a result of British advances in the first fortnight of February 1941, in the north to Keren, in the south to Mega and Kisimayu, the Italian High Command decided to shorten its line of defence in the Western Sector and Nasi ordered the withdrawal of the garrisons of Dangila, Piccolo Abbai and Meschenti on Bahr Dar and of Engiabara on Burye, to commence on 16 February. The forces in Gojjam were to be regrouped into two mobile forces, one under Torelli at Bahr Dar and the other under Natale at Burye, 'with the task of resisting an advance of the rebel forces on Debra Markos'. Whether the assembly of British forces at Belaiya, observed by Italian aircraft, had any influence on the decision to withdraw is not clear. The British at the time believed that this was so, but the Italian official historian and General Nasi say that the reason was the advances in the north and south and this seems more likely. There is no doubt though that the withdrawals from Dangila and Engiabara, the forts covering the escarpment, were in accordance with orders, which, coinciding exactly with the arrival of Gideon Force on the escarpment, played into Wingate's hands.

Before this happened Mission 101, reinforced by the arrivals of

Simonds and Thesiger, half the Ethiopian mortar platoon, and Brown's No 1 Operational Centre, had been active in cooperation with the Patriots. Early in February Thesiger, with the mortars, Brown's centre and 1300 of Mangasha's Patriots, attacked Engiabara. The attack went in at 3.30 a.m., after a mortar bombardment, which set fire to buildings, and Sergeant Burke led a bombing party into the native lines and caused considerable havoc. Then, according to Simonds's report to Sandford, the Patriots refused to attack, so 'shelling and LA fire were completed and our troops withdrew. Brown and Thesiger are convinced we could have had the whole show.... Mangasha [was] rather sheepish and said none of the 1300 [were] any good.'

After this near success Brown moved his centre to the Lach river between Burye and Dambacha to assist Nagash, in particular in operations against Mamu's *banda*. Makonnen Desta was operating with other patriot forces west of Burye; Thesiger was about to operate near Dangila with Mangasha, and Simonds, Drew and Kabada were at Faguta, all evidence of the wide-ranging nature of Mission 101's activities. In a letter to Sandford at Belaiya of 8 February Drew passed on a report from Kabada confirming that Ras Hailu had been to Bichena trying to win over Belai Zelleka, asking urgently for aerial bombing of Bichena and Debra Markos, 'or he is afraid Belai Zelleka might go over'. This suggests that, despite his reported submission, Belai Zelleka was still nominally in the Emperor's camp.

Thesiger's operations with Mangasha's Patriots near Dangila came about in the following way. Before Wingate took over command Sandford and Boustead at Belaiya had planned an attack on Dangila with three SDF companies supported by mortars and aerial bombardment in which Mangasha's Patriots were to be asked to cooperate. Simonds was ordered to organize the attack and sent word to Thesiger to see Mangasha and make the necessary arrangements with him. This Thesiger did, and he then received further orders from Simonds to meet Boustead at Dir Ambo at the foot of the escarpment on 9 February to discuss plans for the attack, now to be made at dawn on 14 February. Travelling 'by forced marches' he reached Dir Ambo on the evening of 8 February, and on the morning of 9 February he met first Harris, and then Boustead, Acland and Critchley. How these officers got there must be explained.

Boustead had sent off three Frontier Battalion patrols to find a route up the escarpment suitable for camels, leading the first himself with Acland from Dir Ambo towards Dangila, sending Harris from Dir Ambo up the escarpment to Tumha, and Omar Effendi, an officer of Johnson's company, to Matakal. Omar Effendi found that the Matakal route was suitable for lightly loaded camels and that is the route Gideon Force eventually followed. Neither of the other routes was fit for camels and Harris had his first brush with the enemy on his patrol. He had with him a platoon from his company and 40 Patriots led by Dori, Fitaurari Teffere Zelleka's brother, and on the escarpment they met a strong Italian patrol with mortars and machine guns. Leaving Dori to keep the Italians occupied Harris climbed the escarpment further south, hoping to catch them in the rear, but by the time he reached the Italian position early on the morning of 6 February it was deserted and all he found were 'cartridge cases, mortar caps and some bloody clothing. Dori's men had done their stuff.'

Harris then did a march round the villages of the Tumha tribes to show the flag, finding the people friendly but the chiefs close to Dangila unwilling to commit themselves openly to the Emperor and that the local influence of Torelli and his garrison was strong. His Sudanese plainsmen marvelled at the grass and trees and running water and fat cattle on the plateau. Harris returned to Dir Ambo early on 9 February, to be greeted by the rest of his company 'with huge grins and many handshakes ... this is the way of the Sudanese', and to be told that Thesiger, whom he had not previously met, had arrived. The meeting is the occasion of another Thesiger story. Harris went to greet Thesiger, found him bathing in the freezing river and invited him to breakfast when, 'after informing me that he had lived on the country for the past two months and could not imagine why people troubled to take rations with them, he proceeded to finish my last tin of grapenuts, half my remaining supply of sugar, and most of my one and only remaining pot of marmalade.'

At 11.00 a.m. the five officers sat down to a conference. The original purpose of this had been to coordinate plans for the attack on Dangila on 14 February, but Critchley, who was on his way to rejoin Mission 101 having had treatment for his eyes, brought the news of Wingate's appointment to command. Because of this, as Thesiger records, 'Colonel Boustead refused to attack Dangila as previously arranged, since Major Wingate was now in command, and the plan, which had been made by Colonel Sandford, had not been sanctioned by him.' If any further evidence is needed that Sandford was a soldier as well as Wingate here it is. This was a very good plan but the withdrawal of the three companies of Sudanese regulars, albeit possibly for correct reasons, torpedoed it completely.

Thesiger and Critchley left immediately for Mangasha's head-quarters, arriving on 12 February, still unsure if the RAF would attack on 14 February. Understandably Mangasha, whose army was gathered near Dangila, refused to attack without the regulars or an assurance of RAF support, and suggested as an alternative an attack on Piccolo Abbai supported by the mortars. When Simonds on 13 February received confirmation that the RAF would attack Dangila on the 14th and passed this to Thesiger, Mangasha still refused to attack Dangila, but Thesiger managed to persuade him to leave four *fitauraris* with their men to block Torelli should he move out of Dangila to help Piccolo Abbai. No inkling of the Italian intention to evacuate Dangila on 16 February seems to have reached British intelligence.

The four heroic *fitauraris* deserve to have their names recorded in any history of the war of liberation. They were Aiyellu, Ain Ingeda, Mogus and Adama.

At 3.00 a.m. on 16 February the attack on Piccolo Abbai went in after a reconnaissance by Thesiger and Sergeant Body on the evening of 15 February. The plan was, after a mortar bombard-ment, for Body and a demolition squad from his centre to blow up the road bridge over the Abbai under cover of an attack by 800 of Mangasha's Patriots. The plan miscarried. The mortars overshot and caused no damage; Body got to within 20 yards of the bridge under heavy fire but his men would not follow him and the Patriots fired off a lot of ammunition but refused to get to close quarters or attack. The Italians had reinforced both the bridge and the fort in anticipation of Torelli's withdrawal from Dangila.

Mangasha withdrew his forces at dawn and dispersed them to collect food.

At 8.00 a.m. Thesiger and Body heard very heavy and continuous firing from the direction of Dangila. At 1.00 p.m. they received news that Torelli had come out and was being engaged by the four *fitauraris* and their men, who, as Thesiger wrote, 'opposed every yard of his advance until he fought his way into Piccolo Abbai at 6.00 p.m.' Mangasha, under Thesiger's strong persuasion, sent all available forces on to the road between Piccolo Abbai and Meschenti, 34 kilometres further along the road to Bahr Dar. The Patriots closed in on Piccolo Abbai but Torelli fought his way out. His force marched across the open plain and was ambushed by the Patriots at Aba Aragwat at 8.00 a.m. There followed a very severe battle lasting three hours in which Torelli was forced off the road and his brigade was in serious danger but was saved by two bombing raids by Savoias from Bahr Dar. Under cover of these Torelli regained the road and fought his way to Meschenti, which he reached at 6.00 p.m. after 12 hours' continuous fighting with the Patriots attacking all the way.

Thesiger could not persuade Mangasha ('he is no soldier') to move in person between Torelli and Meschenti, but his *fitauraris* 'fought magnificiently, as did the rank and file of the Ethiopian forces', captured many prisoners, including two Italian officers, one out of four lorries, and many machine guns and rifles. Thesiger, who did not like the Italians, commented, 'Fitaurari Ain Ingeda captured and saved the lives of two Italian officers, which is more than the Italians have ever done to Abyssinian prisoners.'

Torelli's force numbered at least 5000, four good colonial battalions, one CCNN battalion, with artillery, cavalry and *banda*, and he was a strong commander. His casualties from 16 February to 30 April were 201 killed and 605 wounded, including an estimated 100 to 150 at Bahr Dar, thus the losses in the retreat from Dangila were probably 650 to 700, making this one of the most significant actions of the whole campaign, fought by Patriots alone. Ethiopian casualties are not known, but must have been heavy as they were attacking against fierce fire for two days for the distance of 63 kilometres over the open plain between Dangila and Meschenti. Nor are their numbers known; Mangasha's total strength was probably 5000. There is another good reason why the Dangila operation is important. Many times in the Gojjam campaign and afterwards there will be criticism of the Patriots by British officers and complaints of being let down, often justified. Here the boot was on the other foot. The Gojjam Patriots were let down by the regular forces and had to fight a formidable battle on their own. It was also an opportunity lost. If Boustead's three companies, 600 Sudanese raring for a fight, had joined in this action, this could have been the end of Torelli. A resounding victory at this stage could have had incalculable consequences for the Emperor's cause. Wingate decided otherwise, that the main thrust should be to Debra Markos and beyond, a bolder plan in the long term. It does seem though that Wingate thought little of what Sandford had been doing and ignored the possibilities at Dangila. Sandford allowed himself the mild comment afterwards that it was a pity Torelli was not 'put in the bag'; his plan could well have achieved this result.

On hearing of the evacuation of Dangila, Simonds initiated further actions against Engiabara and Burye, reported to Sandford that Engiabara had been occupied by Kabada on 17 February with a small force of Mission 101 soldiers, and suggested that Mission 101 should move to east Gojjam to stir up patriot activity there. All this was to change, however, with the arrival of Wingate at Faguta on 21 February to take command of Mission 101. Let us see how he got there.

Gideon Force: The Advance into Gojjam*
Wingate had decided to use the Matakal route up the escarpment and assembled his force at Lower Matakal at the foot of the escarpment on 17 February, now reduced to about 1000, 600 men of the 2nd Ethiopians and about 400 Sudanese of Nos 1, 2 and 4 patrol companies' Frontier Battalion under Boustead with Acland as his staff officer. Jarvis and No 3 patrol company had been sent north in pursuit of Torelli, and the bulk of No 4 remained to garrison Belaiya under Maxwell because, so Boustead said, 'they had had all the fun so far'. The Italian withdrawals from Engiabara

---

* See General Map 2 inset.

and Dangila, carried out on 16 February, allowed Gideon Force to climb the escarpment unopposed, and Johnson went up on 17 February with lightly loaded camels and some help from Gumz tribesmen, now veering towards the stronger side, leaving a notice at the bottom, 'THIS WAY TO THE PROMISED LAND'. on the evening of 17 February, the day, it should be noted, when Mangasha'a *fitauraris* were still fighting a desperate battle against Torelli up to the gates of Meschenti, Wingate held a conference with the remaining officers at Boyle's headquarters and outlined his plans. As recorded by Harris, Wingate gave a remarkably inaccurate account of events at Dangila, ignoring the battle being fought by Mangasha's men, and saying that while Jarvis was pursuing Torelli, the Patriots refused to join in, being far too occupied with looting. (There certainly was looting, but not by those pursuing Torelli.) He believed, as we now know incorrectly, that Torelli had evacuated Dangila because of an erroneous idea of Gideon Force's strength. The whole line of forts from Engiabara to Debra Markos and beyond was now open to them and he intended by 'attacking secretly, often, and from all directions, ... to create in the minds of the defenders the same erroneous impression as to our strength. ... This was playing for much higher stakes than the mere harrying of a defeated enemy.'

Although he was wrong about Dangila, probably because, as Sandford generously said, he took over command too late in the day, Wingate's plan for the future sets out exactly what he did in fact achieve at Burye. Harris was most impressed with Wingate, commenting that, 'His hair was long and he was far from clean ... but he was a remarkable character, clever and full of drive and a most daring commander.' Luyt confided to his diary, 'We hope to push hard at Burye and straight on — our ambitious aim being to reach Addis Ababa in six weeks.' All this Wingate was proposing to do with a force of about 1000 men and supply and communication dependent on the 200-mile camel journey from the escarpment to the road head at Um Idla. Wingate intended to, and often did, overcome the supply problem from enemy sources, issuing an order of the day on 18 February, 'The comforts which we now lack and the supplies which we need are in the possession of our enemies. It is my intention to wrest them from him by a bold stroke.' He also issued a less felicitous address to the Ethiopian

Patriots, urging them to 'Rouse yourselves and put an end to your bickerings and disputes, which have disgraced your Ethiopian name among future generations.' Divisions there had been and still were among the Patriots, but what they had achieved on their own since 1937, and with Mission 101's help since September 1940, seems to have counted for nothing with Wingate.

After fatigue parties had improved the worst places in the track, Gideon Force climbed the escarpment with its camels on 18 and 19 February, a climb of three hours for marching troops and four-and-a-half hours with lightly loaded camels. Getting the camels up the precipitous track was hard work, and Luyt left this sensible comment: 'Many a time have I been undeservedly furious with a man. . . . One always gets away with it because one is European but it does no good. . . . I must strive to be more civil and patient. Major Chapman-Andrews was a good model in this respect.'

Wingate climbed the track on 18 February and, ordering his force to concentrate at Engiabara, went there himself with Akavia, a section of Sudanese and a platoon of A company's 2nd Ethiopian Battalion under Lieutenant Enko Haile Mariam. There he found Sultan Effendi with the propaganda section, Kabada and his men, and considerable evidence of patriot looting. Kabada struck an immediate rapport with Wingate and recorded that Wingate's 'approach to work and strategy' was different from that of Sandford. 'Col. Sandford put considerable effort into all he did, but even so his work was not straightforward; it was wrapped up in politics. Col. Wingate, however, was concerned only with how to attack the enemy and win victory; political matters were not his concern.' Here again is the view, still current today, of Wingate the fighter and Sandford the politician. The view of Wingate the fighter is a more popular image, appealed more to Kabada and is entirely correct. Wingate was suspected later by Cunningham of wanting to meddle in politics and hustled out of Ethiopia, but this was entirely unjust. He never did so. Sandford had to be a politician by the nature of his work, but he was also very much a soldier and this is not appreciated today.

Leaving Enko with his platoon to garrison Engiabara, the first independent command by an Ethiopian officer, Wingate and Akavia set off for Faguta on mule back on 21 February, Wingate insisting that for security reasons Akavia should follow him two hours behind. The picture, as decribed by Akavia, of the eccentric British colonel riding through the Gojjam Highlands followed by his civilian clerk carrying his portable typewriter on his mule is almost comic. 'Wingate on his mule with the Ethiopian colours on his topi and totally unarmed raising his hat now and then and saying *Ingie* [English] and *Tena Yistilia* [Health may God give you] went a distance of 25 miles through enemy country.' In fact the Patriots controlled the territory and Sandford and his officers had been riding about it for months, but this was good drama; eccentric behaviour, if coupled with effectiveness, commands great respect in Africa, and Wingate is certainly remembered.

On arrival at Faguta Wingate took over Mission 101 from Simonds whom he ordered to proceed to Beghemder and cut communications between Gondar and Debra Tabor and between Debra Tabor and Dessie. This was an early example of long-range penetration by Wingate and a remarkably correct strategic prognosis, particularly with regard to Dessie. Whether on Platt's orders or his own initiative Wingate's plan resulted later in the Dessie garrison's line of retreat being cut off. Simonds's force became known as Beghemder Force and would include Jarvis's No 3 patrol company, and later Fitaurari Birru's Patriots and No 2 Operational Centre. Before he could reach Beghemder Simonds had to prise Torelli out of Bahr Dar, and these operations will be described in the next chapter.

While Wingate was at Faguta Grey collapsed from exhaustion. He had a blackout and went temporarily blind. He had been working the wireless sets, often single handed, for five months without a break, operating by day and enciphering and deciphering messages by candlelight and having very little sleep. He recalls with gratitude that Wingate and Simonds looked after him after he passed out and Wingate arranged for him to be flown back to Khartoum for 14 days' leave. He recovered fully and rejoined the force at Burye.

Wingate and Akavia returned to Engiabara on 22 February, again riding separately, and found Gideon Force assembled there having marched from Matakal where it had left a detachment as garrison under Peter Hayes, Johnson's second-in-command. The cold nights and green fodder did not suit the camels and they lost several on the march. The column also met the Coptic Church, the priest in each village holding out the cross to be kissed by the passing troops, giving them his blessing and receiving a small donation from them. Luyt, who carried a Bible and read part of the Gospels daily, found the Church gave 'excessive attention to rites and ceremonies, confusing the outward show with the real principles involved'. (There spoke the Calvinist South African!)

At Engiabara they met the Australians of No 1 Centre, Luyt being glad to see Ted Body, last seen in Khartoum, 'a grand fellow, who handed on all the news re the enemy'. Despite patriot looting Engiabara was full of food. Harris and Johnson collected six camel loads of biscuit for their companies, found Wingate lunching and 'joined him in a meal off tinned delicacies washed down with excellent Chianti'. Tutton and Body also went in on an authorized looting expedition, collecting flour, tea and sugar for the men and tinned delicacies for themselves, and seeing 'great drifts of macaroni and case upon case of tinned goods and piles of great Parmazan cheeses'. They invited Body to a six-course supper, cooked by Tutton's orderly, Tadessa.

Mission 101 North

At the end of November 1940 Bentinck had moved east to Ankar, and there on 10 January 1941 Foley left him to join Gideon Force, much missed by Bentinck who felt that if his mission had been given more assistance he could have undermined the enemy position at Gondar more effectively. Meanwhile, Mohamed Effendi, based at Debarech south of Wolchefit, continued his attacks on the Gondar–Asmara road, causing losses to vehicles and casualties to personnel. During February Bentinck moved further east and established his headquarters at Maana and made contact with the local patriot chief, Ras Wubneh. He asked to be relieved because he was unwell, and on 24 February was joined by Bimbashi L. F. Sheppard who was to take over from him. On 27 February the two officers with 17 of their men and 50 of Ras Wubneh's Patriots occupied the Italian fort of Kech from which the garrison retreated. The news of the raising of the Ethiopian flag on this fort reached the British press and was written up as the daring capture of an Italian fort in the heart of Ethiopia. At that dismal period of the 1940/1 winter any minor success was welcome news. This was the limit of eastern penetration by the mission, which then returned to Maana.

More Volunteers: Ringrose and Railton

Two more officers and several British non-commissioned officers responded to the call for volunteers for the operational centres. These were sent by Platt straight into the Gondar area, the first being Major Basil Ringrose of Notts Yeomanry (Sherwood Foresters), who entered Ethiopia at Um Hagar on 8 February 1941 with three sergeants from his regiment, Cottle, Callis and Perkins, 12 Ethiopian soldiers and a Lewis gun. They travelled initially in 15 cwt trucks, but soon switched to mules. Ringrose's orders from the *kaid* were to harass communications and cut the Gondar–Asmara road between Debivar and Dabat.

The other officer was Second Lieutenant Andrew Railton, 1st South Staffs serving in the Western Desert, who was posted to the 3rd Ethiopian Battalion, which was forming in Khartoum in February 1941 under Lieutenant Colonel Ker from *ascari* deserters at the battles of Gallabat and Kassala during Platt's advance. Railton took over C company, a complete company of a colonial battalion, which had deserted to the British en bloc at Gallabat. They were re-equipped with Springfield rifles and Hotchkiss light machine guns, and Railton, with two sergeants, Burns and Curry, was given three weeks in which to retrain them. They retained their *graduati* who were given British warrant officer and NCO ranks. With this unit Railton was to enter the Gondar region and join Sheppard and Mission 101 North.

Gideon Force: The March round Burye

Gideon Force started the march south from Engiabara on 24 February. Meanwhile in Eritrea the first assault on Keren by two brigades of the 4th Indian Division had ended in stalemate on 14 February, the British had withdrawn to regroup, leaving a force holding Cameron Ridge, and Platt would soon resume the offensive with two divisions (the 4th and 5th Indian) against the strong Keren defences held by 40,000 Italian regular and colonial troops.

In the south Cunningham's army of three divisions from Kenya was advancing on a two-divisional front (11th and 12th African) against seven Italian divisions totalling 90,000 men. The line of the Juba river had been forced in a three-brigade advance against two Italian divisions. Mogadiscio was occupied on 25 February, and the advance to the Marda Pass, the gateway to Ethiopia, had begun.

In Gojjam Gideon Force was proposing to advance against two colonial brigades, while Beghemder Force pursued the 3rd Brigade northwards. Measured against the perspective of the other advances Gideon Force was a very minor effort, although fitting into the total picture, important politically as a rallying point for the Emperor, and surprisingly effective militarily, despite the enormous odds, because of the boldness of Wingate's methods. Wingate gave out his orders for the advance in the camp near Engiabara on the afternoon of 23 February. Gideon Force was to bypass Burye marching by night and take up a position five miles to the northeast of Burye, invest and if possible capture Mankusa, and harass Burye in the hopes that the Italians would surrender. The light coloured desert camels were to be camouflaged by covering them thickly with mud, a job carried out amid much groaning from the camels and ribaldry from the men, and camel loads were not to be removed at any time during the night march. Harris protested at the last order, anticipating sore backs in the 14-hour march, but Wingate was adamant, though he gave way over a similar order regarding the horses, which Harris insisted must have their loads removed every three hours.

The force set off on the evening of 24 February, the 2nd Ethiopians leading, for *political* reasons, as both Boustead and Harris emphasize in their accounts! Immediately against them in Burye were six colonial battalions of the 19th and 3rd Colonial Brigades, one company of the 10 CCNN, the 37th Battery of 65-millimetre guns and 81-millimetre mortars, the Burye mounted *banda* of irregular cavalry, at least two armoured cars, and Mamu's *banda* of between 1500 and 2000 men. Beyond Burye, the forts of Mankusa and Jigga each had garrisons of about 250 men, and in Dambacha there were the three remaining companies of the 10 CCNN, about 500 men. Altogether Natale had about 6000 regular troops, excluding Mamu's *banda* and the garrison at Dambacha. Against him Wingate had one and a half battalions, two three-inch mortars, Kabada and his 50 men, No 1 Centre, and 200 of Nagash's Patriots under Fitaurari Zelleka Desta — excluding the Patriots about 1300 men. The Italians had close and regular air support from bases at Addis Ababa and Bahr Dar. RAF Wellesleys bombed Burye by night on 21 and 28 February, but Wingate had no close tactical air support, and in fact no more air support at all until they reached Debra Markos. The advance was a bold, indeed impudent, move, impossible without the whole-hearted support of the local population.

It was soon pitch dark with no moon and they were ordered to keep in touch by using a recognition signal, whistle or flashing torch. (Tutton wrote, 'Wingate is nuts on it. Boustead thinks its tommy rot. Tonight it proved most useful.') There were no difficulties on the first night's march and Wingate called a halt at midnight at the Fatham river where the road bridge had been destroyed by one of Brown's demolition parties, and where there was good cover in riverine forest. He warned the force to expect air attack soon after dawn, and sure enough at 7.00 a.m. two Capronis came over, circling low, but, as Harris records, 'They failed to spot us ... as soon as we realized this everyone got up and there was a burst of laughter.'

During the morning of 25 February a crossing was made for the camels over the river and in the afternoon Wingate gave out his orders. His plan was to make straight for Mankusa, striking across country north of Burye, and he proposed to go ahead with a local headman as guide and an Ethiopian platoon, dropping *askaris* off at intervals who would light beacon fires after dark to guide the column and also indicate their presence by whistling the recognition signal. One unforeseen difficulty of the extraordinary night that followed was that the Ethiopian *askari*, who were not provided with whistles, were physically unable to make more than a faint sound by whistling. This did not matter on the first part of the march as the fires proved disastrously effective. In those ecologically happier days long and very inflammable grass covered the Gojjam plateau at the end of the dry season.

The column set off at 4.30 p.m. on 25 February, Wingate having gone ahead with No 13 platoon of Tutton's company (Lieutenant Haile Mariam). They reached the first three marker fires successfully, D company leading. At 9.00 p.m. they were held up for a time making a crossing for camels over a river bed, and as they approached the second marker after the crossing the fire caught the long grass around it and began to spread, driven by the high wind. Boyle detached C and D companies to try and put it out, and they tackled it with branches but in spite of their efforts the fire spread towards a village, which had to be evacuated, and haystacks and grass houses went up in flames. Harris, marching an hour behind the Ethiopians, saw 'miles ahead an enormous fire break out and spread rapidly, lighting up the sky all round'.

Harris managed to follow the markers to the rendezvous, eventually, to his great joy, spotting a flashing torch and hearing 'a string of English oaths uttered in Boustead's unmistakeable voice followed by a torrent of Arabic'. Boustead was cursing an unfortunate Sudanese soldier whom he had left to guide in Boyle's two missing companies and had lost them in the darkness. Harris reported to Wingate, 'who proceeded to tell me what he thought of Ethiopians in general and Boyle's battalion in particular. ... He was far from polite and I was sorry for Boyle who was sitting, looking rather dejected, well within earshot.' The missing companies were C and D, delayed because of the fire, who did not reach the rendezvous until after midnight.

It was 3.00 a.m. on 26 February before the column was sorted out and ready to move again, Harris's company now in the lead, 'the Ethiopians being in disgrace'. Tutton continues, 'Wingate was in a great temper. ... He cursed Boustead. ... He cursed Boyle. ... He openly said that he was sick of the 2nd Ethiopians.' Wingate led as before, dropping off marker guides. Harris had great difficulty following the line, on one occasion luckily blundering into an Ethiopian marker 'shivering with cold and trying to produce a breathy whistle through his chattering teeth', but the column kept together and at 6.45 a.m. made camp in a forested valley five miles northeast of Burye. By 9.00 a.m. Italian planes were out looking for them.

The night march of Wingate's long column of 1500 men, 700 camels and 150 horses spreading over four miles, advertising its presence by blowing whistles, flashing torches and starting an enormous grass fire, all within five miles of the Italian commander's headquarters, must go down in history as one of the wierdest operations on record. The most extraordinary aspect was the failure of the Italians to intervene. The march across country in total darkness was not only a bold gamble, but a great achievement for Wingate's leadership. He got his force where he wanted it and cannot be blamed if he was angry when his plans were bungled. The unwieldy nature of the force confirmed the Italians' belief that it was much larger than in fact it was. The swathe in the long grass trampled by the 700 camels and 150 horses must have suggested to the Italians, when their spies reported, the presence of an enormous force. In addition the Emperor's party and various operational centres had left Belaiya and were now moving up the escarpment, indicating that British reinforcements were close behind.

After a short rest (all diarists thankfully record their first sleep for 48 hours), Wingate held a conference on the afternoon of 26 February. He had decided that his force was too unwieldy for guerrilla operations, and he wished to keep the Italians guessing and make them nervous about their communications. Boyle was ordered to leave that afternoon and go forward with two objectives, to harass communications between Burye and Debra Markos, and to liaise with Thesiger who had already been sent forward by Wingate to persuade the local patriot leader, Fitaurari Haile Yusus, to invest the fort at Dambacha. Boyle left at 3.00 p.m. with A, C and D companies of his battalion, commanded respectively by Second Lieutenant Syd Downey, Lieutenant Ken Rowe (nicknamed Jiggsa), and Second Lieutenant Tutton. Wingate himself, with the remainder of the force, including B company of the 2nd Ethiopians under Lieutenant A. S. Beard, with two Vickers medium machine guns, planned to bypass Burye and invest Mankusa.

Thesiger, with his Sudanese orderly and Ethiopian interpreter, found Haile Yusus at Farasbiet, a cold bleak spot in the Choke mountains, and describes him as 'a typical Abyssinian aristocrat, small, with delicate features ... incisive and commanding ... a fighting leader'. Thesiger put Wingate's request to him, to which he agreed, and moved with him and his men, numbering about 1000, to Seccolo Mariam, a large flat-topped hill about 1000 yards north of the fort of Dambacha. They were spotted by the Black-shirt garrison who opened up with machine guns and then attacked. The Patriots counter-attacked, drove the Italians back to the fort, broke into the native village to the east of the fort, which housed an irregular *banda*, set fire to the huts and drove off cattle and mules. They then returned to the hill. The operation had had the effect desired by Wingate, to worry the Italians about their lines of communication, and for the next two or three days they attacked the hill with fighter aircraft. The Patriots avoided casualties by squatting on the edge of the cliff below the crest, on the advice of Thesiger, who recalled reading in *Seven Pillars of Wisdom* how Lawrence had done this with his Arabs to avoid Turkish aircraft. Thesiger sent a message to Wingate, reporting his position and asking for a Vickers gun.

Meanwhile Wingate, who had sent Johnson forward with one platoon to ambush the Burye–Mankusa road, left the position northeast of Burye with his column soon after dawn on 27 February and skirted north of Burye, keeping the fortifications just out of sight. The Italians made no attempt to interfere with this movement in broad daylight of what was still a sizeable force with 500 camels, not even by aerial attack. At midday the column halted and unloaded the animals in a wood within two miles of one of the outer forts. Here Wingate detached Boustead with Harris's company and Sergeant Body and a mortar section to demonstrate against this fort, while he and Acland went on with the rest of the column to an agreed rendezvous.

Boustead deployed his company and opened up with the mortar on the fort at 1000 yards. This brought an immediate response in machine-gun and mortar fire from the fort, and after an exchange of fire for about half an hour an enemy shell set fire to the long grass in front of Harris's position (the long grass again a tactical factor), 'causing a thick smoke screen to drift across our front and then a blood-curdling sound smote my ears — that of galloping horses accompanied by the high-pitched luluing of savage horse-men as they bore down on us through the smoke.' This was a troop of the Burye mounted *banda*, about 50 strong led by a *sciumbasci*, charging at the gallop through the smoke, 'yelling madly and shooting wildly from the saddle as they rode'.

Harris, firing the Bren gun from the hip and the rifles of the section with him, succeeded in halting the cavalry when only 40 yards from them. They wheeled to their left to attack the company *bash shawish*, Hassan Musaad, who had a section of six men 200 yards to Harris's right, and a battle royal ensued until Harris was able to go to Hassan's assistance and their combined fire power drove the cavalry off. It had been a hard fight and at one time Hassan had been attacked from all directions. Hassan had lost one man killed and the section commander badly wounded with a bullet through the neck. They found three dead troopers and ten dead horses within 30 yards of Hassan's position, and 'Hassan insisted on having a handsome saddle stripped from one of the dead horses for my use as a memento of our "blooding".'

In this action Harris lost one killed and four wounded in his company and estimated the enemy losses at between 15 and 20 men and horses. This first confrontation between the steady Sudanese infantry and the colonial cavalry, pressing home an attack quite closely against automatic weapons, shows the quality of the troops and junior commanders on both sides in this campaign. It was now dark and Johnson had appeared to join them, marching to the sound of the guns, and leaving him to harass the Burye forts, Boustead and Harris followed the motor road to their rendezvous with Wingate, carrying the wounded on horseback, the only transport available, borne with fortitude by the Sudanese. Meeting Wingate they lay up till dawn south of the motor road while Johnson moved round the Burye forts, firing on them from different directions and provoking a veritable tornado of firing, which continued until dawn.

At first light on 28 February the force moved south of Mankusa to a large village where they made camp. On the way Harris, with the rearguard, found Clifford Drew, the Mission 101 doctor, camped within machine-gun range of Mankusa fort. When Harris expressed surprise at Drew camping so close to the enemy, Drew replied that he felt safer near the Italians than near 'that madman Wingate', who he thought was taking the most appalling risks. However, Drew joined the force, a most valuable addition, and

Boustead was delighted that his Sudanese wounded could now have proper attention.

Wingate had requested aerial support on 26 February and, in response two RAF Wellesleys, bombed Burye on 28 February. One was shot down, but the raid was a discouragement to Natale and an encouragement to the Patriots. To make the raid the Wellesleys from Khartoum had to use the advanced landing ground at Sennar, and the timing of the raid, two days after the request, was about the best that Wingate could hope for. He could not expect tactical air support in an action; the Italians still could. On 1 March the force moved to a hill position 1500 yards east of Mankusa, which came to be known as Church Hill. To provide greater mobility in guerrilla operations they took only horse and mule transport and four days' rations, sending the camels to a safe harbour five miles south under a Sudanese officer, Yuzbashi El Hag Effendi Musa, with a platoon as escort.

While Wingate was confronting Mankusa, Boyle, with three companies and 200 baggage camels, had reached the fort of Jigga, 19 miles down the road to the southeast on the evening of 28 February. They had no wireless telegraphy; communication with Wingate was maintained for a time by runner. Bypassing Mankusa they left a platoon of C company under Gerazmatch Dabala to cover the fort and try and persuade the garrison to surrender to the Emperor's forces. The Mankusa garrison's response was to open fire, which Dabala returned. Jigga was held by a company of colonial troops, six officers and about 250 men. Patrols went out to reconnoitre the defences, a request was sent to Wingate for one of his two mortars, and Boyle placed ambushes on the road east and west under Rowe and Corporal Wodaju. Rowe's ambush east of the fort was successful on 1 March, surprising a transport column and causing casualties (five killed and several wounded).

Facing Wingate at Mankusa the garrison consisted of No 4 company 72nd Colonial Battalion, two officers, one Italian NCO and 240 *ascari*. They had the standard armament, two Schwartzloze heavy machine guns, Breda light machine guns, rifles and grenades. They were experienced soldiers from a good battalion. The subaltern officer was Tenente Michele Butera. Against this force Wingate had about 300 regulars and was joined on 1 March by Fitaurari Zelleka Desta's 200 Patriots, who had been in ambush positions on the Burye–Mankusa road, and by the propaganda section. Wingate planned an attack by the Patriots at dusk on 1 March, preceded by a mortar bombardment. Although he had an excellent gunner in Body he ordered Harris, who had never handled a mortar before, to take charge of the mortar attack and gave him some quick instruction. The mortar attack went ahead and caused considerable damage, setting houses on fire, but the patriot attack did not materialize, their leader telling Wingate that to take the fort without air support was impossible. Harris's comment was that this was 'typical of the type of assistance we received from the Patriots', but it was too much to expect Patriots to tackle fixed defences or work to a timetable, as Wingate himself acklowledged later in his dispatch.

Investment of Mankusa continued and the garrison showed no disposition to surrender despite heavy casualties from the mortar bombardment and the fire from Beard's two Vickers guns poured into the fort, 85 killed and wounded out of 240 according to Tenente Butera, who was himself wounded by mortar fire. When Sultan Effendi's propaganda section shouted at the defenders through their megaphones to surrender to *Janhoi* (the Emperor), some shouted back that they knew nothing of *Janhoi*. Although the accounts of both Harris and Akavia refer to numerous desertions, Butera is adamant that his men were old soldiers and there were no desertions from his company. There is evidence though that the propaganda was having an effect on the Gojjami irregulars of Mamu's *banda*.

On 2 March Wingate sent one mortar team to Boyle at Jigga with a message, as Tutton records, 'that Mankusa fort ... had been reduced to a heap of ashes by mortar fire but still held out gallantly. We were to go ahead and do what damage we could along the enemy's lines of communication.' Boyle also received the message from Thesiger intended for Wingate, requesting a Vickers medium machine gun, and a suggestion, according to Tutton, for a joint attack on Dambacha with Haile Yusus's men. Wingate's message was the last received by Boyle before the action at the Charaka river, some six miles further down the road, on 6 March against the retreating Italian column. There was no indication that

Burye would be evacuated and no order to take up an ambush position to cut off the enemy. Boyle's orders were to disrupt communications.

Wingate's message, and the decision whether to attack Jigga or go on to Dambacha, were debated at a conference of all the European ranks of Boyle's battalion, including the three sergeants, on the evening of 2 March. The three sergeants, all South Africans, were Botha (A company), Geoffrey Clarke (C), and Dick Luyt (D). The decision reached by a show of hands was to move on, obviously the correct decision but a curious way for Boyle to reach one. He did not consult his senior Ethiopian officers. Boyle moved his battalion after dark on 3 March to a small stream, the Charaka river, arriving at 2.00 a.m. on 4 March, and made camp at dawn on the edge of a patch of acacia forest east of the road bridge on the west (Jigga) side of the stream. Scrapes were dug and machine guns and light machine guns set up for anti-aircraft and ground defence, and Boyle went off to Seccolo Mariam, five miles down the road, to see Thesiger and concert a plan of action with him. This camp was the scene of the action on 6 March.

During the march from Burye Italian aircraft had been busy trying to locate the column, but failed because of the excellent cover, not only of the acacia forest but of the head-high elephant grass which covered much of the countryside, very trying to march through but good for concealment. Most of the time the column was able to march on the road, described by Luyt as 'a very fine substantial road ... raised and banked most of the way, well bridged at every little stream, the road appears to have been made to the pattern of its Roman ancestors.' They saw no Allied aerial activity but some of the men picked up leaflets dropped by the RAF reporting the capture of Mogadiscio and Mega by Cunningham's forces, news which, as Tutton records, 'caused much joy in the camp'. They met armed Patriots on the road, many in captured Italian uniforms, and this prompted Luyt to comment:

This almost pre-Biblical country must endure its pains while our object, the restoration of the Emperor, is striven for. Death, murder, all the worst evils known to man have been brought to these people by their contact with Europe. Now we crown it all by actually making it a battleground between two European powers and range the local people on opposite sides. What a debt we have to repay!

The Worries of Colonel Natale

Gideon's 300 surrounded the camp of the Midianites and blew their trumpets and 'the host of Midian fled'. Gideon Force had surrounded Burye, and forcing Natale to abandon that fortress was one of Wingate's great successes, the result of his policy of long-range penetration and cutting communications. Natale had been ordered to hold Burye but the RAF bombing, the desertion of Mamu's *banda* and, in the words of the Italian historian del Boca, 'above all that Gideon Force, which seemed to have the gift of ubiquity', convinced him that Burye was untenable. The desertion of Mamu's *banda* was a success for the propaganda section, which had bombarded Burye and Mankusa with megaphone messages proclaiming the presence of the Emperor and the imminent freedom of Ethiopia. This had little effect on the regular *ascari*, but the Gojjami *banda* had started to desert 'in dribs and drabs' until, on 1 March, Mamu and the entire *banda* of 1500 men deserted.

The 'ubiquity' of Gideon Force was Wingate's achievement and an important one. The march round Burye, the attacks on Burye and Mankusa, the activities of the 2nd Ethiopians at Jigga (believed also to be Sudanese troops), and the threat to Dambacha from Haile Yusus's Patriots, and the 'Sudanese elements' with them (Thesiger and his orderly!) all contributed to give the impression not only of ubiquity but also of considerable numbers. The previous mining and demolition operations of Brown's centre on the Burye–Dambacha road had added to these worries. Natale signalled Nasi requesting permission to evacuate. Permission to withdraw as far as Dambacha was granted, but no further, and the evacuation fixed for 4 March. These events will be described in the next chapter. First let us go back and see what the Emperor and Nott have been doing.

The Emperor Moves into Gojjam

Back at Belaiya Nott recorded the arrival of other operational centres, first No 2 Centre under Captain Mackay (Canadian

100

artillery), 'a Canadian gunner and mad keen', with five sergeants from the Northern Irish Anti-Aircraft Regiment, followed by No 3, Lieutenant Gordon Naylor and four sergeants of the 1st Beds & Herts, No 4, Lieutenant Bathgate and two sergeants of the Kings Own, No 5, Captain van der Post (Rifle Brigade) and Lieutenant W. E. D. (Bill) Allen (Life Guards) and four sergeants, three Coldstream and one 13th/18th Hussars, and No 6, Lieutenant Welsh and five sergeants of The Buffs (Royal East Kent Regiment). None had their full complement of *askari*, and 'all centres are arriving deficient of stuff such as AT mines, detonators and medical kit'. Fitaurari Birru and Patriots arrived with Mackay.

Nott also welcomed Foley from Mission 101 North, 'his usual bright self', and Riley on his way to rejoin the Frontier Battalion, who had brought 'Birru's braves from Akrib + 350 camels, only lost three'. Lieutenants John Riley and John Bagge had both joined Nott's rear HQ at Gedaref earlier to take charge of arms depots on the frontier. Riley, christened 'Freddie' by Nott because he could not cope with two Johns, had found a vacancy in Johnson's No 1 patrol company. Bagge later met Gideon Force in Addis Ababa and had important duties under the Emperor. Foley and le Blanc started to make a motorable road from Belaiya to Matakal and Nott told them to continue up the escarpment and link up with the Engiabara–Burye road. When this was completed Gideon Force could be supplied by motor transport.

The last word from GHQ Khartoum about the Emperor's move, received on 22 February, was that he could move into Gojjam 'as soon as Wingate thinks the road is clear'. Nott was taken unawares when the Emperor announced on 25 February his intention to move because, not anticipating the early fall of Dangila and with Wingate's approval, he had sent off most of the mules with a supply convoy to Faguta. He and Sandford were summoned to the Emperor's presence and rebuked, but 'when I explained the situation, he repented and said it was Okay. Telegram from Orde saying that the country ahead was full of milk and honey.'

This was the only disagreement Nott had with the Emperor and they remained very good friends. He managed to scrape together 150 mules and 60 saddles and the 'amazing cavalcade' set off on the afternoon of 26 February. The march on 27 February was a long one for the Emperor, starting at 6.30 a.m. and arriving in camp at 6.30 p.m. after dark, but he was a fine horseman and these long journeys were no trouble to him. Nott 'spent nearly all day talking to Lorenzo Taezaz', and there were compensations for travelling with the Emperor. 'Andrew [Chapman-Andrews] broke open one of the Emperor's boxes and we finished a bottle of John Haig in no time. Andrew provided a rattling good dinner.'

The party arrived at Lower Matakal on 28 February. Sandford had left Belaiya separately on 26 February, hoping to find Wingate on the Engiabara–Burye road and discuss with him the forward movement of the Emperor. He failed to find him, not surprisingly as Wingate was by that time operating round Burye and Mankusa, and sent word to Nott on 1 March that 'HIM should stay at the foot of the escarpment until word received from Wingate.' On 2 March Nott went up the escarpment, met Bimbashi Colin Macdonald, adjutant of the Frontier Battalion, and they selected a site for the Emperor's camp at Dura 'by a stream with a waterfall', meeting on the way 'Nagash's men with 380 mules and Mangasha's with 50'. The arrival of the Emperor had stimulated the production of both mules and recruits.

Despite a signal from GHQ Khartoum that 'no rep[ea]t no onward movement [of HIM] should take place until Burye falls', Haile Selassie moved up the escarpment to his camp at Dura on 4 March. Nott was always careful to treat the Emperor with great respect and consult him about the practical details of the journey, but the decision when he should move forward rested with the *kaid* in Khartoum. That at least was the view of GHQ Khartoum, for operational reasons. They could not risk his capture by the Italians, which would be an enormous propaganda coup and would cripple the revolt. The Emperor though had a mind of his own and did not always comply.

From Dura Nott sent off Mackay and No 2 Centre to join Beghemder Force on 7 March with '65 men, 31 mules, also Fitaurari Birru with 300 mules'. Wingate complained later about reinforcements being sent by Sandford to the 'secondary theatre' and not to Gideon Force, but the decision to send Mackay and Birru to join Simonds had been taken by Sandford before Wingate took over, had not been questioned by Wingate, and was now being implemented by Nott. Birru was a most important figure and Sandford had for a long time been wanting him to go to Beghemder to take command of the revolt there. Nott did not get his chance of action until later, but it is evident that as DAA&QMG, with Sergeant Rees to assist him, he was the linchpin of the whole operation, not only having the responsibility for the Emperor, but also trying to maintain contact between Sandford, Wingate and GHQ Khartoum, receiving and giving orders to the operational centres, organizing the animal transport, forwarding arms and supplies and sending recruits back to Khartoum, and generally keeping things moving smoothly. One thing he did not need to worry about was petrol, unlike Cunningham's motorized troops for whom it was one of the most precious commodities.

Notes
1. Plantation Syndicate. The cotton-growing scheme in Gezira province. Agricultural inspectors under 30 were released to join the SDF. Among them were Johnson and Hayes.
2. Waratah – New South Wales.

4

Gideon Force in Gojjam:
The Pursuit

From his position on Church Hill opposite Mankusa on the morning of 3 March Wingate received from Khartoum a message intercepted by Middle East signals that the Italians were intending to evacuate Burye. He ordered Boustead to get ready to move with the bulk of the force to a rendezvous four miles north of the motor road, while he himself remained at Church Hill with three SDF platoons under Bimbashi Desmond Creedon, second-in-command of Harris's company, Akavia, Kabada, Sergeant Body and their men. He also sent a letter to Boyle telling him that the Burye garrison might withdraw and warning him to keep his camels a good distance from the road. This letter was sent by the traditional method, carried by an Ethiopian runner in a cleft stick, and never reached Boyle.

It is not clear precisely what orders Wingate gave to Boustead, but it seems likely that he intended him to intercept Natale's retreating column. Boustead moved with his force to the rendezvous during the night 3/4 March, and at dawn on 4 March moved back cautiously towards the road, expecting to meet Wingate there. By 6.00 a.m. there was no sign of Wingate but they saw three Capronis, which flew over, failed to spot them (they were in good cover), and went on to bomb Church Hill. Then they saw Natale's column, as Harris describes: 'File upon file of troops came marching down the road preceded by four armoured cars ... the road was soon black with troops, animals and transport as far as the eye could see.' Harris wanted to stir up the column with light machine-gun fire but Boustead would not hear of it ('we should have been blown to blazes as soon as we disclosed our position'), and they let the column go by. The column consisted of about 6000 fighting troops, including two armoured cars, 300 Europeans, and 200 cavalry, and was escorted by one Savoia-Marchetti aircraft sent from Addis Ababa. With the column there were 1000 non-combatants, wives and families of *ascari*, civilian employees, and some chiefs who had compromised themselves by their support of the Italian government. There were at least four lorries.

Wingate was still at Church Hill and at 7.00 a.m. the garrison on Mankusa opened up a heavy fire with machine guns on Church Hill supported by 81-millimetre mortars from the battery with the column. At 8.15 a.m. they advanced on Church Hill in open order supported by infantry from the column. Wingate's men lay down and returned fire, Wingate directing the fire with Body standing next to him. When two horses were hit Body suggested to Wingate that it would be a good idea if they sat down and, 'with a wry grin, he did'. Ayana Bire, one of Kabada's men, a great Wingate fan, but no fan of the Sudanese, says, 'Col. Wingate gave his horse to an Ethiopian soldier to hold and joined in the battle firing his weapon. The Sudanese ran away and Wingate was annoyed with them and beat them.'

Wingate ordered a phased withdrawal, which was carried out successfully despite what Ayana says, Akavia being the last to leave with a Sudanese platoon. Wingate himself says, 'I nearly got caught in Mankusa but escaped through fleetness of foot.' He rejoined Boustead at 11.30 a.m. after Natale's column had passed, looking, according to Boustead, 'particularly scruffy and shaken' (Boustead was no Wingate fan), and it is quite clear that there was a serious row between the two colonels, Boustead angry because Wingate had risked his three platoons and Wingate accusing Boustead of failing to inflict damage on the enemy. According to Thesiger Wingate accused Boustead of cowardice and Boustead never forgave him for this. Boustead defended his action later — 'If we had opened fire ... this would have brought the Caproni bombers on us and probably the large force of cavalry with the column' — but it is difficult not to conclude that he should have taken some hostile action. In the event the column had passed unscathed and Wingate sent Boustead, Acland and Harris off in pursuit with a force of about three platoons, Johnson to follow when he had investigated Mankusa and collected stragglers, and Beard, who relied on camel transport for his company, which had not yet rejoined them, was sent to take charge of Burye. Wingate had informed Sandford by signal of the evacuation of Burye who immediately arranged for it to be occupied by Brown's centre and Nagash's Patriots, and looting was prevented. Sandford signalled the Emperor at Dura camp that he was leaving for Burye, suggesting that he should meet himself and Kabada there.

Burye was an important acquisition for the Anglo-Ethiopian forces, and Drew established a hospital there to which the Sudanese wounded were sent. The Italians left behind intact two five-ton lorries and two staff cars and the Australian sergeants took these over and were able to carry supplies to Gideon Force as they followed Natale down the motor road. They also left intact large supplies of petrol, rations and grain for the horses, and the Wellesley bomber, which had been brought down on 28 February with a hole through its oil tank. This was later recovered.

Natale's column went on down the road and camped near the road bridge over the Lach river, the encampment on an open hillside making a marvellous target for air attack had there been air support. Boustead caught up the column at 3.00 p.m. and at dusk sent out small patrols under Sudanese NCOs to shoot up the encampment, provoking a furious response. Meanwhile only 17 miles down the road were the 2nd Ethiopians in their camp on the Charaka river, the two units quite out of touch and ignorant of what the other was doing. Boyle had returned on the afternoon of 4 March from Seccolo Mariam having agreed a plan of attack on the fort at Dambacha with Thesiger and Haile Yusus for the night of 5/6 March. He had been revolted when one of Haile Yusus's men had shown him an arm and leg lopped off some unfortunate Italian straggler. Smith, Downey and Botha were sent to carry out a reconnaissance of the night's attack, and the battalion spent the day of 5 March under cover avoiding Italian aircraft, which were overhead for most of the day. Evidently the Italians had learned of their presence in the area and were trying to locate them.

At 4.00 a.m. on 5 March Boustead got his men into position to fire on the Italian column as it started its march, himself and Acland to the north of the road, and Harris and Hassan Musaad near the road bridge. They watched the column break camp at dawn and march up the road across the bridge and opened up with their Brens, causing casualties and provoking heavy and close return fire from the rearguard. Harris then, rashly as he admits, crossed the river and doubled to the south of the road with one section and fired on the flank of the column, 'moving slowly past and offering such a target as a man might dream about'. The reaction was swift. They saw an Italian officer giving orders and a troop of cavalry charged them and they had to run for it, just reaching the river in time, across which the horses could not follow. North of the road Boustead and Acland had a similar experience and had had to run to avoid being cut off by a foot patrol. Neither was a young man (both about 41), and Harris was much amused by the spectacle of 'a Commanding Officer, a Lieutenant Colonel, in full flight carrying a Bren gun as he went'. On his way to rejoin Boustead Harris found several dead *ascari* with Patriots already stripping the bodies, and 'one badly wounded Eritrean who begged us to put him out of his misery with a bullet. I could not bring myself to do this and left him after tying up his wound with a field dressing.'

Natale's column continued its march and made camp at Amba Tullo, a strong position about one mile east of the river Dirr, across the river from the fort of Jigga, which was burned and its garrison collected as the column went past. Boustead and Acland, with Johnson and his three platoons, who had joined them from Mankusa, followed and made camp about 1000 yards from the Italians. It was now the afternoon of 5 March. Harris joined them in the evening having waited at the Lach river for the rest of his company and his horse transport under Creedon. While they were enjoying a late breakfast Wingate arrived, 'in great heart, having just received Brown's report on the stores left in Burye'. Wingate had with him Akavia and Kabada's 50 men from Mission 101 (but not Kabada himself who had gone to Burye to meet Sandford and await the Emperor). With these men he then followed the Frontier Battalion along the road, not leading from the front as he usually did, but leaving the pursuit to Boustead. He was not in close touch with him and was completely out of touch with Boyle. Certainly on 5 March he sent a signal asking for air support on 6 March, but this must have been a request for general air support in pursuit of the column. No particular action was anticipated on that day. In the light of the claim Wingate made later that at the Charaka river on 6 March he had the enemy 'jammed between my two battalions and hoped in vain for a *coup de grâce* from the air' the effectiveness of the pursuit by Boustead's two small companies needs to be examined. On the evidence of Tenente (later General) Raimondo Barberis of the 65th Colonial Battalion, the rearguard battalion, they suffered some losses from the attacks of the pursuing Sudanese, but not serious, were well able to cope with them, and the march was not disrupted. His evidence is supported by the fact that Natale was able to detach the rearguard without difficulty to take part in the battle on 6 March. Undoubtedly the continual harassment by the Frontier Battalion patrols reinforced Natale's belief that Gideon Force was much larger than it actually was.

Meanwhile, only five miles down the road from the Italian camp at Amba Tullo, the 2nd Ethiopian Battalion, in its camp on the Charaka river, was preparing for its night attack on Dambacha fort, oblivious that Natale was advancing towards them and completely out of contact with Wingate and Boustead. In accordance with plans agreed with Thesiger, Rowe, with Gerazmatch Dabala and one platoon of C company with a Vickers medium machine gun, left in the morning of 5 March to join Thesiger on Seccolo Mariam, followed later by Downey (with another Vickers) and Botha (with the mortar), who took up positions covering Dambacha fort. The plan was that after an opening bombardment with mortar and medium machine gun fire, Haile Yusus's Patriots would attack and burn the *banda* village at 8.00 p.m. and Tutton, with two platoons, would then attack the fort, supported by reserves under Smith and Downey. Fire was opened by the two Vickers and the mortar as planned at 5.30 p.m., the Italians responding with machine-gun and artillery fire, and Tutton got his two platoons into position 200 yards from the enemy wire, ready to attack and waiting for the Patriots. No attack came and, after waiting until midnight and exchanging fire with the garrison, Boyle called off the attack and ordered all detachments back to camp except for Rowe's, which remained on Seccolo Mariam overnight and returned next morning.

The Action on the River Charaka: 6 March 1941*

During the night of 5/6 March Johnson and Omar Effendi shot up the Italian encampment at Amba Tullo while Harris and his company rested. At 3.00 a.m. on 6 March the 2nd Ethiopian Battalion returned to its camp on the Charaka river. Although disappointed with the failure of Haile Yusus (inevitably referred to as 'Highly Useless') to turn up, Tutton was happy with the performance of his men. Luyt and Clarke had been left in charge of the camp and reported, so Tutton records, 'rumours from *shifta* that the Burye garrison had evacuated and reached Jigga'. Boyle failed to appreciate that the large Burye garrison would not stop at the small fort of Jigga, but would go on to Dambacha, and that he was sitting astride its route. He took no special precautions and the battalion retired to rest leaving normal sentries. Its strength was 300 Ethiopians and seven Europeans, eight after Rowe returned, and its armament, in addition to the men's rifles, one three-inch mortar, five Vickers medium machine guns, four light machine guns, and one Boyes anti-tank rifle. They were not in an ambush position facing west, but encamped at the bottom of the slope with the river between them and the Italians in Dambacha, the nearest enemy so far as they knew. A and C companies were near the right bank of the Charaka stream, north of the road bridge, D company about 400 yards further north, and the camel camp under escort south of the bridge. Their position was taken for concealment, not defence, they had no field of fire, and most of the area was covered with elephant grass, shoulder or head high. When the action started they had to stand to fire their weapons over the grass. On the east side of the stream there was a ridge, which would have made a reasonable ambush position but Boyle had not occupied this, not anticipating any advance from the west, save that when the alarm was raised he placed himself and Downey with Vickers medium machine guns east of the stream.

---

* See Sketch 2.

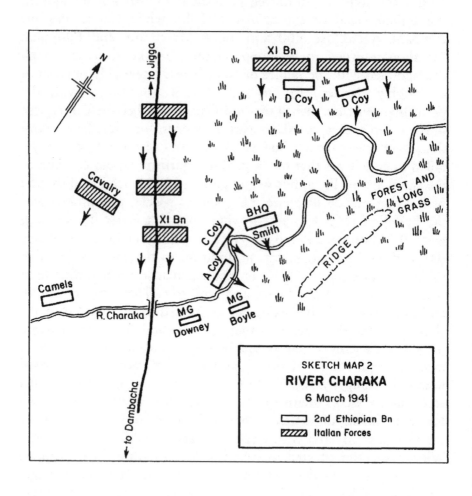

SKETCH MAP 2
RIVER CHARAKA
6 March 1941

▭ 2nd Ethiopian Bn
▨ Italian Forces

Back at Jigga, at 4.00 a.m. on 6 March Boustead took Harris to the fort from which there was a commanding view of the countryside and, as dawn broke, pointed out to him the route he wished him to follow across country to reach a point overlooking the motor road on the line of the enemy's withdrawal. Harris set off to try and cut off the column, leaving his animal transport, the men carrying the heavy weapons. Johnson and his men, after their night operations, followed the column south of the road.

At 5.00 a.m. the Italian column broke camp and marched off, 6000 fighting men against the Ethiopians' 300, with the 11th Colonial Battalion and the two armoured cars in the lead as advance guard. The Savoia aircraft soon appeared to cover the march. Natale's aim was to reach Dambacha, an easy march of 11 miles. He must have known that there was an enemy force ahead, but had no precise knowledge of where it was. Leading the column, the 11th Colonial Battalion covered the ground swiftly at a speedy half run. In command was Captain Annelli, Tenente Volpi commanded No 2 company with Sotto Tenente Marchetti as his subaltern, and a 20-year-old *tenente*, Giuseppe Gallia, commanded No 3 company. There were only three companies, one having provided the garrison for Bichena, now withdrawn to Debra Markos. This was one of the original Eritrean battalions with long service in Eritrea, Libya and Ethiopia, but now, like the other colonial battalions in the two brigades, a mixed battalion with Eritrean *graduati* and Amhara or Tigrean *ascari*. The *graduati* were distinguishable, and vulnerable, because of their red shoulder stripes and badges.

As the 11th Colonial Battalion rounded the bend at first light leading to the final stretch of road before the Charaka bridge, they spotted the camp of D company, the 2nd Ethiopian Battalion, and deployed either side of the road, Nos 2 and 4 companies north of the road and Gallia's No 3 company south. Volpi's No 2 company was on the left flank approaching D company's position, went straight into the attack, and had a rude shock. D company was alert, but only just. Tutton had been wakened at 5.45 a.m. by heavy firing from the direction of Jigga, and decided to take out a patrol while Luyt alerted the company and sent a message to Boyle. He ran into the advancing enemy and managed to double back to his company, where he found that Luyt had given the order to fire and 'was encouraging the men who were yelling with excitement and blazing into the long grass'. After a fierce struggle in D company's camp the enemy were driven out by grenades and rifle fire from the hip at close range. Tutton was hit by grenade splinters in the leg, another grenade hit him but failed to explode, and he saw one of his grenades knock over an Italian officer who was encouraging his men. Ayella dragged Tutton back, and 'some courageous fellow picked up the grenade, removed the pin, and threw it back'. In this first encounter, 'Luyt was ... magnificient ... and Lieut. Taka Wolde of 14 platoon set his men a great example.'

Meanwhile Nos 3 and 4 companies of the 11th Battalion were advancing astride the road against A and C companies' position, and also met fierce opposition. Boyle had placed the rest of his battalion in position with their backs to the stream, A company under Sergeant Botha on the left and C company under Sergeant Clarke on their right. He placed Downey with two men and a Vickers medium machine gun on the east side of the stream close to the bridge, and himself with another Vickers on his right between Downey and A company. The two Vickers were to cover the approaches to the bridge and were to operate with devastating effect. To the right of C company was battalion HQ under the adjutant, Captain Smith, augmented by some men from No 15 platoon, D company, who had retreated without orders when D company was first attacked, but were rallied by Smith and fought well under him.

Boyle must be given credit for his quick reaction and for getting his battalion into the best position he could in the short time available. A and C companies defended the line of the stream with great resolution and No 4 company of the 11th Battalion was driven back with heavy casualties. No 3 company, however, under Gallia, although suffering severely, the *sciumbasci* killed and 30 other casualties, succeeded in crossing the stream south of the road bridge and reaching the road beyond it behind the Ethiopians' position. Then, as Gallia recalls, 'Col. Natale pulled me back. He was afraid of the Patriots intervening.' On the evidence of an artillery lieutenant, Gastone Rossini, some of Haile Yusus's men were starting to gather on the ridge behind the Ethiopians' position, but they played no part in the battle. Even so, recalling Gallia was probably a mistake by Natale. Had he reinforced the encircling movement, he would have made short work of the Ethiopians. As it was he continued to batter away at them frontally.

After the withdrawal of Gallia's company, the two armoured cars were brought forward and they raked A and C companies' positions with heavy and concentrated fire from their six heavy machine guns, but the situation was saved by an act of great individual courage by Lance Corporal Wandafrash of C company who, on his own initiative, ran forward to the road with the Boyes anti-tank rifle, lay down 100 yards from the armoured cars and fired eight rounds, putting both cars out of action and killing or wounding the occupants, including a lieutenant colonel travelling in one of the cars. Heavy fire was directed at Wandafrash, but he returned safely to his company, abandoning the rifle but taking the bolt with him.

Back on D company's front the 11th Battalion mounted a second attack led by Annelli with Volpi still commanding No 2 company although already wounded, this time approaching cautiously through the long grass. Marchetti had been wounded in the first attack and was missing. Luyt played a big part in repelling this second attack. He took over the Lewis gun of No 13 platoon (Haile Mariam), which had jammed, repaired it, and fired it himself from a standing position resting the barrel on the branch of a tree. The Lewis gun fire, with Tutton firing his rifle accurately alongside, and steady fire from Nos 13 and 14 platoons, caused much execution among the attacking troops, particularly among the Eritrean *graduati* whose red shoulder stripes made them visible in the long grass. The ejector mechanism on the old First World War Lewis gun frequently failed to work and Luyt had to prise cartridge caps out of the breech with a penknife. 'These were the really trying moments. All this time bullets dug into the tree behind and beside me.'

In this second attack Anelli was wounded and Volpi was killed leading his *ascari* with great gallantry, as was was his company *sciumbasci*. This phase of the battle was a classic case of fine leadership of good troops on both sides, Tutton and Luyt on the

113

Allied side, Anelli and Volpi on the Italian, an example also of the sad situation commented on by Luyt earlier, 'ranging the people on opposite sides', Ethiopian against Ethiopian. Volpi and Luyt were both singled out and awarded medals, Volpi the *Medaglia d'Oro al VM* posthumously, and Luyt the DCM. The 11th Battalion, driven back for the second time, suffered severely, with three officer and 127 *ascari* casualties. The time was now about 9.00 a.m. and Natale brought up fresh troops with machine guns and the pack battery with their 65-millimetre guns and 81-millimetre mortars and battered away at the Ethiopian positions. The accompanying Savoia also bombed and machine-gunned the Ethiopians and was hit by ground fire. As Tutton records, 'We set up a great shout as it passed over us getting lower and lower.' The plane made a forced landing at Dambacha.

At 9.30 a.m., with their ammunition beginning to run short and the enemy fire unabated, Tutton moved Corporal Wodaju of No 16 platoon with his Vickers medium machine gun from the right to the left of his position so that he could enfilade the Italians, collected about 20 men and led two counterattacks, the men advancing firing from the hip and driving the Italians back some distance. He records that 'the men behaved very well. . . . Rifleman Tadessa Labessa and Follower Tadessa [his young orderly who cooked the dinner at Engiabara!] especially distinguished themselves.'

Meanwhile there had been developments on A and C company's fronts, observed by Thesiger from Seccolo Mariam where he was with Haile Yusus and his Patriots and from where he had a grandstand view of the action. Natale had sent the 21st and 72nd Colonial Battalions against these two companies, but they had been battered by Boyle's machine guns, the 21st in particular suffering severely with one officer, Adjutant-Major Mosca, killed. Thesiger sent a note to Boyle warning him that 'Italian troops are getting round on your left, across the plain in large numbers.' This was the 72nd Battalion and the mounted *banda* who had made a righthanded sweep through the Ethiopian camel camp and captured about 200 camels.

By this time Rowe had arrived from Seccolo Mariam with Gerazmatch Dabala and the platoon of C company and they were soon engaged. As Enko records, 'Dabala was so angry to see his

114

friends being attacked that he ran towards the enemy with his rifle raised and started firing at them. The Italians turned their guns on him and killed him.' The death of Dabala, the highly respected company leader of C company, throwing himself on the enemy like a highland chieftain, was a great loss to the battalion.

When the 21st and 72nd Battalions failed to break through against Boyle Natale sent for the rearguard battalion, the 65th Colonial Battalion commanded by Lieutenant Colonel de Mandato. The fact that they could easily disengage suggests that they were not being closely pressed by the Frontier Battalion patrols. Harris, with his three platoons of tired, hungry soldiers carrying their heavy weapons, was struggling across country north of the road through long grass and over ridges. He was once fired on by the rearguard but was otherwise out of touch with the column. Johnson with three platoons was south of the road, also out of touch, and somewhere behind them on the road was Wingate. None were aware that Boyle was engaged in a major conflict with Natale's column until they were almost on top of the battlefield.

The arrival of the 65th Battalion was the turning point of the action. Barberis recalls, 'LXXII Battalion were weakened by the casualties of their company at Mankusa and could not break through. We hurried forward to help.' Tutton describes a scene, which might have come out of the Peninsular War, how 'the Italian Colonel[1] placed himself at the head of his battalion, a conspicuous and brilliant figure in the full insignia of his rank, and marched down the road towards the bridge. He was shot down but the column pressed on regardless of casualties.' The officers of the 65th Battalion believe in fact that their colonel was knocked over by a grenade thrown by 'an English captain'. This could only have been Smith or Rowe and the report shows the close quarter nature of the engagement.

A and C companies were forced back behind the stream and at the crucial moment Downey's Vickers jammed. After emptying his pistol into the advancing enemy and seeing that one of his men was dead and the other had decamped, he removed the lock from the Vickers and threw himself into the nearest patch of tall grass. Here he was joined by a wounded Italian officer, Sotto Tenente Marchetti of the 11th Battalion, who asked for help. 'I gave him my waterbottle and helped him to loosen his belt.' Their positions were soon reversed when they were surrounded by *ascari* of the 65th Battalion who aimed their rifles at Downey. Marchetti quickly intervened and ordered them to lower their weapons and almost certainly saved Downey's life.

The breakthrough by the 65th Battalion was achieved with heavy loss, indicating the ferocity of the resistance by the Ethiopians, who had already seen off attacks by the other battalions. From the accounts of two surviving officers, now Generals Cicolella and Malara, the 65th Battalion lost 'Sotto Tenente Crispini killed, Tenente Col. de Mandato, Captain Vico, Tenente Cicolella, Sotto Tenente Venditti, and Doctor Sotto Tenente Degli Antonini wounded, and 25 *graduati* and 110 *ascari* killed and wounded.' Downey, now a prisoner, was escorted 'very roughly' to the road, asked, 'Any land mines?' and pushed into the front vehicle, still covered with the Italian officer's blood from attempts to staunch his wound.

D company on the right did not maintain its position for long after the retreat of A and C companies. Fresh troops advanced against it from the 3rd Colonial Brigade and it was now suffering casualties, including the company leader, Fitaurari Garadou, and CQMS Ayella. They had little ammunition left, a shell burst set fire to the long grass in front of their position and the whole place became a blazing inferno, and the Italians drove a wedge between Tutton and Luyt. Luyt's Lewis gun jammed again at a crucial moment with the advancing *ascari* almost on top of him and he was knocked over by an exploding grenade. He picked himself up and retreated with his men across the stream, and Tutton on his right was forced to do the same. The time was now about 11.00 a.m.

Natale's column had achieved their object of breaking through to the Dambacha road. They wasted no time in occupying the Ethiopian camp or in pursuing the Ethiopians across the stream, but pressed straight on to Dambacha clearing the position by midday, taking their wounded, and the captured camels, but leaving their dead unburied and a great deal of equipment lying about. The scattered sections of the 2nd Ethiopians returned and reoccupied their camp during the early afternoon. Certainly by

1.00 p.m., when Harris and the first troops of the Frontier Battalion arrived, Smith was already back in the camp collecting elements of the battalion together. Harris had heard the closing stages of what was clearly a major engagement. He had been joined by Boustead, Acland and Johnson, 'somewhat out of breath', who, thinking that the sounds of the engagement came from Harris's company, had doubled forward with Johnson's company to reinforce him. They then realized that it was Boyle's battalion that was engaged with the enemy and so pushed on to try and get into the fight, but arrived at the road about an hour after the Italians had moved on, 'to be greeted by a "whoop" from Smith, Boyle's adjutant, who was standing below us waving his arms'. Signs of the recent action were evident, dead camels, two wrecked armoured cars, and the 'road was littered with boxes, saddlery equipment, ammunition and dead men'.

The tradition has grown up, believed by Ethiopians today, that Haile Yusus's Patriots took part in the Charaka action. Sadly this is not true. The presence of some of them on the ridge behind the Ethiopian position probably deterred Natale from pursuing an encircling movement, but not only did the Patriots play no part in the action, they moved in as soon as the Italians departed to strip the bodies and loot the 2nd Ethiopian Battalion's kit. Luyt was disgusted, writing in his diary under strong emotion on 7 March, the day after the battle, 'The despicable *shifta*, they who had not raised a finger to help us in the fight — these human vulture rats were in among our stores, looting as hard as they could ... the people we are supposed to be helping, the "loyal" subjects of the Emperor.' Luyt recalls that he and Rowe observed the looting and sent two *askari* back to Boyle urging him to come up with the rest of the battalion as soon as possible. This they did and the looting stopped. D company's camp escaped the worst of the looting largely because of Corporal Wodaju who, with Rifleman Mulugeta (who had been wounded), had remained in his concealed position with his Vickers medium machine gun and had continued to fire his gun after D company retreated, had kept off the Patriots and had even collected a large dump of enemy war material, chiefly arms and ammunition.

Thesiger, who is quite sure the Patriots played no part in the action, wrote to congratulate Boyle on the afternoon of 6 March, 'You put up a magnificient show. I reckon they were 10 battalions strong,' and again on 7 March to apologize for the looting of their kit by the Patriots and that he was trying to get it back, 'It was a very poor show. I suppose they thought the Italians would get it and they might as well take it first. . . . I congratulate you all on a very fine fight. Your men are well seasoned now.' The Patriot looting of their allies was inexcusable. Their failure to fight was understandable, if not creditable. They had been fighting the Italians for four years. Now that the regulars had arrived, their view was, 'Let them get on with it. Why should we get killed at the last minute?'

Passing through the carnage of the Charaka battlefield, the Frontier Battalion pressed on after the retreating Italians, Johnson's No 1 patrol company in the lead. They were tired and hungry, having had little proper food for three days. Discarded tins of Italian food provided sustenance for some, including a seven-pound tin of strawberry jam which was enjoyed, though it made them thirsty. On approaching the hills surrounding Dambacha fort Johnson was fired on by the Italian rearguard, and Boustead sent Harris round to the left to 'do his stuff'. From a ridge overlooking the fort Harris opened up with his Brens on the Italians from the range of 800 yards as they made camp while Johnson did the same from a position near the road. Harris soon came under accurate machine-gun fire from troops sent round to his left, realized that he was in danger of being cut off and decided to withdraw. In doing so he had four men wounded, including the platoon commander, Babikr Bashir, and staying himself with Hassan Musaad and the last section to cover the withdrawal, was knocked over by a machine-gun burst as he was getting up to go and wounded in the chest and left arm. Helped by Hassan and another soldier he managed to make the road, 'crying out with pain' (Hassan was gripping him by his wounded arm), and was told by Boustead, 'Stop making such a bloody row and get on back. This curt utterance had a miraculous effect.' The time was now 4.30 p.m. Leaving Johnson and Creedon with three platoons to cover the Italians Boustead marched the rest of his battalion down the road back towards the Charaka, Harris and the other wounded managing to walk unaided. After an hour they met Wingate sitting on the side of the road who bound up Harris's wounds with field dressings and fed him with 'dog biscuit and tinned tunny fish' from supplies brought up from Burye by one of the Australian sergeants in an Italian staff car. Leaving Johnson to harass the Italians during the night, Wingate moved the rest of Boustead's battalion two miles down the road towards the Charaka, where they met their camel transport and camped and the men had their first proper meal for three days. Drew joined them there and was able to treat the wounded.

The official historian, Colonel Barton, wrote of the Charaka action: 'The Ethiopians fought with fierce bravery for a short while, then broke and fled. ... They lost a quarter of their strength. For practical purposes they were of small value for the rest of the campaign.' This probably derives in part from Wingate's dispatch in which he praised their performance and said that 'the enemy was much impressed', but also said, 'they were immobilized and able to do little further in the campaign'. The foregoing account, based on contemporary diaries and documents and the evidence of survivors, suggests that Barton's judgement needs to be corrected. The action was not briefly over; the Ethiopians resisted for at least four hours and beat back at least two attacks by two colonial brigades causing heavy casualties before the third attack broke through. They then retreated but reoccupied their camp as soon as the Italians passed through. Their casualties were 48 or 12 per cent, not one quarter, and their performance for the rest of the campaign can be judged from the narrative below.

Actual casualties on the two sides were

Allied, officers and British NCOs, one killed (Dabala), one captured (Downey), two wounded (Tutton and Luyt, lightly, remained on duty), total four, Ethiopian, 21 killed, 23 wounded. Total 48.

Italian, three officers killed, ten wounded, two nationals killed, six wounded, 122 *ascari* killed, 201 wounded, total 344. The relatively high proportion of Italian officer casualties shows that they commanded from the front.

119

In his dispatch Wingate accused Boyle of 'sitting down in the line of the enemy's retreat . . . in what must have been one of the worst tactical positions for defence in history.' In fairness to Boyle his position was chosen for concealment, not for defence or ambush. The arrival of Natale's column was to him just as unexpected as his presence was to Natale. Wingate also said:

> I had kept Khartoum informed of the situation and when for four hours I had the enemy jammed between my two battalions and unable to move I hoped in vain for a *coup de grâce* from the air. It is no exaggeration to say that the capture of this force at the moment would have made possible an immediate and successful advance to Addis Ababa.

The most charitable view of this preposterous claim is that Wingate was too far from the scene of action to know what was going on. It would be more accurate to say that while Natale's column battered away at the Ethiopians, the six Frontier Battalion platoons, their attacks no more than a nuisance, were kept at a distance by the rearguard and arrived at the scene one hour after action finished, while the Patriots stood and watched the battle and then looted the camp. If air support was requested Wingate knew very well that from their bases in the Sudan the air forces could not give immediate support to ground troops in Ethiopia. There is no possibility that Natale would have surrendered, even in the unlikely event of an Allied air attack. He had two good brigades with experienced officers and he was merely concerned with breaking through to Dambacha and this he succeeded in doing.

Wingate's immediate reaction was generous, like that of Thesiger. He wrote to Boyle at 7.00 a.m. on the morning of 7 March before he set off again after the Italians, a letter dictated to Akavia and kept by Boyle. He congratulated Boyle and his men on 'a very creditable effort. . . . It is quite evident from the remains on the ground that your men put up a great fight against odds and completely turned the tables on the enemy.' Of the participants, Tutton, a classical scholar, likened the defence of the Charaka to the battle of Thermopylae (481 BC) when 300 Spartans held up the Persian army. Luyt commented that the casualties should have been much higher, 'Bad shooting and the elephant grass saved many lives.' He went to look at the tree where he had stood with his Lewis gun and found '25 bullet holes to the height of 12 feet and quite 8 at a height to have killed me. Something more than luck must have kept those bullets off.' The tradition that British soldiers climbed into trees and fired at the Italians over the long grass persists among local villagers to this day and must have originated with Luyt and Tutton. Luyt was generous in his praise of his company commander, 'throughout the fight Tutton was an inspiring leader and brave example to the men', and on the whole of his men, 'Some of the men were magnificient ... and showed great individual courage. Not all, of course, but some.' Smith singled out Downey and Tutton, 'who led two spirited counterattacks', for particular mention, and Rowe, after his death later, was praised by his *askari* for 'fighting like a lion' at the Charaka. Wingate recommended Luyt for the DCM, Rowe for the MC, and Clarke, Wandafrash and Wodaju for the MM. Only Luyt received an award.[2] It seems true of this action that nearly all did well, though Boyle cannot escape criticism. The action became known as Boyle's battle or Boyle's blunder, and it certainly was a blunder not to have sent out patrols when the Patriots reported that Natale had left Burye, and not to have stood to an hour before dawn. Boyle appears though to have acted swiftly and intelligently in getting his battalion into as good a defensive position as possible with Vickers medium machine guns covering the road. There is little evidence as to his own part in the action and Luyt believes that he lost some respect with the men because he did not play a prominent part like the company officers and sergeants and Ethiopians like to be led from the front.

With regard to Wingate's own position in the action it appears that his two battalions were out of his control on 5 and 6 March and acting independently. Where he was himself from mid-morning on 5 March until the evening of 6 March remains a mystery. Was the action a defeat for Wingate? Luyt believed it was, albeit temporary, and this is the later Ethiopian view. As Major Johannes Abdu, Nott's interpreter, wrote in a letter to the *Ethiopian Herald* in 1973, 'O. W. lost only one hot battle — YE CHEREKA'. The Italians were entitled to claim success having broken through. Their official history refers to the column reaching Dambacha after a 'violent battle against huge forces of Sudanese, Ethiopian refugees and rebels', and Rossini records the action as one in which the *ascari* of the colonial battalions performed with great credit, believing also their enemy to have been Sudanese. Wingate in his dispatch says correctly that 'the enemy was much impressed' with the sturdy resistance, and this, together with the pressure from the Frontier Battalion which followed, induced Natale to disobey orders and abandon Dambacha. The stand of the 300 may not deserve a place in history like Thermopylae, but those who fought there on both sides have reason to be proud.

The Pursuit Continues

After writing to Boyle on the morning of 7 March Wingate advanced again against Dambacha with the Frontier Battalion. In the early hours Johnson's company had occupied the ridge facing the fort, but an attempt to advance further was met by accurate machine-gun fire, the *ombashi* of the leading section was killed, and the section withdrawn, and after a reconnaissance revealed that the position was held in strength, Wingate decided to pull back and pass round to the south. Before this movement could be carried out, Natale evacuated Dambacha on 8 March, abandoning in his haste the Savoia brought down at the Charaka, crossing the Tamcha river five miles further on without destroying the bridge, and going straight on to Gulit (known to the Italians as Dess) 12 miles west of Debra Markos, evacuating on the way the garrison of Emmanuel (known to the Italians as Baremma). None of these steps were approved by Natale's superiors.

Wingate occupied Dambacha on 8 March, was joined on 10 March by the 2nd Ethiopian Battalion, which had managed to move by stages, and on 11 March held a special parade to congratulate the battalion on its performance. Luyt, who had been given the job of reorganizing the battalion transport to replace the lost camels, collecting camels, mules and even ox carts, recorded with pleasure that at this parade, 'to my surprise Wingate came up to me and congratulated me personally, a most surprising and unexpected gesture and hence most welcome.' Also at this parade Wingate announced his intention to recommend Lance-Corporal

122

Wandafrash and Corporal Wodaju for awards. (These were never granted.)

Dambacha was productive of two more Thesiger stories, one on the previous theme. Tutton records a *bon mot* from Boustead, who overheard Thesiger telling Smith, who was feeding him, how easy it was to live off the country. 'Boustead told Smithy. "That's true, Smith. For the last week the country has been me. Now, I perceive, it's you."' The other story is told by Akavia who was immensely impressed with the way Thesiger calmly took charge when Wingate's interpreter and three Sudanese were horribly burned by exploding petrol.

On the afternoon of 11 March Gideon Force marched out of Dambacha in pursuit of Natale, the force consisting of two-and-a-half companies of the Frontier Battalion, C company of the 2nd Ethiopian Battalion under Rowe, Thesiger and his *banda*, Foley, Kabada and Lij Makonnen Desta from Mission 101, and a new arrival, Lieutenant Guy Turrall, an experienced Royal Engineers officer and demolition expert, who took charge of the two mortar sections. A, B and D companies of the 2nd Ethiopian Battalion under Boyle were left in Dambacha to recruit transport animals and repair and clean up the fort. Wingate's original plan was to bypass Debra Markos to the south and cut communications between that centre and Addis Ababa, foreshadowing the long range penetration schemes, which he brought to fruition in Burma. Some of Haile Yusus's men followed the Italians, in Thesiger's words, 'rather half-heartedly', and both he and Belai Zelleka promised help, but not much materialized, none from Belai Zelleka.

Meanwhile, in the rear Drew had operated on Harris and the Sudanese and Ethiopian wounded, the operations being frequently interrupted by air attacks by Caproni bombers. There were no casualties to personnel, but Tutton had a mule killed within 20 yards of him. A feature of this period was the Italian local air superority and how comparatively ineffective aerial attack was. On the evening of 8 March the wounded were moved to Burye in two lorries and a staff car driven by Brown and two of his sergeants where, in Harris's words, 'the genial countenance of Colonel Sandford welcomed us to Burye fort'. From Burye Harris and four badly-wounded Sudanese were flown out to Roseires in a captured Caproni, which had flown in the day before with Brigadier Lush, Colonel Airey and Major Tuckey for discussions with Wingate and Sandford. They had a lucky escape on leaving. Two Savoias arrived to bomb the airfield but failed to spot the Caproni. So ended Harris's part in the campaign and also unfortunately his lively and interesting account. Thanks to the surgical skill of Clifford Drew he recovered from his wounds and later commanded a parachute battalion in Normandy. In the words of Boustead he had 'played an invaluable part in the operations ... and richly deserved the MC which he was awarded.'

The Emperor Moves to Burye

Sandford from Burye kept the Emperor at Dura informed of the progress of Gideon Force and, anticipating the early withdrawal of the Italians from Debra Markos, suggested that he should write to the patriot leaders ordering them to dispute the passage of the Italians across the Abbai, in particular to Belai Zelleka, who 'carried on negotiations with Ras Hailu, but did not submit. I will try and arrange for Wilfred Thesiger to go with him.' Was Sandford interfering in operational matters? Probably not. This was in accordance with the *kaid*'s instructions and Sandford saw Wingate at Dambacha on 11 March to concert plans with him. Furthermore Sandford, in addition to being adviser to the Emperor, had been ordered by Platt to take over 'A&Q', all administrative arrangements for the force this side of the Abbai.

The Emperor's convoy, with Nott and rear HQ, left Dura on 10 March, and arrived at Burye on 14 March. At the same time eight operational centres left Matakal, travelling mainly by moonlight to avoid Italian aircraft. At Engiabara Nott watched and filmed the Emperor holding a review of Mangasha's troops, 'the braves reciting their prowess and strutting the while' and a similar one at Burye for Nagash's men. One would have expected, now that the Emperor was back in Gojjam, to hear about a massive concentration of Patriots under his leadership in cooperation with Gideon Force to round up the Italians, and this is clearly what Sandford had envisaged. This did not happen for a number of reasons, the reluctance of Gojjam Patriots to move out of their own areas, Wingate's policy of going ahead with his striking force, the feeling that they had done their bit, 'Let the others get on with it,' and even, as suggested by General Nega, then on the Emperor's staff, the Emperor's belief that the *ascari* would be more likely to surrender to regular troops than to Patriots. Whatever the reason, Mangasha and Nagash and their men played no further part in the Gojjam campaign.

Sandford and Lush had met the Emperor at the Fatham river, half way to Engiabara, driven out by Sergeant Burke in an Italian staff car, and they brought him into Burye while his mule convoy followed and immediately got down to political discussions, the purpose of Lush's visit. Lush brought back some answers to the points raised by the Emperor at Belaiya, on proclamations and judicial appointments, but there was still disagreement regarding the control by political officers of OETA over liberated territories where operations were continuing on which Wavell insisted. Haile Selassie had to accept this and relations with Lush were still amicable though later they became very strained.

Nott had received an order from Wingate to go forward and join him. This was cancelled by Sandford, certainly interference by the 'Brigadier with the roving commission', but justified. There was no one available to replace Nott in his vital role at this stage. On this occasion Wingate accepted the position, but he won his point later when he took over 'A&Q' and Nott came under his direct command. In any case Nott was unwell with a badly poisoned leg. He visited Drew's hospital in Burye to have his leg dressed and 'spoke to the wounded (21 Sudanese, 19 Ethiopian), and had 80 sacks filled with *tef* hay sent to hospital for them to lie on. Funny that nobody had thought of that before.' Nott's practical good sense, as always, emerges from this extract. Nott also found Critchley in Burye, immobilized by two bad legs.

On 16 March a South African Air Force Junkers arrived at Burye with three Palestinian doctors requested by Wingate, one of whom, Dr Zablany, was posted to the 2nd Ethiopian Battalion, and on the same day the Junkers took Lush and his fellow officers back to Khartoum, taking also Critchley and four wounded. Critchley did not return to Ethiopia. He had done splendid work with Sandford in the early days of Mission 101 but was not fit and asked to be sent out. His path crossed with Wingate's later in the war in

Burma where he fought with Karen irregulars and added the DSO to his MC.

Nott remained at Burye with the Emperor and Sandford and this became Mission 101's rear headquarters and the collecting point for the operational centres. Nott had to hobble about organizing it all, a difficult job for a man with a poisoned leg. Blood poisoning in the days before antibiotics was not a light matter. Burye was an important centre and Haile Selassie could now start to establish his authority over the local chiefs. The airfield enabled an air link to be opened with the Sudan for bringing in mail and some supplies and for evacuating the wounded. Gideon Force, which in the Burye operations had fully earned the title so imaginatively given to it by Wingate, was now moving into east Gojjam for operations around Debra Markos, where the same tactics would be employed, though with less success, since they were now up against a more resolute Italian commander. Before following them let us see what has been happening on other fronts.

In Eritrea, where the 4th Indian Division had been holding grimly onto Cameron Ridge since 14 February, Platt launched his second attack on Keren on 15 March with the 4th and 5th Indian Divisions — an attack which would in the end succeed after an initial repulse and 12 more days' bitter fighting against stubborn resistance. On the southern front Berbera was reoccupied on 16 March by a force from Aden, and on the same day Cunningham's leading brigade, the 23rd Nigerian, reached Jijigga and by 21 March was ready to attack the Marda Pass, the gateway into Ethiopia. These were important advances. The capture of Jijigga gave the South African Air Force a well-equipped airfield and would enable it to give close support to the troops on the ground. The port facilities at Berbera, though limited, could be used immediately for the landing of troops and supplies. British Somaliland was now clear of Italian troops. In northern Gojjam Beghemder Force had followed Torelli to Bahr Dar, which they reached on March 12, and were containing him there.

Colonel Maraventano Takes Command

In east Gojjam Natale's column had come to a halt at Gulit on 10 March. The Italian High Command was dissatisfied with Natale's performance and on 14 March he was replaced by his deputy, Colonel Saverio Maraventano. The command structure was also reorganized. Because of the 'British thrusts from the north and south and the increasing Abyssinian rebellion', Aosta had given orders for the setting up of two fortified zones of resistance, at Gondar and Debra Markos, with the object of keeping Allied forces engaged in Ethiopia for as long as possible and preventing reinforcements being sent to the Middle East where it was hoped that the arrival of Rommel and the Germans would bring about a reversal of fortunes in favour of the Axis, as indeed proved to be the case. Gondar remained under General Nasi; Debra Markos was transferred on 14 March to the command of the Shoan sector commander, General Scala, who was stationed in Addis Ababa. Maraventano therefore had firm orders to defend Debra Markos, which he proceeded to carry out, and Wingate found that he had a much more determined enemy than Natale.

The troops Maraventano took over from Natale amounted to about 14,000 — 2163 nationals, 7153 colonials and 5000 'Gojjami armed irregulars', of which Ras Hailu's *banda* accounted for 4000. The two colonial brigades that had marched with Natale were in position in the fortified hills, good defensive positions, north and south of the road at Gulit, with the *banda* behind and the Blackshirt battalions in Debra Markos and the surrounding forts. At Usciater on the way to the Abbai there was a Blackshirt company with some irregulars, and at the Safartak crossing of the Abbai, 75 miles from Debra Markos, were the 13th Colonial Battalion and an engineer bridging company under Captain Silvi.

Some 70 miles north of Debra Markos, accessible by a track which skirted the 14,000-foot Choke mountains, was the fort of Mota, garrisoned by three companies of the 69th Colonial Battalion, which had been intermittently under siege by Hailu Belao's Patriots since Sandford's visit to east Gojjam in November 1940. Kiero, on the way to Mota, was no longer garrisoned.

Maraventano was confident of the loyalty of the regular colonial troops, mainly Eritrean *graduati* with Shoan and Tigrean *ascari* and some Gojjamis, and his confidence was justified. He was doubtful of the reliability of the *banda*. He found the morale of the troops good, 'their breakthrough at the Charaka proved this,' but was determined to restore discipline and confidence, which had suffered from the hasty retreat from Dambacha.

Against these strong forces Wingate, with his small Gideon Force about 600 strong, advanced with supreme confidence, crossing the Tamcha river by the intact bridge (five miles from Dambacha), and continuing a further 12 miles to Fort Emmanuel, where a garrison of one platoon of No 2 Patrol Company was left under Creedon. Arriving opposite Gulit, a further eight miles, on March 13, his original plan was to leave Boustead to tackle the Gulit positions while he with a small force circumvented Gulit and Debra Markos to the south and made his way towards the Abbai gorge at Safartak to cut communications between Debra Markos and Addis Ababa. He may even have contemplated a dash to Addis Ababa avoiding all strongholds. This plan — 'Addis Ababa in six weeks' — is mentioned by Luyt. There is a current belief, another Wingate myth, that Platt deliberately withheld air and artillery support from Gideon Force to make sure that Cunningham's forces from the south reached Addis Ababa before the Emperor's. This belief may have been fostered by Wingate himself according to a conversation recorded by Kabada, 'Captain Wingate told me that priority for guns and air support was being given to the British Army coming from the direction of Harrar with the intention that the British would be the first to take Addis Ababa. . . . The only way for the Emperor's army to reach Addis Ababa first was not to wait for this support but to bypass enemy installations. . . . I have written this to record the unforgettable friendship of Captain Wingate in being so open with me about his plans for the war.'[3]

The movements of the various forces converging on Addis Ababa and their timing will emerge from the narrative that follows. To suppose that Wingate, with one and a half battalions and with or without air support, could have occupied and held Addis Ababa before the resistance of the main Italian armies had been broken is fanciful.

In the event Wingate changed his plans because his route south of Debra Markos was blocked by Ras Hailu's *banda*. He returned to join Boustead, who was encamped at High Hill camp north of Gulit and who was already sending out nightly patrols against the Gulit positions. On 17 September Wingate carried out in part his original plan, sending Thesiger, Foley and Rowe, with Rowe's No 9 platoon, to disrupt communications east of Debra Markos and to contact Belai Zelleka with a view to blocking the Italian retreat at the Abbai gorge at Safartak. Foley carried on with the mining operations he had done so well in the north, and had some success in blowing up vehicles on the Debra Markos road.

Meanwhile Maraventano was active. He heard from spies of the occupation of Emmanuel by a Sudanese unit and ordered Nuovo, the commander of the 3rd Brigade, to carry out a reconnaissance in force against the fort on 16 March. Nuovo took two battalions, a section of 65-millimetre guns and the Burye mounted *banda* against Creedon's 30 men. Creedon put up a sharp resistance, causing 18 casualties in the attacking forces, and withdrew in good order and Nuovo occupied the fort. He did not stay but returned to Gulit to report to Maraventano that the fort was occupied by '200 Sudanese and 100 rebels'. RAF Blenheims had bombed Debra Markos on 16 and 17 March, the first air support for Gideon Force since the raid on Burye on 28 February, and on 16 March had spotted and reported this troop movement.

The reoccupation of Emmanuel caused some alarm at Dambacha, but this subsided when the Italians withdrew. Boyle was ordered to send a platoon to relieve Creedon, who had moved back into the fort, and Haile Mariam with No 13 platoon of D company was detailed and left at 2.45 a.m. on 19 March. Tutton was pleased that for the first time an Ethiopian officer had been given an independent operational command. In fact Haile Mariam never reached Emmanuel because Maraventano struck again.

Since the second attack on Emmanuel was widely believed by the British to presage an Italian counterattack as far as Dambacha or Burye, it is worth seeing what Maraventano actually says. 'On the afternoon of 17th March His Excellency General Scala asked me on the telephone if I could with my forces undertake the permanent reoccupation of Baremma [Emmanuel]. When I replied in the affirmative he ordered me to carry it out as soon as possible.' There is no evidence that the Italian counter move was intended to go any further than Emmanuel. Maraventano gave orders for an attack on 19 March, informing also Ras Hailu, who asked to be allowed to take part. On 19 March Maraventano marched against

Emmanuel with both brigades, the 37th Battery, the mounted *banda*, and 600 of Ras Hailu's *banda*. Only a skeleton force was left on the Gulit ridge consisting of 140 men of No 3 company 69th Colonial Battalion (the battalion at Mota), and the 5th Battery. It is evident that Gideon Force had not made much of an impact yet and Maraventano saw no danger in leaving Gulit lightly defended, that Ras Hailu was still firmly in the Italian camp, and that Maraventano intended to impress the local population with a massive show of force against a small objective.

The attack was carried out by the 72nd and 11th Colonial Battalions supported by the 37th Battery and the mounted *banda* and lasted from 11.30 a.m. until 3.00 p.m. when Creedon rereated, having again given a good account of himself. Tenente (later General) Giovanni Vallisneri, commanding No 2 company 72nd Battalion, describes how they took Baremma (Emmanuel) to revive the morale of the *ascari* after the retreats, 'I captured two machine-gun posts with riflemen and took prisoner the Sudanese NCO in charge. We did not intend to go any further.' Italian losses were six killed and 22 wounded; Sudanese losses were two killed and eight missing, including a sergeant. Patriot losses are not known, if they took part, and this is by no means clear. The Italians believe that some of Haile Yusus's men were in the fort but there is no confirmation of this from British sources. Some of the Sudanese soldiers captured here were the victims of one of the ugliest incidents of the campaign, untypical and unexplained. Two, possibly three, were shot while POWs at the crossing of the Abbai on 7 April. One managed to escape. The results of this operation were significant. Maraventano stayed with his two brigades at Emmanuel and, apart from a motorized patrol to the Tamcha river, advanced no further. He reported, however, 'an improvement in morale and aggressive spirit of the troops and the restoration of our prestige.' Akavia reports, 'Some Chiefs who joined us are now contemplating treachery.' There is no doubt that the local population, impressed with the massive Italian counter-stroke, was waiting to see who would come out on top.

Operations at Gulit and Emmanuel

Nott at Burye summed up, fairly caustically, the situation on 19

1. ABOVE LEFT. Brigadier D. A. Sandford 2. ABOVE RIGHT. Critchley with
Fitaurari Werku and Patriots, February 1941. 3. BELOW. Drew operating after
Charaka/ Dambacha actions, March 1941.

4. RIGHT. Dambacha, March 1941. Wingate inspecting a soldier of the 2nd Ethiopian Battalion.

5. BELOW. Patriots attacking.

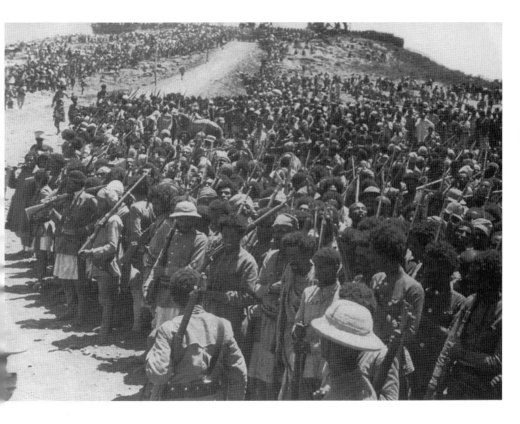

6. ABOVE. Ethiopian Patriots listen to the Emperor at Debra Markos.
7. BELOW.The Emperor returning to camp after a tour of the countryside,
February 1941.

8. ABOVE. (left to right) General Poli, General Nasi and Colonel Richard after the Gondar operation. 9. BELOW. The surrender at Wolchefit, September 1941. Colonel Gonella leads his troops out saluted by Brigadier James and a guard of honour of 2/ 4 KAR.

10. ABOVE. Thesiger, Johnson, Rowe and Howell. 11. BELOW. Benson leading 2nd Ethiopian Battalion behind Wingate and the Emperor in march into Addis Ababa, Tutton marching behind.

12. RIGHT. Johnson and Patriots.

13. BELOW. The Emperor signing
the Anglo-Ethiopian agreement.
Mitchell is seated with Lush
standing next to him. The two
Princes are behind the Emperor.

14. ABOVE. Nott 15 .BELOW. Acland

16. Camel Patrol of the Sudan Defence Force

March. 'Wingate . . . 4 miles N of Debra Markos . . . is out of touch and merely cmdg 2 coys. Brown's centre and 2 Ethiopian Battalion at Dambacha. Enemy at Emmanuel, ½ way between Debra Markos and Dambacha. . . . Flap at Dambacha. Boyle loading lorry with personal kit ready to flit! What complete chaos!' In fairness to Boyle he was loading his kit, not himself. Wingate sent orders for the 2nd Ethiopians to take up a defensive position on the line of the Tamcha river, and Tutton moved with D company on 20 March, having had some problems before moving with 'several men dead drunk and under arrest'. The fleshpots of Dambacha did more harm to the 2nd Ethiopians than the Charaka action and the soldiers forgot the pledge they had made in Gotani camp. They soon recovered, however. Tutton sited his company in good ambush positions south of the river, contacted two local *fitauraris*, Evetu and Alama, who offered to help, and waited for the ground attack which never came. They were, however, bombed and machine-gunned by Italian planes on 21 March but were in good cover and suffered no casualties. They received their first mail since leaving the Sudan, flown in to Burye and sent up by Boyle — 'A breath of home and happiness stole into our camp.' Boyle moved A and B companies to the north side of the Tamcha on 23 March and on his own initiative and apparently without any orders or communication from Wingate started sending out patrols against the Emmanuel positions.

The first of these was led by Tutton and Luyt on 23 March, taking with them Fitaurari Evetu and some of his men, when they reconnoitred the Italian positions on what they called Church Fort, one and a half miles west of Emmanuel. They returned next day with No 15 platoon under Kenyasmatch Ababa and a newly joined British NCO, Sergeant Glover of the Coldstream Guards, with a Lewis gun on a mule. At the same time Smith, now commanding A company, led a platoon under Enko against positions further north. Tutton's patrol to Church Fort caught some of the *ascari* of the garrison in the open playing football and Glover with his Lewis gun did considerable execution, causing a number of casualties. Luyt afterwards felt that this was very unsporting, but recognized that the effect on the morale of the very reluctant Patriots accompanying them would have been disastrous if they had not fired.

131

With Evetu's men Tutton had noticed that the fear of the Italian strength, the result of their retaking Emmanuel, was obvious, and most of them refused to go near the fort. As it was they were delighted with this success and on their way back Tutton's men were entertained to food and drink by Evetu at his house where 'the men had a fine evening and put back a lot of drink. I left them to it, chattering like magpies ... and no doubt exaggerating the occurrences of the afternoon.'

Smith and Enko's patrol north of the road had also been successful, as Enko records: 'We went with 10 soldiers and attacked the Italians with hand grenades — a surprise attack at night. Captain Smith was a major assistance on this occasion.'

During the night of 24/25 March at 2.00 a.m. Tutton and his men heard heavy artillery, machine-gun and rifle fire from the direction of what they thought was Fort Emmanuel; this was in fact Wingate's force attacking Gulit eight miles further to the east, as we shall learn shortly, an illustration of the complete lack of communication between the two battalions.

Meanwhile from High Hill camp Wingate intensified his raids on the Gulit positions and the forts north of Debra Markos, leading at least one personally. One such raid led by Acland gives a good illustration of the *askari*'s code. Acland took with him men from No 2 Patrol Company whose sergeant was of the Beni Amer tribe from the border country between Eritrea and the Sudan. Learning that the troops defending the position to be raided came from the 69th Colonial Battalion, which had many Beni Amer, including the sergeant's brother, Wingate suggested that our soldiers should try to persuade their relatives to desert, but, as Acland recalls, 'our troops were most indignant at the suggestion. They did not intend to try to persuade their brothers to break their oath.'

It has been advanced in support of Wingate's reputed brilliance as a commander in this campaign that it was as a result of these repeated raids that Maraventano gave up ideas of any further advance. There is no evidence to support this or that Maraventano was contemplating any further hostile move. Furthermore he had the bulk of his forces with him at Emmanuel, which Wingate was not raiding. His reaction to the reports he received of enemy activity at Gulit was to send Nuovo back to Gulit with two battalions to protect his lines of communication. This move was completed on 24 March. This left Maraventano with four battalions on Emmanuel to face Boyle's three companies and Nuovo on Gulit with two battalions and one company to face Wingate who also had three companies. Between 19 and 24 March the force opposing Wingate on Gulit had only been one company and one battery, and of this Wingate had been quite unaware.

In the early hours of 25 March, unfortunately for the Allies just after Nuovo had returned to Gulit with his two battalions, there took place what both British and Italians agree was the most serious action of the Debra Markos operations. (They do not agree as to who came off the better!) This was the action heard by Tutton from the other side of Emmanuel. Had Wingate attacked 24 hours earlier he could well have taken the position and cut Maraventano off from Debra Markos. Wingate attacked with 300 Sudanese and Ethiopian regulars in three prongs, Acland with No 2 Patrol Company and some of No 4 against the Addis position north of the road, Johnson with No 1 patrol company against the centre, south of the road, and Clarke with C company, 2nd Ethiopians against the southern flank. Acland has left his account of the attack on Addis, the eastern height and main bastion of the defence. After overrunning a minor position from which the defenders fled, they approached the main position by a narrow ridge and were fired on as they crawled towards it in the darkness, Acland leading the company. 'My runner advised me to put my head in a hole. I said if I did this they might hit my arse. The troops following heard this and there was a great cackle of laughter, which the Italians must have heard.' Three men fell down the ridge and were killed. Acland also fell down but was stopped by a tree and pulled up by his *shawish*, Tumbul. They attacked the position from close quarters with Mills grenades and the defenders threw grenades in reply. Acland was knocked down by an Italian grenade as he was about to throw a Mills grenade, 'the shock of being hit made me grip my grenade tighter instead of dropping it so I was still able to throw it instead of being blown up.'

The attack faded out when Acland was knocked out about ten yards from the main Italian position, which was evacuated. Tumbul and his men helped Acland back to High Hill camp, where the other assaulting companies assembled after having also pressed their attacks to grenade-throwing range. Johnson, himself less seriously wounded by grenade splinters, thought Acland looked like 'a badly shot pheasant.' Maraventano reported' a successful defensive battle after two hours desperate fighting', and received the congratulations of General Scala. His casualties were eight *ascari* killed and 34 wounded. Within the limitations of Wingate's policy (attack, cause damage and withdraw), the operation was a success for Gideon Force. Allied casualties were three Sudanese killed, two officers wounded (Acland and Johnson who remained on duty), 11 Sudanese and one Ethiopian soldier wounded. Acland was awarded the MC and Shawish Tumbul the MM. Acland was evacuated and did not return to Gideon Force. He did not think much of Ethiopians, nor of Wingate, but he was a most effective officer and Boustead's right-hand man. At 41 he was beyond the age and seniority when duty required that he should lead platoons against defended positions, but he still did it and could make his men explode with laughter under fire.

Events in Eritrea now had an influence on Mission 101 and Gideon Force. Platt's second attack on Keren, launched on 15 March, was repulsed. Desperate to prevent any reinforcements reaching the Italians, Platt signalled Wingate on 19 March urging him to take all steps to prevent any troops reaching Keren from Beghemder or Gojjam. Wingate was out of touch at High Hill camp. Sandford received the signal and after trying for a day and a night to contact Wingate on horseback and failing, decided on his own initiative to send No 6 Operational Centre (Welsh and five sergeants of the Buffs, no men) to reinforce Simonds at Bahr Dar. The centre left on 22 and 23 March. This was no more than a gesture, but reinforcing Beghemder Force was all that Sandford could do to help the *kaid*. Wingate reacted furiously to this 'interference'. Sandford signalled Khartoum for help in resolving their differences and Nott recorded, 'Rude and stupid letters from Wingate. . . . I am utterly sick of Wingate's orders and letters. He expects the most impossible things without considering the A&Q difficulties. He is out of touch and has no clear picture of things.' The result was a signal from Khartoum on 25 March congratulating Wingate on his conduct of the Debra Markos operations but requesting his return to Burye 'so that he may be able to control the whole effort . . . and put in order the supply system.'

Wingate handed over his force to Boustead on 26 March and arrived at Burye on 27 March after spending the night at Boyle's camp on the Tamcha river. An exchange of letters between Boyle and Sandford at this time, in which Boyle complained of being 'completely in the dark', shows that he had received no orders from Wingate save to move to the Tamcha. Wingate had concentrated on Gulit, leaving Boyle to fend for himself. Boyle also had asked Sandford to send back some deserters who had gone to see the Emperor, a sign of trouble brewing in his battalion. Sandford very properly told Boyle to contact 'Col. Wingate, OC Mission 101, who is directing operations, for orders', said that the Emperor had already sent back his men, adding 'I have assured HM's Secretary that you will not shoot or flog them.' Reading this remark of Sandford's takes us back with a shock to the 1914–18 war, only 20-odd years before these events, when deserters were shot, though not on the orders of commanding officers. In 1941 a KAR commanding officer still had the power to flog, but it was a power that was seldom used and it soon disappeared.

Nott recorded, on Wingate's arrival at Burye on 27 March, 'Orde suddenly appeared without warning and was out looking for blood. However, his magnetic personality dominated and dispelled all disgruntled thoughts, although he was *very* critical of the things [that] had been sent forward from here.' Also on 27 March came great news from other fronts. 'News that Keren and Harrar had fallen — great excitement.'

The immediate cause of Wingate's anger was the dispatch of No 6 Centre to Bahr Dar. To quote from David Rooney's new biography, Wingate 'complained to Colonel Airey, "Sandford has cancelled every order that I have sent back, which was not in accord with his own views. . . . Since we came up the escarpment not a man, not a weapon, not an animal has reached me from the rear".' In his dispatch after the campaign he complained of 'the passage of what centres were available to the theatre second in importance.' The facts are that Wingate had been joined by three good officers, Foley, Turrall and Makonnen Desta, and the following reinforcements, as recorded by Nott, were on the way, 'March 20 Naylor and his Centre and 100 camels to join Wingate. 24 March Bathgate and his Centre and 100 camels, Riley and 34 camels to Dambacha. 25 March Maxwell with 20 camels, Barlow with 59 camels, Hayes with 60 camels left to join Gideon Force.' Sandford, writing in 1950, said that, in response to Platt's urgent signal, 'as Wingate had disappeared into the blue ... I took upon myself the responsibility of sending Centres No 2 and 6 [under McLean and Pilkington] to join Birru ... for which I received bitter reproaches from Wingate.' Sandford has got his facts wrong and does not do himself justice. He only sent No 6 (Welsh) to Bahr Dar; No 2 (Mackay) had already gone, and McLean to replace Mackay and Centres No 5 and 10 under Pilkington were sent later with Wingate's concurrence.

Wingate's other cause of complaint against Sandford concerned the issue of rifles to Patriots, 'who could not and did not make use of them.' He objected particularly, again quoting Rooney, that 'Sandford had issued 561 Springfield rifles to the Patriots and none to him.' What the 600 men of Gideon Force would have done with 561 extra Springfields is difficult to imagine. Sandford also complained to Khartoum that Wingate would let him have no weapons and asked for a special allocation for the Emperor and the Patriots. Sandford had good reason for wanting to build up the Emperor's bodyguard to 3000 to enhance his prestige.

The result of this disagreement, the most serious since the change of command at Belaiya, was a rebuke to both men from the *kaid*, and the decision that Wingate should keep his HQ on the road so that he would be accessible, and that he would be responsible for his own 'A&Q', Sandford to remain Haile Selassie's chief military and political adviser. This suited Nott. At least he now had only one master. He respected Wingate's ability and knew how to get on with him. Wingate decided to move his HQ to Dambacha, and Nott went to take his leave of the Emperor and his entourage 'who seemed genuinely pleased to see me up and about again'. Let us now see what has been happening in what Wingate called the theatre second in importance — Beghemder.

While Gideon Force was attacking Gulit and Emmanuel, Simonds was with equal impudence confronting Torelli at Bahr Dar, 400 regulars and some Patriots against a colonial brigade (see

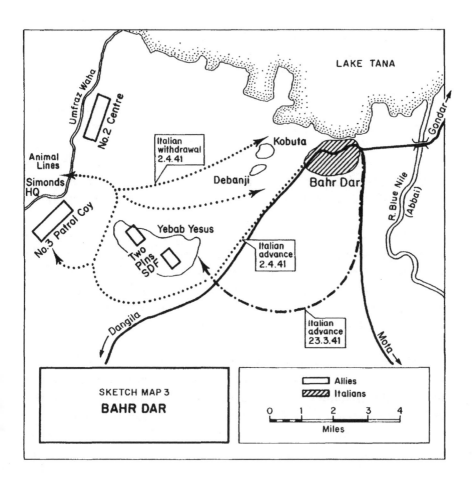

LAKE TANA

Umfraz Waha

No.2 Centre

Italian
withdrawal
2.4.41

Kobuta

Debanji

Bahr Dar

Gondar →

Animal
Lines

Simonds
HQ

R. Blue Nile
(Abbai)

No.3 Patrol Coy

Yebab Yesus

Two
Plns
SDF

Italian
advance
2.4.41

Dangila

Italian
advance
23.3.41

Mota →

SKETCH MAP 3
BAHR DAR

Allies
Italians

0   1   2   3   4

Miles

Sketch 3). A defensive perimeter of six to seven miles included the town and lake shore, with inner defences round the town. Two hills west of the town were occupied, Kobuta and Debanji. Simonds disposed his forces with his HQ and the animal transport lines west of the stream Umfraz Waha, Mackay and No 2 Centre east of the stream, and No 2 Patrol Company east of Simonds's HQ, with two platoons on the hill Yebab Yesus. Mackay had five British sergeants and 120 men, Jarvis had a strong company of 250 men and another British officer, Major John Holcombe, a Middlesex territorial who had volunteered for the operational centres, had joined him at Belaiya. In support were two sections of the Ethiopian mortar platoon and Fitaurari Birru with 500 Patriots. Against this force Torelli had four colonial battalions, one company, 2 CCNN, the 44th pack battery, the regular Bahr Dar *banda* 300 strong and an iregular *banda* from Beghemder of 1000, a total force of about 5500. As in the Debra Markos operations, the irregulars supporting the Italians considerably outnumbered those supporting the Anglo-Ethiopian forces at this stage.

On 18 March, while Jarvis was carrying out a reconnaissance in force against the main Italian positions, Mackay was badly wounded by shell fire when patrolling towards the west of the enemy positions and had several men killed and wounded. Simonds was not then in wireless communication and sent a mounted Sudanese with a message to Nott at Burye asking for help. The Sudanese arrived on 21 March, on foot and carrying his saddle having left an exhausted horse behind him, and Nott sent Dr Haggar, a Syrian doctor who had recently joined Mission 101, to treat the wounded, and arranged for Mackay to be evacuated by air from Dangila by the South African Air Force. Mackay, in Simonds's words, 'an incredibly tough Canadian', recovered from his wounds and passes out of this story, but is one of the characters who made a deep impression on his Ethiopian soldiers. One of them, Alemaiyu Hailu, describes him as, 'a brave man. He had a flat nose and was of solid stature and always marched ahead. ... When he was wounded we tied up his wounds and offered him a horse to ride but he refused to mount and walked on his feet.' Lieutenant Neil McLean, Royal Scots Greys, a 22-year-old regular cavalry subaltern, who had arrived at Burye with No 7 Centre,

138

was ordered to take over from Mackay and joined Simonds after he had arrived at Debra Tabor. In the meantime Sergeant Morrow took charge of No 2 Centre.

On 23 March, while Jarvis and Holcombe were on a horseback reconnaisance of the Italian positions, Torelli launched an attack on the two platoons on Yebab Yesus. A young Sudanese second lieutenant, Hamid El Nil Effendi Defalla, had been left in charge of the company, and Simonds went to his support with the Centre troops and Patriots. The attack was beaten off with some difficulty, the *ascari* approaching to within 50 yards of the Sudanese positions. Simonds, who described the enemy as 'well led', and the successful defence as 'due to bravery and good discipline of Sudanese troops', hastened the departure of the Italians by setting fire to the long dry grass with a Verey light, and they retired, pursued by the Patriots. (The grass was again a feature of this battlefield.) Jarvis and Holcombe heard the firing and succeeded in rejoining their company late in the action in which Hamid Effendi had commanded with great skill and coolness. The Sudanese found ten bodies when the Italians withdrew and their own casualties were two killed and two wounded. There were casualties among the Patriots, including a subchief whose funeral Simonds attended next day, 'the service was in Ge'ez, the ancient Ethiopian language'. Hamid Effendi was awarded the MC, and the two sergeants commanding the platoons on Yebab Yesus the MM, for their parts in this action.

As with Maraventano's reoccupation of Emmanuel, Torelli's attack was thought by the British to be part of a general counter-attack in Gojjam, but it does not seem that this was the case and that Torelli was only concerned with inflicting damage on his enemy and reducing pressure on his troops. Both before and after 23 March No 3 patrol company was active in night fighting patrols against the Italians and Holcombe remembers taking part in several of these, often with the *bash shawish*, Nur-L-Bella. Once they raided the Italian transport lines and captured 16 big Cypriot mules, and on another occasion just as they were setting off a message was brought to Holcombe, sent up from Dangila, which read, 'Son born 21.3.41. Both well.' I told Nur I had a son and he said, 'It doesn't matter if you get written off tonight.'

On 26 March Simonds, whose wireless was now working, received a signal from Wingate ordering him to 'march into Beghemder and cut the Gondar–Debra Tabor–Dessie road and isolate the garrison', leaving No 3 patrol company to contain Torelli in Bahr Dar. Simonds took with him Fitaurari Birru and his Patriots, his bodyguard of 24 men, No 2 Centre (Morrow with four sergeants and 90 men), and No 6 Centre, which had just arrived from Burye (Lieutenant Welsh, five sergeants and 90 men transferred from No 2 Centre). The centres had been brought up to this strength by local recruitment. This was the day when Keren was about to fall, when Cunningham, having taken Harrar, was approaching Dire Dawa, and Wingate was on his way back from Gulit to Burye in a rage to confront Sandford for 'interference'. It is remarkable that Wingate had the strategic foresight to send this order, confirming his previous order to Simonds in February, which resulted in the line of retreat of the Dessie garrison being cut off when they were attacked by the 1st South African Brigade in April. (Dessie fell on 26 April.) Wingate has been given little credit for this initiative.

Simonds and his force had to cross the Abbai gorge where it widened out to a ford by a precipitous track only wide enough for one laden mule, and where at the bottom, Simonds recalls, 'it was a different world — full of bird song'. Crossing the ford, where the water was saddle high, 'I have a mental picture of Fitaurari Birru, an elderly and dignified figure, crossing still sitting on his mule held up by four of his bodyguards with water up to their chests. We were about 2000. We advanced into Beghemder, a beautiful country.'

Keren fell on 27 March, the most important event of the whole campaign and the action in which the most casualties occurred — Allied 3765, Italian 8000 and 3500 prisoners. Asmara was occupied on 1 April and Massawa on 8 April, but Platt's army was still a long way from Addis Ababa and of far more immediate concern to the Italian High Command was the advance of Cunningham's troops from the south. After the capture of the Marda Pass and Harrar by the 23rd Nigerian Brigade, Dire Dawa was occupied by the 1st South African Brigade on 29 March, leaving the Awash gorge as the only remaining obstacle before Addis Ababa. On 2

April the South African Air Force bombed Addis Ababa aerodrome and destroyed or damaged a total of 32 aircraft, an Allied success, which significantly altered the balance of air power in their favour. The road and rail bridge at Awash were demolished, but the crossing was forced by the 5th KAR on 3 April, Brigadier Fowkes's 22nd East African Brigade having taken over the lead from the South Africans, who ran out of petrol. There was nothing now to stop Cunningham's troops who entered Addis Ababa on 6 April. Their arrival first had nothing to do with any deliberate withholding of support for the Emperor's forces, as Wingate believed. The opposition in the south crumbled. In Gojjam it had remained firm.

These momentous events had an immediate and important effect on the Gojjam campaign, as we shall see in the next chapter.

Notes
1. Tutton believed that the Italian colonel was Colonel Borghese, but there is no doubt that it was de Mandato. Colonel Borghese commanded the Granatieri di Savoia and was killed at Ad Teclesan near Keren. The author is grateful to Colonel Barone Amedeo Guillet, the gallant survivor of a cavalry charge against Indian artillery in Eritrea, for this information.
2. Luyt felt strongly that Tutton should have received an award and wrote to his sisters about this after his death.
3. From then on Kabada, when referring to Wingate in his book, used the informal personal pronoun in Amharic, indicating his close personal regard — the author is grateful to Diana Spencer for this information.

5

Gojjam Evacuated[*]

After Wingate's departure Boustead continued nightly raids on the Gulit positions while Boyle moved his battalion closer to Emmanuel and also continued attacks. These operations were again not coordinated and Luyt recalls one night attack on Church Fort with Tutton when he suddenly wondered if the Frontier Battalion was in occupation. Maraventano recorded 'increased enemy activity on all fronts', and also his concern over the 'increasingly disloyal attitude' of Belai Zelleka. To forestall any attempt by Belai Zelleka to cut his communications with the Abbai he sent the cavalry squadron and irregulars to occupy Mount Dick, and ordered Ras Hailu to send reliable emissaries to Bichena to probe Belai Zelleka's intentions.

Then on 29 March Maraventano was summoned to Addis Ababa. He travelled early on 30 March in a plane sent up for him and saw the Chief of Staff, General Trezzani, at 8.30 a.m., who explained the 'grave military situation' and warned him that Gojjam would probably have to be evacuated. He was then taken before Aosta when 'His Royal Highness expressed his satisfaction with the operational activities of my troops' and confirmed the order to evacuate Gojjam. Maraventano was to concentrate his forces at Debra Markos prior to departure, send the two CCNN battalions to Addis Ababa, discharge the irregulars and discharge or transfer to Ras Hailu's *banda* the regular Gojjami *ascari* according to their wishes, and leave to Ras Hailu such material as

[*] See General Map 2 and Sketch 4.

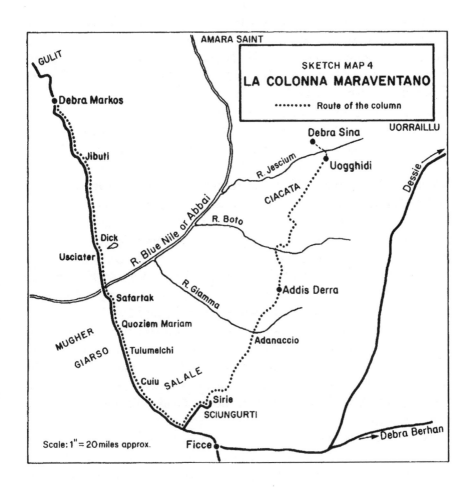

AMARA SAINT

GULIT

● Debra Markos

SKETCH MAP 4
LA COLONNA MARAVENTANO
········· Route of the column

UORRAILLU

·Jibuti

Debra Sina
●

R. Jescium

●Uogghidi

Dessie

CIACATA

R. Boto

R. Blue Nile or Abbai

·Dick ◁

Usciater

R. Giamma

●Addis Derra

·Safartak

·Quoziem Mariam

MUGHER

·Tulumelchi

Adanaccio

GIARSO

·Cuiu SALALE

·Sirie

SCIUNGURTI

Scale: 1" = 20 miles approx.

Ficce ●

→Debra Berhan

143

they could neither carry nor destroy. On departure he was to destroy all radio and telegraphic equipment and the column was to follow the route Debra Markos–Ficce–Debra Berhan–Dessie. If Debra Berhan was already occupied by the enemy he was to reach Dessie via Ficce and Uorrailu. These orders were precisely followed by Maraventano's column in retreat except that he could not reach either Ficce or Dessie before these places fell to the Allies. The route is shown on Sketch 4. Maraventano returned to Debra Markos by plane early on 31 March and immediately started putting these orders into effect. The troops on Emmanuel were ordered to retreat to Gulit on 31 March and the combined force from Gulit to Debra Markos on 1 April.

Between 27 and 29 March the 2nd Ethiopian Battalion kept up the pressure against the Emmanuel positions, patrols being led by Tutton, Luyt, Smith, Gerazmatch Asfau of D company and Basha Worku of B company. Then, on returning to camp on the morning of 29 March after a night patrol, noting the onset of the dysentery, which was to plague him for the rest of the campaign, Tutton learned that 60 men of A company, now commanded by Smith, had mutinied and some had gone to see the Emperor. On his own initiative Boyle had decided to move his battalion to the Diadeb river south of Emmanuel to cut communications between Emmanuel and Gulit. The move was planned for the night of 30 March, D company as usual in the lead. Very sick with dysentery Tutton got up at 5.30 p.m. to check on his company's preparations to find that No 15 platoon and one or two of No 16 had followed the mutineers. 'Several others were dead drunk and incapable of moving. The CO [Boyle] knocked down Geake Tadeh who was in this condition.'

Tutton moved to the Diadeb with the rest of his company arriving at 10.30 p.m. on 30 March, and was followed by Boyle with the battalion. On 31 March the Emmanuel garrison moved to Gulit but the Ethiopians were not on their route and there was no confrontation, though Brown's centre ambushed part of the column and caused some casualties. Luyt took a patrol to Gulit and confirmed that it was still occupied; the fact that this was necessary is again evidence of the lack of communication between the two battalions. Tutton remained in camp and was treated by the newly arrived medical officer, Dr Zablany, with 'castor oil, opiates, and liquid diet'.

Boustead, at High Hill camp, had heard through his liaison officer, Makonnen Desta, of the Italians' intention to withdraw from Gulit and made plans to interfere by an attack on the Addis position at Gulit on the night of 31 March and by sending Clarke's C company of the 2nd Ethiopians to Prospect Hill to ambush the withdrawal. The attack on Addis, the position where Acland was wounded, was led by Colin Macdonald, the Frontier Battalion adjutant, and Guy Turrall, with two platoons of No 2 Patrol Company. After Macdonald and Turrall and their men had approached to within a few yards of the position and thrown grenades, Macdonald was killed by the first burst of return fire. After that, in Maxwell's words, 'the attack was rather a shambles as most of No 2 company ran when they saw Colin fall.' Turrall, himself wounded in the head with grenade splinters, and the two platoon sergeants carried Macdonald's body back to High Hill, arriving exhausted at midday on 1 April — a brave effort. Macdonald was buried at High Hill church the next day, Boustead reading the service; in Maxwell's words, 'three volleys were fired over the grave; it was a beautiful service and most moving. It's a terrible loss; he was a grand lad.' Macdonald, the very able and well-liked young Sudan Political Service officer, 'an Arabic Scholar with the prospect of a brilliant career', had had to take a back seat as adjutant until then and was sadly killed in almost his first action. The behaviour of No 2 Patrol Company was a rare lapse by troops who had consistently done well.

The incident involving Clarke's men (actually two platoons of C company, 60 men) was also something of a shambles and a blot on the battalion's record, although this was not entirely the men's fault. On the evening of 31 March they advanced to within 1000 yards of the selected point and then refused to go any further, saying that the position was too exposed. Clarke sent a message to Boustead which did not reach him. The result was that when the watchers from High Hill saw the Gulit garrison stream out onto the plain at 7.00 a.m. on 1 April, not a shot was fired at them. The Ethiopians' failure to obey orders cannot be excused, but one questions whether the orders were sensible. In no way could two platoons have destroyed two brigades or seriously interfered with their retreat. The Ethiopians had proved their courage at the Charaka but did not believe in taking on hopeless odds. Boustead himself had declined to tackle these same troops when they left Burye, and in three days' time Johnson would let the same column go past unmolested and no one would question his courage. No disciplinary action was taken against C company save that one Ethiopian officer was court martialled, and they were not involved in the mutiny in the rest of the battalion.

Wingate at Dambacha, sick with malaria and poisoned legs, was, in Nott's words, 'furious' when news of the desertions from Boyle's battalion reached him. He sent orders relieving Boyle of his command, appointing Beard to take temporary command, and 'also Adjt Smith is to be removed for ill-treating the men'. Nott went forward to Emmanuel on 2 April, picking up Beard on the way, where he 'found 113 of Eth. Bn having refused to obey Boyle's command to march forward but decided to attack Emmanuel. They paraded in good manner and sober. After refusing to rejoin the Bn I asked them if they would go forward under Beard — to a man they said they would. So off they went.' All credit to Nott for the way he handled this and to the Ethiopians for the way they responded. Beard, described by Nott as 'an awfully nice man, Irish — was in Connaught Rangers in last war', shows up well in this incident too, a good officer, respected by the men.

Beard went forward, taking the former mutineers with him, took command of the battalion on the Diadeb, and moved on to join Boustead before Debra Markos. The fact that the men went forward willingly under Beard, and indeed had mounted their own attack on Emmanuel (abortive because the Italians had already left) shows that the true reason for the mutiny was mishandling by Boyle and Smith. Boyle was a bad commanding officer and should never have had the command, and both he and Smith used their fists on the men too freely. Wingate was right to dismiss them, though it was ironic that it was Wingate who did so since he was himself guilty of striking soldiers on several occasions without any apparent diminution of his prestige. Indeed General Nega said of him, 'Wingate was our father. If he struck us it was to correct us so that we would not err again.'

There was no more trouble in the 2nd Ethiopian Battalion under Beard nor under the new commanding officer, Lieutenant Colonel Benson, who arrived to take over at Debra Markos on 5 April. The ring leaders were disciplined on 9 April, but no other action was taken and the effect of the mutiny was short lived. Boyle and Smith were flown out to Khartoum and pass out of this story. Wingate's intemperate comment in his dispatch is quite wrong. Discussing the refugee battalions he said, 'the best of these was the 2nd Ethiopian Battalion and they spent a considerable part of the campaign in a state of mutiny. On one occasion only were they of much use.' The mutiny lasted in fact from 29 March to 2 April.

Between 1 and 3 April Boustead sent patrols led by Turrall, Kabada, Makonnen Desta and Clarke against the forts north of Debra Markos, continuing the pressure. Clarke with his two platoons redeemed their failure on 1 April by a raid on Abima Fort, which caused 18 casualties. On 2 April Boustead sent Johnson with two platoons, Kabada and his men, and a mortar section southeast of Debra Markos to ambush the Italians as they withdrew. On the same day Grey on Wingate's orders sent by wireless telegraphy a signal to the Italians at Debra Markos threatening a forward movement of 'vast masses of patriots', and inviting them to surrender. There is no record of any reply to this message. On 3 April the Emperor and Sandford moved from Burye to Dambacha and the 'vultures', as Luyt might have described them, started closing in on the kill. Fitaurari Haile Yusus and others arrived in the Debra Markos area and were allotted sectors to cover by Boustead. Mangasha and Nagash still attended on the Emperor, jockeying for position in the takeover of Gojjam as the Italians withdrew, their large forces a potential threat but quite inactive, and at times a nuisance on Gideon Force's lines of communication, sniping at vehicles, and once murdering a messenger for his rifle. Wingate had no help from Patriots in the fighting round Debra Markos. In contrast Maraventano not only had Ras Hailu's *banda* but also numerous other bodies of irregulars under chiefs still loyal to the Italian government.

Meanwhile Maraventano was preparing for evacuation. He sent detachments of Ras Hailu's *banda* to guard the road against inter-ference by Belai Zelleka, and 'on his own account' Ras Hailu sent

147

messages to Belai Zelleka to hold to his promise not to disrupt the column. 'The *Ras* assured me that Belai Zelleka would be loyal to his word.' On the evening of 1 April Maraventano was informed by a signal from General Scala that the 13th Colonial Battalion at Safartak and the Engineer Company would remain in position until the column passed and then come under his command. On 1 and 2 April he sent the two CCNN battalions to Addis Ababa. They lost one vehicle and some casualties to one of Foley's mines. At the same time the regular Gojjami *ascari* were discharged or transferred to Ras Hailu's *banda* and the battalions reorganized, most being reduced to three companies.[1] On the afternoon of 2 April Lieutenant Colonel Tremontano of the operations' staff telephoned from Addis Ababa to ask Maraventano if he could speed up his withdrawal. Maraventano declined and said he would move on 4 April as planned. On 2 April the South African Air Force bombed Addis Ababa aerodrome and the KAR was approaching Awash. It is not surprising that the High Command asked Maraventano to hurry. It is quite clear though that although he was under some pressure from Gideon Force the pressure was not severe and he could afford to take his time.

Johnson, ordered by Boustead to 'get in front of the Italians and do what damage he could', had taken up an ambush position with his small force on the ridge known as Jibuti or Dumbuka 28 kilometres from Debra Markos through which the road to the Abbai runs and waited for the Italian column. They were facing towards Debra Markos but had two sentries watching the road behind them. At dawn on 3 April Maraventano's transport column left Usciater to return to Debra Markos, having delivered one of the CCNN battalions. The column consisted of 30 empty lorries and a Red Cross vehicle, escorted by two armoured cars, a platoon of Blackshirts and 50 of Ras Hailu's *banda*. As they approached the Jibuti ridge from the south they were spotted by Johnson's sentries. Johnson turned his men round, let the Italians get within range, and opened up with Brens and an anti-tank rifle. The leading armoured car attempted to return fire but could not elevate sufficiently, and the escort got out and returned fire from behind rocks. The two armoured cars were knocked out by the Boyes anti-tank rifle and 25 trucks were destroyed. The remaining five trucks were turned round and the survivors went off in them in the direction from which they had come. Italian casualties were seven nationals killed and one missing, five *banda* killed and 12 wounded. Johnson's force suffered no casualties. The result of this highly successful ambush was that Maraventano's withdrawal plans were disrupted and he could not carry all the supplies he needed, though by using civilian transport, 'I was able to load four days' rations.' Johnson was awarded an immediate DSO for this action.

After Maraventano had taken leave of Ras Hailu and his daughters and loyal chiefs and subchiefs ('the older faithful ones wept'), his column started its 800-kilometre march to Dessie at 9.00 a.m. on 4 April having been assembling since dawn. Ras Hailu assured him again that his march would not be disrupted this side of the Abbai. In addition to his seven colonial battalions[2] and 1000 national troops, the column included, '4000 women and children, the families of *ascari*, 500 native civilians who had compromised themselves by acts done in our favour, and about 100 nationals from the towns of Engiabara, Burye, Dambacha and Debra Markos. As most carried their own belongings, you will have a faint idea of how this crowd encumbered the march of the column.' They also had the 200 Ethiopian baggage camels captured at the Charaka river. Despite these encumbrances they covered the ground with remarkable speed.

While Maraventano departed unmolested from Debra Markos, Gideon Force was poised to move in. In the town Ras Hailu, the old Lord of Gojjam, performed a double act, displaying a most remarkable authority. He saw Maraventano off the premises, made sure that neither Belai Zelleka nor anyone else molested him on his way to the Abbai, put his men in to take over the forts and prevented looting in the town, and awaited Boustead and the Emperor. Boustead sent Hayes in at midday on 4 April with two platoons of No 1 patrol company. As Hayes approached the fort, 'I was met by a large crowd and Ras Hailu. They started kissing my feet and Ras Hailu took me in to a small inn and plied me with *tej*.' Boustead and Nott followed with Gideon Force, placed guards on all stores and allotted areas to the gathering patriot chiefs in the surrounding forts. Among the chiefs was Nagash with his men, designated as governor of Debra Markos by Haile Selassie, who arrived on 5 April. With this authority he demanded that Boustead should remove his troops from the fort. Having had no help from Nagash in the fighting Boustead and his officers dealt with him and his men fairly sharply. Boustead refused to remove his troops, and when Nagash's men started looting the hospital, 'Jock Maxwell shot one dead at 300 yards and scared off the others, making them drop their loot as they ran.'

Nott and Kabada went back to Dambacha in one of Ras Hailu's trucks to report to Wingate and the Emperor. Although flying the Ethiopian flag, they were sniped at by Patriots. Nott stopped and 'warned the various posts not to fire'. Nott returned in the truck with Wingate, and other arrivals at Debra Markos on 5 April were Lieutenant Colonel Geoffrey Benson OBE, Royal Ulster Rifles, to take command of the 2nd Ethiopian Battalion, and Sandford and Kabada to see Ras Hailu, assess the political situation, and prepare for the Emperor's entry on 6 April.

When Sandford and Kabada, who, despite what Kabada wrote afterwards, were working together effectively and amicably, met Ras Hailu, the *ras*, who had a sense of humour, greeted Kabada with the words, 'You will pursue me to my grave!' Kabada, as court chamberlain, had been his gaoler under Haile Selassie. Sandford told him that the Emperor was pleased with his action in surrendering the town and maintaining law and order, and Hailu replied, as Sandford reported to the *kaid* in a letter of 8 April, with 'a long story explanatory of his attitude over the last few years, and in particular detailing his manoeuvres over the last few weeks for hoodwinking the Italians so as to be able to come over when the time was ripe.' He also said that the Emperor should defer his entry into Debra Markos for fear of aerial attack. Sandford saw through this last remark as a ploy by the *ras* to consolidate his position with Nagash's *fitauraris* before the Emperor arrived.

On 6 April 1941, the same day Cunningham's forces entered Addis Ababa, Emperor Haile Selassie entered Debra Markos in a car driven by le Blanc in a convoy of six cars, which le Blanc had led up the Matakal escarpment on 2 April, the first vehicles to travel on the road he had been constructing. The date 6 April remains a significant one in Ethiopian history, the 'Day of Liberation' under the Mengistu regime (1974–91), the day on which

British troops entered Addis Ababa and the day the Ethiopian flag first flew over a provincial capital. But it had a more ominous significance at the time; it marked the recapture of Benghazi by Rommel and Axis troops signalling the beginning of the reversal of Allied fortunes in North Africa.

Haile Selassie arrived at the fort at midday and was greeted by Wingate and a parade of the two battalions of Gideon Force commanded by Boustead. After Haile Selassie had taken the salute, Ras Hailu was to make his submission, but, awkward to the last, he kept the Emperor and the parade waiting for half an hour. Then, as Tutton records, 'he drove up in a motor car and got out. He bowed stiffly, a formal obeissance to the Emperor, and muttered something, and then stood upright.' Nott was also watching the scene; 'Haile Selassie then read an address in which he praised the Fr. Bn and 2nd Eth. Bn. He then sat on the Palace steps — which we had hastily cleaned as his dwelling — and held a reception of notables.' We can speculate how many of those notables who said goodbye to Maraventano with tears in their eyes on 3 April came to greet the Emperor on 6 April. In the evening, on hearing that Cunningham's troops were in Addis Ababa, the Emperor invited all officers to a 'champagne [captured] reception'. So ended an eventful day.

Next day Nott extracted petrol from Ras Hailu, who was still holding the petrol supplies — 'He gave me a good reception and some inferior cognac before breakfast' — and Haile Selassie held a review of patriot forces, eliciting a comment from Maxwell, which was unflattering but fair as far as the Debra Markos campaign was concerned: 'HM received patriots who danced before him, reciting their prowess, mostly lies except for Azaj Kabada and his boys.' Ras Hailu's *banda* also paraded before the Emperor.

Maraventano's column reached its first camp near Jibuti, the scene of the Johnson ambush, at 4.00 p.m. on 4 April after a march of 28 kilometres. 'There was no disturbance by the enemy. This fact, together with the birth of a baby boy to the wife of a *Sciumbasci*, were judged to be good omens.' Johnson was still in position with his force on the Jibuti ridge, but he moved out of the way when the column approached. He was content with the destruction of the transport column, and, like Boustead at Burye and Clarke's men at Gulit, thought the main body too large to tackle.

Maraventano's men saw the burned-out vehicles and found and buried seven national soldiers, and then marched on to the Abbai, arriving on 6 April and crossing on 7 April. Johnson followed with his force on 5 April but was delayed for 24 hours by hostile, or at least uncooperative, tribesmen who refused to let him pass and insisted that he and his men stay in their village overnight. During the night Johnson's interpreter 'overheard the Ethiopians discussing whether to kill us'. Next morning Johnson insisted that they must go on after the Italians and they were allowed to go, but evidently, even at this late stage, with the Italians about to evacuate Gojjam, the discipline of five years' administration and the strength of the Italian forces caused some Gojjamis still to hesitate over which side to back.

Wingate and Boustead were confident that Belai Zelleka would fall on the Italian column as it approached the Abbai gorge. Thesiger had found Belai Zelleka, who at first agreed to ambush the Italian column, then made excuses and finally said it was his army and he would move when he was ready. When Thesiger learned to his dismay that the Italians had crossed on 7 April unmolested he returned to Debra Markos to report to Wingate, noting 'Boustead was furious but Wingate was unexpectedly understanding'. Knowing Thesiger's strong personal feelings about Ethiopian freedom Wingate gave him another chance and sent him back to the Abbai to join Johnson in the pursuit of Maraventano. Thesiger wrote to Sandford after crossing the Abbai, reporting on the political situation, and commented, 'Having seen the escarpment I feel confident that Belai Zelleka could have completely destroyed the Italian force.'

Belai Zelleka was an effective and much feared leader of patriot resistance in Gojjam between 1937 and 1940 and had a well-trained and well-armed army of between 2000 and 7000 men. He is today the great hero of the patriotic war, and the road out of Addis Ababa to Gojjam is named after him. It is difficult for Ethiopians to believe that he was a traitor to the cause of freedom. There is no doubt, however, that he was seduced by Ras Hailu and that his failure to cut off the column was because he had received a very strong inducement from the *ras*, namely (according to contemporary reports) the promise of marriage with Ras Hailu's granddaughter, a bait which was, as Thesiger says, 'irresistible to his peasant mind'.

Back at Debra Markos Boustead handed over the fort to the 2nd Ethiopian Battalion, removing his Frontier Battalion from the temptations of champagne and Chianti of which Debra Markos was full, and this was the end of the campaign for the Ethiopian battalion, except for Rowe and his platoon with Johnson, as they were required to be in attendance on the Emperor until his entry into Addis Ababa on 5 May. Tutton heard with envy of Johnson and Rowe pursuing Maraventano beyond the Abbai, lamenting 'this vile illness'. Dr Zablany recommended his evacuation to Khartoum, but 'Wingate and Drew refused to hear of it'. Tutton was made adjutant to the new commanding officer and promoted captain, as also were Rowe and Beard. Luyt, Clarke and Shaw, who had returned from Kwara, were commissioned in the field by Wingate, and Luyt took over D company.

On 9 April the final act in the mutiny and the failure of Clarke's men on 1 April took place. The ringleaders of A company's mutineers, and Lij Kassa, one of Clarke's platoon commanders, were brought before the new commanding officer, Benson, and, as Tutton records, 'All sacked from the army with ignominy. Lij Kassa found guilty of disobeying an order and cowardice in the face of the enemy.' Examples have to be made in wartime, but we are left with the feeling that in neither case were the men entirely to blame.

On the other fronts news arrived of the capture of Adowa by Platt's forces in the north and the pursuit by Cunningham's forces of the retreating Italians from Addis Ababa northwards towards Dessie and southwest into Galla-Sidamo. In North Africa and the Mediterranean the news was not good. Having recaptured Benghazi Rommel was advancing towards Derna, and the Germans invaded Yugoslavia and Greece. These advances did not then affect the situation in East Africa, but later the Italians would be encouraged to continue resistance.

The Frontier Battalion suffered 29 casualties in the Debra Markos operation, one officer killed and two wounded, five other ranks killed, 13 wounded and eight missing. The 2nd Ethiopian Battalion suffered five, four killed and one wounded. The Italians suffered eight nationals killed and two wounded, 29 *ascari* killed and 145 wounded. Of these eight *ascari* were killed and 32 wounded in Wingate's attack on Gulit on 24/25 March, and one national and five *ascari* killed and 34 *ascari* wounded in the attacks on Emmanuel by the 2nd Ethiopian Battalion of 26–30 March. These figures suggest that both battalions inflicted about equal damage on the enemy and refute the belief held by most historians that after the Charaka action the 2nd Ethiopian Battalion were of small value for the rest of the campaign. The Frontier Battalion suffered more severely, probably because they saw more action at close quarters under Wingate and Boustead than the Ethiopians did under Boyle, although facing inferior forces at Gulit to those against the Ethiopians at Emmanuel. The Ethiopians played a part consistent with the ability of their commander. Tutton and the other patrol commanders were immensely keen, but lacked proper direction from Boyle as to what they should be doing, and he in turn from Wingate who ignored him.

Boustead was in no doubt that it was the repeated attacks of his Sudanese that led to the evacuation of Gulit and the retreat to the Abbai. Wingate made the same claim in his dispatch: 'I forced the enemy to evacuate [Gojjam]. Had he remained, the issue at Keren would have been affected.' Wingate clearly believed this claim, but it cannot be substantiated. The issue at Keren was decided on 27 March at which time Maraventano was still firmly entrenched at Emmanuel and Gulit and resisting Gideon Force attacks. What caused his withdrawal were the orders of the High Command, which he received on 30 March, issued because of the Allied advances in the north and south. In west Gojjam Wingate's tactics forced Natale's withdrawal from Burye. In east Gojjam Gideon Force attacks and the threat of the Patriots may have been factors in the situation but the reasons for the evacuation were the victory of Platt at Keren and the advance of Cunningham on Addis Ababa.

To the Italians the Patriots represented a threat but in fact they played a negligible part in the Debra Markos operation. Some of Haile Yusus's men may have helped to garrison Emmanuel, and after Emmanuel was reoccupied Fitauraris Evetu and Alama gave some help to the 2nd Ethiopian Battalion. Mangasha and Nagash attended on the Emperor and played no part. Wingate tried to involve Belai Zelleka, but he failed. In contrast the Italians had strong support from irregulars, largely because of Ras Hailu, whose influence in east Gojjam was important. Ras Hailu was a man of commanding presence and great authority, greater probably than any patriot leader except for Ras Kassa, in character an amusing and time-serving rogue. Long at odds with Haile Selassie, who had treated him with clemency, he had thrown in his lot with the Italians hoping to achieve under them the status and power Haile Selasie would not give him, including the title of *negus*. For a brief period in Gojjam, as a result of Nasi's suggestion, he did enjoy that status, serving the Italians with apparent loyalty. When it was clear though that the Italians were going to be defeated he made his belated submission to the Emperor who again treated him with clemency.

The reasons why the Patriots failed to play any part have been considered in the previous chapter and undoubtedly an important reason was the fundamental difference on policy between Sandford and Wingate. Sandford was in favour of the Emperor and the Patriots being forward, Wingate preferred to go ahead with his strike force and, since he was in command, his policy prevailed. Sandford made some comments on this after the war in a letter to the official historian, Colonel Barton. He thought that the correct military solution in Gojjam would have been to pin down and destroy or capture the Italian forces.

> But this could only have been done by using patriot forces to the full and this needed the presence of the Emperor, Sandford and Kabada, who were left too far behind in Wingate's advance. Wingate preferred to use his own little force as a striking force and it was too small to be more than an irritant and a spur to flight, which were not wanted from the *military* point of view. But *politically* this ... evacuation was all to the good.

It enabled the Emperor to establish his authority in Gojjam.

The Debra Markos operation was the last in which Gideon Force operated together, and although the latter cannot be given the entire credit, as claimed by Wingate and endorsed by Sandford, for forcing the Italians out of Gojjam, its continuous night attacks put pressure on the Italians and were a hard test for officers and men and a fine effort for this small force. The final stages at Gulit were very much Boustead's battle. He it was who planned and executed the final attacks, sent Johnson in pursuit, and occupied Debra Markos. In his autobiography Boustead acknowledges that it was for the Debra Markos operations that he was awarded the DSO and this was well deserved.

While Wingate and Gideon Force were operating before Debra Markos, Simonds and Birru (with Centre troops and Patriots) moved to Debra Tabor to contact local chiefs and cut the road north and south as ordered by Wingate. With Simonds was Ato Getahun Tesemma, one of the original officers of Mission 101, enormously helpful as liaison officer and interpreter. Jarvis, with No 3 patrol company, remained opposite Bahr Dar containing Torelli and harassing him with continual raids and night attacks. These forces were under Wingate's control, albeit remote.

North of Gondar Mission 101 North was still at Maana under Bentinck and Sheppard, encouraging patriot resistance and trying to win over the Kamant, following Sandford's original orders. Further north Ringrose and Railton were about to march in to the Wolchefit region to stir up resistance there, Railton with orders to report to Sheppard and Ringrose under direct orders from Platt, and initially without any knowledge of each other! These guerrilla forces had nothing to do with Wingate, indeed he probably did not know of their existence, but all had the same objectives, the return of the Emperor, the encouragement of resistance, and the disruption of Italian communications.

On 2 April Torelli attacked No 3 patrol company again at Bahr Dar, a more serious attack than that on 23 March (see Sketch 3). The attacking force followed the Dangila road, bypassed the Kebab Yesus hill and swung up to No 3 patrol company's positions, penetrating between the animal transport lines and the forward posts. The mounted infantry and muleteers had to withdraw and lost some equipment and saddlery. The Sudanese infantry were being attacked from several directions and, as Holcombe recalls, drove the Italians back with accurate rifle and light machine-gun fire. It was a 'very tricky business', the Sudanese were 'very good', and the enemy 'attacked vigorously, some Italians but mainly Eritreans[3] who were good'. The attackers withdrew to Bahr Dar north of Kebab Yesus through Kobuta, leaving 29 dead on the field, and having had many wounded, including Torelli, two other officers and an Italian NCO. No 3 patrol company lost one killed and four wounded. Simonds heard later that Torelli had himself driven round his men's positions propped up in a staff car to dispel rumours that he had been killed. He had been wounded when personally leading the attack, a gallant effort by the 54-year-old brigade commander. This was the fourth time that Torelli had been wounded in action in Ethiopia and he was certainly one of the heroes on the Italian side in the campaign. He was awarded the *Medaglia d'Oro al VM* after the war.

For several days after the attack on 2 April the Italians were quiet and appeared to be assembling forces for another attack, which Jarvis could not have withstood because of shortage of ammunition. Then Boustead arrived on 12 April from Debra Markos to visit his company, a journey with mules of three and a half days, bringing with him several mule loads of ammunition, and the situation was saved. Jarvis occupied Kobuta, from which fire could be brought to bear on the Italian positions, and increased his pressure by fighting patrols and raids. Torelli's attack, though courageously executed, had not succeeded even in the limited objective of relieving the pressure on his brigade.

North of Gondar Mission 101 North had continued to try to win over the Kamant without success. Taezaz Haile, who had succeeded Wolde Giorgis as the Emperor's representative, was fired on when he approached the Kamant on 3 March, and on 26 March the Kamant attacked the camp at Maana and were only driven off with difficulty by Bentinck's small force consisting of himself, Sheppard, four Sudanese, six Yemenis, and Mohamed Effendi and his *banda* of 25 soldiers. On 4 April Sheppard formally took over Mission 101 North from Bentinck who left to return to the Sudan. On the way at Wahni he met Lieutenant Colonel Ker and the 3rd Ethiopian Battalion who had entered

Ethiopia from Gallabat and were going to attack Chilga with the Composite Battalion of the SDF. This force was to be known as Kerforce. Bentinck arranged with Ker for Railton with C company of his battalion to be detached to reinforce Sheppard.

Major Humphreys of the Sudan Artillery, serving with Kerforce, watched Bentinck entering their camp, 'badly crippled with a 1914–18 leg wound, wearing a much darned khaki shirt and a Wolseley helmet with a large badge of the Coldstream Guards, his mules in perfect condition, he said goodbye to each mule by name as they went past.' During his seven months in Ethiopia Bentinck had had a role which was minor compared with that of Sandford, but important and difficult. He had operated in areas where there was no effective leader, where many chiefs were more interested in banditry than in fighting for the Emperor and Haile Selassie's writ had never run strongly, and where some tribes, like the Kamant, were actively hostile. He had not seriously disrupted the movement of troops to Keren, but despite his age and disability he had done his best to carry out Sandford's orders.

Railton took over Bentinck's mules, left Wahni on 3 April with C company, and reported to Sheppard at Maana. His orders from Ker were to 'move to the Gondar–Asmara road to operate against communications and outlying Gondar defences.' He got no orders from Sheppard whom he found a 'shy, helpful, friendly man, but no soldier', and, hearing that Mohamed Effendi was operating near Amba Giorgis on the Gondar–Wolchefit road, decided to go and find him. From patriot chiefs on the way he learned that there was a strong Italian garrison at Wolchefit and that a British officer was in the area. This was Ringrose, but he did not learn his name until he met the man who was to become the patriot leader, Dejasmatch Ayelewu Birru. The advance of the 20-year-old Railton leading a company of ex-enemy *ascari* into enemy occupied territory with very little briefing may seem in retrospect a very rash move, but it worked and the very confidence of the move impressed the Patriots.

The local political situation was even more complicated, and the chiefs more in conflict, than in Gojjam. The chiefs of Armachaho (between Chilga and Amba Giorgis) had never submitted to the Italians, and were traditional enemies of the Wogera chiefs

(Dejasmatch Ayelewu Birru and Dejasmatch Arayia) who had. The Armachaho chiefs expected to be rewarded for not submitting and did their best to undermine the usefulness of Ayelewu and Arayia. A further complication were the Kamant who were still supporting the Italians. Ayelewu Birru will be remembered as the pro-Italian former governor of Gondar under Haile Selassie who had put up a show of fighting in the Italian war and had submitted as soon as he decently could. He was a leader of similar status and authority to that of Ras Hailu in Gojjam, and it was essential to detach him from his allegiance to the Italians. Ringrose had arrived near Dabat on the Gondar–Asmara road on 18 March and had started a secret correspondence with Ayalewu who insisted on receiving a letter from the Emperor. The Emperor was then in Gojjam, but with the help and initiative of Dodds-Parker in Khartoum a letter was obtained from the Crown Prince, which was dropped on Ringrose by air and delivered to Ayalewu, who agreed to defect from the Italians on 12 April with Arayia and all their men. Both had large armies equipped with Italian rifles and machine guns. Arayia had had a leg broken in an RAF raid on Gondar, was impressed with British strength (he bore no grudge) and was quite ready to change sides.

Thus the end of the first week in April 1941 saw Platt established in Asmara, Cunningham's forces in Addis Ababa, the Emperor in Debra Markos with part of Wingate's force pursuing Maraventano, Simonds stirring up the Patriots to cut off Debra Tabor, and Sheppard, Ringrose and Railton north of Gondar and about to be joined by the important forces of the defecting chiefs, Ayalewu and Arayia. The Italians still held Dessie, Amba Alagi, where Aosta had his headquarters, and Gondar, where Nasi was in command, and there were important forces still to be defeated in southwest Ethiopia, but the tide was turning against the Italians. Let us now return to the pursuit of the Maraventano column across the Abbai (see Sketch 4).

Maraventano had crossed the Abbai on 7 April unmolested under the protection of the 13th Colonial Battalion. Johnson arrived at the gorge with his force on the same day after the column had crossed, finding there Thesiger, Rowe with No 9 platoon, and Sergeant Howell with part of No 1 Operational

Centre. Boustead and Nott were also there, having come by road from Debra Markos, and they found sad evidence of the death of some of the Sudanese prisoners captured at Emmanuel. 'Found an escaped Nafar of No 2 company who pointed out ... a dead *Shawish* and *Ombashi*, captured, like himself at Emmanuel. They had been shot and fallen down the cliff. He escaped by rolling over the top.'

Johnson's orders were to cross the Abbai with his force, to be known as Safartak Force, abbreviated to Safforce, and pursue Maraventano, but before he did so his force was reduced by the refusal of his Nuba soldiers to cross the river. 'They said it was not their job to cross the Nile; they had been away from their wives long enough. The Arab soldiers were not affected.' Johnson sent the Nubas back to report to Boustead and they marched off under their sergeant. He was left with one officer (Riley), 56 soldiers and 12 muleteers of the Frontier Battalion, Rowe and 27 men of No 9 platoon with 10 muleteers, Howell with 15 men of No 1 Centre, Thesiger with one Sudanese orderly and nine *banda*, and two mortar men, a total force of 137. They had 41 mules and 22 horses on which they carried rations, ammunition and the heavy weapons, which consisted of one three-inch mortar and 24 bombs, two Boyes anti-tank rifles, one Vickers medium machine gun, 14 light machine guns, and 141 Mills grenades. Their small-arms ammunition was of three varieties, .303, .300 and 7.92 millimetre. All these details were carefully recorded by Nott in his diary when he took over. Against this minute force Maraventano had eight colonial battalions, including the 13th, one CCNN battalion, two batteries of 65-millimetre guns and 81-millimetre mortars, the cavalry and mounted *banda*, and some HQ troops, including a company of *carabinieri* (CCRR), and, after the Abbai crossing, the pontoon company of engineers under Captain Silvi and a Sudanese company under Tenente della Rovere who had been working with them and who decided (in Silvi's words) to 'follow Maraventano rather than surrender to the English, stipulating only that they would be required to fight against the rebels, not against their compatriots'. In all Maraventano had about 1000 European and 6500 colonial troops, and to pursue and harry this force were indeed seemingly preposterous orders for Johnson. The column was, however, impeded by large numbers of non-combatants, and Safforce was not the only enemy. Once the column crossed the Abbai it was under continual attack from Patriots.

Safforce crossed the Abbai on 8 April, losing one man in the crossing, which was defended by the 13th Colonial Battalion, whose casualties were seven killed and 13 wounded in disputing the crossing and repelling patriot attacks. Meanwhile Maraventano had reached Quoziem Mariam where he learned of the occupation of Ficce by British troops, blocking the one motorable route to Dessie. During the night 8/9 April Patriots attacked the 3rd Colonial Brigade, and on 9 April the 13th Battalion had a very sharp engagement in the Mugher valley attempting, on orders from the Shoa commander, to rejoin their brigade in Galla-Sidamo, losing 44 *ascari* killed and 83 wounded. The battalion gave up the attempt and rejoined Maraventano's column. Ahead of the column patriot forces were gathering in Giarso and Salale, Ras Kassa's fief, Thesiger reporting, 'The Italian force is retreating towards Ficce and being considerably shot up by *fannus* and *banda*.' Behind the column Johnson was following closely with his men and continuing the practice, which he had adopted against Natale in the retreat from Burye, closing up and firing into the Italian camp at night.

The date 10 April was an eventful one for the column. Leaving Quoziem Mariam at dawn, the column reached Tulumelchi at 10.30 a.m. after a march of 18 kilometres and relieved the garrison of *carabinieri*, having had to repel patriot attacks on the flanks on the way and remove the telegraph poles, which the Patriots had cut down to block the road. At 10.00 a.m. the column was spotted by two Harts of No 41 squadron of the South African Air Force from Addis Ababa, who reported finding the column of '200 white Italians, 12,000 natives and 50 vehicles'. Fearing aerial attack, Maraventano speeded up his march and reached Cuiu at 4.15 p.m. after a march of 45 kilometres and relieved the garrison of 250 *banda* under Tenente Cantalamessa after a cavalry charge by his cavalry commander, Major Torielli, had scattered a patriot force of about 1000, which had been besieging the garrison for the past week. At 5.00 p.m., after the column was dispersed and in position, seven Allied aircraft appeared, five Harts and two Gladiators of No 41 squadron of the South African Air Force, and bombed and machine-gunned the column for 35 minutes. Although Maraventano says his casualties were 'relatively light', reduced by the good discipline of the troops and the hot fire opened on the aircraft, they were in fact considerable, according to his record, two officers wounded, one national killed and 12 wounded, 24 *ascari* killed and 68 wounded, two civilian nationals wounded, and ten native civilans killed and 50 wounded. In addition, in actions against Patriots on the march, the column suffered 16 *ascari* killed and 34 wounded and six horses killed and eight wounded (in the cavalry charge). The column had no anti-aircraft weapons, only rifles and the light Breda light machine guns fired from the shoulder, but the pilots reported, 'the return fire was fierce. One Hart was hit 33 times.' Allied reports claim that the column was dispersed, abandoned its vehicles and made for Dessie, but in fact the vehicles were not abandoned until later at Sirie.

On the evening of 10 April Maraventano signalled Italian HQ at Dessie asking for an airdrop of ammunition, and sent his adjutant, Captain Lancia, to offer the Cuiu *banda* the choice of discharge without weapons or to continue with the column, and ordered the march to be resumed at 12.30 a.m. on 11 April. The *banda* all deserted during the night taking their rifles, but Lancia had taken the precaution of removing their light machine guns and spare ammunition. The march resumed as ordered at 12.30 a.m., helped by a full moon, in a silence 'broken only by the rumbling of the overloaded lorries'. Some of these were now carrying the wounded, their loads of ammunition having been distributed among the marching *ascari*. They reached the hilly country of Salale at 7.30 a.m., where they would find cover from air attack after the advanced guard had driven a 'substantial body of rebels' out of the way. At 8.15 a.m. a single Hart from No 41 squadron, piloted by Lieutenant Collins, appeared over the column, sent to find the remnants of the force 'believed by the pilots to have been completely destroyed ... the previous day'. Collins attacked the column with bombs and machine-gun fire at low altitude but was brought down by ground fire and he and his sergeant observer were made prisoner. Rossini saw the plane come down and sent some of his *ascari* to run towards it to capture the occupants. At the same time he noticed that Patriots who had been following the column were streaking towards the plane. He and his fellow officers were much amused to see that the two airmen, seeing Patriots and *ascari* converging on them, actually ran towards the red-tarbushed *ascari*, apparently not liking the look of the Patriots, thus making themselves prisoners of war. Collins and his observer were well treated by their captors, who bore no rancour for the bombardment of the previous day.

The events of 10 and 11 April give a good picture of Maraventano's column on the march. This large force, with its mass of non-combatants and wounded, after quite severe casualties from air and ground attack on 10 April and a 45-kilometre march, moved off half an hour after midnight next day in a disciplined way and ready for action. At this time Allied forces elsewhere in Ethiopia were victorious and had complete command of the air, and the Ethiopian people were everywhere rising up against the Italian government. Maraventano had some desertions, but the bulk of his colonial troops, mainly Ethiopian, remained disciplined, loyal and ready to march, fight and take casualties until the column surrendered on 23 May. This says a good deal for the quality of the Italian colonial army, officers and *ascari*, and of the commander.

It is evident also that patriot forces made determined efforts to harass and halt the Italian column on the east bank, once it had crossed the Abbai, unlike Belai Zelleka on the west bank. This increased activity can be ascribed in part to the desire to join in the pursuit of a defeated enemy, in part to Sandford's letters in the Emperor's name encouraging the Patriots to attack the Italian column, and also to the fact that the column had moved away from Ras Hailu's influence to a region where Ras Kassa was dominant.

On the night of 11 April Maraventano received orders by wire-less to make his way to Dessie across country by Deraa, still in Italian hands, because Debra Berhan, as well as Ficce, had been taken by the 'English', thus completely blocking his route to Dessie by road. He decided to move north to Sirie by a motorable track, which was reopened by Silvi and his engineers, and reached Sirie on 16 April after a sharp attack by the 72nd Colonial Battalion had put to flight a 'substantial force of rebels'. On the way, on 13

April, he received a signal from General Frusci, former commander at Keren and now commanding at Dessie, in reply to his request for an airdrop of supplies; 'Bravo Maraventano. Possibility can help you. Signal daily the position you will reach each day.' Frusci instructed him to repeat his signals to commander Dessie sector, 'to whom you are answerable'. This was the Scottish sounding Colonel Anderson, who was not going to be of much help to Maraventano in the weeks to come.

On the night of 15 April Maraventano had suffered the first serious desertion of regular troops; '165 *ascari* of the 4th Gruppo Squadrone taking six light machine guns, also about 10 from other units in the brigade and about 50 from the garrison Coy at Quoziem Mariam'. This left him with only about 100 regular cavalry and the Burye mounted *banda* of 200. The measures he took against desertion, 'control of dependents, continual inspection and daily talks by officers and *graduati*' did not eliminate the problem but 'contained it within fairly modest limits'.

Maraventano remained at Sirie from 16 to 24 April, spending the time investigating the route to Deraa and recruiting food supplies. The local population had left taking their cattle but leaving granaries full of cereal crops, which the Italians collected. On 17 April Frusci signalled that he was hoping to send a plane, and on 19 April a single Caproni arrived and dropped by parachute tea, sugar and several thousand rounds of Mannlicher ammunition, followed by a second Caproni on 21 April, which dropped tea, sugar and jam. A lone Caproni was shot down over Debra Markos on the same day by South African Air Force Gladiators and if this was the same plane it was a sad end to a daring mission. These air sorties by the Regia Aeronautica, which had few planes left, were brave efforts and raised the spirits of the troops. Maraventano was lucky not to have had more attention from Allied aircraft, which were seen, but there were no more air attacks except for an abortive one on 24 April. We will leave Maraventano at Sirie, fending off Johnson and the Patriots, and see what has been happening on other fronts.

Allied advances had continued elsewhere in AOI. In the south the 12th African Division advanced into southwest Ethiopia while the 11th African Division pursued the Italians southwest from

Addis Ababa. In the north Massawa had been captured on 8 April, thus freeing the Red Sea (one of the main strategic benefits of the campaign), and Platt's forces then advanced south into Tigre towards Amba Alagi, where Aosta had his headquarters. Ras Seyum of Tigre had collaborated with the Italians, like Ras Hailu, but went over to the Allies as their forces approached from the north with his 7000 well-armed followers, a blow to the Italians and an accretion to the Allied strength. In North Africa and the Mediterranean the war was not going well for the Allies. Greece had been invaded by the Germans on 7 April, overrun by 27 April and the Allied forces (sent from North Africa to help) evacuated, and Crete was in danger. Rommel had pushed the depleted desert army back in Cyrenaica and Tobruk was threatened. Wavell needed more troops and the 4th Indian Division was ordered back to North Africa, to be followed by the 5th Indian Division as soon as the operations in northern Ethiopia were concluded and the three South African brigades. The 2nd and 5th were already on their way, and the 1st South African Brigade was marching north from Addis Ababa to attack Dessie and join the 5th Indian Division in the attack on Amba Alagi before joining Wavell's command.

Beghemder Force at Debra Tabor

Thanks to Wingate's strategic foresight the escape route for the 10,000 Italian troops in Dessie northwest towards Debra Tabor and Gondar had already been cut. Simonds with Fitaurari Birru and Beghemder Force had arrived near Debra Tabor at the end of March, and had been joined there by Lieutenant Neil McLean to take over No 2 Operational Centre. Debra Tabor was an important administrative centre on the road from Dessie to Gondar, well fortified with a seven-mile perimeter, and garrisoned by 6000 men commanded by Colonel Ignazio Angelini. Between 1 and 10 April Simonds booby trapped the road on each side of Debra Tabor while he and Birru contacted chiefs. On 11 April he set up an ambush at Limado, a hill three miles north of Debra Tabor, which led to a sharp action with an Italian supply column from Gondar. McLean, with Sergeants Morrow and King and 90 men from No 2 Centre and an energetic local patriot leader, Fitaurari Danyo, and 100 men, took up an ambush position on the road, which was mined, and prepared a bridge for demolition, which was covered by Sergeant King with a platoon. The Italians spotted the ambush, debussed, and attacked King's platoon. McLean went to his assistance with the Centre troops and Patriots and a fierce engagement ensued. Then Italian reinforcements arrived from Debra Tabor and McLean ordered his force to withdraw to Limado. Sergeant King, with great gallantry, ran forward and detonated the explosives on the bridge with his pistol and the bridge blew up. He was badly injured and captured. Two days later Simonds received a letter from the chivalrous Italians informing him that, 'Sgt King of your army has died of his wounds received in battle and has been buried with the honours of war. He was a very brave man.'

Simonds wrote to Wingate recommending King for the VC and Wingate forwarded the recommendation, and both Simonds and McLean wrote to his widow, Mrs Violet King, in Londonderry. Nothing was heard of any award. This was a substantial action in which the Italians lost one truck destroyed, 15 *ascari* killed and five wounded, and the Allies one British non-commissioned officer and 13 other ranks killed and 13 wounded. Simonds records that, 'Patriots and Centre troops fought well. Incident had good effect on waverers.' The result was that no further attempts were made by the Italians to run convoys from Gondar into Debra Tabor. The relieving troops from Debra Tabor were the 79th Colonial Battalion, later, after the fall of Debra Tabor, commanded by McLean as the 79th (McLean's) Foot!

Leaving McLean in charge at Debra Tabor, Simonds went south, contacted Patriots and drove hostile *banda* off the Dessie road, effectively cutting the road and the line of retreat for the Dessie garrison in accordance with Wingate's orders. He then moved north towards Gondar, blocking and mining the road and obtaining the submission of the hostile district of Deraa. Many Patriots came to join him so that, 'my force [was] never less than 4000'. He then moved back to Limado to rejoin McLean where on 24 April he was reinforced by Lieutenant Mark Pilkington, Life Guards, and his combined 5th/10th Operational Centre. On the departure, sick of van der Post, Pilkington had taken over his No 5 Centre in addition to his own No 10 and arrived with three sergeants, Preedy (Life Guards), MacDonald (13th/18th Hussars) and Edge

(Coldstream Guards), and 60 *askari*. Pilkington and McLean, both Old Etonian cavalry subalterns, were to form a splendid and irreverent partnership, which continued until the end of the Gondar campaign. With these forces Simonds settled down to invest Debra Tabor.

The Capture of Mota

The Italian fort of Mota, 70 miles north of Debra Markos, was still being invested, not very closely, by Hailu Belao's Patriots. On 10 April Wingate ordered Brown's No 1 Centre to go north to stimulate patriot activity, but there was trouble in the ranks and 58 men refused to march. They were arrested and disarmed, and when their sergeant, Burke, complained to Wingate about their treatment, 'Wingate went through him like a dose of salts,' as Nott records. The men were dealt with by court martial the next day, together with two soldiers of the 2nd Ethiopian Battalion who had been caught stealing bombs for resale to Patriots ('a profitable racket at two dollars a bomb!') and sentenced to be discharged from the army with ignominy. As Nott describes, 'The men were marched up, their sentence read out — with a warning that they would be shot if they enlisted again — stripped of all uniform except shorts and chased down the ranks out of the fort while the big drums in the corner of the fort were beaten. HIM watched through window crack.'

Brown went off to Mota after the court martial with Burke and the remaining men and contacted patriot leaders, and on 18 April Wingate ordered Boustead to 'mop up' Mota. Bill Allen, now the battalion animal transport officer, describes how Wingate's orders arrived at Boustead's mess, 'near midnight. We had dined very well and over Italian champagne and cognac were lamenting the fate of King Edward VIII.' Boustead left on 19 April with 400 men of Nos 1, 2 and 4 patrol companies, and Turrall with two mortar sections, and arrived at Mota on 21 April. Allen had supplemented the mules with 60 camels and had bought corn for their use, and blankets, groundsheets and cigarettes for his Sudanese, all Italian stores, from an Armenian trader who was Ras Hailu's agent. The old *ras* continued to make a profit out of the English even after submission! The track to Mota skirted the 14,000-foot Choke mountains on the west side. The corn-fed camels 'waltzed up the hill', but despite Allen's comforts the Sudanese spent a miserable night in a blizzard and many went down with mountain sickness. They recovered when they reached the plain next day, and Allen managed to shoot a buck to supplement their diet.

Boustead contacted Brown and Lij Anderji, the Emperor's representative with the Patriots, and spent the day reconnoitring the fort and making a plan of attack. Then, on the evening of 21 April, a message arrived from Wingate ordering Maxwell with the bulk of the Frontier Battalion to return to Debra Markos in order to take part in the Emperor's triumphal entry into Addis Ababa, planned for 5 May, leaving Boustead with two platoons, Brown's centre, Turrall's mortars and the Patriots to reduce Mota. This was a typical Wingate order, taking a calculated risk that bluff and pressure would still induce the Italians to surrender even though two thirds of the besieging force had marched away. Maxwell marched off back to Debra Markos on 22 April.

The bluff worked. After two days of bombardment by Turrall's mortars, which set most of the buildings inside the fort on fire, with the Sudanese pouring in light machine-gun fire, and an exchange of polite letters with the Italian commander, Major Mazzorella, terms of surrender were agreed. Some 11 Italian officers and NCOs were escorted to Debra Markos by Brown's centre, and 340 *graduati* and *ascari* were recruited into the Emperor's army. Allen gave the honours for the Mota operation to Turrall and his crews, 'who worked the mortars tirelessly, and to the Sudani subaltern, Mustafa Effendi Kamali, in action for the first time'. Turrall was awarded the MC for the Mota and Debra Markos operations. On hearing of the surrender of Mota Wingate sent orders to Boustead to go north to Bahr Dar, enforce the withdrawal of Torelli, and then join Simonds at Debra Tabor and, if possible, enforce the surrender of the garrison.

Operations at Wolchefit[*]

The stronghold of Wolchefit, 110 kilometres north of Gondar, was commanded by Lieutenant Colonel Mario Gonella, a tough and

---

[*] See Map 2 and Sketch 8.

enterprising Alpini officer, with a garrison of about 5000 men, half national and half colonial, with 30 guns and mortars. The position was a very strong one, almost impregnable on the north side where there was a 4000-foot escarpment down to the plain, now climbed by the motor road from Asmara, an incredible feat of Italian engineering. Anticipating an attack from General Platt's forces in the north, General Nasi ordered the withdrawal to Wolchefit of all outlying garrisons in Simien and the demolition of the road up the escarpment. These withdrawals were carried out between 2 and 7 April under attacks from the air and also from patriot forces on the ground. A typical incident was that at Zaremma where the forces of Dejasmatch Nagash (not to be confused with the Dejasmatch Nagash of Gojjam) besieged the garrison, which consisted of an irregular *banda*, commanded by Sergeant Major Sante Angelo Bastiani. After a bitter struggle, in which Bastiani lost 40 killed and many wounded, the Patriots were so impressed with the courage of the defenders that they allowed a truce for Bastiani to bury his dead, collect his wounded and retreat to Wolchefit, an unheard-of privilege. This was an action similar to that at Kwara, where the Patriots fought on their own without any British or imperial support, and similar also in its ferocity. Bastiani, known to his men as 'Ras Bianco' and to Ethiopians as 'Diabolo Zoppo' (the limping devil), had a high reputation as a *banda* leader, and had commanded his *banda* of about 1500 men since 1937, mainly Amhara from the Dessie region with some Eritrean *graduati* and Gojjamis, an unusual command for a warrant officer. He wore no badges of rank, only a green scarf, which all ranks wore with pride, and he and his men had fought in many actions against the 'rebels' in which he had been five times wounded (hence the 'limping devil'). The 'Banda Bastiani' was to play a major role in the forthcoming siege of Wolchefit.

Platt's forces from the north, consisting of a heavy machine-gun company of the SDF and the Sudan light battery, secured the road as far as Debivar, patrolled towards the escarpment, and opened regular artillery fire on the Italian positions from 17 April onwards, but this was only a holding operation and they did not attempt to go any further. South of Wolchefit the attacks were to come from British-led patriot forces. Ringrose, in correspondence with Ayalewu, had secured his agreement to come over to the Allies on 12 April and join in an attack on Dabat, held by a mixed force of about 500 Italian troops, on 13 April. Ringrose had by then collected a force of about 3000 Patriots. The attack was successful, despite an Italian counterattack, and Ringrose then moved north near Debarech and established his lines of communication with Platt's HQ in Asmara by sending Sergeant Perkins to form a rear base at Zaremma. Henceforth supplies were sent to him by road to Zaremma and thence by mule convoy west of Wolchefit to his camp.

Further south Railton, with C company had crossed the Gondar–Wolchefit road and met Mohamed Effendi, 'a tough and vigorous soldier', east of Amba Giorgis on 13 April. Together they went on to see Dejasmatch Arayia and then Dejasmatch Ayalewu who 'was delighted to see a British officer and gave us a royal reception'. Railton was the first British officer to meet Ayalewu, all Ringrose's contacts having been by correspondence. Ayalewu convened a meeting of chiefs and Patriots on 15 April at which there were about 10,000 present. At the end of a day of speeches Railton proposed a night attack on Amba Giorgis on 19 April, which was agreed, but the plan was abortive because Ayalewu was summoned north by Ringrose to take part in an attack on Debarech, an order by a more senior British officer with which he had to comply. Railton, and Sheppard who had joined him, had to be content with raiding and investing Amba Giorgis for the time being. Then on 5 May Railton planned an attack on Amba Giorgis with C company alone, having first sent in a letter to the Italian commander demanding surrender. The Italians evacuated the position and C company moved in without firing a shot, and henceforth it became Railton's base. Ringrose having taken Dabat, Wolchefit was now effectively cut off from Gondar.

La Colonna Maraventano: The March to Deraa

At Sirie Maraventano had concluded that the best route to Deraa lay through Adanaccio across the Giamma river, and he gave orders for five days' cereal to be distributed to the *ascari* and their families and for the march to resume on the night of 23/24 April. Meanwhile Johnson had sent his second-in-command, Riley, to

Addis Ababa to seek help. Riley found his way to Addis Ababa, commandeering an Italian lorry in Ficce, and saw Major General Wetherall, commander of the 11th African Division, and as a result a force of two Nigerian companies with artillery, known as Arkcol, was formed under the command of Major T. L. Fasson, Border Regiment, which returned with Riley with orders to cooperate with Safforce.

On the night of 21 April Johnson carried out a succcesful night attack on the Sirie positions, confirmed by Maraventano who reported three killed and ten wounded, and on the evening of 23 April Arkcol artillery opened fire on the Italian positions causing considerable casualties. (Maraventano reported 31 *ascari* killed, two officers and 82 *ascari* wounded.) The Italian 65-millimetre pack guns with a range of 6000 yards were completely outranged by the field battery's 18–25 pounders with a range of 12,000 yards. Shelling was resumed at dawn on 24 April followed by an aerial attack by the South African Air Force at 7.00 a.m., but the column had departed during the night, the positions were empty and the attacks abortive. The column had reached the end of the motorable track and would rely henceforth on animal transport. During the afternoon of 23 April the remaining lorries had been destroyed by fire and arrangements made for the transport of wounded on stretchers or on horseback. Having no animal transport Arkcol could not follow and returned to Addis Ababa, leaving the pursuit to Safforce and the Patriots.

The column moved on towards Adanaccio under continual patriot attack, kept off by counterattacks in which the Debra Markos training battalion and the Sudanese company distinguished themselves. One such counterattack was observed by Silvi who with part of his company took a wrong path and lost contact with the main column. They came under fire from Patriots on a hill and while they took cover and wondered what to do a formation from the column came to the rescue and attacked and drove off the enemy. Silvi describes the agile *ascari* in the attack. 'To see a group of our *ascari* attack a dominant position on the run was a marvellous spectacle. Climbing and leaping like goats ... they shot and threw grenades with such *élan* as to throw the enemy into confusion.'

171

The column reached Adanaccio on the south side of the Giamma river gorge on the evening of 24 April and, because of the exhaustion of the national troops, remained there on 25 April where they again came under patriot attack. According to Maraventano's account casualties on the march were two nationals killed and two wounded and eight *ascari* killed and 22 wounded, and at Adanaccio three nationals wounded, 18 *ascari* killed and 48 wounded. These figures show the scale of the patriot attacks. It must be said though that at this point Safforce was out of touch and there is no Allied confirmation of these attacks.

Back at Debra Markos Wingate had sent off No 3 Operational Centre under Naylor, with Sergeants Cannon, Goode, Lewis and Bartlett and 40 *askari* to reinforce Safforce on 23 April, and on 25 April, on hearing of the intervention of Arkcol, ordered Nott to go forward and take command 'to see that our forces got their share of the spoils'. Nott left immediately, taking four men but not, to his regret, his interpreter Johannes Abdu who was sick, hitched a lift to the Abbai where le Blanc was working on the crossing, and marched to Cuiu arriving on the evening of 26 April. There he found Naylor and also Ras Kassa 'who joyfully received me and gave me some fine *tej* and enjoyable conversation, his son Asrate Kassa interpreting', and Thesiger, 'who let me share his small tent and stew pot'.

On 26 April Maraventano had started to cross the Giamma and Safforce was out of touch. Nott quickly got a grip of his force, sending written orders to Johnson, who was camped five miles away, to dispatch Riley and Naylor in pursuit of the column, and seeing Johnson himself early on 27 April. He found Johnson, 'in his own words, browned off. . . . I felt at the time a slight feeling of resentment of my taking over from him but with it . . . an air of relief of responsibility. Johnson had been at it longer than anyone else and had done extremely well.'

Nott then marched to Sirie with Thesiger and Asrate Kassa, arriving at 4.30 p.m. on 27 April to find Ras Kassa already there with his army, but to be told by him that he had been ordered by Haile Selassie not to cross the Giamma, which was his feudal boundary. The reason for the Emperor's order is not clear, but he did not then want the forces even of his most loyal chief to operate outside his feudal territory. Nott was much weakened by Ras Kassa's refusal, but was undeterred and permits himself a mildly purple passage in his entry of 28 April. 'And so I left Ras Kassa and his army at Sirie on this day at 0630 hours and with Thesiger I sallied out to do battle.' Nott reported his intentions to Wingate with a remarkably accurate assessment of the opposing strengths: 'Enemy strength estimated at 6000 rifles. I have 150 rifles. They have 8 guns and 2 mortars. I have one mortar with bum sights and few shells.'

Nott caught up with Johnson and his force at the Giamma gorge at 1.30 p.m. on 28 April, gave the officers a 'three minute pep talk', and by 4.30 p.m. was bathing in the Giamma — 'how grand it was!' Finding that his wireless set would not work, he sent it back with four men: 'Nobody is going to stop me having a crack at the enemy.' For Nott's small force the 3000-foot descent was difficult enough down a precipitous path so narrow that guns and other equipment at times had to be unloaded and manhandled. For Maraventano's unwieldy column of 12,000 humans and 5000 animals, which crossed on 26 and 27 April, the difficulties were much greater, and patriot sniping caused about ten casualties. Transporting the many wounded was an enormous problem and tied up a great number of men in porterage duties. Silvi had three stretcher cases in his company. He placed an officer in charge with an NCO and 16 men for each stretcher in four shifts, the four bearers changing over every 20 to 30 minutes. Maraventano had given strict orders that no one must be left behind, and Silvi used 'physical methods' when necessary to deal with men who tried to fall out or evade porterage duty. 'In prison camp afterwards I met several of my soldiers who thanked me for the slaps and kicks on the bottom, which I had given them on those occasions.'

After sending Major Calvi, commander of the 13th Colonial Battalion, ahead with two battalions to secure Addis Derra, 30 kilometres from the Giamma, Maraventano joined him there with the column on the evening of 28 April after a difficult ascent during which they lost 60 horses and mules. He describes Deraa as a 'vast plateau with steep sides ... 300 to 400 metres high, dominating the surrounding region. The plateau, lightly undulating, was well watered and dotted with small acacia woods.' There were 'ample stocks of food, and the mainly Muslim population seemed friendly'. There was an Italian fort, recently vacated, which they reoccupied. On the way Maraventano had heard the unwelcome news that Dessie had surrendered on 26 April and a farewell message from Frusci regretting that he could not help him any more, concluding, 'Courage: your goal is not far off.' In fact his goal was now a good deal further, Amba Alagi until that stronghold fell, and then Gondar. The news about Dessie was bad because two-thirds of his *ascari* came from the Dessie region and he could expect some effect on their morale, although in fact this did not happen.

Nott followed with his force and from now on we can balance Maraventano's *diario* with Nott's diary. For the next two weeks these two professional soldiers confronted each other at Deraa, Maraventano showing a disposition to stay until events elsewhere forced him to move (as in Gojjam), Nott with his small force containing and harassing him, but lacking the strength to force his surrender until Wingate arrived with Ras Kassa and patriot reinforcements.

Turning to other fronts, Dessie with its garrison of 10,000 had surrendered on 26 April to Brigadier Pienaar's 1st South African Brigade, assisted by 500 Shoan Patriots under Captain Campbell, the Black Watch. These were some of Ababa Aregai's men and they went on under Campbell to fight at Gondar. Amba Alagi still held out, as did Gondar and its outlying garrisons, including Chilga, towards which Kerforce was moving. Axis successes in Greece and Cyrenaica encouraged the Italian High Command to consider a counter offensive and Nasi was asked on 24 April whether he could mount an operation to recapture Addis Ababa with a force of ten colonial and three CCNN battalions raised from the Gondar garrison. With the fall of Dessie, however, this plan was abandoned since the road to Addis Ababa was now closed. In the south the KAR was advancing southwest through the lakes, while the Gold Coast Brigade, advancing north towards them, was engaged in an extremely tough fight against the Italian position at Uaddara, which they had reached on 19 April.

Boustead had arrived at Bahr Dar on 1 May from Mota to find Jarvis and No 3 patrol company in possession. Torelli had been recalled to Gondar by Nasi and had moved out on 27 and 28 April. After taking the submission of the pro-Italian Dejasmatch Ijegur at Kalala, Boustead moved his force to Debra Tabor and joined Simonds and the combined force settled down to besiege the garrison. Beghemder Force had done well at Bahr Dar. The young soldiers of No 3 patrol company, recruited and trained by Bill Harris, had fought courageously under the effective leadership of the two British officers, Jarvis and Holcombe, and outstanding Sudanese officers and NCOs. The Ethiopian Centre troops, mortar men and Patriots had all played their part. Casualties in No 3 patrol company for this period were three killed and five wounded, in No 2 Centre at least five killed and a number wounded. Patriot casualties are not known. Against them Torelli's brigade is estimated to have had 100–150 casualties. In the next chapter we will deal with the return of Haile Selassie to his capital, the political climax of the campaign.

Notes

1. Captain Gallia of the 11th Battalion took over Volpi's No 2 company and appealed successfully against its disbandment on the grounds that 'if this happened it would be as if Ten. Volpi and the *sciumbasci* died twice.'

2. The colonial battalions were the 11th, 23rd, 30th (3rd Brigade), the 21st, 15th, 72nd (19th Brigade), training battalion, with 5th and 37th batteries, the 4th Gruppo Cavalry, Burye mounted *banda*. The national units were Blackshirts and *carabinieri*. They were joined at the Abbai by the 13th Battalion, the Engineers and the Sudanese company. There was one white woman with the column, a 19-year-old Italian girl from Addis Ababa who was caught up by the war when visiting friends in Gojjam.

3. Eritreans — in fact mixed units.

6

Haile Selassie Enters Addis Ababa: The End of Maraventano's Odyssey

hile Safforce was confronting Maraventano at Deraa and Boustead with part of the Frontier Battalion had joined Simonds at Debra Tabor, the rest of Gideon Force, and Sandford and Wingate, remained with the Emperor in Debra Markos for most of the month of April 1941, the Emperor receiving the submission of chiefs but immediately demanding that he should be allowed to enter his capital. Before dealing with this question we will mention two problems which caused the Emperor and Sandford much concern even before they entered Debra Markos, the paucity of the Emperor's personal troops, and the fact that it was the British, not the Emperor's troops, who were getting all the credit for winning the war. Haile Selassie complained to Sandford that he 'is being made to cut a very poor figure before his people, which is not only galling to him now but dangerous for him in the future.'

Sandford had always advocated that the Emperor should have not less than 3000 household troops. Writing to Lush on 29 March he said that Wingate wanted to take all regular troops with him across the Abbai, 'destination Dessie ... he has strong views and rides roughshod over anyone who holds different views. He said today that political consideration should carry no weight in wartime!' This would leave the Emperor with his bodyguard of

176

350, 'insufficient to overawe Mangasha and Nagash if they started squabbling'. Belai Zelleka had written deploring the fact that the Emperor had come with less than 3000 troops 'like a *shifta*', and the Italians had put out damaging propaganda, 'that it was the British, to whom he had sold his country, who were winning the war while he appeared in the eyes of his people inferior in strength to any other Ethiopian leader.' In contrast to his own small force the Emperor had heard that the principal collaborators, Ras Hailu, Ras Seyum, Ras Getachew and Dejasmatch Ayalewu Birru had all received large grants of arms from the Italians, which he considered very dangerous.

Sandford urged that the 4th Ethiopian Battalion and 500 Shoan deserters in Khartoum be sent forward, and that the bodyguard be increased to 500. Although these additional troops were not sent, Sandford's efforts to increase the household troops had some limited success. In Debra Markos the bodyguard was increased to battalion strength by incorporating Nos 4 and 8 Operational Centres — Bathgate (King's Own) and Stanton (Yorks Hussars) — and Beard from the 2nd Ethiopian Battalion was appointed to command. An Indian army colonel, Colonel Morrogh-Bernard, was appointed to command the Emperor's household troops. The 2nd Ethiopian Battalion (except for Rowe's platoon) remained in attendance on the Emperor instead of pursuing the Maraventano column, much to the disappointment of Tutton. Later, Wingate's capture of the Maraventano column was a significant success for the Emperor's troops, which could be set against the British successes.

The entry of Haile Selassie into his capital was the most important political and symbolic event of the campaign. It was necessary to show the Ethiopian people, and the world, that the *negus negusti*, Haile Selassie I, had returned to his seat of power, which many people still thought he should not have left in May 1936. Apart from the symbolic importance of his return there was a pressing military reason why he should establish his government in Addis Ababa as soon as possible and that was the possibility of a British defeat in North Africa where, during April 1941, British forces had been driven back by Rommel from Benghazi towards the Egyptian frontier. A British defeat might leave the Emperor without support in Ethiopia against both Italian and German enemies. As Sandford wrote to Lush on 8 April, 'He [the Emperor] feels very strongly that he must get to Addis Ababa as quickly as possible, form his government and raise a standing army.'

A popular legend about the Emperor's entry into Addis Ababa, still current in Ethiopia as another Wingate myth, is that Wingate brought him in against orders from the British military establishment. The following account is based on contemporary records, which provide the best evidence. The decision when the Emperor should enter was delegated by Wavell to his chief political officer, Sir Philip Mitchell, in consultation with the local military commanders, Cunningham and Wetherall, and his deputy, Brigadier Lush. Cunningham insisted on delay for security reasons. Lush would have the task of conveying this decision to the Emperor who never accepted it, nor did Sandford and Wingate who saw no good reason for delay. Lush and Sandford were brothers-in-law and old friends. They found themselves frequently in conflict over policy, but this disagreement did not affect their personal relationship and it was to the advantage of both Britain and Ethiopia that Sandford and Lush could agree to differ, remain friends, and try and find ways of resolving difficulties. Wingate stuck to operational matters and kept out of the political argument, a fact that may seem surprising in view of his involvement with Zionism in Palestine and that makes his later treatment by Cunningham even more unfair.

Mitchell flew into Addis Ababa immediately after its capture to confer with Cunningham and Lush. He did not fly on to Debra Markos to see Haile Selassie (the person most concerned), which he acknowledged afterwards was a mistake. As a result of Mitchell's visit Sandford received a signal dated 8 April from GHQ Khartoum: 'Emperor will *not* rpt *not* be allowed into Addis Ababa until active operational stage regarding which I cannot give details has developed and arrangements regarding disposal of italian civilians have been made by GHQ ME.' The operational factor referred to was that fighting was still going on in Shoa, Maraventano was still on the Debra Markos–Addis Ababa road (the Emperor's route to the capital) until 14 April and at Sirie within striking distance until 23 April, and Addis Ababa contained

178

20,000 Italians, 12,000 armed. Surrounding the city was a ring of forts still in Italian hands, and outside them Ras Ababa Aregai's army of 7000 Patriots. Cunningham, on military not political grounds, insisted that the Italians must be disarmed before the Emperor could be allowed into the capital, fearing a bloody conflict between armed Italians and Patriots if they flooded into the city to greet him. He and Wetherall were unsure of what the Patriots might do, although assured by both Sandford and Lush that Ababa Aregai's Shoans would respect Italian lives and property (correctly as it turned out). There were some grounds for the British commanders' fears. At Dire Dawa in early April seven Italians had been murdered by *ascari* deserters, and near Aselle on 11 April the advancing KAR found on the road the naked and mutilated bodies of 14 Italians, including the *residente*, murdered by Arussi Galla. To senior British officers all Ethiopian Patriots looked alike, they did not appreciate that the Amhara of Shoa had different standards of behaviour from the Arussi Galla, and they were not taking any chances.

The other factor was the presence of 5000 Italian civilians, and in particular, in those more chivalrous days, of large numbers of Italian women and children. On his approach to the capital Cunningham had tried to enter into negotiations with Aosta about the safety of these, Wavell signalling to Aosta on 31 March, 'Anxious to avoid danger to Italian women and children. Gen. Cunningham authorized to contact you.' The negotiations came to nothing but the civilian population remained an important factor.

The decision, as recorded by Lush, was that before Haile Selassie could be allowed to enter his capital the Italian troops must be disarmed and interned, the forts handed over to Ethiopians under British control, and the women and children concentrated in four safe areas. Silvi's wife and daughter Rita, aged 16, were among the women and children and were billeted in the Hotel Imperiale where they were at first guarded from the depredations of the Patriots by ancient Italian waiters issued with rifles they did not know much about handling. In fact, as Rita Silvi records, they were in more danger of annoyance from the amorous intentions of some allied officers drinking in the hotel bar, but this was stopped by an appeal to the 'English General' (almost certainly Brigadier Lush), who listened to the applicant ladies 'with great courtesy', and put an armed sentry on their quarters.

Lush flew to Debra Markos on 10 April to see the Emperor, travelling with his party in two South African Air Force Harts, and seeing Maraventano's column on the south side of the Abbai ('lovely bombing target — but *no* bombs'). Cunningham's decision to delay his entry into Addis Ababa and the reasons for it were explained to Haile Selassie by Lush at a conference attended also by Sandford, Wingate and Nott, Nott recording that 'Addis was not yet safe for HIM to go there.' On this occasion Sandford and Wingate accepted the decision. The Emperor did not, nor the security reasons for it. To him all was quite simple. He had come back and wanted to resume his position as Emperor. Next day he informed Wingate that he intended to go forward to the capital and asked for 100 mule saddles. Wingate's reply is not recorded but he and Sandford must have persuaded the Emperor to be patient.

The Emperor cooperated to the full over the other matter raised by Lush at the conference, patriot support for the remaining operations against the Italians in which Cunningham was anxious that they should play a full part. Sandford returned with Lush to Addis Ababa to see Cunningham and discuss with him the Emperor's proposals. As a result Ababa Aregai was ordered to take over the Addis Ababa forts with his men and send 500 men to cooperate with the 1st South African Brigade at Dessie (these were the Shoan Patriots under Campbell who did take part in the attack), Gurassu Duke and his Patriots were ordered to cooperate with the 22nd East African Brigade in the southwest, and Kabada Tesemma was put in charge of Patriots in the Lechemti area west of Addis Ababa.

Nott flew to Addis Ababa on 13 April (noting the destruction of 'about 30 planes' on the airfield) bearing the Emperor's written orders to put these plans into effect with two officers to assist in their implementation, Lij Makonnen Desta, who had fought throughout with Mission 101 and Gideon Force, and Lij Asfau, and the promise of more officers to take over the forts by the next plane. Nott also reported on Gideon Force to Wetherall's HQ, commenting, 'one realized from there how small our little effort is in Gojjam — although it all fits into the picture.'

Nott returned to Debra Markos the same day while Lush put into effect the agreed security measures with great vigour with the help of British police and administrative officers. This involved, as Lush records, 'disarming and interning 12,000 armed Italians, enlisting and training 1000 Ethiopian police, arranging for the taking over of the forts by 1500 Ethiopian Patriots, and the removal of 5000 Italian civilians into safety zones.' Meanwhile the Emperor waited impatiently at Debra Markos where he was joined by his sons, the Crown Prince and the Duke of Harrar, the latter appointed governor of Harrar with Chapman-Andrews as his political adviser. On 19 April Nott invited the Emperor and his two sons to a drinks party attended by Wingate, Morrogh-Bernard, Benson, himself and Lieutenant Colonel Ben Tarleton, a visiting staff officer who later administered patriot forces under Sandford. Wingate's felicitous toast, made in 'champagne cocktails [captured]' and recorded by Nott in his diary, is worth preserving:

> I rise to propose the health of Your Majesty, which will be drunk in the wine of the discomfited aggressor. Myself and the British officers under my command have born their part with the patriot Ethiopian forces in this campaign in the knowledge that, in so doing, they were supporting that same cause for which England is fighting throughout the world. The right of the individual to liberty of conscience, the right of the small nation to a just decision at the tribunal of nations, these are the causes for which we fight. Until ETHIOPIA was liberated the major wrong, which brought in its train the present war, had not been righted and success for our arms could not be expected.

Wingate sadly did not survive the war. He died before the D-day landings in Europe and the defeat of the Japanese in Burma and did not see the victory of the Allies in the causes for which they were fighting. The generation who fought and did survive can look back 50 years and take pride that they did fight for these causes, so eloquently expressed by this remarkable man. Wingate could also relax. Two days later, on 21 April, when Sandford returned from Addis Ababa, Nott records, 'Orde and Dan had a big crack at night over glass of whisky. Orde and I stayed up late discussing matters and drinking innumerable brandies. Brilliant brain he has. He will be CIGS or I am a Dutchman.'

Sandford had flown back with a flight of seven South African Air Force planes sent to escort the Duke of Harrar to his new post as governor of Harrar (one Junkers, three Gladiators and three Hurricanes), and the 'crack at night' took place after a ceremonial parade at which Haile Selassie had conferred the ranks of lieutenant general on the Crown Prince, major general on the Duke of Harrar, and colonel on Asrate Kassa. The Gladiators of this flight shot down a lone Caproni that appeared on that day, possibly the plane that had dropped supplies on Maraventano. Two problems confronted Sandford on his return, both the result of blunders by the British, which upset the Emperor. The first was the appointment of Ras Seyum as governor of Tigre, approved by Mitchell, without reference to Haile Selassie. Sandford protested vigorously about this in a letter to Lush, insisting that it was vital for the Emperor's authority that the two leading collaborators, Ras Hailu and Ras Seyum, should make public submission to him in Addis Ababa. 'I have not mentioned the matter to HM yet as I know it will provoke a first-class explosion and I want to avoid this at the moment.'

The other was a BBC announcement reporting that Cunningham had told Aosta that unless the Italians surrendered he would not be responsible for their safety because he would not be able to hold back the Ethiopians from massacring them. 'The Emperor resents deeply such things being said by official British sources. He is quite confident that he can prevent any ... ill-treatment of Italians when he enters the capital.'

On the question of Haile Selassie's entry letters from both Sandford and Wingate survive showing that Sandford consistently urged that he should be allowed in earlier, that both tried to persuade him to accept the British commanders' reasons for the delay, and both in the end conceded that they could not hold him up any longer. Wingate writing to Sandford on 22 April, said:

> The Emperor sent for Morrogh-Bernard and myself this morning at 10 o'clock and a long discussion took place. ...

He is feverish and not really in a condition to work. He announced categorically that he intended to move on Thursday by mule and to proceed straight to Addis Ababa. After pointing out various difficulties there was nothing to do but acquiesce.

The rest of the letter deals with the security and operational aspects of the journey, which Wingate regarded as his concern and which depended in any event on the Emperor recovering from the malaria from which he was suffering.

Sandford wrote to Lush on the same day, 'The Emperor is determined to leave here on 24th and again I advise that he should not be stopped. I . . . hope that you will be able to work to the 1st May', and again on 26 April, 'The Emperor thinks you are all wrong in delaying his arrival. He does not believe in the dangers which the British authorities fear and thinks that any delay is dangerous to himself and the general military situation.'

It is quite clear that Wingate did not bring the Emperor into the capital against orders, nor did he ever claim to have done this. The security measures insisted on by Cunningham were completed by the end of April, and the date finally decided for the Emperor's entry was 5 May 1941, the fifth anniversary of the entry of Marshal Badoglio on 5 May 1936. The Emperor would be escorted by his bodyguard and the two battalions of Gideon Force, hence the summons to the Frontier Battalion to return from Mota.

The Emperor and his staff left Debra Markos on the morning of 27 April in two trucks with Wingate and Morrogh-Bernard, followed by Akavia in a 15-cwt truck escorting Ras Hailu, and arrived at the Abbai in the afternoon. There the Emperor joined the 2nd Ethiopian Battalion and the bodyguard who had marched on foot, covering the 72 miles in two and a half days, and camped with his troops. The Frontier Battalion left Debra Markos on 28 April, also on foot, with its camel and mule column moving more slowly behind. The pontoon bridge over the Abbai had been burned by Silvi's engineers when they left, and the road up the escarpment demolished, and Foley and le Blanc had completed a new bridge, observed by Nott when he crossed on 25 April, and were working on the escarpment. On the evening of 27 April le Blanc reported that the demolitions were just passable, and on 28 April the Emperor's trucks went through empty, driven in turn by le Blanc 'with great courage ... within a few inches of the precipice, inch by inch', as Tutton decribes. At one point they had to be hauled up an 'almost perpendicular slope' by 150 men of the 2nd Ethiopians with a long rope. The baggage was carried by the *askari* and the Emperor walked. Akavia recalls helping to carry the baggage and push the trucks, and how Ras Hailu 'saw me sweating in the heat and sent me a bottle of *tej* by a servant'.

Half way up the long escarpment Tutton, marching with his men, came across a group of 11 Italians, prisoners of the Patriots. He spoke Italian and learned from a Sicilian sergeant of the 13th Colonial Battalion that they had been in patriot hands for some time and had marched 200 kilometres. There are two points of historical interest in this small incident, first Tutton's comment in his diary, 'It is a sad sight to see white men, whatever their sins in the past, at the mercy of black men, especially wretches like the patriots.' The racial remark is historical, typical of young Britons of the time, and should not be considered offensive. The other point is that the Italians were prisoners and were still alive.

At the top of the escarpment the battalion was met by John Bagge, who had come out from Addis Ababa driving 'a fine Alfa Romeo', and Tutton, still weak from dysentery, was glad to accept the job of going back to the city with him to take over barrack accommodation for the force. The march of the rest continued on foot to Ficce where they were met by trucks and transported to Entoto, a fort in the hills above Addis Ababa, where they assembled in readiness for the march into the city on 5 May. Luyt describes the end of the journey.

> We are here at last! Through the efforts of others the final miles have been quick and safe, but we felt ... a thrill of pride as we looked down on the Abyssinian capital. We had done our little bit and 18 of our fellows lay in testimony near Dambacha and others elsewhere. ... We had arrived as we had set out to do with Gojjam conquered and the Emperor with us. ... The stage was set for a new era in Ethiopian history.

184

Lush had made Ababa Aregai, the great patriot leader who had kept the flame of resistance burning in Shoa since the Italian occupation, responsible for the Patriots in the capital during the Emperor's entry, and the 7000 men of his army were to line the streets to greet their Emperor — a wise choice, and, in Lush's words, 'he played his part magnificiently.' Tutton, while waiting with his battalion on the Ficce road, watched Ababa Aregai's army marching in.

> It was a real symbol of the old regime — there were thousands of them of all types in a motley collection of clothes, many ferocious looking men with huge mops of black hair standing out from their heads ... some of their leaders were gigantically fat and rode along on mules, which carried their weight with difficulty. There were decent looking men amongst them and I will say that they were quiet and well behaved. ... Ras Ababa's son, an urchin of about 12, in full patriot dress with rows of cartridges round his waist and a revolver, brought along a small squad of children of about the same age.

Horses were sent out from the city for Wingate and the battalion commanders to ride on the march. The Emperor decided to enter the city in an open touring car, driven by le Blanc and accompanied by Wetherall. Wingate was to lead, mounted, followed by D company 2nd Ethiopian Battalion under Luyt, then the Emperor's party, then the rest of the 2nd Ethiopian Battalion, the Frontier Battalion and the bodyguard. The press brought up the rear, travelling in the municipal fire engine, provided by Lush who took a chance that there would be no fire. The march started at midday along the Ficce road (today the Belai Zelleka road!) to the Old Ghibbi (the Old Palace) where Cunningham was waiting to greet the Emperor, the streets decorated with triumphal arches and lined with Ababa Aregai's Patriots and South African and Nigerian soldiers and enthusiastic crowds of Ethiopian 'men, women and children' (as Luyt describes) 'singing and wailing their own peculiar note. ... Flags, bunting and paint proclaimed the popularity of the royal green yellow and red, while one saw an occasional though usually misshapen Union Jack and several pathetic but courageous emblems of fallen Greece.'

After the two-hour march the Emperor entered the Old Ghibbi, as did Wingate who beckoned Akavia to follow, so he observed the ceremony. So also did the unrepentant Ras Hailu, who rode in one of the cars behind the Emperor. After Cunningham's greeting the Emperor made a long speech reviewing the events of the past five years, finishing with generous praise for the armies of generals Platt and Cunningham. The leaders then moved into the assembly hall, and, as Akavia records, there was a long delay while Ethiopian officials tried to sort out who should be admitted. 'In the end, the ceremony of the toast etc. took place without any other Ethiopians, except the Emperor and *Ras Hailu*, who somehow got himself admitted.' So Ras Hailu, the *enfant terrible* of Ethiopian politics, the most loyal supporter (until the last minute) of the Italian regime, ended up not in prison nor on the scaffold, but riding in the Emperor's triumphal procession, and the only Ethiopian notable present to drink the returning Emperor's health!

Haile Selassie was thus restored to his palace in the capital captured for him by Cunningham's South African and African forces while Platt's British, Indian and Sudanese troops had borne the brunt of the fighting in the north. It was fitting though that the Emperor should be accompanied by his own little army, Gideon Force, demonstrating the part it had played, and that the Patriots, who had kept the flame of resistance alight for four years, should line the route of his march. This was Wingate's day of glory, and rightly so. Sandford, in contrast, was merely one of a group of senior officers standing with Cunningham to greet the Emperor — not that he would have minded this in the least provided that his Patriots were represented in the parade, as they were. To Sandford, though, the return of the Emperor was the culmination of years of work, and the part played by him should not be forgotten.

In the photographs and in the documentary film of the march, *Lion of Judah*, Wingate can be seen leading the march, wearing his large sun helmet and riding his white horse rather uncomfortably in shorts. Behind him is the sturdy figure of Acting Captain Luyt, the South African Rhodes scholar and Oxford rugby football blue, dressed in KAR bush hat, khaki jersey and shorts, boots and puttees, and wearing webbing belt and revolver. Marching on his left was Akavia, a shorter man of similar build in khaki bush shirt and shorts and Bombay bowler, also with a holstered pistol but without insignia of rank, and behind them the Ethiopian officers and D company. Behind the Emperor's cortège was Benson on a white horse leading the rest of his battalion and behind him Tutton, marching very smartly like a guardsman despite his illness (this must have been a fearful effort for him) wearing Sam Browne belt and bush shirt. The officers were clean shaven, orders having been given, rather to Tutton's regret, that beards must come off before the march. Behind the Ethiopian battalion was Maxwell *Bey* wearing an *emma* (turban) at the head of the 'gallant SDF' (Luyt's words) riding a black charger. He would have preferred his faithful mule, who had carried him from the frontier, to the horse that 'took a dislike to the flowers in the street and pulled like a train'. Also in the pictures are the Patriots and the ruffianly group of junior Patriots under Ababa Aregai's son, showing off their weapons in mock battle, and the vast ululating crowd near the Old Ghibbi, interspersed with Nigerian soldiers and South African military policemen, standing smartly with sloped rifles and coming to the 'Present' as the Emperor passed. After the parade the Patriots dispersed peacefully to their camps outside the city and there were no incidents of any sort, confirming the correctness of the assurances given by the Emperor and Sandford.

Gideon Force's animal transport under Allen arrived at Entoto on 7 May and so missed the Emperor's parade. There, on Wingate's orders, the surviving 53 camels were shot. It was a hard order for Allen, who had nursed his camels across the Choke mountains to Mota and back and had set off from Debra Markos with 120 fit camels, but the order was clearly necessary. There was no food for camels at 8500 feet, the altitude of Addis Ababa. These were the survivors of 18,000 camels recruited in the Sudan and the force could not have moved without them, but the wastage of animal transport in the Gojjam campaign was appalling. Against the anxious world events of 1941 the fate of a few thousand camels may seem of small importance, but we should spare a thought for these great-hearted animals who made the Gojjam campaign possible. In Colonel Angus Buchanan's book on the Sahara there is a dedication, 'TO FERI N'GASHI. ONLY A CAMEL, BUT STEEL TRUE AND GREAT OF HEART.' If Gideon Force camels had a communal grave, it should bear some such epitaph.

Wingate did not dally in Addis Ababa and left on 9 May to join Safforce in the pursuit of Maraventano and was followed by Ras Kassa, who had obtained Haile Selassie's sanction to cross the Giamma and cooperate in the pursuit. On the way past Entoto Wingate saw Allen who asked if he could go with him with the fitter mules. Wingate declined, saying that the mules had done enough, so Allen missed the last stage of the campaign, much to his regret and to posterity's loss. He would have added a splendid last chapter to his book. The Frontier Battalion under Maxwell left on 7 May for Dessie to relieve the 1st South African Brigade, ordered to Amba Alagi and then North Africa. The 2nd Ethiopian Battalion took over barracks in Addis Ababa. This was the beginning of the end for Gideon Force, save for Safforce, to whom we must now return.

La Colonna Maraventano: The End of the Odyssey*

We left Nott and Maraventano about to confront each other at Deraa. Maraventano had disposed of his forces with the two colonial brigades on the edge of the plateau facing south and west, a central reserve under his control, and a Blackshirt company in the fort. Nott reached the foot of the Deraa escarpment at 10.15 a.m. on 29 April and got his small force onto the escarpment by a classic piece of deception. He sent Rowe forward after dark to light bogus camp fires and keep them going until dawn, 'lay low on April 30 and quietly chuckled' while the enemy shelled the bogus camp, and in the evening sent two patrols to the spurs facing them, one under Sergeant Howell and the other under Naylor and Sergeant Goode. Naylor's patrol climbed the escarpment with difficulty in the dark and shot up the Italian positions with light machine-gun fire. They were counterattacked, and 'Goode did well' holding up the pursuers with his Hotchkiss to enable the patrol to escape.

Meanwhile Nott, having feinted against the enemy left, moved

---

* See Sketch 5.

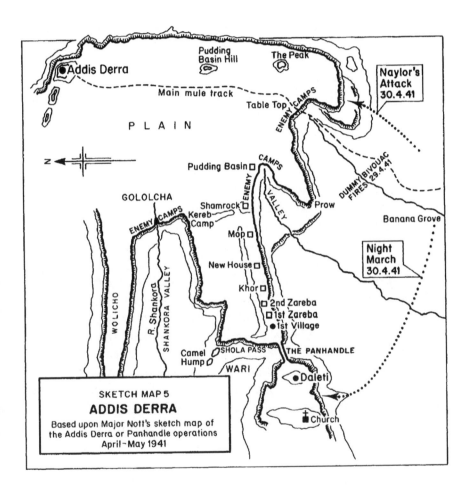

Addis Derra

Pudding Basin Hill

The Peak

Naylor's Attack 30.4.41

Main mule track

Table Top

ENEMY CAMPS

P L A I N

Z

Pudding Basin

CAMPS

ENEMY

VALLEY

Shamrock

Prow

DUMMY BIVOUAC FIRES 29.4.41

GOLOLCHA

ENEMY CAMPS

Kereb Camp

Mop

Banana Grove

Night March 30.4.41

New House

WOLICHO

R. Shankora

SHANKORA VALLEY

Khor

2nd Zareba

1st Zareba

1st Village

Camel Hump

SHOLA PASS

THE PANHANDLE

WARI

Daleti

SKETCH MAP 5
ADDIS DERRA
Based upon Major Nott's sketch map of
the Addis Derra or Panhandle operations
April~May 1941

Church

189

the rest of his force against their right by a difficult march across broken country, scaled the cliff in the early hours, and was established on the top at Daleti by sunrise on 1 May. His force then took up defensive positions with a Coptic church behind and overlooking a causeway or panhandle, which divided them from the Italian positions. Their climb was unopposed, but they lost a horse over the cliff with its load of a Bren gun, a loss they could ill afford. Thesiger went over the causeway with his *banda* and clashed with an enemy *banda* patrol, wounding two and killing one, 'which they brought into camp on two poles — like a leopard.' Nott 'signalled' Wingate reporting his position and asked for aerial support; there was no air support then or afterwards. Without wireless telegraphy Nott had to send a runner to Ficce from where the message would be transmitted by wireless telegraphy to 'Affidavit', the Emperor's wireless set, on the march between Debra Markos and Addis Ababa, and after 5 May in Addis Ababa.

On 2 May Nott, the regular soldier, applied his training to improving his defences, camouflaging his seven remaining Bren light machine guns and insisting that the Sudanese Bren gunners made out range cards, and siting the Vickers medium machine gun of the Ethiopian platoon below the crest, like Wellington siting his batteries at Torres Vedras. These precautions paid dividends next day. Naylor arrived with his centre, having been delayed by a bad attack of malaria, and was placed in reserve near the church, so Nott had his force complete. On the evening of 2 May Nott and Thesiger led a bombing and mortaring raid on the Italian positions, while a local patriot leader who had joined them, Basha Talam Worq, carried out a night attack causing casualties.

Nott's presence on the plateau ('numerous Sudanese troops commanded by English officers') was reported on the afternoon of 2 May to Maraventano who ordered Nuovo to 'carry out a probing attack at dawn on 3 May to determine the strength of the enemy'. Otherwise Maraventano concerned himself with establishing his defences, set up a political office under Lancia and sent out patrols to inform the locals of the reoccupation of Deraa and to purchase food. These brought back reports that 'rebels' were converging, that Ras Kassa had threatened death against anyone supplying food to the column, and that the locals ran when they saw the *ascari.* Nonetheless Maraventano was clearly then contemplating a lengthy stay. In a long signal of 2 May to Frusci, then with the viceroy at Amba Alagi, he proposed to make Deraa a firm base 'and await events and the end of the long rains [September–October]. Pray approve.' He received no reply to this signal. Medical problems also engaged his attention, in particular an outbreak of dysentery, which was causing up to 100 men to report sick daily. The doctors lacked medicines and had to improvise, and a concoction was prepared from the aloe plant by one of Silvi's officers 'who had a degree in pure chemistry', which gave some relief. They also had insufficient bandages for the many wounded. 'To provide these the officers gave up their sheets.' Nott and Thesiger, living in shirt and shorts, sharing a small bivouac tent and sleeping on the ground, would have been amused to learn that their adversaries slept in sheets.

On 3 May Nuovo carried out his probing attack, described by Nott as 'the most thrilling day of my life'. He had a force of battalion strength, supported by sections of heavy machine guns and 65-millimetre guns — about 750 rifles against Nott's 70 or 80 actually engaged — under the command of Major Comito, commander of the 23rd Colonial Battalion. Nott was in his camp interviewing the chief Muslim sheikh of Borena when he heard his Brens open up at 8.30 a.m. and a messenger reported the attack. Ordering the camp to be struck and the animals taken to the Coptic church, Nott ran forward to find the attack in progress. He had 40 Sudanese in the firing line with seven Brens, Rowe with his Vickers medium machine gun behind, and Thesiger and his *banda* joining in the defence. The Italians had advanced onto the panhandle and, not seeing any opposition, had come forward with their machine guns on mules. The Sudanese held their fire until they were within 300 yards and caught them by surprise. 'However, their attack was determined inspite of the withering fire from our MGs. Those that got down tried to work up to our position and round our flanks. One got killed by a Mills bomb just below our central guns.' The enemy kept up a 'continuous MG fire and very accurate shell fire but were forced to withdraw at 12.30 leaving considerable dead on the field. Our casualties one killed two wounded.' Johnson described the action as 'quite a battle.

That was a close run thing' (a typically Johnsonian understatement) and praised his company sergeant major, Musa, who was awarded the Military Medal. Nott reported to Wingate that 'Sudanese troops very steady in face of heavy MG and arty fire and heavily outnumbered.' Maraventano also praised his troops, 'particularly 2nd company of XXIII battalion...who pressed forward to the closest quarters with superb courage and dash... and III brigade HQ platoon under Ten. Cosentoni.' Italian casualties were one officer wounded, 19 *ascari* killed and 53 wounded, a heavy loss for a small action. Italian estimates of Nott's force were wildly out, 'about 1000, of whom 700 were Sudanese with 20 automatic weapons'. As at the Charaka river the colonial troops and regimental officers showed great bravery in pressing the attack, but the leadership was inept, battering away frontally when an outflanking movement would have forced Nott to withdraw.

The immediate effect of the action for Nott was to improve his standing with the locals, 'who have swarmed in with gifts of cattle, sheep, eggs, *tej*, honey, bread and bananas. Several have offered to fight for us.' Expecting further attack Nott had his force standing to at 4.00 a.m. on 4 May (35 minutes before first light at 4.35 a.m.) and continued this practice daily. On 5 May, the day of Haile Selassie's triumphal entry into Addis Ababa, he received a reply from Wingate to his message of 1 May, 'Have requested air action — hope to send you reinforcements 4/5 — organizing patriot support. Well done to date. Follow up.' Nott replied asking for his interpreter Johannes to be sent up, for a wireless telegraphy set, and again for aerial support. He continued active patrolling — Thesiger had to 'leg it to avoid being cut off by enemy cavalry' — noted that the enemy were digging in suggesting a long stay, and that 'it's going to be a hard nut to crack by irregular tps without arty support', but reconnoitred the enemy positions with a view to attacks when reinforcements arrived. Through the local Muslim sheikh he tried to persuade the Muslim *ascari* that they were backing a lost cause, and to counter the 'widely believed rumour that Germany is going to win the war and Italy will be back shortly'.

Maraventano did not accept that his cause was lost, nor did his *ascari* 'allow the propaganda inviting them to desert, or the loss of Dessie, to affect them or to shake their faith in a final victory which would ... drive away the English and the *Negus* from the Empire. With such troops I could look forward to the future with confidence.' The bulk of his colonial troops did remain loyal though he had a few desertions, recording eight Shoans, one Eritrean *graduato* (the first and last) and one national engineer, and Nott obtained useful intelligence from a Tigrean *ascari* and a *carabiniere*. Maraventano had to concede that the political and military situation was deteriorating rapidly although he still believed on 4 May that the correct course of action was for all outlying garrisons to withdraw on Deraa and suggested this to Colonel Anderson, formerly sector commander and *commissario* at Dessie, and now at Magdala Tanta.

The country north of Deraa was a vast highland plateau broken by many tributaries of the Abbai to the west, roadless and traversed only by mule tracks. Four days' march (about 100 kilometres) north of Deraa was Debra Sina or Agibar, which still had an Italian garrison, as did Tanta, 300 kilometres further north, near Theodore's old capital of Magdala. The region was largely populated by Muslim Galla people who had supported the Italian government but that support was beginning to fall away now that the Italians were losing.

On 6 May Maraventano received a request from Anderson to send two battalions to relieve Tanta, which was under siege by 'rebels', and although concerned that this force would have a difficult 300-kilometre march beyond Debra Sina through 'rebel' infested country he agreed that it was right to try to relieve Tanta and sent off Calvi with the 13th and 65th Battalions with a mortar section of the 37th Battery. The *ascaris*' families, sick and wounded, and surplus animals of these units remained with the main column. Anderson disagreed with Maraventano's suggestion for withdrawal on Deraa and proposed instead that the final bastion should be Uorrailu. Maraventano argued that although his column was strong enough to resist attacks at Deraa, it was not suitable for movement over difficult country because of his mass of 'impedimenta', and signalled High Command at Amba Alagi asking for a directive and liberty of action. He was told, unhelpfully, by Aosta's chief of staff, General Trezzani, 'You are answerable to Anderson who will give the required directive.' Amba Alagi was already under attack but the shifting of responsibility for the Maraventano column was feeble and the result was that Maraventano was without orders until after the fall of Amba Alagi on 19 May when he came under General Nasi at Gondar who was more helpful. Anderson's intervention lost Maraventano two good battalions and led to the withdrawal of the column from Deraa and its eventual surrender.

Meanwhile Nott was beginning to receive more patriot support and by 10 May had 500 armed Patriots willing to fight. He organized them in raids and attacks on the enemy's flanks and, with his own patrols, in ambushing foraging parties. In addition to Basha Talam the patriot leaders were Balambaras Hapte Mariam, his brother Bezabe Banjo, Fitaurari Kibra Selassie and Kenyasmatch Redda. There were problems over food; they lived mainly on boiled chicken with *wat* sauce, highly spiced, and eggs, 'once Wilfred and I ate 24 eggs for breakfast with bananas and honey.' They all had lice and it was now raining nearly every night and very cold. On 8 May Nott sent off a mule convoy to Cuiu to collect mortar bombs, dollars (to pay the Patriots) and 'sandals for the poor Sudanese who have been marching barefooted over these bloody stony wastes'. He had asked for sandals when he took over the force on 26 April but none had been sent. Surely a plane could have been found to drop supplies. The Italians managed it so long as they had any planes left.

On 11 May it rained all day and there were no operations, but from 12 to 14 May there was intense activity by Safforce and Patiots, recorded by Maraventano as 'repeated attempts by the enemy to infiltrate our lines with battalions supported by automatic weapons — always promptly driven back.' On 12 May Riley got to within 50 yards of Shamrock with three Brens under cover of mist and 'belted the tents. Italians came streaming out into their trenches, quite a number were bowled over. They opened up with MGs. Riley slipped away in the mist.' Meanwhile Patriots attacked on both flanks. In the Shankora valley Hapte Mariam was counterattacked by a colonial battalion with artillery but stood firm supported by Rowe with his platoon who 'did some good shooting with his MG.' Nott reported the day's events to Wingate (he had received a wireless telegraphy set on 11 May), adding, 'believed two bns enemy left for Debra Sina where rest of force expected go shortly.' On the evening of 12 May in rain and bitter cold Nott took Thesiger, Riley, Rowe and Naylor on a 'recce of the enemy's positions so that they would have a clear picture of the attack, which I am planning for the near future'.

Nott was right that two battalions had left, but wrong in believing that Maraventano on 12 May was contemplating moving with the whole column to Debra Sina. This decision was forced on him on 13 May by a signal from Calvi reporting that the *ascari* of his column, after an hour's march from Debra Sina, had halted and refused to go forward without their families who had remained at Deraa. Maraventano replied that he would move with his entire column on Debra Sina on the morning of 15 May and from there march to relieve Tanta with his whole force including the Calvi column. The only way he could prevent the disintegration of the two battalions was to join them with the column, restoring their families to them, and embark on an expedition of rescue for which his large and unwieldy column was, as he himself had said, totally unsuited. On the afternoon of 13 May he gave orders to unit commanders to be ready to move on 15 May 'all ranks to carry 5 days' cereal ration, if possible reduced to flour'.

On 13 May Patriots again attacked up the Shankora valley and patrols led by Naylor and Sergeants Howell and Lewis bombarded Italian positions. On the morning of 14 May Nott received a note from Wingate to say that he was on his way, and went to meet him at the Coptic church. Wingate had marched without pause since leaving Addis Ababa on 9 May. He brought with him Akavia, Johannes, a Sudanese section, a wireless set, and the news that Ras Kassa was close behind him with 1200 Patriots. Nott took him round the forward positions and briefed him on the situation, noting in his diary, 'Though pleased to have him commanding I must admit that I would have liked to see the showdown now that we have sufficient tps to take the enemy on.' Wingate's arrival has been described by his biographer, Sykes, as 'throwing his own fire into the dispirited force . . . a fitting prelude to his most spectacular achievement in Ethiopia.' Thesiger and Nott both agree that Wingate's arrival, with the strong reinforcement of Ras Kassa and his men, and his greater authority as commander of the Anglo-

Ethiopian forces under the Emperor, made an enormous difference. Also the fact that a full colonel was now commanding against him, soon known to Maraventano, probably persuaded the Italian commander to believe that Wingate's forces were larger than they actually were. Nott does not agree that they were a dispirited force, and indeed the evidence is that this was not the case and that morale was excellent with the force increasing in confidence and numbers. Johnson had a more mundane recollection of Wingate's arrival. Hayes, his second-in-command, had tried to send some champagne by Wingate, but Wingate refused to take it saying, 'Johnson can have beer', and had brought a few bottles for the British officers and NCOs. He also brought two mule loads of Italian tinned meat for the troops, but since they were marked with the Christian Coptic Cross they were no good to the Muslim Sudanese who, in Thesiger's words, 'threw them down in disgust'. They must have been welcome to the Christian Ethiopians but Wingate, who had commanded a Sudanese company, should have known better.

As to the rounding up of the Maraventano column, this was certainly a great achievement, but for the third time in this campaign Wingate was incredibly lucky. Torelli withdrew from Dangila and Engiabara on orders just before Wingate climbed the escarpment into Gojjam; Maraventano was ordered to evacuate Gojjam before Wingate forced him out, and now has had to leave the strong position of Deraa to save his two battalions.

Nott and his small force, half Sudanese and half Ethiopian, deserve high praise for the Deraa operations. It was miserably cold at the altitude of Deraa (about 9200 feet), with the long rains starting. All ranks were in tropical kit with one blanket and one groundsheet, used as a bivouac. Many were barefoot until sandals arrived and without proper rations, living largely off the country. There was not a word of complaint, and in these conditions against a greatly superior enemy the performance of all ranks was remarkable.

On other fronts Aosta at Amba Alagi was under attack by the 5th Indian Division and the 1st South African Brigade. In the southwest operations against the strong Italian forces under General Gazzera were continuing, the 11th African Division advancing southwest from Addis Ababa supported by Gurassu Duke's Patriots, and the 12th African Division advancing from the south, also supported by Ethiopian irregulars and by Belgian African forces further west. On 3 May, the day of Nott's exciting day at Deraa, two companies of the 5th KAR stormed the Italian position at Fike in the lakes in a classic bayonet charge, a brisk action, which gave the Italians a healthy respect for the KAR and deterred the local commander, General Bertelli, from a counterattack he was planning. On 11 May the 5th KAR suffered a reverse when counterattacked by Italian medium tanks at Bubissa, but on 19 May at Golito Sergeant Nigel Leakey, a Kenya-born sergeant serving with the 6th KAR, showed how to deal with tanks by climbing onto one and shooting the occupants with his revolver. He was killed attempting a second tank and awarded a posthumous VC, the second won by East African forces in the Second World War. On 10 May the 24th Gold Coast Brigade of the 12th African Division captured the strong position of Uaddara after a hard 21-day battle, and on 22 May the two divisions met at Uondo ready for the next stage of the operations, the crossing of the Omo river and the capture of Gimma. The operations in the southwest have usually been dismissed as mopping-up operations, but in fact there were some considerable actions and occasions when the Italians resisted with bravery and tenacity.

Elsewhere the war was not going well for the Allies. The German grip on the Balkans was now complete and British intelligence reported the build-up of troops on the Russian frontier. By the end of May 1941 Crete had been evacuated and in North Africa Rommel's forces had reached the Egyptian frontier and Wavell's army was back where it had been before the victory against the Italians, save for Tobruk, which still held out. It is not surprising that rumours had reached the Deraa tribesmen that Germany was winning the war. The German threat to the east would only be stemmed in Syria, where the Vichy French would be defeated, and Iraq, where Rashid Ali's pro-Axis revolt was thwarted.

Against the background of these weighty events the end of the Maraventano column will be described. Safforce played its part but the main casualties in the final actions were suffered by the Patriots, mainly Ras Kassa's Shoans, fighting against Shoan and

Tigrean *ascari* under the Italian flag, both sides with equal courage. It was fitting that Ras Kassa, who had fought as a boy at Adowa in 1896, with Ras Tafari against Negus Mikael at Sagale (not far from the route of the column) in 1916, and had commanded the northern armies against the Italians in 1936, should have been present in this last battle.

On the evening of 14 May Maraventano confirmed his orders for the column to move on the night of 15/16 May. He had received intelligence that 'an English colonel and armed irregulars commanded by Ras Kassa' were now on Deraa. His intention was to march to Debra Sina, collect the Calvi column, which was halted six miles beyond it, and go on to relieve Tanta. In the event Tanta surrendered on 19 May, as did Amba Alagi, so his objective was limited to reaching Debra Sina. This in itself was a formidable undertaking for his unwieldy column, involving a 100-kilometre march along a rough mule track and crossing two deep gorges, the rivers Boto and Jescium.

Wingate's intention was to enforce the surrender of the column, an intention Cunningham's HQ did its best to frustrate by an extraordinary signal, which Wingate received on 15 May. By this Wingate was ordered to proceed to Debra Tabor to join Boustead, Nott to report to Addis Ababa for other duties, and Johnson to break off the engagement and proceed to Dessie to reinforce the SDF garrison there. Wingate replied asking for the message to be repeated, and when it was, in the same form, he dictated to Akavia a long appreciation to be signalled, assuring Cunningham that he could put Maraventano out of action within ten days. The reply to this was that he must obey orders, to which Wingate responded by referring to his previous signal and closing down his set. All one can say about this episode is that it shows Cunningham's HQ to have been totally out of touch, and Wingate's Nelsonian response justified by events. He was never in fact taken to task for this insubordination.

Maraventano's column left the plateau as ordered, the advance party leaving at 11.30 p.m. on 15 May and the rearguard leaving Deraa Fort at 11.30 a.m. on 16 May. Rumours of the enemy moving reached Wingate and Nott on the morning of 16 May. Rowe was sent to reconnoitre, found the enemy had left the villages, and went on with Naylor and Hapte Mariam to the fort, which they reached just after the rearguard had left. Wingate 'leapt on his horse and ordered a general advance', and Nott mobilized Ras Kassa and his men and brought them along, reaching the fort at 4.00 p.m., 'finding it on a cliff, one of the most inaccessible places I have ever seen. They could have held it until the cows came home.' Later, at the surrender, Wingate told Silvi that the Italians must have been mad to give up Deraa.

Wingate, Nott and Ras Kassa spent the night of 16/17 May in the fort while the Italian column streamed down towards the Boto river, crossing at dawn on 17 May. From the fort they heard firing as Patriots attacked. At 9.00 p.m. Wingate sent for Thesiger and ordered him, in Thesiger's words, 'to leave at once and march without stopping until you get in front of the Italians, then engage them and make sure you inflict at least 200 casualties.' He himself would follow the column and attack from the rear. Thesiger took his orderly, Muhammad, nine *banda*, Rowe and No 9 platoon, five sergeants and 55 *askari* of the two centres and 300 Patriots under three leaders, Ayalou, Makonnen and Birru. The senior NCO in No 9 platoon was Corporal Wandafrash, who had knocked out the armoured cars at the Charaka river. They carried two days' rations and took no baggage animals and for this reason Rowe's Vickers was left behind. Each man carried a rifle and the force numbered about 400 rifles. They had one Hotchkiss light machine gun, carried by the British sergeants, and some Mills grenades (see Sketch 6).

Thesiger led his force down the escarpment to the east of Deraa during the night of 16/17 May, arriving at the bottom at dawn on 17 May, and followed the valley northwards with the Ciacata plateau on his left. They were sniped at by Muslim Galla tribesmen from the cliff tops, formerly pro-Italian, now waiting to see who would win. In the late afternoon they reached a point in the valley due east of the *banda* fort of Uogghidi and learned from Ayalou that there was a guard post on top of the escarpment. At dawn on 18 May they climbed the cliff and Thesiger and Rowe went ahead and surprised the guard post, finding an old man and his five sons asleep. They learned from the old man that another of his sons was with the 1200 *banda* in the Uogghidi fort and Thesiger told him

199

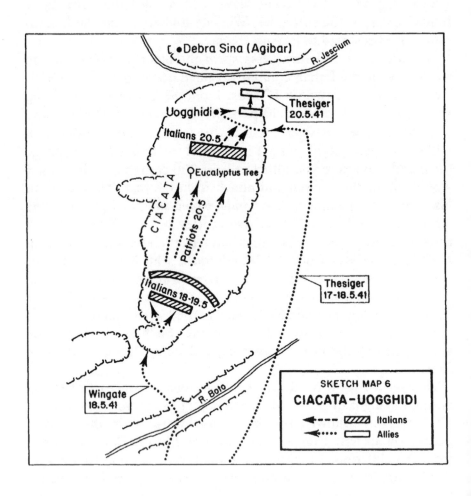

SKETCH MAP 6
CIACATA-UOGGHIDI

that the Emperor was now back on his throne and behind them was a great army and he should go at once to the fort and 'advise the *banda* to escape before it was too late'. The old man went off and Thesiger and his men spent the day of 18 May lazing in the sun, pleasant at that altitude of over 9000 feet. After dark a rocket went up from the fort and the old man returned to report that the *banda* had deserted and the fort was empty. On the morning of 19 May Thesiger occupied Uogghidi. As ordered by Wingate he had placed himself ahead of the Italian column and astride their line of march to Debra Sina.

By dawn on 18 May the Italian column was established on the Ciacata plateau, with the 3rd Colonial Brigade facing towards Deraa, after a long hard march from the Boto river (described by Maraventano as the 'Via Crucis'). At 7.00 a.m. the commander of the 3rd Brigade, Nuovo, reported 'several thousand' enemy advancing in attack formation, including a Sudanese unit. He opened fire with his battery, 'causing confusion without impeding the advance'. This was Wingate's force with Ras Kassa's 1200 rifles, which had set off in pursuit of the column on the morning of 17 May, climbing onto the Ciacata plateau at dawn on 18 May. After leaving the Boto river Nott records, 'No water to drink but one of Kassa's men gave me a bottle of dry champagne.' Johnson recalled the shell fire, 'The first salvo went over, the second fell short. We ran forward and avoided their third salvo.' Nott records:

> We saw clearly the enemy's masses. . . . Johnson's boys were sent forward to feel round the left flank and also 300 picked patriots, who all advanced steadily in open formation in the face of heavy MG and Arty fire. . . . Our HQ, where Wingate, Kassa and I were [having built *sangars*], were heavily shelled. Our forces unable to pass the wall of MG fire.

Other patriot forces advanced against the right flank but were held up by heavy machine-gun fire. Johnson's Sudanese were withdrawn in the evening having suffered losses of one killed and three wounded. Company Sergeant Major Musa again distinguished himself, bringing forward ammunition under fire and taking the wounded to safety. Patriot losses were 40 killed and 100 wounded, and the survivors of the 300 Patriots on the left flank 'who had crept forward to within a short distance of the enemy MGs, could not be extricated, and remained there until the enemy retired two days' later.' Maraventano confirms the facts of the British accounts. The patriot attacks were repelled by the 3rd Brigade without calling on reserves, that on the left flank being driven back by a counterattack by the 23rd Battalion in which 'Tenente Genovese, Adjutant Major of the battalion, met a glorious death.' After firing ceased at 5.00 p.m. the Anglo-Ethiopians buried their dead and recovered their wounded from close to their lines, but many had to lie out and 'their groans and cries for help' were heard by the Italians. Maraventano records his own casualties as one officer and 32 *ascari* killed and 78 *ascari* wounded, puts the enemy numbers at 4000, and concludes, 'the glorious victory had caused a fearful void in ammunition of all arms; that was the bitter note of that splendid day.'

Wingate withdrew his force two miles for the night as a security measure. His forces had been unable to cross the 'wall of fire' and had suffered more severely than the defenders, but the Patriots were quite ready to resume action next day, as the *ascari* were to receive them. On 19 May the Patriots renewed their attack while the SDF were rested. The Italians replied with machine-gun and artillery fire, and 'Wingate prepared a letter demanding surrender.' Nott noted the difficulties of operating with patriot forces who, although extremely brave, had their own way of doing things. On 18 May he had had to quell fighting between two tribes of Ras Kassa's men waiting to go into action, and on 19 May found that the patriot leader covering their front had only one man in the line of *sangars*. 'The rest of his men were half a mile away in a village having breakfast!' Johnson, watching the battle while his men rested, remembered Ras Kassa, 'a very respectable old gentleman, charming manners. ... He sat on his shooting stick like an English country gentleman watching a pheasant drive.'

Maraventano had received reports from *ascari* sent out in plain clothes exaggerating the strength of the Allied forces. Ras Kassa was reported to have 15,000 men, Thesiger at Uogghidi 500 Sudanese and 3000 'rebels', the almost mythical Belai Zelleka was coming with 4000 men. Calvi signalled that Debra Sina was besieged by 'rebels' who had been joined by the deserting *banda* from Uogghidi. Maraventano saw his own situation as extremely grave because of the reported strength of the enemy and the shortage of ammunition and supplies, particularly 'the total lack of medicines and bandages for his 1200 wounded of whom 500 were serious cases'. He decided, after a personal reconnaissance with half the cavalry, to retake Uogghidi with the main column and join Calvi at the Jescium river after Calvi had relieved Debra Sina, hoping to find at Debra Sina the supplies he needed. He gave out orders to this effect at 5.00 p.m. on 19 May and signalled his intentions to General Nasi at Gondar. So the stage was set for the decisive battle on 20 May.

Maraventano started his march from Ciacata at dawn on 20 May, the 3rd Brigade breaking off contact with the Patriots and passing through the 19th Brigade, which became the rearguard. In the advance guard under Major Torielli were the cavalry and mounted *banda* and the training battalion. Making an early reconnaissance Wingate and Nott discovered that the Italians were withdrawing. 'Orde ordered a general advance. ... The Patriots were already following up.' Wingate kept the Sudanese and mortar section in reserve in case of counterattack, and, as Akavia describes, a 'running fight ensued, conducted entirely by patriot forces, who ... displayed great courage and frequently ran in among the enemy's troops,' pressing home their attacks and suffering many casualties from enemy machine guns in the open plain.

Meanwhile Thesiger in Uogghidi had been warned by his scouts of the approach of the advance guard, and, not wishing to be penned up in the fort, moved his force to a low ridge near the edge of the plateau. As they took up their positions they saw 'the Italians advancing across the plain in dense formation'. The Italians then halted and opened with artillery fire; the first shell landed near Thesiger and knocked him over and he received a shrapnel wound in the right leg. The infantry then attacked, but the combined fire of Thesiger's 400 rifles and the British sergeants' one Hotchkiss light machine gun (described by Thesiger as 'a First World War weapon, often unreliable, which on this occasion did us well'), brought the attack to a halt. Maraventano believed that Thesiger's force had 'numerous automatic weapons arranged in emplacements'.

This attack was followed by a cavalry charge at about 10.30 a.m. led by Tenente Luigi Fiorilli, which Thesiger dismisses as 'rather a half-hearted charge by native cavalry', but which in fact was pressed closely to grenade throwing range and Thesiger acknowledges that it was the British sergeants, Goode, Lewis, Bartlett and Cannon, and the Australian Howell who were the mainstay of the defence. They stopped the cavalry with the Hotchkiss and drove them off with Mills grenades. The trouble taken by the adjutant of the 1st Beds & Herts Regiment to select good men for No 3 Centre paid off on this day and without them Thesiger would have been in difficulty. Thesiger remembers Cannon, who was also wounded by a shell splinter, as a particularly good man to have with him. Goode and Cannon were recommended for the Military Medal by Wingate, but the awards were not made.

In 'this happy episode' (*'questo felice episodio'* — Maraventano's description) Tenente Fiorilli 'fell gloriously' and also killed were several troopers and 20 horses, but the charge had an effect, scattering the Patriots who retreated in some confusion. Fearing that his force would be surrounded Thesiger decided to withdraw northwards to a second ridge, which formed the northeast corner of the plateau overlooking the Jescium river gorge, 'hobbling back' supported by Muhammad. There he stood firm, and 'beyond shelling' the Italians left them alone. In the withdrawal Rowe, who was suffering badly from blistered feet, could not keep up with his men and told them to go ahead and followed slowly, turning round from time to time to fire his weapon at the pursuing enemy. While thus retreating he was shot through the base of the heart and left for dead. He was, however, only severely wounded and was taken prisoner by Italian *ascari*. This was the end of the road for Captain Rowe of the KAR Reserve ('Jiggsa'), described by Nott as 'rough, tough and brave', who had marched on his feet since crossing the frontier at Um Idla on 20 January and whose feet had been giving him trouble as far back as Jigga (4 March) but who had gone on without complaint or rest. Two other men died in his platoon, Rifleman Haile Abatu and Corporal Wandafrash Falaka, who had behaved with such gallantry at the Charaka river and who again, in the words of the battalion war diary, 'showed considerable courage and devotion to duty'.

Thesiger also lost about 30 Patriots killed or missing, and six killed and 15 wounded from the two centres. Although he had had to retreat in the face of the first attack, he had held the second ridge, effectively blocking Maraventano's route to Debra Sina as ordered by Wingate. As to whether he had carried out the second part of Wingate's orders (to inflict at least 200 casualties), 'when I eventually rejoined Wingate, he said with his grim smile, "Well, you got your 200, indeed rather more, I think".'

Meanwhile Maraventano had reoccupied Uogghidi and at 2.30 p.m. launched two battalions, the 72nd and the 21st, in a counter-attack against Ras Kassa's Patriots who were pressing his rearguard closely. According to Rossini, 'The enemy attacked bravely and came up close. We fired with our guns into the multitude but they still came on. LXXII drove them back;' and Vallisneri of the 72nd, 'We drove the enemy back for six kilometres and captured many mules. I had to restrain my *ascari*.' Whether the counterattack went quite so far is doubtful. Certainly by 4.00 p.m. firing had died down and Akavia records that when Wingate went forward to reconnoitre, 'Maraventano's 7000 fighting men were being contained on the south side by 1500 Patriots, 35 Sudanese and the Mortar Section, and on the north by Thesiger's 400.' Italian casualties for the day were one officer and 12 *ascari* killed, three officers and 165 *ascari* wounded, 20 horses and eight mules killed or wounded. Maraventano again claims a victory 'against forces three times our number and aggressive'. Nott records the Patriot casualties on the south sides as 'several hundred'. This was a considerable engagement and the over-estimation by Maraventano of the numbers against him illustrates the intensity of the patriot attacks.

On the afternoon of 20 May Wingate had sent to Maraventano a letter informing him of the surrender of Aosta at Amba Alagi on 19 May and giving him 24 hours in which to decide whether to surrender, saying that he had orders to withdraw all British personnel and leave the conduct of operations to the Patriots. Maraventano replied that he would resist to the last cartridge and sent to General Nasi at Gondar a long appreciation of his situation with a copy of Wingate's letter, concluding that there was grave anxiety for the 500 stretcher cases, the political situation was without hope, and to continue resistance he needed ammunition and medical supplies. Nasi had four aircraft and was continuing to supply Wolchefit and Debra Tabor from the air, but evidently decided against attempting a supply drop on Uogghidi, a much longer flight. He replied on 21 May, 'decide according to conscience and tradition how you think best.'

Maraventano called a council of war of all senior officers down to battalion and squadron level to decide whether to surrender on terms or fight on. The delegates unanimously agreed that further resistance was impossible, 'but they trusted themselves to my decision'. Maraventano lamented having to surrender to an enemy 'I had constantly beaten ... to avoid the extermination of my brave soldiers and their families by the rebels when the control of the English had been taken away.' Wingate meanwhile had called off hostilities and sent, as Nott records, 'another stronger letter ... demanding instant surrender or he would take away the whites and leave the Patriots to finish it off. As the Patriots had damn all ammunition left it was a superb bit of bluff.' Maraventano's reply, that he had authority to submit on honourable terms, reached Wingate at 6.00 p.m. on 21 May, and arrangements were agreed for a meeting of delegates next day to discuss terms.

On 22 May Major Nott, representing Colonel Wingate, met Lieutenant Colonel Nuovo, representing Colonel Maraventano, who came forward under a white flag with interpreter Captain Daverio escorted by an Italian sergeant and 12 cavalrymen. The meeting, held at a eucalyptus tree on the plateau, lasted two hours and the following terms were agreed:

- Honours of war to be conceded.
- Colonial troops to be discharged to their homes.
- Sick and wounded to be evacuated to Addis Ababa.
- Until arrival at Ficce all officers, national troops and 500 colonial troops to be left with their arms, 'in recognition of their valour shown'.
- Safety of column guaranteed until arrival at POW camp in Addis Ababa.
- The same terms to apply to Debra Sina.

Nott conceded the right to carry arms to the nationals for security against possible patriot attack on the way back, and to the 500 colonial troops 'as a token of their gallantry'. Conceding honours of war meant a guard of honour for Maraventano, at least a company strong. 'As our total regular troops were only a platoon or so the joke was too good to miss. I replied [to Colonel Nuovo] with a straight face that a suitable guard would be there.' When Nott went back to report to Wingate, 'he was furious about the Italians and colonial troops being armed but later agreed that it was perhaps the best thing to do.' It is evident from all Italian accounts of the campaign that the concession of honours of war and the right to bear arms were of immense psychological and historical importance and enabled the Italians to salvage some pride from their defeat in the campaign. After Nott had reported, Wingate sent Riley with an Italian lieutenant to Thesiger with news of the agreement and orders to proceed straight to Debra Sina and enforce the surrender of that garrison.

The day 23 May started badly with a series of explosions from the Italian lines, the *ascari* throwing away their hand grenades. Wingate sent Lij Yohannes, Ras Kassa's liaison officer, at the gallop to tell Maraventano that he would order a general advance if the destruction of war material did not stop. Maraventano replied that he was coming at once to the place of surrender with his staff (this was the eucalyptus tree). Nott had scraped together a guard of honour of ten muleteers and had the regular Sudanese behind. Nott describes

> the amazing sight, first Colonel Maraventano and his staff
> ... a guard of honour of 10 *hamla* men did a ragged present
> arms. Then came the national and colonial troops ... they
> dumped their arms in great piles, guarded by the Sudanese.
> ... By 1700 hours we had a column of 10,000 prisoners ...
> camped within our lines guarded by a handful of Sudanese
> and patriots.

Wingate received Maraventano on horseback with Ras Kassa beside him and his 'staff' (Akavia!) behind, both also mounted. Wingate believed that the colonial troops did not want to

207

surrender and Rossini agrees, 'In the war they had been fighting against the Patriots there was no surrender. You either won or you lost. In the recent fighting they considered that they had won. Besides they were afraid of Ras Kassa.'

Both Rossini and Silvi recorded their impressions of Wingate at the surrender, Rossini not very complimentary, describing him as '*un ometto insignificante, dall'aspetto miserabile*' (an insignificant little fellow of miserable appearance), though later in prison camp 'the anger I felt against this man who had humiliated us ... turned to respect and esteem.' Rossini recorded a different impression of

> the tall, straight, soldierly figure of Major Nott standing next to Wingate and Ras Kassa, who spoke to me in the language of Vergil and I understood he was asking how we had transported the guns up such difficult hills. I indicated the National mules. '*Muli optimi*', he commented and held out his hand, which I took. Thus I got to know this brave officer, now a General in retirement at Worcester, who was less fortunate than us because after having made us prisoner he suffered the same fate twice himself.[1]

Silvi records Wingate's generous tribute to the colonial troops. 'The English Colonel, whose face was completely obscured by a beard and a large helmet, raised his hand in salute. Then he moved towards the group of officers with outstretched hand and said, "I have never before fought against such gallant colonial troops".'

Lieutenant Collins and his observer, shot down at Cuiu on 11 April, were handed over to Wingate at the surrender, with the badly wounded Rowe. Among the Patriots who had joined Nott at Deraa and followed Wingate to Ciacata was Zaudi Flati with his 11-year-old son Wudineh Lodi, who had gone with his father to carry his rifle. Wudineh had watched with amazement while the Patriots and *ascari* slogged away at each other on the Ciacata plateau and remembers seeing Rowe, 'Abba Jiggsa', being carried on a stretcher by four white Italian soldiers. 'He raised his head as he arrived and greeted his friends.' Rowe and the two airmen were transported to Ficce and from there flown to Addis Ababa. Silvi tells a pleasantly human story about this, the airmen repaying the humane treatment they had received while prisoners of the column. 'Being informed that some of us had families in Addis Ababa the two aviators offered to take letters, a sympathetic gesture of which we took advantage. I sent a letter to my wife and daughter.'

To anticipate events, here is the sequel. Silvi's letter never reached his family, but because his mule was captured with all his papers a report reached them that he was dead. His daughter, Rita, did not believe the story, and

> with the confidence of youth (I was 16) I went out into the streets of Addis Ababa every day to watch the soldiers and prisoners marching in. One day I saw my father marching on foot with a column of prisoners. He was ill and suffering from malaria but I went up and greeted him and walked with him some way. Then I went back and told my mother.

A sadder sequel is the story of Rowe, and again we will anticipate events. Rowe arrived at the seventh South African casualty clearing station in the American Hospital in Addis Ababa on 26 May. Both Tutton and Luyt were in the same hospital and able to talk with him. He appeared to be recovering and was particularly cheerful on the morning of 31 May, but then had a massive haemhorrage and died. He was buried with full military honours at the Gulela cemetery in Addis Ababa on 1 June, Wingate, Benson and Nott attending the funeral with a firing party from Rowe's company. Nott records: 'At 3.00 p.m. we attended poor Rowe's funeral. . . . It was quite an impressive affair. Benson read the service as there was no C of E chaplain here. Some of the *askaris*, who liked Rowe, sobbed out loud as they marched away.' Rowe appears in a group photograph as a tall strong figure wearing the bush hat and 'shorts long', which were the standard and sensible KAR uniform at the time. He was a fine soldier, highy regarded by his brother officers and by his men, and 'Jiggsa' is remembered by old soldiers, and by boys like Wudineh, to this day, 50 years later. What better farewell could a brave soldier have than that his men should weep at his burying.

Thesiger received Wingate's order from Riley in the afternoon of

22 May and set off for Debra Sina at dawn on 23 May. On arrival he sent Riley and the Italian *tenente* into the fort under a white flag to require the commandant to come out and meet him. The two battalions of the Calvi column, the 13th and 65th, had redeemed their refusal to march northwards by fighting their way into the fort against the Galla Patriots encircling it and relieving the garrison but were then themselves besieged. Several hundred of these Galla, assembled near the fort under their *dejasmatch*, started hurling insults at Thesiger's Shoans and then started shooting. Thesiger dealt with this problem in a typically robust manner. He went forward to confront the mob with his interpreter and a bodyguard carrying the Ethiopian flag, yelled at the Galla to stop firing, and told the *dejasmatch* 'he would hang if he fired on the flag of his country and he was to remove his rabble. He did.'

When Riley returned with the Italian commander, Thesiger insisted on unconditional surrender, went into the fort with his men and disarmed the *ascari*, and had the bolts removed from their rifles. Two of his own Patriots, whom he had left outside, were caught looting. He had them flogged and warned his chiefs that the next man caught would hang. He then marched the 2500 strong garrison out, the *ascari* carrying the boltless rifles with the bolts in boxes on the mules; he reached Ficce without incident on 31 May and handed over his prisoners thankfully to Wingate. Before leaving the fort he had allowed his Shoans to go in and collect ammunition, not wanting this to fall into the hands of the Galla peasantry.

Wingate had set off from Ciacata with his column of prisoners on 24 May on the long march to Ficce, which they reached on 29 May, 'old Ras Kassa beating us by a short head'. Johnson led, and Wingate and Nott brought up the rear riding captured Italian chargers. Relief at the end of a hard operation and the pleasure of riding good horses made it a cheerful journey and Wingate showed remarkable histrionic talent, entertaining his companions with long extracts from Shakespeare's plays. Wingate and Nott did not fraternize with the Italians. Johnson accepted an invitation to dinner at the Italian officers' mess, where Maraventano, whom he decribed as a 'very nice man', asked him why he had not put his troops on both sides of the road at the Jibuti ambush. 'I explained

210

that I had so few troops that I did not like to split them. He thought that was a fair answer.'

At Ficce Maraventano's troops still had to undergo their final ordeal. A message was received from the Emperor to say that he wished to hold a parade of his prisoners. Against the background of the much publicized victories of Platt's and Cunningham's forces it was important for the Emperor's prestige that there should be a public show of the prisoners captured by his own small army. Thesiger was sent to inform Maraventano of the Emperor's wishes. The colonel protested that it was barbarous to humiliate prisoners. Thesiger was the very last Englishman to receive such a protest kindly and records how he lost his temper, reminded the colonel of Italian misdeeds and told him to be on parade with his men next morning. Nott records that some of the Italian officers, perhaps imbued with the Fascist, un-Italian colour bar introduced by Mussolini (aping Hitler) in 1938, 'begged the British officers to spare them the indignity of marching with their men (*les noirs*) . . . who had fought for them so gallantly.' This was refused, although according to Silvi the 198 officers marched separately when the column filed past the dais on which the Emperor stood with the Crown Prince, Ras Kassa and his surviving son, Asrate Kassa. Silvi's account gives a curious slant to the story, emphasizing again the fear of Ras Kassa, felt by the *ascari* at Uogghidi, and the power of rumour. After the parade Silvi records that a rumour circulated among the officers that Ras Kassa had wanted to kill all 198 Italian officers in revenge for the murder of his two sons at Ficce in December 1936, but 'the *Negus*, who had no hatred for the Italians, on the contrary he admired them for what they had done, convinced him to be content with this demonstration.'

The three-day fight at Ciacata and Uogghidi from 18 to 20 May, with which the operations of Safforce and the march of the Maraventano column ended, was a substantial engagement. In terms of casualties the only actions to come near it in severity in the Gojjam campaign were the retreat from Dangila and the Charaka battle. The Allies here suffered three British wounded, of whom Rowe died, one Sudanese killed and three wounded, eight Ethiopian regulars killed and 15 wounded, 200 Patriots killed and 500 wounded, a total of some 730 casualties. The Italians suffered two officers and 64 *ascari* killed, three officers and 243 *ascari* wounded, a total of 312. The Patriots tackled the greatly superior forces of the Maraventano column with reckless courage, and without their sacrifice Wingate's bluff in bringing about the surrender of the column would not have succeeded. They suffered nearly 50 per cent casualties and deserve a high place of honour in the annals of the war of liberation. While it is right to praise the Patriots, the plan and direction was Wingate's. The whole operation was a good example of the support of guerrilla forces by a regular nucleus, and bringing about the surrender of the column was Wingate's most spectacular achievement in Ethiopia.

The achievements of Safforce were later recognized by the awards of the DSO to Nott and Thesiger, a second DSO to Johnson, and, very much later, the award to Wingate for the whole campaign of a bar to the DSO, which he won in Palestine. Of the other ranks the only award known for certain was that of the Military Medal to Company Sergeant Major Musa. Wetherall, Wingate's immediate superior, gave Wingate and his force a well-deserved accolade in his dispatch for the action at Uogghidi. 'This brilliant action ... as a feat of arms carried out by a minute regular force supporting irregulars in very difficult country against an enemy greatly superior in numbers and armament can have few parallels.'

Maraventano's odyssey was militarily irrelevant but it was a fine performance to lead and keep together his heterogeneous column and he must go down in history as a good commander who deserved well of his country. He and his men had fought fairly, save for the one deplorable incident involving the Sudanese captured at Emmanuel, and were entitled to go into captivity with honour, the nationals to prison camps and the *ascari*, who had fought so gallantly right up to the end, released to their homes in accordance with Wingate's promise.

Note

1. Nott was captured near Tobruk in 1942, imprisoned in Italy, escaped on the Italian armistice in 1943, at liberty for five months, betrayed and recaptured and spent the rest of the war in a German POW camp.

7

The End of Gideon Force:
Wingate's Role Assessed

S afforce reached Addis Ababa in early June 1941, following
Wingate and Nott who had attended Rowe's funeral on 1
June. No congratulatory messages were received from
Cunningham's HQ, but the Emperor appreciated what Safforce
had done. He put a house at the disposal of Wingate and Nott,
and, as Nott records, 'produced champagne and *tej* for our
parched throats. ... He congratulated me personally on the operations at Addis Derra and Debra Sina. I dined with him a few days
later with Chapman-Andrews, Johnson, Riley, Dan Sandford and
Wilfred Thesiger.' A notable absentee at that dinner was Wingate.
Nott records that on the afternoon of Rowe's funeral Wingate had
been told by Wetherall that he no longer had a command, that
Gideon Force was to be dispersed, and that he was under orders to
fly to Force HQ at Harrar immediately. 'Orde flew to Harrar to
see General Cunningham, take a few days' rest and badger Middle
East to let him go to Palestine to raise the Jewish Army, as he told
me Ben-Gurion had requested of him. What went on at HQ I do
not know but Wingate flew to Khartoum *en route* for HQ Middle
East shortly afterwards.'

Evidently Cunningham's headquarters could not get Wingate out
of Ethiopia quickly enough. Peter Molloy, then a staff captain,
recalls meeting Wingate at Force HQ, 'an unimpressive, scruffy,
bearded figure. Everybody in Force HQ distrusted him. He had
brought the Emperor in. They wanted him out as soon as possible

... they were afraid he would meddle in politics.' As recently as 15 May Cunningham had ordered Wingate to Debra Tabor and it was clearly his intention then that Wingate should go on to Debra Tabor and Gondar. What made him change his mind is not clear, but it was probably the belief, based on the knowledge that Wingate had meddled in Zionist politics in Palestine, that he would do the same in Ethiopia. This was a wholly unfair judgement. At no time in Ethiopia did Wingate concern himself with politics. He left political matters always to Sandford, while he concentrated on operational matters himself.

Wingate was ordered to fly direct from Harrar to Khartoum *en route* for Cairo and was not even allowed to go back to Addis Ababa to take leave of the Emperor. This probably saved his life as it deprived him of a weapon that might have ensured the success of his suicide attempt in Cairo a few weeks later. Akavia had given Wingate a small Italian Beretta pistol as a present for his wife. Wingate had the pistol with him but the ammunition was left with his kit, which was with Akavia in Addis Ababa. He arrived in Cairo in the first week of June 1941, where he was told he had reverted to the rank of major and where he was joined by Simonds on 16 June. Both men were angry at the way they had been treated, Simonds for being ordered away from near success at Debra Tabor to take up a job that no longer existed, Wingate because the achievements of Gideon Force seemed to count for nothing. Amid the deteriorating war situation, with the Germans in Greece and Crete and Wavell's armies in retreat in Libya, Wingate and Simonds found, as Simond records, that they 'were received with cold indifference by GHQ staff officers', who were uninterested in their little battles in Ethiopia. Wingate wrote his dispatch on the Gojjam campaign in which his clear and imaginative exposition of how a guerrilla force should operate is marred at times by inaccuracies and immoderate language. In extenuation it must be said that the dispatch was written by a justifiably angry man. He was seen about the dispatch by Wavell, who was critical of the immoderate language but promised to look into the grievances mentioned about allowances for his men and decorations recommended and not awarded. Wavell left Middle East Command on 7 July, so the grievances were lost sight of, but Wavell clearly held neither the dispatch nor his attempted suicide against Wingate because he sent for him for Burma in 1942.

On 4 July Wingate attempted to commit suicide in his Cairo hotel room by cutting his throat with a knife. He was discovered unconscious, taken to hospital and survived. At the hospital, where he was given a blood transfusion, a blood sample was taken which was 'swarming with malarial parasites' and he was found to have cerebral malaria. The fact of the attempted suicide is quite clear. This was an attempt to kill himself, which, had he had ammunition for his Beretta pistol, would probably have succeeded. The motives are less clear. In his own account Wingate says that he felt a sense of failure in Ethiopia. Instead of achieving Ethiopia's freedom he had handed the country over to the 'inept diplomacy' of the Occupied Enemy Territories Administration with talk of a protectorate. 'I thought our treatment of Ethiopia cold and tyrannical and our talk of liberation miserable cant. ... I thought my death by my own hand would provide a point ... and would make people pause and think.' There was talk of a protectorate, later and not in Wingate's time, and soon squashed, but this self-justification after the event simply does not ring true. The first exploratory meeting to discuss an Anglo-Ethiopian agreement between Haile Selassie and the chief political officer, Sir Philip Mitchell, took place on 23 May when Wingate was at Ciacata. After this Mitchell returned to London to discuss the Emperor's requests with the British cabinet. Wingate left Addis Ababa on 2 June, and even if he had known of this meeting, all the evidence is that he did not concern himself with political matters, leaving them to Sandford. He was *'functus officio'*. He had brought the Emperor into his capital, rounded up Maraventano, and was looking for new challenges, 'to badger Middle East to let him go to Palestine to raise the Jewish Army'. It is inconceivable that Ethiopia's future, about which nothing had been finally determined save for the promise of independence, could have weighed on his mind at that time to the extent of attempting suicide as a gesture.

The truth of the suicide attempt seems to be simpler and more creditable to Wingate. He had completed a hard, uncomfortable and very successful campaign. He had shown courage, professionalism and strategic ability of a high order, worthy of the recognition all professional soldiers seek. Instead of receiving praise he had been hustled out of Ethiopia by Cunningham as though he were a delinquent, had met with indifference in Cairo, and the rejection of his claims for allowances for his men, and (so he thought) his recommendations for awards. His understandable anger and frustration at the disgraceful way he had been treated combined with his sense of failure and his serious medical condition to tip the balance of his brilliant but at times unstable mind in favour of self-destruction.

Wingate was visited in hospital by several of his officers, including Nott who recalls that when asked why he did it, 'he looked very sheepish and after a long pause said, "I've made a bloody fool of myself."' He made a quick recovery and on 22 July was examined by a senior psychological consultant, G. W. B. James, who reported that he was not responsible for his act of attempted self-destruction, which was the consequence of 'a depressed state to which he was prone, aggravated by malarial fever', that he was no longer suicidal and had recovered his mind completely. On 12 August he replied to a letter from Tutton who had asked if there was a chance of serving under him again, 'It is pleasant to find someone who enjoys the hazards of war. You can depend on me to ask for you if I have a chance of employing you.' He went on to say that he was over a recent illness, that he had written to Rowe's mother, 'who seemed pleased to get my letter', and concluded, 'Remember me to everyone in the 2nd Ethiops, especially to Clarke and Beard. Best of luck.' The letter shows that by that time he was completely sane, helpful and rational and shows also his good side, writing to Rowe's mother despite his personal problems. On 18 August Wingate was boarded Category D by a medical board and sent back to England by sea to convalesce, and on the way he again showed the same caring side of his character. How he managed it with wartime security is not clear, but he got a message to Luyt's parents, who lived 100 miles from Cape Town, asking them to come and see him when his ship docked. They came, and Wingate told them what their son had done, and this must have given them enormous pleasure.

With the departure of Wingate Gideon Force ceased to exist, although Beghemder Force with the mortar platoon and some elements of Mission 101 (the centres) continued to operate. Johnson, Riley and the Sudanese joined the Frontier Battalion at Dessie and thence back to the Sudan. Naylor joined the 2nd Ethiopian Battalion, still in Addis Ababa except for B company under Shaw, which was operating with Gurassu Duke's Patriots near Gimma. The Beds & Herts sergeants went back to their regiment, Howell and the other Australians back to the 6th Australian Division, and Akavia followed Wingate to Cairo. Nott was posted as GSO2 to the 11th African Division with responsibility for patriot forces in southwest Ethiopia but by the time he arrived at Gimma on 4 July this had already been occupied by the 22nd (East African) Brigade, after it and the Nigerians had forced the crossing of the Omo river. Nott returned to Addis Ababa where, 'Johannes begged me to stay and command the Ethiopian army!'

General Gazzera had surrendered with all forces in the southwest on 4 July and it is worth comparing the numbers involved in this campaign with those in Gojjam. Allied forces in the southwest consisted of three African brigades and, for a time, two South African battalions, assisted by Gurassu's Patriots. Italian forces were 40,000 regular troops and *banda*, the remnants of seven divisions. Prisoners taken before the final surrender were 12,852 at Soddu, 3900 at Omo river, and 12,000 at Gimma, including General Scala, three other generals and eight brigade commanders. The scale of these operations was considerably larger than those of Gideon Force, though under the indifferent leadership of Gazzera the troops in the southwest gave up more easily than those under Maraventano.

Back in Addis Ababa Nott noted the arrival of Major General Butler to command the British military mission, of Mitchell for discussions with Haile Selassie about the Anglo-Ethiopian areement, and of Wavell to receive the Order of Solomon from the Emperor on his way to India to take up his post as commander-in-chief, having handed over Middle East Command to General Auchinleck. Wavell, like Wingate, is remembered as a good friend to Ethiopia. One of Auchinleck's first actions was to appoint Cunningham to command the Eighth Army in the Western Desert. Wetherall succeeded him temporarily in command of East Africa Command until after the Gondar operations when Platt took over.

On 28 July Nott was ordered to fly to Cairo for a 'special mission', and left after farewell dinners with Ras Kassa and at the palace where he was guest of honour; 'It was all very sad.' In fact he went back to his regiment, 1st Worcesters, in the Western Desert and was soon in action again. Sandford had a continuing role during this period, not only as the Emperor's political adviser over the Anglo-Ethiopian agreement, but also as his military adviser on patriot operations, sending out orders to patriot leaders in his name, and intervening when difficulties arose between them and the regular forces.

It is time to make a final assessment of Wingate and Gideon Force. Wingate claimed in his dispatch, 'I forced the enemy to evacuate [Gojjam],' and this claim is supported by the official historian, Colonel Barton. 'By the end of April the whole enemy force had been driven from Gojjam. ... This was *not* to conform with movements elsewhere.' We have seen that this is at most only a half truth. Wingate did force Natale from Burye, he did not force Maraventano to evacuate Debra Markos. This movement *was* to conform with movements elsewhere, i.e. the advances of Platt and Cunningham. Wingate was not to know of the orders to Maraventano and believed his claim, as did many others, including a retired Italian general, General Gonella-Pacchiotti, who wrote to the author about 'this splendid soldier who conquered Gojjam and turned the situation in Burma when he created the Chindits.' Both these points, particularly the second, are still the subject of historical debate, but it is a fact that Wingate's campaign in Gojjam enhanced his reputation as a leader of unconventional forces, that this is in the main justified and that even if he did not do all he claimed, what he did remains a considerable achievement.

We have to try and answer one question, mentioned in Chapter 1. Did Wingate's policy of going ahead with a small *corps d'élite* succeed, as opposed to that of Sandford (dismissed by Wingate as a pedlar of war material and cash), which was to arm the Patriots and have the Emperor well forward in command? Sandford never had the chance to prove his policy, but he believed, with justification, that Torelli could have been 'put in the bag' at Dangila and Maraventano at Debra Markos. As it was Torelli's brigade went on to fight at Bahr Dar and Gondar, and Maraventano took a lot

218

of rounding up. Gideon Force, fighting alone without Patriots, as it did for most of the Gojjam campaign was too small, in Sandford's words, 'to be more than an irritant and a spur to flight'. The answer to the question is therefore that the *corps d'élite* did achieve limited success in Gojjam, and only full and triumphant success in Wollo in the rounding up of the Maraventano column as the regular nucleus of a much larger irregular force. The same principle, the desirability of a regular nucleus, emerged again and again in the Gondar operations, which will be described in the next chapter.

Gideon Force may not have achieved all that Wingate claimed, but it achieved a great deal. It entered Gojjam against formidable physical obstacles and superior Italian forces, the men marching on their feet with unwieldy animal transport, without artillery and with virtually no air support. They were constantly engaged against the enemy in harassing actions, mainly at night. By their ubiquity they induced the Italians to believe they were cut off and thereby created the myth of a superior 'Anglo-Sudanese' force. Although in the light of after knowledge their influence on events was not as great as they believed, from Wingate downwards they did believe it to a man. Their morale was high and their tails were up. For such a small force against such odds their achievements were remarkable.

Gideon Force, the *corps d'élite*, was Wingate's idea and his creation. The concept of an independent self-contained column marching in to disrupt communications was based on the old idea of a cavalry raid. The guerrilla tactics (the harassment of the enemy by small parties) were designed to force the enemy to withdraw and they achieved this at Burye. The expedition was the precursor of Wingate's first Chindit expedition, the long-range penetration column behind the lines in Burma in 1943. In the handling of Gideon Force Wingate showed great boldness and originality, but in Gojjam at times tactical weakness. For example, the night march round Burye was brilliant, if chaotic, but at Man-kusa he underestimated the Italian will to resist and only escaped 'by fleetness of foot'. The Charaka action happened because he sent Boyle's column ahead to disrupt communications, a correct conception, as was the order to Thesiger to mobilize Haile Yusus's

Patriots at Dambacha, but in the period leading up to the battle he lost control of both his battalions and afterwards in his dispatch made the wholly fictitious claim that he had the enemy 'jammed between his two battalions and unable to move and hoped in vain for a *coup de grâce* from the air'. In the Debra Markos operations he again failed to coordinate the actions of his two battalions, which were operating some eight miles apart quite independently at Gulit and Emmanuel.

Wingate owed his success in Gojjam in great measure to the previous efforts of the Patriots and Mission 101, which enabled him to move freely away from the main forts, and also to the threat of the Patriots, even when they were inactive. He also owed a good deal to luck, the order to Torelli to withdraw from Dangila and the order to Maraventano to withdraw from Debra Markos, and to the advances of Platt and Cunningham, which gave rise to these orders. But he acted boldly, exploited his luck and deserved his success. In Wollo he again owed something to luck when Maraventano withdrew from the strong fortress of Deraa because of the muddle over the Calvi column, but with the strong assistance of Ras Kassa and his Shoans the pursuit and capture of the Italian column was brilliantly executed. If we judge Wingate's command in Ethiopia as a whole and balance the credits against the debits, Wingate emerges as a bold, imaginative and successful commander in operations, which, albeit in a minor way, contributed to the Allied success in East Africa.

With regard to personal views of Wingate in Ethiopia, next to Wingate and Sandford the two outstanding men in Gideon Force and Mission 101 were Nott and Thesiger. Both appreciated Wingate's strengths and abilities; neither particularly liked him. Both, however, are of the opinion that no one other than Wingate could have achieved what he did in Ethiopia. Of others, his greatest admirers were Simonds and Akavia, who had known him in Palestine, recognized his weaknesses, his ability to upset his superiors and staff officers so that he was often his own worst enemy, but nevertheless remain as convinced today as they were 50 years ago that the man they served was a great leader whose like would not be seen again. To some Gideon Force officers, loyal to their own battalion commanders, Boustead and Boyle, with neither of whom

Wingate got on, Wingate appeared as an unsmiling, unorthodox, scruffy commander who did not appeal. Even so, where Wingate was there was action and both Tutton and Luyt asked to serve under him again, and Railton, not directly under Wingate in Ethiopia, served under him in Burma in 2nd Chindit force.

It is from the NCOs that we get views of Wingate that more closely approximate the respect and confidence in him as a leader many Chindit officers and most Chindit other ranks held. Grey admired him greatly, though he found him unusual and different from the regular British officers he had known. ('If you have a leader who gets results you back him which we did.') The Australian sergeants of No 1 Centre all asked to continue to serve under Wingate but were sent back to the 6th Australian Division. In a letter to the author former sergeant Ted Body wrote, 'I had the greatest respect and highest regard for Wingate as all us Australians had. . . . He had no fear — liked to shock — was extremely restless and had a very kind side to him. . . . I think a lot of his moods and poses we read about could have been to emphasize a point.' Body raises an interesting point. Wingate could be verbally aggressive. He was also physically violent, in Ethiopia often striking and manhandling soldiers. Was this done for effect? He certainly believed in instant discipline and some of his outbursts may have been calculated, but some were sheer bad temper.

To Body and Grey Wingate's eccentricities, which so offended some of his fellow officers, were irrelevant. What mattered was that he got results. To Ethiopians it was the same. To them Wingate was the fighter, the single-minded champion of Ethiopian freedom, the man who brought the Emperor in, a legend then and a legend still today. If he struck them, 'He is our father; he does it to correct us so that we do not err again.' The evidence is in Kabada's book and in the hearts of countless old soldiers with their memories of Wingate like Shambul Ayana Bire. It is a remarkable record for a man who spent less than six months in Ethiopia. In trying to assess Wingate in Ethiopia the author is conscious himself of having veered from side to side, praising him for what he did, criticizing him for his immoderate language and exaggerated claims, Wingate was not a man with whom one could ever be comfortable. He was rude, aggressive, often violent and subject to black fits of temper. He was intolerant of obstruction or incompetence, was often scruffy in appearance and often made exaggerated claims in writing of events in which he had participated. He was not, however, a charlatan or a liar. When he made claims he believed them to be true. Against these faults must be set his virtues and they are formidable. Wingate was a brilliant innovator, had great strategic insight, and had the power to inspire and lead first-class subordinates and to make them trust and believe in him. Personally he could display great charm and erudition, and at times be a great play actor and very good company, as on the long ride back to Ficce with the Maraventano column. Looking back on Wingate over 50 years and all the evidence about him, the author comes firmly down on the side of the Wingate men and would have been proud to have been numbered among them if he had measured up to Wingate's exacting standards.

Nott's considered judgement on Wingate in Ethiopia contrasts succintly his faults and his virtues, and although one may disagree with the catalogue of faults there is evidence to support them in these pages.

> Wingate was the most complex character I've ever met. He had a driving passion and was unnecessarily impatient. Generous yet self-promoting with enlarged claims. He had a phenomenal memory and loved holding the stage. Some of his personal habits were a bit *outré*. He had great strategic vision but his tactics were poor. He was not a lovable person but he was a great leader.

Nott goes on, and we should remember he is writing about the obscure gunner major of 1941, not the great Chindit leader of 1944, 'I have such a photographic memory of all these characters — Dan Sandford, Wienholt, Arthur Bentinck, Tim Foley, Critchley, Boustead, Thesiger, Johnson, Riley, Gillespie, Jack, the *kaid* et al. But Orde was the man who stood out.'

As a postscript to Wingate in Ethiopia we must complete the story of Beghemder Force at Debra Tabor, an operation still under Wingate's control and where he would have been sent had not Cunningham changed his mind. Debra Tabor was closely invested by Boustead, who had his Sudanese and Turrall with the mortar platoon in position two miles west of the town, while Simonds was three miles north at Limado with the Centre troops, Fitaurari Birru and 5000 Patriots. Both forces carried out nightly harassing raids against the Italian positions with light machine-gun fire and mortar bombardment by Turrall's mortars, supplemented by fire from an ancient muzzle-loading Italian cannon (made by Ansaldo in 1890), captured by the Patriots and resurrected and repaired by Morrow and his fellow sergeants. The first time they fired it the gun reared up and fell over backwards, but Morrow soon got the measure of it and the gun performed quite useful service. Like Nott's men at Deraa the Sudanese suffered badly from the cold of the high altitude (about 7500 feet) but morale remained high, Holcombe recalling, 'Whatever the conditions the men always remained cheerful.'

On 17 May, when Boustead had been reinforced by two platoons of No 4 company under Carroll-Leahey, bringing his strength to two full companies, No 3 and No 4, he and Simonds planned a joint attack on the Italian positions. Before this was launched news was received of Aosta's surrender at Amba Alagi on 19 May, and they invited the garrison commander, Colonel Angelini, to surrender; but he declined, for he was under orders from General Nasi to continue resistance. Then Simonds was ordered to report to Cairo for 'other duties', and on 20 May Boustead was ordered to hand over operations to the senior subaltern, Pilkington, march his two companies to Dessie, join Maxwell and return to the Sudan. The march to Dessie took nine days and they received an airdrop of supplies on the way, the steady Sudanese marching out as strongly as they had marched in six months earlier. As Simonds recorded laconically, 'Abandonment did untold harm and discouraged patriots. Reached Cairo 16.6.41 to find job filled.' This left Pilkington with his combined No 5/10 Centre, McLean with No 2, Welsh with No 6, Birru, Danyo and some Patriots to continue the siege, but patriot support dwindled and many left to cultivate their land. This force was henceforth called Northern Force. Had Wingate been in command at Debra Tabor he would no doubt have turned a blind eye to the order to abandon the siege, as he had with Cunningham's signal at Deraa.

Beghemder Force had had a secondary role to that of Gideon Force, but had performed it effectively, containing Torelli at Bahr Dar, encouraging patriot resistance, cutting off the line of retreat from Dessie, and investing Debra Tabor, though the latter operation was left incomplete by the withdrawal of the Frontier Battalion. Like Wingate, Simonds left Ethiopia with a grievance, but he had shown energy and imagination in his command of Mission 101 at Sakala and had effectively carried out Wingate's orders in Beghemder, a difficult assignment well performed and deserving of more recognition than he was accorded. In terms of awards, whereas Gideon Force[1] was generously treated with six DSOs and three MCs, in addition to one CBE, two MCs and one MBE for Mission 101, the only award to Beghemder Force, apart from the MC and two MMs awarded to Jarvis's company at Bahr Dar, was a mention in dispatches for Simonds. In his mission Simonds had been greatly helped by Fitaurari Birru, a leader of great presence and authority, and by Ato Getahun Tesemma, whom he described as 'a faithful friend and a first-class and conscientious officer and servant of his country'.

Boustead never forgave Wingate for accusing him of cowardice at Burye and the picture of him is marred by his encounter with Wingate in the Cairo hospital where Thesiger records that he looked at Wingate and said, 'You bloody fool. Why didn't you use a revolver?' Setting this aside he emerges as a fine trainer of men and the energetic commander of a first-class battalion. As a soldier he had great experience but the command of a battalion was about his limit and undoubtedly Thesiger is correct when he says that Boustead 'lacked Wingate's originality of thought and bold imagination'. He and his fine battalion now leave the scene, and with the departure of Wingate and Gideon Force and the return of Haile Selassie it may be asked what is there left to tell. The answer is that there are still operational centres and the mortar platoon, part of Mission 101, in Northern Force, the 2nd Ethiopian Battalion still has a part to play, Sheppard with Mission 101 North and Ringrose and Railton are still operating, and the Patriots will have an important role in the final operations at Gondar. Furthermore Sandford, with whom this story started, not only has a continuing military role, but will have a vital role at the end in the negotiations for the Anglo-Ethiopian agreement. The story would be incomplete without rounding off these matters and this will be done in the two final chapters.

Note
1. *Gideon Force*
   DSO: Wingate, Thesiger, Nott, Boustead, Johnson (and bar)
   MC: Harris, Acland, Turrall
   Mission 101
   CBE: Sandford
   MC: Critchley, Foley
   MBE: Grey

8

Gondar*

The last days of May 1941 had seen Axis victories in Crete and in the Western Desert, the sinking of the German battleship *Bismarck* and the collapse of the pro-Axis revolt in Iraq. In June Wavell tried, but failed, to recover lost ground in the Western Desert by operation 'Battleaxe', and on 22 June Hitler attacked Russia, bringing the Soviet Union into the war as an ally of Great Britain. Between May and November 1941 the real possibility of a British defeat in North Africa encouraged continued resistance by the remaining Italian forces in AOI, both to detain British troops who might otherwise go to North Africa and in the hope that the Germans might come to their assistance. These remaining forces were concentrated in the Gondar sector under the resolute General Nasi and consisted of about 40,000 troops in Gondar and the outlying garrisons, Wolchefit, Kulkaber, Debra Tabor and Chilga. There was also a garrison at Gorgora at the northern end of Lake Tana, and several fortified positions between Gorgora and Gondar, including a *banda* garrison at Gianda. Immediately north of Gondar there were strong garrisons at Tukul Dinga and Ambazzo-Uollaich (or Uollag). Nasi's troops were about one half colonial and one half national, the latter mainly Blackshirt militia with some units of the Royal Army. He had 40 guns, four aircraft and some homemade tanks, tractor bodies with metal superstructures carrying machine guns. Nasi made great efforts to instil a spirit of resistance in his troops, the 'Gondar

---

* See General Map 2 and Sketch 9.

226

spirit', and all the garrisons except for Debra Tabor resisted strongly. In the final assault the KAR, which formed the bulk of the regular attacking forces, had harder fighting and suffered more casualties than it did in Cunningham's advance from the south. With the help of the Vichy French governor at Jibuti, an aerial courier service was maintained with Rome, the aircraft flying to Gondar, going on to Jibuti to refuel, and returning to Rome via Gondar. The sector included a settled and largely submissive population of peasants and there was plenty of food for the garrison and fish from Lake Tana. Four motorable roads or tracks met at Gondar, the road from Asmara via Wolchefit in the north, the road from Dessie via Debra Tabor and Kulkaber in the southeast, the track from the west from Metemma via Chilga, and the track from the northwest from Kassala through Um Hagar. Only the Wolchefit road was an all-weather road so that so long as Wolchefit held out Nasi could expect no attack by regular motorized forces until the long rains ceased in October. The shortest approach was from the west, and the first attempt to open a crack in the Gondar defences was made against Chilga, 40 kilometres from Gondar, by Kerforce from the Sudan (see Sketch 7).

Chilga was a very strong natural defensive position of which the main feature was a 2000-foot escarpment, which any attacking force from the west would have to climb. It was held in strength by the 5000 men of the 4th Colonial Brigade commanded by Lieutenant Colonel Miranda under the garrison commander, Colonel Martinelli. Had Brigadier Slim's attack on Gallabat succeeded in November 1940, the Italians would have had to retreat to this line and the campaign would have taken a very different course. The attacking force was commanded by Lieutenant Colonel Ker, the officer commanding the 3rd Ethiopian Battalion, and consisted of his battalion, less Railton's C company now at Amba Giorgis, commanded on this occasion by Major Wicher, the Composite Battalion of the SDF commanded by Lieutenant Colonel Johnny Gifford, Dorsetshire Regiment, and consisting of four companies, two Nuba and two Arab, and C troop of the Sudan Artillery with four 3.7 inch howitzers, commanded by Major Humphreys. One of the SDF Nuba companies was No 5 patrol company of the Frontier Battalion commanded by Bimbashi Guy Campbell, sent

227

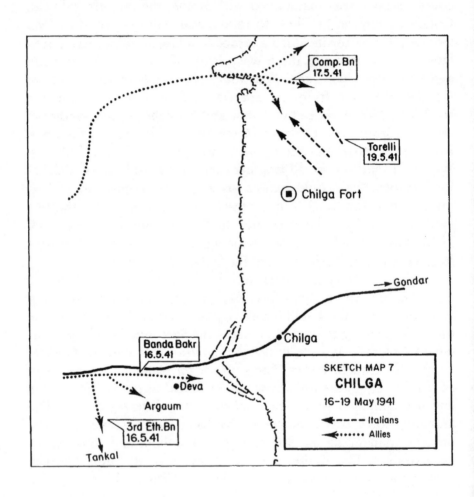

Comp. Bn
17.5.41

Torelli
19.5.41

⊙ Chilga Fort

→ Gondar

Banda Bakr
16.5.41

• Chilga

• Deva

Argaum

SKETCH MAP 7
CHILGA
16–19 May 1941

◄ - - - Italians
◄ • • • • Allies

3rd Eth. Bn
16.5.41

Tankal

off by Wingate from Um Idla in January 1941 to protect Gideon Force's right flank. Kerforce was 1400 strong, a small force with which to attempt such a strong position.

On 16 May the 3rd Ethiopians tackled the escarpment eight miles south of Chilga at Tankal, and the SDF's *banda* Bakr company made a holding attack against Argaum and Deva. The main attack, led by Gifford, was made by the remaining three SDF companies with one Ethiopian platoon. They made a daring approach march by a mule track to the northern flank of the Italian positions, the Sudanese soldiers carrying two dismantled 3.7 howitzers on tree saplings, attacked in the dawn mist on 17 May, took the Italians completely by surprise and overran the positions. They held off counterattacks, the guns giving good support, and by the afternoon of 17 May were established on the escarpment, having captured seven Italian officers, 400 *ascari* and a complete four-gun pack battery with its mules. Had it been possible to reinforce Gifford it seems likely that the rest of the position, including the Chilga fort, might have been captured, and the way to Gondar opened.

Nasi at Gondar reacted sharply to the danger and sent Torelli's 22nd Colonial Brigade and Braca's *banda* group in motor transport from Gondar to reinforce the Chilga garrison and mount a counterattack. The *banda* group had been brought up to strength since its heavy casualties in the relief of Kwara and was under the command of Captain Schreiber, the second in command, Braca being in hospital. During the night of 17/18 May both defenders and attackers on the Chilga escarpment watched the headlights of the approaching motor vehicles. The relieving force arrived on 18 May and counterattacked at dawn on 19 May. By that time Gifford, after referring to Colonel Ker, had ordered a withdrawal. He had not been able to make any further progress; his men were tired and he was suffering casualties. The Italian counterattack coincided with the British retreat but Gifford extricated his force successfully and, by 22 May, all four SDF companies were back at their starting point, taking their prisoners with them, and using the captured Italian mules to carry the 3.7 howitzers. The 3rd Ethiopians had climbed the escarpment at Tankal and had made some progress but were also counterattacked by *banda* and Kamant tribesmen and retreated to their starting point. Casualties were not light. The Ethiopians suffered two killed and three wounded. The Composite Battalion suffered 14 other ranks killed, eight missing and one officer (Guy Campbell) and 100 other ranks wounded. Bimbashi Hanks was captured in the retreat. Italian losses were three officers and 100 *ascari* killed, seven officers and 400 *ascari* captured, and about 400 *ascari* wounded.

After this action the Composite Battalion returned to the Sudan for rest and reinforcement while the 3rd Ethiopians remained opposite Chilga to contain the Italians. The action is claimed, correctly, as a victory for the Italians, whose counterattack swept Gifford's companies back off the positions they had gained. The assault was, however, a brave attempt to breach the Gondar defences, a daring attack courageously executed against superior forces occupying a position of great natural strength, and deserves a prominent place in the campaign record.

There were contemporaneous operations at both Debra Tabor and Wolchefit. We will deal with Northern Force at Debra Tabor first, of whose daily activities Pilkington's letters home give a good picture. Pilkington was encamped north of Debra Tabor astride the Gondar road with McLean watching the Ifaq road to the west and Birru and the Patriots behind him. The Centre troops and Patriots carried out frequent night raids on the Italian positions, on one of which on the night of 21/22 May Sergeant MacDonald was captured. There followed a courteous correspondence between Pilkington and Colonel Angelini, the latter reporting the capture and that 'the *Sergente* is being handled like it is between civilized peoples.' Pilkington replied thanking him for the good treatment, 'which I hope I shall be able to repay', and sending a mule with the sergeant's kit, which MacDonald acknowledged in terms the modern British Army might find curious, 'I feel an awful fool to be in a situation like this but I must say that the Italians have treated me most kindly and courteously. I am, Sir, Your Obedient Servant Ernest MacDonald, Sgt.' Pilkington also corresponded with Birru, addressing him as 'Your Excellency', treating him with great respect, keeping him informed of the situation and suggesting moves for the Patriots, and with McLean and his gunner sergeant, Morrow, who had under command two sections of the original mortar platoon and the old cannon. Sending letters by courier had its hazards. One letter to McLean was delayed because, 'three men went. One had a rifle. The other two set on him, took his rifle, tied him to a tree and ran away. He has just come in.'

On his way to Cairo through Asmara Simonds had persuaded Platt's staff to lay on an air strike on Debra Tabor on 12 June and on the strength of this Pilkington invited Angelini to surrender, which he declined, planned an attack, and reported his intentions to the 12th African Division in Addis Ababa, saying that he could raise 1500 Patriots, but that it was 'impossible [to] keep patriots much longer for agricultural reasons'. When the attack went in the Centre troops bore the brunt of the fighting and had several casualties, as did the mortar platoon. Pilkington was disappointed with the patriot effort, 'Dej. Belai never stood at all. Danyo did better and certainly fought for a bit,' but the Centre troops did well, and 'it was a really good scrap; we used up all our ammo. We must have given them a pretty good knock.' He also did not think much of the air strike. The Italians, again confusing regular Ethiopian troops with Sudanese, reported an attack 'by 3000 rebels and 200 Sudanese under British officers supported by air attack repulsed with serious losses'. They reacted sharply, the *banda* counterattacking and burning villages, and Nasi's two fighters attacked Birru's camp and caused 20 casualties. Good news for Pilkington was that the Wollo *banda* from Angelini's garrison had started to desert — '32 came out the night of 11th June' — and reinforcements arrived, 'Major Douglas with 1200 good patriots from Shoa — well off for LMGs. He thinks Wingate *may* be here later.' Wingate, of course, was already in Cairo, but here is more evidence that Cunningham had contempleted sending him to Debra Tabor and Gondar. Major Dougal Douglas, of the Highland Light Infantry and the 4th KAR, was, in Molloy's words, 'a hopeless regular soldier but being large and flamboyant had considerable success in commanding irregulars'. His success was in fact doubtful. He quarrelled with the dignified and tolerant Birru and eventually had to be removed from his command. He arrived in fact with 2000 Shoans under Fitaurari Haupte Selassie and 800 Wollo Galla. The Shoans were part of Ababa Aregai's army, of whom 500 had gone with Campbell to Dessie. Douglas had taken his force north of Dessie and accepted the surrender of Colonel Anderson at Magdala Tanta and from there had been ordered to Debra Tabor where it was contemplated Wingate would take over.

Regular reinforcements were also on the way. Platt had decided that the capture of Debra Tabor was operationally necessary and it was thought that Angelini would be more likely to surrender to regular troops. Legs Force was sent from the 5th Indian Division still at Dessie, consisting of one and a half armoured-car squadrons of Skinners Horse and a company of the 3rd/2nd Punjabis under the command of Major Guile, and arrived on 16 June. Two attempts were made to mount joint night attacks on the Italian defences with the Shoans supported by air strikes. The first was abortive because of bad weather, and in the second, on the night of 23/24 June, the Shoans declined to take part, their leader, Haupte Selassie, being unimpressed, like Pilkington, with the scale of RAF support. The planes had to fly 300 miles from Asmara and could not linger over the target because of Nasi's two fighters at Gondar. Douglas was furious, blaming Birru and the Beghemder leaders, and the reputation of the Patriots with the regulars plummeted, but the British commanders failed to learn from Wingate the lessons of Gojjam, which were that Patriots could be brilliant in open warfare but should not be asked to tackle strong fixed defences on their own.

In the event no further attack was necessary. While Pilkington maintained the pressure, negotiations opened with Angelini and, despite a last minute intervention by Nasi who sent a Caproni on 2 July with supplies and a message to Angelini urging him to continue resistance, surrender terms were agreed and the garrison marched out on 6 July past a guard of honour of Skinners Horse. Legs Force returned to Dessie with the Italian prisoners, while the majority of the *ascari* in the two colonial units agreed to enlist in Douglas's force. These were the 79th Colonial Battalion, a regular unit recruited mainly from Eritrea and Tigre, which had fought McLean at the Limado bridge in April, and now came under his command as the 79th or McLean's Foot, and the Wollo *banda*, a regular *banda* group recruited in Wollo, which came under Pilkington's command. Both officers were promoted to captain. McLean had under his command 200 Centre troops and 800 ex-

ascari; Pilkington had Sergeants Preedy and MacDonald, the latter released on the surrender of Debra Tabor, 200 Centre troops and 1500 Wollo *banda*, the numbers having been increased by the enlistment of Wollo Galla who came with Douglas. The *ascari* kept their own weapons, Italian drill, and their own *graduati*, the *sciumbasci* becoming company commanders and the *bulukbasci* platoon commanders. These two formidable units formed the essential regular nucleus for patriot activity until the end of the Gondar campaign. Pilkington in addition had a strong gunner unit, the Irish sergeants Morrow and McLure with the mortar platoon, three captured 65-millimetre guns, two Breda anti-aircraft guns and 60 ex-*ascari* gunners.

Nasi's comment on this re-enlistment was that they joined the British '*per amore o per forza*'. McLean agrees that the men really had no choice. It was impracticable to send them home, but there was no compulsion. One of McLean's soldiers, Zaudi Hunegnaw, later a colonel, recalls, 'We sent the Italians to Dessie and we heard they went to Kenya and built a good road. We kept the *Banda* to help us in the fighting and changed them into good soldiers.' Nasi was critical of Angelini's surrender, reporting the armistice to Rome on 5 July, 'I already have reservations about the conduct in command of this officer, which should be investigated after the war,' and again on 8 September, 'Debra Tabor surrendered prematurely not having had any considerable losses.' A number of *graduati* escaped capture and made their way to Kulkaber and thence to Gondar. Depositions were taken from these men by a colonel on Nasi's staff and sent to Rome by the courier plane, which confirm that losses were relatively light and that the 'English' attacks were not pressed to close quarters. What happened to Colonel Angelini after the war as a result of these investigations is not known. Among the *graduati* who escaped was one Muntaz Unatu Undisciau (Amhara) of the 79th Battalion, who became a great hero. He reached Kulkaber badly wounded from a land mine explosion, refused to hand over to the commander, Lieutenant Colonel Ugolini, the battalion flag, which he had brought with him wrapped round his body, and died in hospital in Gondar still declaring his loyalty to the Italian flag and exhorting his fellows not to surrender, '*non fare resa*'. He was awarded the *Medaglia d'Oro al* VM posthumously, one of only two colonial soldiers to receive this award, the other having been a naval rating at Massawa.

Douglas's force, to be known as Dougforce or Douglas's Patriots, was now 7000 strong, consisting of 3000 regulars or ex-*ascari* and 4000 Patriots, 2000 under Fitaurari Birru and 2000 Shoans under Fitaurari Haupte Selassie. He now came under the *kaid*'s HQ at Asmara and his intention was to move northwest and invest Kulkaber. There was some communication but little coordination between the various patriot forces operating in the Gondar sector, and what was needed was a central commander, a 'Wingate', to control the diverse operations of Dougforce, Sheppard, Mohamed Effendi, Ringrose and Railton. In a paper entitled 'Notes on Patriot Cooperation in Operations in Gondar' dated 26 August 1941, Sandford recommended that the Crown Prince, Asfaw Wossen, should take command of all patriot forces in the Gondar sector, assisted by a British director of operations, 'he, the Crown Prince, would have great confidence in Major Nott if this officer could be loaned for this purpose.' Sandford's advice was not taken, Nott was by that time back with his regiment in North Africa, and control of operations remained loose and unsatisfactory.

North of Gondar Ringrose and Railton between them controlled the Gondar–Asmara road between Uollaich and Debarech, Ringrose operating north from Dabat against Debarech assisted by Dejasmatch Ayalewu and his 7000 Patriots, and Railton operating south from Amba Giorgis against Uollaich, assisted by Dejasmatch Arayia's force of 3000. Railton was also in contact with Mohamed Effendi and Sheppard and sometimes operated with them. On 12 May Railton went to see Ringrose at Dabat, a 40-mile mule ride, meeting him for the first time at Ringrose's request. Ringrose had a wireless telegraphy set and was in touch with the *kaid*'s headquarters at Asmara and could call on air support. Railton agreed to mount an attack on Uollaich to divert attention from an attack planned by Ringrose on Debarech on 14 May. Air support was promised but not before 11.00 a.m. Railton hurried back to Amba Giorgis, another 40-mile ride, sent word to Arayia to join him and marched on Uollaich with C company early on 14 May, taking the Italians completely by surprise. His leading platoon could have marched straight in but he held it back because of the airstrike planned for 11.00 a.m., a decision he had to make but much regretted. By 11.00 a.m. when the aircraft attacked (and did little damage because the Italians were well dug in), the defenders were thoroughly prepared and all that Railton could manage was a demonstration in force. As C company withdrew, the Kamant, who had been watching, joined in against them, but Arayia and his men, marching speedily to the sound of the guns, arrived in time to cover their retreat.

Ringrose's attack on Debarech had some initial success, but the Patriots were driven back by a counterattack and lost 18 killed and 27 wounded. A second attack was planned for 21 May and again Railton was asked to mount a diversionary attack on Uollaich, again covered by an airstrike at 11.00 a.m. Railton would have preferred a dawn or night attack, but the Patriots had great faith in air power and insisted on waiting for the RAF. The attack was a disaster. At 10.00 a.m. the Armachaho chiefs, whom Sheppard had persuaded to join in with 1200 men, walked off the field, apparently annoyed with Arayia. At 11.00 a.m. the RAF bombed Railton's camp at Amba Giorgis, 12 miles away, by mistake and 'the fire went out of the Patriots'. C company attacked alone with great courage led by the warrant officer while Railton, the 20-year-old subaltern, tried to exercise some control over the whole battlefield. One platoon got through the wire but it suffered heavily and Railton called off the attack. The Kamant again attacked as did two of Nasi's homemade 'tanks', which were extremely troublesome. Mohamed Effendi, who had been sent with 150 men to cut the Uollaich–Gondar road, had been wounded and was evacuated and C company suffered 23 killed and 30 wounded out of 140 engaged, 37 per cent casualties. Railton returned to Amba Giorgis to recruit and train reinforcements. He had no doctor and his wounded were looked after by the women in the local villages and most survived. He resumed raids and mining operations against the Gondar defences and concluded that patriot penetration north of Gondar offered better prospects than battering away against the fixed defences of Wolchefit as Ringrose was attempting. Ringrose's attack on Debarech on 21 May had been anticipated by the Italians who struck first, causing severe casualties (80 killed and 100 wounded) among the Patriots who were Ayalewu's men and also the men of Dejasmatch Nagash, Bastiani's opponent at Zaremma, who had agreed to join Ringrose if supplied with arms and on payment of 50,000 dollars.

Then the Italians struck a blow from which the Allies would take some time to recover. Gonella never had any trouble from Bastiani's irregular *banda* who remained completely loyal. The Banda Altipiano, a regular *banda* with a full complement of Italian officers, was troublesome. There were 100 desertions and the main body refused to fight and requested discharge. Exercising, in Nasi's words, 'his vast authority', Gonella persuaded the men to return to duty and ordered a sortie to raise morale and break the ring of encircling Patriots, sending the two *banda* groups with two Blackshirt companies to raid Ayalewu's camp. The attack went in at dawn on 22 June and took the Allies completely by surprise. Ayalewu was wounded and captured, the capture being graphically described by a young patriot eye-witness, Jemmere Wonde Admassu; 'I saw Ayalewu being dragged away by *banda*. He had been wounded and the *banda* were mounted and two horsemen carried him between them, one holding his arms and one his legs.' One of Ayalewu's sons, Dejasmatch Merso, was killed, and his elder son, Dejasmatch Zaudu, was wounded but escaped, as did Ringrose, who was slightly wounded by grenade splinters in the mêlée. Nasi claimed 336 'rebels' killed. British sources do not confirm this figure but certainly a number of Patriots were killed and wounded and some of Ringrose's bodyguard. Bastiani and his *banda* are credited with playing a big part in this attack, and Bastiani with the personal capture of Ayalewu. Bastiani was commissioned in the field by Nasi as Sotto Tenente Bastiani and after the war was awarded the *Medaglia d'Oro al VM*, the citation referring to this incident. The effect of this Italian success on the Patriots and the local population was devastating. Ayalewu's men dispersed within a few hours. Ringrose withdrew to Zaremma and thence to Asmara where he had treatment for his wounds, which had gone septic. He sent word to Railton to withdraw to Zaremma also. The effect on Railton's Patriots had been equally devastating ('They now believed the Italians were going to win the war') and Arayia and his men disappeared into the hills, leaving Railton and

C company at Amba Giorgis with 50 Patriots who elected to stay, daily expecting an Italian attack. Railton declined to withdraw to Zaremma, and in any event 'my mind was made up by the soldiers of C Company who flatly refused to contemplate withdrawal.' Railton's retention of his base meant that the patriot effort could be rebuilt. Gradually the Patriots started to come back, first Arayia with 2000 men after ten days, then Zaudu with 3000. By early July Railton had a force of 6000 men, had established that an approach to Gondar from the north was feasible, and had reopened correspondence with the Kamant and met their chiefs. He hoped that Ringrose would come and take command.

Ringrose, however, had other plans, which sadly led to another debacle. He had blamed the capture of Ayalewu on the treachery of the local people, writing to Pilkington of 'a treacherous attack led by peasants on to our camp'. Bastiani emphatically denies this and there is no evidence to confirm Ringrose's belief. This was simply a well-executed surprise *banda* raid. Nevertheless Ringrose remained distrustful of the locals. He also believed, as evidenced by the surrender of Debra Tabor on 6 July, that Colonel Gonella would be more likely to surrender to regular forces, and while in Asmara had arranged with Platt's headquarters for regular support. He returned to Zaremma with a battalion of Indian infantry from the 5th Indian Division, the 3rd/14th Punjabis, commanded by Lieutenant Colonel Shute, and a British 25-pounder field battery, and from there marched to Bosa on the southwest flank of the mountain (see Sketch 8). From there it was planned to attack Wolchefit on 16 July with the Indian troops, Railton's C company, which Ringrose had sent for, and any available Patriots. By that time a patriot force had reassembled under the command of Dejasmatch Nagash, who had taken over the mantle of Ayalewu. Railton arrived at Bosa ahead of his company and on 14 July guided the Punjabi battalion up to Mortar Fort. From there B company of the Punjabis was sent ahead to occupy Passo Cianch (Surprise Fort), not then held by the Italians, while Railton with Colonel Shute, Captain White, forward observation officer (artillery) of the battery, and a British lance bombardier climbed a ridge above the fort to reconnoitre the attack and plan the artillery support. It was a wet, misty day and visibility was poor. Bastiani was

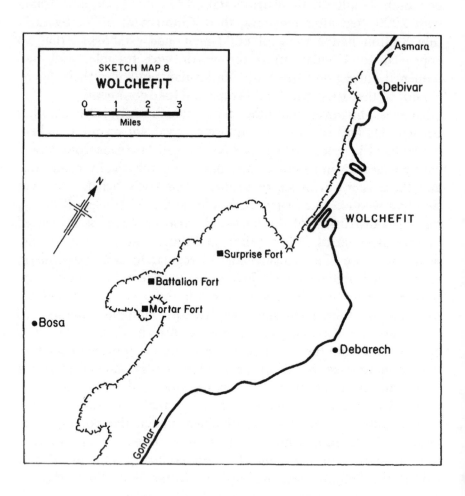

on patrol with his *banda*, surprised the Punjabi company at Surprise Fort while they were having lunch, attacked and put them to flight. Returning with his companions from the reconnaissance and when about 100 yards from the fort, Railton heard firing and 'saw the Indians running back like mad led by a British officer who was throwing away his equipment'. Shute and Railton both fired their revolvers at the officer running away and missed, and then followed the Punjabis. While Shute and Railton were running side by side Shute was hit in the back of the neck by a stray bullet and killed. The lance bombardier was also hit in the thigh but escaped. Major Furney, second in command of the Punjabis, brought up two more companies and recovered the colonel's body, but by that time the Banda Bastiani had disappeared with their loot, which included 'weapons, ammunition, a radio set, and documents revealing the British intention to attack on 16 July'. The Punjabis then moved half way down the escarpment where, at a conference with Ringrose, it was decided to call off the attack and the Punjabis returned to Zaremma. Their casualties, in addition to the colonel, were one NCO died of wounds and 22 other ranks wounded. Ringrose again believed that there was treachery, this time by some of his bodyguard who, he alleged, led the *banda* on to the Punjabis. Railton does not believe that there was treachery, but if the bodyguard were present, of which he is unsure, the fact that they were dressed the same as the *banda* may have caused confusion. 'This was simply a successful *banda* attack.' Bastiani is equally emphatic and down to earth. 'There was no treachery; we were hungry and wanted the food so we attacked.' The story of the 3rd/14th Punjabis is a sad one but a campaign history should tell the facts 'warts and all'. This fine battalion had fought well at Keren, but things can go wrong even with the best of units when taken by surprise in unfamiliar surroundings. What was even worse than the panicky retreat of the leading company was the decision to abandon the attack. To Railton the retreat and withdrawal were bitter disappointments and he felt deeply ashamed that British officers and regular Indian troops 'behaved in front of my men in such a way'.

On 15 July, the day after the Punjabi debacle, Railton with C company was sent to hold Battalion and Mortar Forts, which they occupied successfully after being ambushed by Bastiani's *banda*, suffering some bruises and broken bones from having to 'escape ignominiously down the cliff. A providential mist saved us,' — a third score by Bastiani's men. Down at his camp at Bosa, which was 3000–4000 feet below the forts, a two to three-hour climb, Ringrose, distrustful of his Ethiopian bodyguard, had requested and been sent as his personal bodyguard a platoon of 51 (Middle East) Commando, a unit, which had recently arrived to reinforce the troops investing Wolchefit from the north. This was a commando recruited in Palestine from Jewish and Arab Palestinians, a combination inconceivable today. On 21 July, the 100th day of the siege, Ringrose wrote to Gonella inviting him to surrender and congratulating him on his 'heroic resistance ... it will be an honour to meet you when this war is finished.' Gonella declined. On the same day Nasi signalled his congratulations, concluding, 'Wolchefit, be the MONTE GRAPPA of Ethiopia! Hold fast and they shall not pass.'[1]

On 1 August Gonella, wishing to raise the morale of his colonial troops (he had had more trouble with the Banda Altipiano), and in order to show that the national troops were doing their share of the fighting, led 700 Blackshirts supported by a mortar section against Battalion and Mortar Forts. The Italians left their positions at 3.00 a.m. and the attack went in at 7.30 a.m., led by First Seniore Gavazzi. To Railton this was (as well as being his 21st birthday!) the most important action of the Wolchefit campaign, the only occasion when they were seriously attacked by white troops, who suffered a defeat and whose morale then collapsed. Italian accounts agree on the facts but not on the collapse of morale. The positions were occupied by three platoons of C company, each about 50 strong, two in Battalion Fort and one in Mortar Fort, armed with Springfield .300 rifles. They had no mortars or light machine guns. Both forts were of stone with thick loop-holed walls, cliffs to the south and west, a narrow interconnecting path, and a panhandle to the north about 50 yards wide along which the attack came. Railton had spent the night 31 July/1 August at Ringrose's camp at Bosa, left at 5.00 a.m. on 1 August to rejoin his company, and arrived at Mortar Fort at 8.00 a.m. by which time the attack had started. There was then a field telephone link with Ringrose's camp and Railton asked for patriot assistance, which Ringrose sent up. The Patriots responded promptly and arrived at midday, and, taking a chance while the attack was in full swing, Railton, who had by then moved to Battalion Fort, sent them round to cut off the Italians' retreat. 'By 2.00 p.m. their horns were heard on top of the escarpment and the Italians had to abandon the attack and were hotly pursued. C Company had about 10 rounds left each. The Italians fought bravely but . . . did not get closer than 200 metres. They left 24 dead and 12 prisoners were taken. It was a resounding success.' Bastiani, who supported the Blackshirts with his *banda*, recalls that they were unfit and very tired after the long approach march. It is to their credit that they went forward bravely. The steadiness and good rifle shooting of C company deserve mention. It was reported to Nasi that the defenders had 20 machine guns. Railton tells a story, which illustrates the high morale of his Ethiopian soldiers. After the action a corporal was brought to him by the warrant officer who had been 'court martialled' by the men in his platoon for leaving his post when slightly wounded. 'They insisted that he be dealt with. He was stripped of his uniform and told to go home and not to attempt to re-enlist on pain of death.'

We will break off briefly from the story of Wolchefit to catch up with the operations of Dougforce, which had moved north of Kulkaber in mid July, less Welsh and No 6 Centre who had been left to garrison Debra Tabor (see Sketch 9). Douglas had been ordered by the *kaid* to isolate Kulkaber and Fercaber, to prevent food from Dembia (the area between Gondar and Lake Tana) from reaching Gondar, and to isolate Gondar on the south and east sides. Douglas, from his headquarters at Dancaz, passed these orders on to Pilkington and McLean and allowed them to run their operations, acting himself more as a liaison officer with the *kaid*. Pilkington made his base at Dagoma, north of Kulkaber, with the Wollo *banda* minus two companies that were watching the bridge over the Gumara river on the road between Kulkaber and Gondar, which had been partly demolished by Mohamed Effendi. Morrow, with the guns and some of the Centre troops, was northeast of Kulkaber in a position from which he could open artillery fire on the Italian defences. McLean, with the 79th Foot, was further

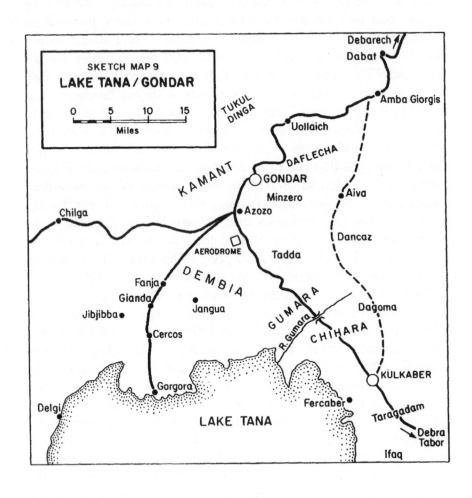

SKETCH MAP 9
LAKE TANA / GONDAR

0 5 10 15
Miles

north patrolling the southern Gondar forts and into the Kamant country west of Gondar. The blockade was clearly beginning to have some effect and, on 24 August, the Italians mounted a big operation to take supplies into Kulkaber from Gondar by road, the convoy consisting of 58 lorries escorted by two battalions of Torelli's 22nd Brigade, Braca's 1st Gruppo Bande and the 14th Gruppo Cavalry.

The two Wollo companies stationed at Gumara tried, but failed, to stop the Italians crossing the river, which they did by laying planks across the broken bridge. Pilkington at Kagoma heard the news and went to help with the rest of the Wollo and his Centre troops, sending word to McLean to join him (the message did not reach him in time) and finding the two Wollo companies still heavily engaged. A running fight ensued and the convoy got through with considerable losses. On 25 August Torelli fought his way back from Kulkaber, having delivered the supplies, reaching his base at Minzero in the evening after heavy fighting all day against the Wollo *banda* and Patriots who came to help. Reporting on the two-day action to Fitaurari Birru, who was still at Debra Tabor, Pilkington wrote, 'the Wollo were superb, the chief honour must go to them. They fought until they had no ammo left.' He reported, 'ten trucks smashed, six Italian officers killed, and many *askaris*, MGs, rifles, ammo and mules captured . . . a number of prisoners taken with one Italian Lieutenant. We had 14 killed and 39 wounded. Fit. Haupte Selassie fought well and was wounded in the leg.' The running through of this convoy to Kulkaber was regarded as another success for the energetic Torelli, and for Braca who received a third *Medaglia d'Argento al VM* for his conduct. Nevertheless, losses were such that they did not repeat it. Captain Celi of the *carabinieri*, stationed at Kulkaber, wrote that from then on supplies were sent to Gorgora, then by boat to Fercaber, and then, since they had few fit mules 'carried by soldiers in loads of 20 kg to Kulkaber, a distance of 20 km there and back'.

Dougforce maintained the blockade of Kulkaber, which was effective except on the side of Lake Tana, but was itself having problems, mainly because of lack of food and pay for the troops. Wollo *banda* and some Tigreans started deserting back to the Italians and there was a danger that all the Wollo *banda* might desert. This was averted by Pilkington, who assembled the *banda* and made an impassioned speech to them. They listened in silence and then, as Douglas described in a letter to Pilkington's mother after his death, 'suddenly chaired him on their shoulders and carried him to their tents, where Ethiopian style every man seems to have shaken his hand and grovelled on the ground.' Eventually an airdrop of dollars was arranged, though the RAF would not drop ammunition and Pilkington had to send a mule convoy to Amba Giorgis to meet supplies sent from Zaremma. The month of August ended for Dougforce with the problems of supply unresolved, but at least some pay for the troops, and this, with Pilkington's oratory, seems to have put an end to the desertions.

Meanwhile at Wolchefit the end of the siege was close. The blockade by C company and the Patriots on the south and west was effective and, although the garrison obtained some supplies by raids on villages and airdrops from Gondar (31 airdrops totalling 86,780 kilograms of supplies), they were running out of food. At the beginning of the siege Gonella had told Nasi that his supplies would last until 1 September with care. On 15 July he had placed the garrison on half rations and ordered the slaughter of transport mules to start. On 3 September he reported that he could not make the rations last beyond the end of September. Signs of scurvy and other disorders associated with malnutrition were beginning to appear, which were affecting the efficiency of the troops.

Action on the Wolchefit southern front during late August and September was concentrated at Surprise Fort. This had been garrisoned by a Blackshirt company since the withdrawal of the Punjabis. In response to Railton's jibes 'to see what they could do besides run away', Ringrose's Ethiopian bodyguard, which stayed down at his camp well away from the fighting, agreed to attack Surprise Fort in cooperation with C company. The attack went in before dawn on 26 August and was a brilliant success. C company made a noisy frontal attack while the bodyguard commander and 150 men slipped round the back and took the position by assault. Some 105 Italian prisoners were taken, with a mortar, two machine guns and signalling equipment. The attackers suffered 27 casualties, mainly from anti-personnel mines. On 18 September Gonella, aided again by Bastiani, evened the score against Ringrose. On a wet afternoon an Italian force drawn from the two *banda* groups with some national volunteers put in a surprise attack and the bodyguard was 'driven helter-skelter' back to Battalion Fort in the same manner as were the Punjabis. Casualties were not heavy though their commander was killed.

On the northern front 2nd/4th Battalion KAR from the 25th (East African) Brigade (Brigadier James) took over from the SDF company on 15 September. This was from the 12th African Division, commanded by Major General Fowkes, formerly commander of the 22nd (East African) Brigade, who took charge of the final operations against Gondar from 15 September, and the intention was that the KAR brigade would advance on Gondar through Wolchefit as soon as this surrendered. As the blockade tightened and his rations diminished Gonella was in regular communication about a surrender with Nasi whose instructions were, 'Sortie — seek an armistice to prolong negotiations — surrender.' On 23 September a fighter plane dropped on Gonella's headquarters Nasi's farewell message, conveying his admiration and gratitude to all ranks 'for the tenacity and loyalty with which you have carried out your duty of holding out to the last crust of bread'. On 25 September, following Nasi's orders, Gonella led a sortie against the Patriots at Uochen, causing casualties and suffering three *ascari* killed and 16 wounded. At 5.30 p.m. Gonella sent emissaries to Ringrose to request an armistice to negotiate for a surrender, who were received by Railton at Surprise Fort and conducted by him to Ringrose. Hostilities ceased at 2.00 p.m. on 26 September.

At 7.00 a.m. on 28 September Colonel Gonella marched out with the honours of war at the head of a representative contingent of his force, saluted by Brigadier James and a company of 2nd/4th KAR. Ayalewu Birru was released to the British and 71 officers, 1560 national troops and 1450 colonial troops went into captivity, including Sotto Tenente Bastiani and his *banda*, to whom he had offered honourable discharge a few days before the surrender but who had all elected to go into captivity with him. He felt that this was a great honour. Italian casualties from 14 April to 27 September were 364 nationals and 1340 colonials killed, wounded, deserters or missing, a total of 1704. Anglo-Ethiopian casualties are not known accurately. Apart from the 3rd/14th Punjabi debacle, these were suffered by C company, the bodyguard and the Patriots and were not light. C company alone suffered 50 per cent casualties. In contrast to the surrender of the Maraventano column, which was made to Wingate and Ras Kassa jointly, the Patriots were excluded altogether from the surrender ceremony, nor indeed did Ringrose and Railton attend. Practically this would have been difficult as the surrender took place at the northern end of the positions, several hours' march away across uncharted minefields, but it seems that the Patriots were deliberately excluded, and there was little recognition by the regular commanders of the part played by the Patriots in bringing about the surrender.

Nasi listed during the siege '31 actions and engagements, 25 aerial bombardments and 16000 artillery shots'. The artillery and air strikes were all from the north, the ground actions all with the forces from the south. At one stage Ringrose had 24,000 Patriots on his pay roll, including those with Railton, but Admassu believes that some chiefs inflated their numbers and the true number was between 8000 and 10,000. Even so this was a considerable number, and at ten dollars a man per month a very large payout. Railton's C company was eager to go on to Gondar but it was decided that, after six months' campaigning, it deserved a rest. Railton paid a generous tribute to his men. 'They never failed. Their cheerfulness was never daunted. ... Led by someone who knew nothing of Ethiopia and little of war their loyalty never faltered.' He is modest about his part but the fact is that his men were well led. Good officers are necessary in any army but with colonial troops the quality and personality of the leader was of paramount importance, whether he be a 21-year-old English lieutenant or a 28-year-old limping Italian sergeant major, whose brilliant leadership of his *banda* was properly rewarded by his country's highest military award. Ringrose, who had been pro-moted Lieutenant Colonel, was awarded the DSO, a proper award for the commander of what was in the end a successful operation, and recommended Railton for the MC and Sergeants Callis and Perkins for MBEs. The latter awards were not approved, though Railton was mentioned in dispatches. There were no other awards to anyone in Ringrose's force. The road to Gondar was now open to the 25th (East African) Brigade. Its brigadier and Ringrose took part in a social event that could only have happened in this extra-ordinary war. The *kaid* gave 24 hours' parole to all the captured officers from Wolchefit, and Ringrose recorded, 'Gonella gave a cocktail party to them and their wives in his flat [in Asmara] to which Brigadier James and I were invited and went and enjoyed.'

We will return to Dougforce. Late in August Pilkington had moved to Dancaz and McLean to Aiva while Sheppard remained at Amba Giorgis. Birru was still at Debra Tabor, though urged very respectfully by Pilkington to come north and organize food supplies for Dougforce with the local chiefs. ('I have had the privilege of knowing your Excellency for some time so I trust your Excellency will accept this letter in the same spirit in which it is written.') Douglas was less respectful, complained about Birru to the *kaid*'s headquarters and signalled Pilkington from Asmara on 9 September, 'Birru must provide food and mules...by end September or go. Birru being placed under my orders. Future rosy. Troops coming.' Birru did move to Dancaz by the end of September and the provision of food and supplies by the locals did improve. One is struck though by the different attitude of British military commanders towards patriot leaders in Gondar from that in Gojjam. In Gojjam it was recognized that this was their war too, that they had been fighting the Italians for much longer than the British, and their help was important. In the Gondar campaign they were treated more as auxiliaries under command and of limited value at that. The main campaign had been won, the KAR regular brigades were on the way, and patriot assistance could be dispensed with. For example, Ringrose wrote to Pilkington on 9 September, 'I have got the OK from Asmara to get rid of all patriots and just work with *banda* — now I am having difficulty in persuading the former to go!' Douglas's talk of getting rid of Birru would have been unthinkable in Gojjam under Sandford or Wingate and indeed such a suggestion was wholly inconsistent with the Emperor's authority. Ringrose never carried out his threat to get rid of the Patriots and they in fact finished up strongly at Wolchefit. Reports of the disagreement between Douglas and Birru did, however, reach the Emperor in Addis Ababa from Birru himself and the Emperor was very concerned with what he heard. He instructed Sandford to investigate and Sandford sent for Captain

John Millard, whom he had known as the commander of irregulars (Millard's Scouts) in southwest Ethiopia. He ordered him to go to the Gondar area to investigate and report. He was briefed by Tarleton and arrived in the Gondar area with the KAR in October.

After the fall of Wolchefit Ringrose's Patriots were dispersed and Sheppard, Pilkington and McLean were left to continue pressure on Gondar and Kulkaber. There is no doubt that had Wingate been given the command, or a director of operations under the Crown Prince been appointed as advised by Sandford, there would have been effective coordination of all patriot efforts and the fortress could well have fallen earlier. One Wingate method, which was well proved by the Gondar operations, was that there must be a regular nucleus, a Gideon Force, for any irregular operation. Dougforce had this, as did Railton. Ringrose did not. He only had a bodyguard of a few good men and many scallywags, and the fragility of unsupported patriot operations was demonstrated by the way his force vanished into thin air after the Ayalewu disaster on 22 June 1941, whereas Railton's nucleus stood firm. Sheppard had no regular nucleus either, only Mohamed Effendi and a small *banda*. Sheppard left no account of what he did and it would be unfair to dismiss his efforts as negligible, but certainly the impression he left with his fellow officers was that, apart from Mohamed Effendi's sabotage activities, he did not achieve very much. Pilkington and McLean were not very respectful about their colleagues in their letters, referring to Welsh as 'the schoolmaster' and to the 36-year-old Sheppard as the '*bimbashi*' or the 'Old Bim', and thought his discomfiture in a raid on his camp by the 25th Colonial Battalion from Gondar on 8 October a great joke. McLean, who was camping nearby and did his best to help with the six men he had with him, wrote, 'You would have laughed like hell yesterday. The great *bimbashi* lost all his kit and most of his money. All his soldiers ran away except . . . his Sudani *hamla* men who got badly cut up.' Sheppard evaded capture and retired to Debarech. In fairness to a very gallant man there was no need for a Cairo University lecturer to have volunteered for this dangerous job, nor to have gone on to serve under the Special Operations Executive in Greece, where he was killed in 1944.

While Pilkington enforced the blockade of Kulkaber, assisted by

Morrow and his guns, who kept up an intermittent fire from the northeast, McLean and his battalion raided the Kamant and the Azozo forts and mined the approach roads to Gondar. McLean also drew excellent maps of the southern and eastern Gondar forts, which were of great value to the KAR brigadiers when Gondar was attacked. One of his soldiers, Shalaka Alemaiyu Hailu, remembers McLean as 'a serious man. When we were not fighting, at night he would read books and draw maps.' Pilkington wrote home to his parents in England describing the countryside and people with his thoughts on various matters. He had a high regard for Birru, 'a delightful person — a great figure in Ethiopia, second only to the Emperor.' His description of highland Ethiopia in 1941 after the long rains is evocative and sad; 'cold and sparkling streams ... fields blazing with yellow or shimmering with blue ... thousands of brilliant butterflies ... heavy contented humped cattle browsing in the lush grass.' This description would have been true when Bruce visited Gondar in the eighteenth century and for centuries before that, but not sadly today in most of highland Ethiopia. He wrote to his father about courage, 'the only quality that really matters in a man ... anything can be forgiven to the brave in heart and nothing can atone for an ungallant spirit. ... Before I had taken courage so much for granted, never believing that it could be lacking — save possibly in races much inferior to my own. Now I look on it as something beyond value.' As with a remark quoted from Tutton earlier, the belief of the English that they were superior to other races is a historical fact. Perhaps at heart they still believe this!

The lonely operations of Pilkington and McLean were about to come to an end. The 25th (East African) Brigade had cleared the demolitions on the Wolchefit pass, had moved to Amba Giorgis, and by the end of October were in contact with the Gondar defences at Uollaich. On 4 November Pilkington had orders to move south to cooperate with a regular force in an attack on Kulkaber. The final phase of the Gondar operations was about to begin.

Gondar: The Final Phase

The opposing forces in the final phase were as follows. In addition to the surviving outlying garrisons of Chilga (four battalions with artillery), Gorgora (one battalion), and Kulkaber (three battalions with artillery), Nasi had 20 battalions and 16 batteries in the main Gondar defences. Of these one battalion and a battery were at Tukul Dinga, five battalions and four batteries at Uollaich, and 14 battalions and 11 batteries in Gondar itself, a total, excluding the outlying garrisons, of 22,500 troops and 40 guns, according to Italian intelligence sources. The number of prisoners plus casualties suggests that the total was nearer 25,000. Against these forces Fowkes had in the 12th African Division nine and a half battalions of infantry, two East African 25-pounder batteries, two Indian mountain batteries (3.7 howitzers), the Gold Coast medium battery (60-pounders), the Kenya Armoured Car Regiment, and South African light tanks, engineers and a road construction company, in total about 15,000 men. The bulk of the infantry were KAR, seven and a half battalions, with a Pioneer battalion, half a battalion of Argyll & Sutherland Highlanders and about the same number of Free French. Under command were the 2nd Ethiopian Battalion, advancing up the west side of Lake Tana, and the Composite Battalion SDF (now known as Sudancol) advancing again against Chilga, and five patriot groups, all given military designations as follows:

Shepforce	Sheppard and his Patriots
Dougforce	Douglas and his Patriots
Camforce	Captain Campbell and the Shoans
Ellforce	Captain Elles and irregular cavalry
Veeforce	Captain van Veen and Patriots with Sudancol

Another irregular force, Henfrey's Scouts commanded by Captain Henfrey, arrived on 15 November in time for the final assault after a long march from the Kenya border. Fowkes's divisional intelligence officer was Lieutenant Colonel Michael Biggs, Royal Engineers, whose intelligence reports are an important source.

The Italians were superior in numbers of infantry and guns and most of Fowkes's infantry were new KAR battalions, untested in battle, but the Allies had almost complete aerial superiority. Fowkes's force was a real polyglot army, the infantry Sudanese,

Ethiopian, Scottish, Free French, with the bulk KAR, Africans from Kenya, Tanganyika, Uganda and Nyasaland under British officers; East African, Indian and Gold Coast gunners; Kenyan armoured cars and South African light tanks; South African, East African, Gold Coast and Sudanese engineers and pioneers; Northern Rhodesian field ambulances; last, but certainly not least, the Ethiopian Patriots under their leaders, erratic, but in the end playing a major role in the final assault; the whole force supported by the Royal Air Force and South African Air Force.

Fowkes's original plan was for one KAR brigade to advance on Gondar through Wolchefit from the north and the other from Debra Tabor through Kulkaber from the south, but this was changed because the long rains continued well into October and the road from Dessie to Debra Tabor was not passable by a large motorized force. The final plan was for both KAR brigades to go in from the north through Wolchefit, and a smaller force, known as Southforce, was to come up from Dessie as soon as the road was passable and tackle Kulkaber in conjunction with Dougforce. The 2nd Ethiopian Battalion, advancing up the west side of Lake Tana, was to cut communications between Gorgora and Gondar to stop supplies reaching Kulkaber, and from the west Sudancol was to make a further attempt on Chilga.

First into action was the 2nd Ethiopian Battalion, officially now the second battalion of the Ethiopian Army, but we will keep the old name (see Sketch 9). The battalion had moved from Addis Ababa to Debra Markos in September 1941, thence to Dangila, less one company left to garrison Dambacha, and arrived at Delgi on the west side of Lake Tana late in October accompanied by Ellforce, an irregular cavalry unit 50 strong, mixed Sudanese and Ethiopian, commanded by Captain Elles, Political Officer Gojjam. Benson still commanded the battalion and Dr Zablany was still medical officer, but of the original British officers who had entered Gojjam only Tutton remained, back commanding D company. Captain Gordon Naylor, formerly of No 3 Centre, was adjutant. Of the other company commanders two were from the KAR and one from the Leicesters, and the British NCOs were all from British regiments. With Tutton in D company was Sergeant Symmonds. Of Ethiopian officers Gerazmatch Asfau and

Lieutenant Haile Mariam were still with D company and Captain Werku Desta and Lieutenant Enko Haile Mariam with B. Although reorganized on British Army lines in April 1941 the battalion had no three-inch mortars and no supporting weapons other than Vickers medium machine guns, a serious omission, which resulted in many good men's lives being wasted when they were required to attack a strongly fortified position. There were plenty of captured guns and mortars available and it is difficult to understand why Benson did not make a fuss about this. Certainly neither Wingate nor Nott would have accepted this situation, nor, to give him his due, would Boyle.

Benson's orders were to disrupt communications and stop the movement of supplies between Gondar and Gorgora in either direction. The Italians had a battalion at Gorgora, posts at Cercos, Gianda and Fanja on the new road to Gondar, and a battalion at Jangua, eight miles to the east of the old road. Benson decided he must eliminate the central post of Gianda in order to carry out his duty of disrupting communications. This was a formidable task for his small force, having regard to the strength of the Italian forces in the area. He had 350 men in the three companies of his battalion and 50 irregulars under Elles. Gianda was garrisoned by a *banda* of about 120 men, all Ethiopians from the area, under Lieutenant Ugo Collarini. The post consisted of an outer perimeter and an inner fort, the old *Residenza*, a two-storey stone building with a verandah which was sandbagged and wired, the whole making an effective blockhouse.

Benson left Delgi on 30 October led by Elles with a screen of mounted infantry. After losing one *askari* killed in a skirmish with the enemy they halted on a start line ordered by the divisional commander, and assembled at Jibjibba, three miles west of Gianda, on 10 November. On 11 November, while Ellforce went east to block any reinforcements that might be sent from Fanja or Jangua, the 2nd Ethiopians attacked Gianda at 5.00 a.m. The attack was successful to start with and the outer perimeter occupied, but the inner blockhouse was very strongly defended and the attacking companies were held up and suffered casualties. Early in the assault Tutton, in the lead with D company, was hit as was Gerazmatch Asfau, and Lieutenant Haile Mariam was killed.

Tutton and Asfau were assisted back to cover by Sergeant Symmonds and two *askari*. By 9.00 a.m. the attacking companies were making little impression on the defence. Some of the leading troops were as close as 40 yards from the blockhouse, exchanging fierce small-arms fire with the defenders. The lack of mortars was severely felt and the men could not lob grenades beyond hand-throwing range as the Springfield rifles, which they still had, could not be fitted with grenade dischargers, like the British Lee Enfields. Elles left some of his men to guard the Fanja road and came back to help in the assault. At this point Naylor arrived with a message from Benson that if the fort did not surrender in half an hour he would signal divisional headquarters and call off the assault. Then Naylor, who was reputed to be a good cricketer, succeeded in lobbing two Mills grenades onto the verandah of the blockhouse, which caused considerable damage and casualties. A British sergeant set fire to a building adjacent to the blockhouse with a cigarette lighter and a Verey pistol, and an RAF plane, one of a force which had raided Jangua, appeared overhead. The Ethiopians resumed their attack, and under these combined pressures the garrison surrendered at 9.45 a.m. Enko gives the credit in the final assault to Werku[2] Desta, who 'attacked the Italian camp with hand grenades and killed many Italians and raised the Ethiopian flag'. The divisional intelligence report of 11 November records, 'a fierce engagement lasting four hours. . . . Ethiopians are reported to have behaved magnificiently.' Ethiopian casualties were one Ethiopian officer and 14 *askari* killed, one British officer (Tutton, who died of his wounds), one Ethiopian officer and 27 *askari* wounded. Ellforce suffered two Ethiopians killed and one wounded and two Sudanese wounded. Italian casualties were 17 *ascari* killed and 30 wounded, and Lieutenant Collarini and 56 *ascari* captured. After the action the 2nd Ethiopians drove back an Italian force advancing from Jangua and then concentrated at Jibjibba. The Italians then evacuated Jangua and Cercos and retired on Gorgora where the Ethiopians followed them. By this time the Gorgora garrison was 1500 strong, too strong for Benson to attempt an assault with the 300 regulars and 40 irregulars left of his force, and he remained investing and raiding the position until Gondar surrendered.

The result of this small but very sharp action was that communications were effectively cut between Gondar and Lake Tana, as was the line of supply to Kulkaber, and the first crack in the Gondar defences had been made. If Benson had had mortars the attack would have succeeded more quickly with fewer casualties to the attackers, but the 'magnificient' performance of the 2nd Ethiopians at Gianda wiped out any stigma remaining from the Charaka action (if there was any) or from the mutiny, and overturned the verdict of historians that the battalion was of no use after Charaka. Here also was another case, as in Gojjam and Wollo, where Ethiopians were ranged against each other under different European leadership, giving complete loyalty to their leaders. Collarini's men did not give up until ordered to do so. Leading the assault against him was Tutton, who commanded equal loyalty from his men. Politically the victory had significant consequences. Biggs reported on 13 November, 'Capture of influential *banda* leader at Gianda is said to have had exellent morale effect in that area.' The Kamant surrendered to Sheppard on 15 November. The connection cannot be proved, but seems likely.

Tutton had been shot through the groin and his intestine perforated. Arrangements were made to evacuate him to hospital and a South African Air Force Hart piloted by a young Cape Town pilot made a daring landing on a hastily-cleared landing strip near Jibjibba. While Tutton lay on a stretcher waiting for the plane he asked to see the officer in charge of the fort. Collarini has left his own account of his meeting with Tutton in a letter written in Addis Ababa on 24 November 1941.

The wounded man said these words to me in Italian, 'I am happy to make the acquaintance of a courageous soldier and I wish to shake his hand,' I replied, 'If the Abyssinian formations had not been commanded by you and the other English officers with such bravery it is certain that I would not have lost the battle.' I bid him farewell and wished him a speedy recovery. 'Yes', he replied, 'apart from the war there must be no grudge between men [*oltre la guerra fra gli uomini non deve essere rancore*].'

Tutton was flown to base hospital at Dabat and operated on, but died the next day on 12 November and was buried at Dabat, although a few months later his grave was moved to the War Graves Commission cemetery at Asmara, where it still is. A moving tribute to Tutton, and to Rowe who died after Uogghidi, comes from an Ethiopian comrade, Colonel Enko Haile Mariam, interviewed in 1989, 48 years after these events, but yet with clear memory and strong and genuine feeling. Colonel Enko wrote out for the author, in Amharic and without hesitation, the names of the British officers who entered Gojjam with his battalion.

> Captain Tutton was a good man. We took him to be a religious man. He was constantly advising us. When we moved from Um Idla he came to greet me to shake my hand and said, 'Good luck. I am sure you will do some heroic deeds.' He bid us farewell as we marched into Ethiopia. Unlike Boyle and Smith, Tutton when he met the soldiers of the battalion gave them hope, saying, 'You will have your independence in a short time!' At Gianda after he was wounded he told us to go on fighting. He called out, 'I am going. I am wounded. Go on fighting.' We carried him back to safety because we liked him. Tutton and Rowe [Jiggsa] were the two people most loved by the Ethiopians. Jiggsa was buried at Gulela. Ethiopian soldiers wept at his burial. I was present when Jiggsa was buried.

Tutton took to war with the same enthusiasm with which he had pursued his other interests before the war. He had dedicated his life to the service of Africa and would have made his mark, like his comrade, Dick Luyt, had he survived. He understood that Ethiopian soldiers must be led by example and not driven, appreciated that to them the campaign was a crusade to free their country, and consistently showed a fine example and great courage. With Tutton died also Haile Mariam, one of the original officers of D company, who, according to Luyt, had formed a close friendship with Tutton and it was perhaps appropriate, if they had to die, that they should die together.

The next task for General Fowkes was to try and eliminate

Kulkaber and for this purpose Southforce assembled at Debra Tabor on 11 November, consisting of the 1st/6th KAR, the 1st Battalion of the East African Pioneers under Lieutenant Colonel Michael Blundell, the 51st (Gold Coast) Medium Battery (60-pounders), one squadron of the Kenya Armoured Car Regiment, and the 9th Field Squadron of the South African Engineers under Major Gilson. The force was commanded by Lieutenant Colonel Collins, the officer commanding the 1st/6th KAR. With Southforce was Captain John Millard, appointed liaison officer between the regular forces and the Patriots, with orders to report to Sandford on the relations between Douglas and Birru. While Fowkes's forces closed in on Gondar, Biggs's intelligence reports reveal, from intercepted signals, that Nasi was being urged by Rome and, in turn, was urging his troops to hold on for another two months in the hopes that the Germans would come to their help. The last days of Gondar were being affected by events of immense gravity elsewhere. By the middle of November 1941 the Germans had advanced to within a few miles of Moscow. In an attempt to draw some pressure away from the Russians, the Eighth Army in North Africa attacked and, by 18 November, had driven Rommel back to El Agheila. Rommel counterattacked and this started a British retreat, which ended in June 1942 with the British back on the Egyptian frontier. This was too late to save Gondar, but the Axis advances encouraged resistance and in November 1941 the idea of rescue was not completely fanciful.

The defenders of Kulkaber totalled 1910 men of all ranks from three battalions under Lieutenant Colonel Augusto Ugolini, an infantry officer of the regular army, in the 67th Colonial Battalion, one of the battalions of Torelli's 22nd Brigade, 240 CCNN, and the *carabinieri* battalion (CCRR), half Italian *carabinieri* and half Zaptie, Ethiopian or Eritrean military police. The CCRR were, and still are, part of the regular army and have fought as infantry in all Italy's wars. On Fercaber there were 609 nationals from 14 CCNN and 88 colonial machine-gunners. Kulkaber, the 'place of the Euphorbias', was a mountainous position of ridges and peaks, Fercaber lower but also formidable (see Sketch 10). Both positions had strong defences with barbed wire and many booby-trap mines. General Nasi's orders were to hold fast. A unit, if cut off, should

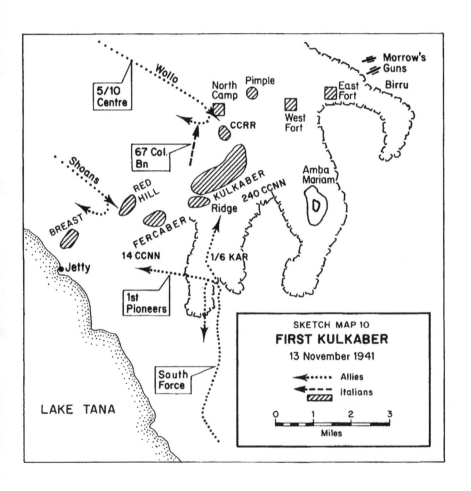

SKETCH MAP 10

FIRST KULKABER

13 November 1941

←····· Allies

←--- Italians

0   1   2   3
Miles

hold out and wait for the counterattack. Collins's plan for the attack was for the 1st/6th KAR under its second-in-command, Major Robertson-Glasgow, to attack from the south supported by the Pioneers who would make a holding attack against Fercaber from the east. Pilkington's Wollo *banda* and Centre troops would attack Kulkaber from the northwest, while Haupte Selassie's Shoans would attack Fercaber from the west. Birru's Patriots with Morrow's guns were in position northeast of Kulkaber to support Pilkington's advance. The South African sappers of the 9th Field Company supported both attacks, not only in their normal role of dealing with mines and booby traps, but also two sappers were posted to each platoon of the infantry battalions to act as junior leaders and performed very valuable service. The Kenya Armoured Car Regiment's armoured cars, supported by 'mock-up' tanks (bulldozers camouflaged as tanks), would demonstrate against Kulkaber from the east. McLean with his battalion was at Tadda, placed to stop any assistance reaching Kulkaber from Gondar.

Douglas and Pilkington were critical of Collins's plan, which, they maintained, was made without proper reconnaissance and no provision for communication between the attacking forces, nor between Southforce and its supporting artillery, the Gold Coast 60-pounders. Millard accompanied the 1st/6th KAR HQ with 25 men from No 2 Centre with four light machine guns to act as liaison officer with the Patriots, but in fact liaison was impossible with the two attacking forces advancing from opposite sides of the mountain and no wireless telegraphy communication, and things turned out just as Douglas and Pilkington had feared. After bombardment by the 60-pounders and heavy aerial attack on 12 November, the attack went in at dawn on 13 November. The 1st/6th KAR, after a long approach march, which started at 1.30 a.m., cleared the Italians off the position shown as 'Ridge' soon after dawn, but were then held up by heavy fire from positions overlooking them on both sides and made no further progress. On their left the Pioneers advanced steadily against Fercaber, taking positions and prisoners, but Blundell noted that all was not well with the 1st/6th KAR. Looking down into a valley on his right, he saw 'groups of *askaris* sliding down into the valley in twos and threes'. Lieutenant Roger Swynnerton, adjutant of the 1st/6th KAR on that day, confirms that most of the right flank company retired without orders, leaving only one platoon with 12 men in position. Meanwhile from the northwest Pilkington attacked with the Wollo *banda*, supported by the centre machine guns, the mortar platoon and Morrow's guns, aiming at North Camp, held by the *carabinieri*. The Wollo, in Pilkington's words, 'put up a staggeringly good show', getting through the wire and past the mines and taking many posts from which the 'Italians picked up their MGs and buzzed off.' Some posts held, as ordered by Nasi, notably that of 'Brigadiere Salbatore Sansi' who held out 'clinging to his weapon and firing to his last breath' (one of Captain Celi's men and his description). Then the 67th Colonial Battalion counterattacked under their commander, Major Garbieri, and fighting swayed backwards and forwards at close quarters. The Wollo failed to take the fortified high ground, described by Pilkington as 'fantastically strong positions, sheer murder for a frontal attack', and in late afternoon withdrew with difficulty under cover of their machine guns. The Wollo suffered severely, 21 killed including three *sciumbasci* company commanders, and 71 wounded. Sapper Lance-Corporal McPhee with the Wollo was badly wounded and later died. On their right the Shoans fought well at Fercaber, losing 17 killed. They had been joined by Captain Karl Nurk, a Kenya white hunter who had served with the 3rd Ethiopian Irregulars in southern Ethiopia, winning an immediate MC. He was to serve with the Shoans for the rest of the campaign. Birru's Patriots also played some part, advancing from the east and drawing artillery fire, which was diverted from the main battle.

On the south side of Kulkaber the 1st/6th KAR was stuck on 'Ridge'. Robertson-Glasgow could not communicate with the Gold Coast battery nor with Dougforce. At one stage he asked Millard to get a message through to Pilkington to renew his attack, but as Millard was getting a patrol ready (it was now late afternoon), changed his mind and ordered evacuation. The men from Southforce trailed back down the hill to their bivouacs, which they reached at midnight. Collins blamed the Patriots for the failure of his attack, but the relative casualties (Southforce had very few) and the evidence of Colonel Ugolini and Captain Celi do not support this view. Whereas Southforce made some limited penetration these attacks did not worry the Italians, who again thought the enemy were Sudanese. The attack of the Wollo *banda*, whom they identified as such, did, however, cause them much concern and was extremely dangerous. The Wollo failed in their brave attempt to take North Camp, but this made no difference to the performance of Southforce. A good word must be said for the Italian defenders. The *carabinieri* and Zaptie followed Nasi's precept and held out even when surrounded and the *ascari* of the 67th Battalion counterattacked with vigour. The day was for the garrison a notable success.

The failure at Kulkaber caused Fowkes to change his plans. He needed the armoured cars and the Gold Coast gunners for his assault on Gondar and they could not get through to help until Kulkaber was taken. The 26th (East African) Brigade took over the Uollaich front and the 25th Brigade was sent to join Southforce and Dougforce at Kulkaber by an old track through Aiva, which was cleared by working parties. Brigadier James took command of the whole force and a second attack on Kulkaber was planned for 21 November. Sudancol was asked to demonstrate in force against Chilga on 20 November to divert attention from this attack. Before this came off there were changes in command. Crown Prince Asfaw Wossen arrived at Fowkes's headquarters on 18 November with his chief of staff to represent his father and to coordinate all patriot forces. At this late stage he could be no more than a figurehead but his presence was welcome. Also on 18 November Douglas's command was terminated, officially because he was sick after a fall from his mule, but actually because of his disagreement with Birru and other reasons. Douglas's command was divided for the Kulkaber battle between Millard, who took over all patriot forces west and north of Kulkaber (those of Pilkington, Nurk, Haupte Selassie and McLean), and Captain Peter Molloy (Somerset Light Infantry and 4th KAR), who was to lead Birru's men on the east side with Morrow's guns. Both men would admit that Pilkington, McLean and Nurk knew their jobs so well that their own functions were more as liaison officers with brigade headquarters than as commanders. Also on 18 November Sheppard had a success. His Patriots captured a hill overlooking Uollaich and the submission to him of the Kamant tribe was confirmed.

260

The second attack by the SDF Composite Battalion (Sudancol) on Chilga on 20 November was, in the words of Guy Campbell, 'a bit of a shambles', a gallant attempt against impossible odds. Gifford's Composite Battalion and B troop of the Sudan Artillery were the attacking force while 300 Pioneers and Patriots led by a Belgian officer, Captain van Veen, made a feint to the north. The attack went in at dawn on 20 November after Sudancol had made the same long difficult march up the escarpment (see Sketch 7). The Italian positions, still held by the three battalions of the 4th Colonial Brigade under Colonel Miranda and 502 CCNN, were now heavily wired and the wire was unaffected by the artillery bombardment, as our troops had discovered in the 1914–18 war. Some inroads were made in the defences, but casualties were heavy. Bimbashi Boyer, commanding No 3 Idara, was killed trying to lead his company over the wire by throwing an army blanket over it. After four hours hard fighting Gifford ordered withdrawal, the battalion having lost one officer and 25 Sudanese other ranks killed and 62 wounded of whom 16 were left behind. Although costly, the attack succeeded in its object of drawing reinforcements away from Gondar. Torelli's 22nd Brigade was again sent to assist, but was not needed although it did get involved in heavy fighting with Patriots on the way. Italian casualties were 70 killed and 150 wounded. The Composite Battalion remained in position west of Chilga patrolling and raiding the Italian positions until 28 November (the day after the surrender of Gondar) when Miranda surrendered in response to an order from Nasi dropped on him by a British aircraft.

Brigadier James's plan for the second attack on Kulkaber on 21 November was for Norcol (2nd/3rd KAR, supported by 2nd/4th KAR and 18th Indian Mountain Battery) to attack from the northwest where Pilkington had attacked on 13 November while Southforce attacked from the southeast from the direction of Amba Mariam. Nurk and the Shoans would attack on the right of Norcol, Pilkington and the Wollo *banda* would attack Fercaber, while Birru's Patriots, led by Molloy, would attack on the right of Southforce at dawn supported by Morrow's guns and take Pimple whose capture was essential to enable the 1st/6th KAR to reach its objective, the ridge to the west. The South African sappers were again in support as were the South African light armoured detachment, five Bren gun carriers with Norcol and three light tanks with Pilkington. The attack was preceded by a very heavy aerial bombardment (Ugolini says that there were 57 aircraft) and artillery bombardment by the 60-pounders (see Sketch 10a).

The part of the attack involving Birru and his Patriots went wrong from the beginning. Birru had not been consulted and when Molloy, a young officer quite strange to him, arrived at his headquarters on the evening of 20 November with two sappers and two KAR *askari* with a Boyes anti-tank rifle and explained the brigadier's orders he was non-committal and not impressed with the ability of the Boyes rifle to penetrate the Italian blockhouses. Molloy spent the night trying and failing to get through to the brigadier on the wireless set to warn him that Birru might not march. At dawn on 21 November Molloy was ready with his two sappers, Sapper J. A. Brenner and Sapper J. P. Pienaar. As Molloy records, Birru simply said, 'We will see', and after half an hour's fruitless argument Molloy set off for Pimple with the two sappers hoping to shame the Patriots into following. Some 100 men did follow for a time, but 'sprinted back when we came under mortar fire'. On the way to Pimple Molloy met Captain Ted Onslow with a platoon of the 1st/6th KAR, which had been sent to attack Pimple from which his battalion was pinned down. They agreed that Molloy should wait ten minutes while Onslow, taking Sapper Pienaar, tackled Pimple from the northeast, and he and Sapper Brenner would then go straight up the hill at the position. Onslow came under heavy fire from West Fort, a blockhouse covering Pimple, and Pienaar was shot in the face while attempting to cut the enemy wire. Onslow was severely wounded while trying to rescue him and was pulled to safety by an *askari* from his platoon, while Pienaar was rescued by another sapper, Sapper Treharne. All this happened under heavy fire from Pimple and West Fort, four noteworthy acts of bravery in Fowkes's polyglot army. Another extraordinary act was to follow. Onslow reappeared, carried by his men on a stretcher, and Molloy decided to attack Pimple alone with Brenner. His plan was to creep up and try and push a grenade through the embrasure of the corner pillbox. They reached the wire five yards below the pillbox without being spotted and then

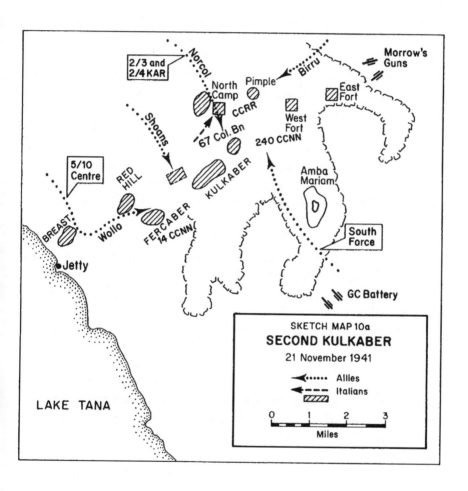

SKETCH MAP 10a

SECOND KULKABER

21 November 1941

◄·····　Allies

◄----　Italians

0　　1　　2　　3
Miles

were seen from West Fort while Brenner was cutting the wire, were fired on and Brenner was wounded. Molloy dragged him back 30 yards to the shelter of a fallen tree. The Italians exploded aerial bombs wired up as land mines all round them and they were left for dead, lying out in the blazing sun for four hours with Brenner only conscious at intervals.

The 2nd/3rd KAR's attack from the northwest against North Camp, held by the *carabinieri* and 240 CCNN, made good progress and made a breach in the defences. As Ugolini describes, 'Across this breach charged an East African unit courageously led by English officers. Furious hand to hand fighting followed . . . and the *carabinieri* were overpowered, but the English left many dead, including an English officer and two English NCOs.' Ugolini ordered a counterattack by the 67th Colonial Battalion, which drove the KAR back, and in retreating they were bombed by their own aircraft. They were rallied by the 2nd/3rd KAR's second in command, Major 'Bombo' Trimmer, West Yorks Regiment, who led them back up the hill in a second successful attack. Assisted by two companies of the 2nd/4th KAR, the 2nd/3rd KAR retook North Camp and held it against several further counterattacks by the 67th Colonial Battalion in the last of which Major Garbieri was killed. The *carabinieri* battalion commander, Major Serranti, was also killed in the confused fighting.

Meanwhile on the east side Southforce, held up by the eastern forts, was preparing to renew its attack, and Birru had been watching the battle. At 3.00 p.m. Molloy, still lying out on the hillside with Brenner, heard a lot of firing and cheering and saw 'the Patriots streaming up the ridge led by Fitaurari W. Kassa, Birru's bodyguard commander'. The Patriots took Pimple, their attack coinciding with the the KAR taking the remaining positions on the summit, including Ugolini's headquarters and the capture of Ugolini himself. The Shoans had kept abreast of the KAR on their right, supported by the five South African Bren-gun carriers, and cooperated in the final attack. Southforce was on the point of resuming its attack when Pimple and the summit fell, and the converging units rounded up many prisoners between them. During the last stage of the fighting in the eastern forts Seniore Alberto Casselli, commandant of 240 CCNN, was also killed, thus all three battalion commanders fell on that day. Molloy took two KAR stretcher bearers, recovered Brenner and took him to the first-aid post, and made his way back to Birru's camp.[3] In the attack on Fercaber Pilkington, supported by three South African light tanks and Lieutenant Barton-Bridges of the 9th Field Company with ten sappers, took Breast with the Wollo under covering fire from Sergeant Macdonald and the machine guns of the combined No 5/10 Centre. They went on to tackle Red Hill, but were beaten back by tree mines (aerial bombs in trees attached to booby traps on the ground) and artillery fire 'at point blank range'. Millard had succeeded in joining Pilkington's battle headquarters, accompanied by his bull terrier Bullet who went everywhere with him, and recalls a lighter incident during the attack on Red Hill when a flock of guinea fowl landed between them and the enemy. Tadessa, Pilkington's orderly, went out with his rifle, knocked over two, sprinted 50 yards to pick them up, strolled back with his bag and handed them over to Pilkington's cook, and then resumed his place in the firing line next to Millard grinning happily. Unlike the mountainous Kulkaber the terrain was suitable for tanks, which went on and silenced the guns, and tanks, Wollo and Centre infantry went on together, the tanks crushing the wire and silencing machine-gun posts until they ran out of ammunition. By this time the defenders, Blackshirts of 14 CCNN with *ascari* machine-gunners, were concentrated near the lake, still in strong positions. Pilkington sent in a Wingate-style message to their commander, Seniore Lasagni, that he would withdraw and let the Patriots finish them off. The threat worked and Lasagni surrendered with 700 prisoners. Pilkington is full of praise for the Wollo and Centre troops. 'They did magnificiently, all of them ... the Wollo thrilled with the loot, every man with a huge sack on his head, quite immobile as a fighting force.' The price in casualties was high. Patriot casualties, including the Shoans, were 55 killed and 120 wounded, but many Wollo leaders were killed in the attack on Red Hill and one South African NCO. Pilkington also praises the South Africans: 'Bridges and his sappers did a really good job and Lt Gage in charge of reserve tank crews, ex-Irish rugger international, did a superb job (not his own) going with the Wollo and taking charge at a time I was not there. ... Had a lovely bathe in Lake Tana.'

The Wollo had a deserved reputation, but a word should be said for the Centre troops of Mission 101 attacking here and taking casualties like seasoned infantry, still with one of their original British sergeants, Sergeant Thornton MacDonald of the 13th/18th Hussars, who had come in with van der Post's No 5 Centre. An old Centre soldier, Colonel Zaudi Hunegnaw, remembers Fercaber: 'There was fierce fighting at Fercaber; many British machine-gunners came to help us with tanks, also Kalasingha with guns.' (The 'British' were of course South Africans, the 'Kalasingha' the Sikhs of the 18th Indian Mountain Battery, great favourites with East African troops.) Millard's final comment on the Kulkaber/Fercaber actions was, 'I fear the Italians got what was coming to them. The Shoans took few prisoners and the Nandi regulars, after being bombed by their own planes, were in no mood for clean fighting.' (The 'Nandi regulars' were in the 2nd/3rd KAR, a Kenya battalion, and there were some Nandi in the 2nd/4th KAR, a Uganda battalion.) An Italian officer complained to Millard that his troops were 'very cruel', but the evidence is that once the white flags went up they were respected and although Ugolini reported 'robberies' by the Shoans there were no atrocities by them or by the KAR.

Italian casualties were, on Fercaber killed 25, wounded 55, missing 1, total 127, and on Kulkaber killed 3 officers, 142 nationals, 339 *ascari*, wounded 6 officers, 107 nationals, 244 *ascari*, missing 9 nationals, 51 *ascari*, total 901 out of 1910 troops engaged or 47 per cent. The *carabinieri* and the 67th Colonial Battalion suffered most severely, bearing the brunt of Norcol's attacks and carrying out the counterattacks. The 240 CCNN, mainly opposite South-force, remained in its positions and suffered less. On Kulkaber the fiercest fighting was on Norcol's front where the 2nd/3rd KAR took the strong positions, which the Wollo, unsupported, had failed to hold on 13 November, receiving Biggs's accolade like the Ethiopians at Gianda, 'Bde Cmd reports Norcol fought magnificently, particularly the 2nd/3rd KAR.' Norcol casualties were, killed one officer, 14 *askaris*, wounded eight officers, three British NCOs, 79 *askaris*, total 105. This was a harder fight than any in the earlier campaign and, apart from the 26th Brigade in the attack on Gondar on 27 November, the sort of opposition the

KAR would not meet again until Burma in 1944. Nurk, with Haupte Selassie and the Shoans, did well in support of Norcol, but Southforce, which suffered quite severe casualties in tackling the eastern forts, could say with justification that on this occasion it was badly let down by Birru. If Birru had ordered an advance his men would have obeyed without doubt, and the true reason for this failure probably lies with Birru's unhappy relations with Douglas. He was fed up with Douglas and disinclined to cooperate with him or with his successor for this battle, the immensely keen but new and untested Molloy, who was sent to him as the bearer of the brigadier's orders about which he had not been consulted. Birru was a considerable personage and should have been treated with more consideration, as indeed Pilkington had always done. Here again we see the different treatment of the Patriots in the Gondar campaign, as auxiliaries to be ordered about, not as allies to be consulted. The way was now open for the armoured cars and the Gold Coast battery to go through. The battery had played an important part in the Kulkaber action, with Morrow's guns and the Indian 3.7 howitzers. Molloy has vivid memories of the cheerful, muscular Gold Coast gunners throwing the 60-pound shells about as though they were footballs, and Ugolini was, to his great pleasure, invited to visit the battery after his capture by its commander, Major Stephens.

To the Italians Kulkaber was an epic battle, first the successful defence on 13 November, then the strenuous resistance on 21 November, marked by the high casualty rate including the death in action of the three battalion commanders. The *carabinieri* celebrate the action to this day with an annual reunion. Ugolini was awarded the *Medaglia d'Oro al VM* for his conduct in the action, as was (posthumously) Major Garbieri, commander of the 67th Colonial Battalion. One well-deserved award on the Allied side was that of an immediate DSO to Major Trimmer for rallying the 2nd/3rd KAR after Garbieri's first counterattack. Nasi's last fighter plane, a CR32, struck the last blow at Kulkaber, attacking the staff car carrying Biggs and the CRA, Lieutenant Colonel John Ormsby, on their way back from Kulkaber where they had been collecting identifications. Ormsby was killed and Biggs slightly wounded.

Gondar: The Final Assault

To the British the capture of Gondar, the last pocket of resistance, was a necessary, but not particularly important, divisional operation. To the Italians it was the final and sad moment when the curtain came down on their 58 years of empire in East Africa. Kulkaber having fallen Nasi anticipated, correctly, attack from the south and east and brought down two national batteries from Uollaich, including his one battery of 104-millimetre guns, and kept Torelli's 22nd Brigade, now reduced to two battalions, in reserve. Fowkes's plan was for the 26th (East African) Brigade under Brigadier Dimoline to attack the Daflecha Ridge on a two-battalion front and advance on Gondar from the east, while the 25th (East African) Brigade under Brigadier James advanced from the southeast astride the Kulkaber–Gondar road.

Dougforce, still so designated despite the change of command, would advance in the two-mile gap between the two regular brigades. The attacking forces benefited greatly from the accurate sketches of the Gondar defences prepared by McLean over the past weeks. Millard was now in command of Dougforce in place of Douglas, but, being a gunner, had obtained the brigadier's permission to shoot the guns with Morrow. Molloy substituted for him, regarding himself more as liaison officer with brigade headquarters than as the commander of the three experienced subordinates who formed his force, Pilkington, McLean and Nurk. Birru was left out, according to Molloy, 'in disgrace for his failure at Kulkaber, but his men got in on the looting'. In the north two other forces had parts in the assault. Anforce (the Argylls and the 3rd/6th KAR) would contain Uollaich, supported by Sheppard and his Patriots, the original Mission 101 North, in at the bitter end. Attacking on the right flank of the 26th (East African) Brigade were Campbell and his Shoans, men from Ababa Aregai's army who had fought at Dessie and Magdala (see Sketch 10b).

Attacks by the whole force started at dawn on 27 November, supported by a heavy aerial bombardment on Gondar itself. From a vantage point Molloy watched and recorded the advance of his forces. 'Typically the Wollo were off the mark, first going for the Fantar forts.' They took the first fort, then 'moving amazingly fast in their bare feet, they went straight on for the second fort and

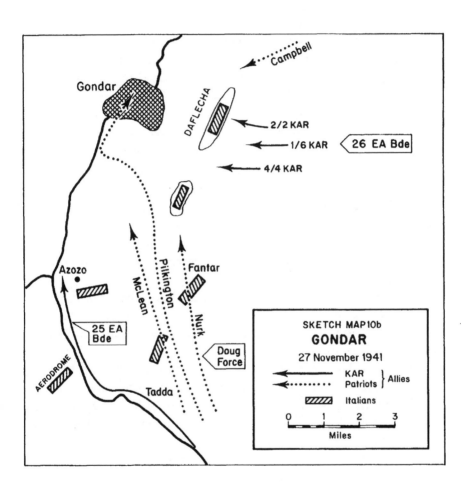

SKETCH MAP 10b
GONDAR
27 November 1941

KAR
Patriots } Allies

Italians

0   1   2   3
Miles

took this too, though with heavier casualties. The opposition were mainly Blackshirts who fought bravely and were mostly killed.' McLean's Centre troops and 79th Foot kept pace on the left of the Wollo. Millard and Morrow had got their three guns into position and Millard was shooting the guns, firing mainly in support of McLean, often over open sights. He watched the KAR regulars on McLean's left 'going in on their objectives with LMGs blazing and fixed bayonets', but McLean's men moved with such speed that it was difficult to keep the artillery fire ahead of them. 'The Italians fought like tigers for a short time but we moved too fast for them, swept over their forward defences and on.' On the right Nurk and the Shoans came up against stiff opposition. 'They occupied the big bluff opposite Fantar ... but were blown off it by accurate mortar fire; however they stuck to their position on the lower slopes in spite of heavy casualties, and eventually overran the bluff once more.' Millard and his gunners were being shelled by the big 104-millimetre guns from Gondar, but 'we were far too busy and excited to worry about that. Old Morrow by this time was cheering in broad Irish, his great red beard flying in the wind, and shaking a colossal fist at one enemy battery, which continued to plaster us on the ridge.'

By 12.15 p.m. Pilkington and McLean had taken the day's objectives and it had been envisaged that the battle for Gondar would take two days. Pilkington had other ideas and sent a message to Molloy at 1.00 p.m. that he was going for Gondar. 'I was appalled. Not only was it against orders, but he had to go up an open valley, overlooked by positions on both sides and commanded by the 104 mm guns from Gondar.' Molloy watched Pilkington's progress up the valley, being pounded by the heavy guns and also being strafed by allied aircraft that mistook him for fleeing enemy. At 2.00 p.m. Molloy signalled brigade headquarters, 'Shell bursts on old road to Gondar mark Pilkington beating Brigadier to it.' (The brigadier's comment on receiving this rather cheeky signal with the pun on Mark Pilkington's name is not known!) In Gondar Nasi launched his reserve against the southern attack but for the first time he records that Torelli's 22nd Brigade, which had fought so gallantly in so many actions, failed him. 'Reduced to two battalions, demoralized by an air bombardment, which had taken it by surprise that morning, its intervention was hardly effectual.' Because of the failure of his reserve, Nasi decided at 2.30 p.m. to send envoys to the British commander to ask for an armistice. At 3.15 p.m. Pilkington, after taking the high ground on each side of the road and the Addis Alem cavalry station, signalled Molloy that he was entering Gondar. 'We were in Gondar hours ahead of the regular African Brigades! We had some fighting at the old Portuguese castle where the *carabinieri* held out, but this was soon over and I went off to see General Nasi. It was a great day for the Wollo *banda*.' Pilkington found Nasi in the town hall. His envoys had not yet returned but, after some argument, Nasi had agreed to surrender unconditionally when Major Yeatman of the Kenya Armoured Car Regiment arrived with a squadron, sent by James to find out what was happening. Yeatman took the surrender, and Nasi's sword, which was later handed over to James. It was 4.30 p.m. when the Union Jack and Ethiopian flag were raised over Nasi's headquarters. The first regular infantry to enter Gondar was the 3rd/4th KAR, which arrived at 6.45 p.m.

Supported by the 'Patriots' on its right the 25th (East African) Brigade took its objectives, the Azozo forts, on 27 November without great difficulty. (The regulars always referred to Dougforce as 'Patriots' although they contained a significant proportion of regulars or ex-Italian regulars.) It was not so with the 26th (East African) Brigade, which had some very hard fighting. In the attack on Daflecha Ridge the 2nd/2nd KAR, a new Nyasaland battalion, attacking on the right with the 4th/4th KAR, a new Uganda battalion on its left with the 1st/6th KAR in support, suffered losses of two British officers, one British NCO and 15 *askaris* killed, 96 *askaris* wounded and six missing. The 4th/4th KAR also suffered casualties, but not so severely. This was a fight quite as tough as Chilga or Kulkaber and with comparable casualties and the objectives were not taken until 3.00 p.m. by which time events elsewhere had brought about the surrender. Molloy records a tail-piece of the battle of Gondar. Early on the morning of 28 November he went into Gondar with the 25th (East African) Brigade HQ to occupy the castle and went in search of his British patriot commanders. He saw, 'advancing up the road to the Castle a body of horsemen, unmistakeably Wollo, with at their head a bearded British officer on General Nasi's magnificient white charger. This, of course, was Mark, entering Gondar for the second time, and in style, as though leading his troop down the Mall for guard duty at Horse Guards.'

British casualties in the Gondar operation (mostly KAR) were eight officers and 108 other ranks killed, 15 officers and 370 other ranks wounded, total 501. Ethiopian and patriot casualties are not recorded, but were considerable with the Wollo and Shoans suffering most. Italian casualties were ten officers killed, nine wounded and three missing (total 22), 138 nationals killed, 214 wounded and 143 missing (total 459), and 599 colonial killed, 944 wounded and 444 missing (total 1248), an overall total of 1765. Prisoners taken, excluding Kulkaber, were 655 officers, 9379 nationals, and 12,956 *ascari*, total 23,008. The KAR historian, Colonel Moyse-Bartlett, sums up the operation as 'causing the heaviest casualties of the Abyssinian campaign ... the *askaris* were required again and again to attack ... static positions of great natural strength, manned principally by European troops under the best of the Italian generals.' This is a fair report of what the KAR did, although the casualty figures suggest that while the Italian national troops did fight well, the *ascari* suffered three times as many casualties, and these men, mainly Ethiopians, like Maraventano's troops remained loyal to the Italian flag right up to the end of the empire. The report also ignores the patriot contribution, as also apparently did the British commanders. James caused ironic amusement in Dougforce by a circular, copied to Dougforce, praising his units for 'achieving a victory, which is, in many ways, unique in its speed, dash and finality.' Platt, in a message to East African Command, which he took over in December 1941, praised 2nd Ethiopian Battalion for its conduct at Gianda and Gorgora, but did not mention the Patriots, nor did he mention them in his final dispatch. The facts are quite different. The Patriots played an important part at Kulkaber and at Gondar, and in the final assault on 27 November without any doubt they beat the 25th (East African) Brigade to Gondar, moving faster in their bare feet and bandoliers than the KAR in marching boots carrying Bren guns and mortars. Pilkington's men went bald headed at all obstacles, disregarding casualties, and reached the town first, and McLean's

Tigreans kept pace on their left. The intervention of these two units was decisive and probably shortened the battle, although the part played by the KAR and its supporting armour, artillery and engineers, particularly the 26th (East African) Brigade on 27 November, must also deserve high praise, and the other patriot forces all made contributions. Finally the air cover provided by the allied air forces (even though they strafed the Wollo streaking for Gondar!) was a sure shield and major contribution to victory. Many elements contributed to the winning of the battle of Gondar, but the important, indeed decisive, role of the 'Patriots' should not be ignored.

Notes
1. Monte Grappa – the central bastion of the defences in northeast Italy on the Austrian front in the 1915–18 war, which never fell.
2. The Patriots believe that 'the British gave Werku a gold medal,' but this has not been verified.
3. Both the brave young sappers, Brenner and Pienaar, made miraculous recoveries from their wounds and are still alive and live in South Africa.

9

The End of the Story:
The Anglo-Ethiopian Agreement

After Gondar the argument as to who had won the battle, the KAR or the Patriots, rumbled on. The Emperor wished to hear at first hand what the Patriots had done, and Pilkington and McLean were invited by Sandford, as ex-head of Mission 101, to come to Addis Ababa to see him. As McLean records, 'The KAR reckoned they had done all the fighting at Gondar and rather frowned on us and the Patriots so Sandford wanted the Emperor to hear what we had to say.' They recounted their exploits to the Emperor who thanked them and invited them to join his army, but understood that they wished to return to their regiments. Pilkington also raised the question of sending Ethiopian troops to North Africa. 'The Emperor seemed much taken with the idea,' and it was later announced that he was prepared to send a brigade with one of his sons; a brigade was in fact selected to be trained for the Sicily landings and Boustead was offered the command. Then rebellion broke out in Tigre and the Emperor wanted his troops, so unfortunately the idea came to nothing.[1] Neither Pilkington nor McLean in fact rejoined their regiments. McLean joined the Special Operations Executive, parachuted into Albania and was awarded the DSO. Pilkington joined Glubb's Arab Legion and while on detachment with the New Zealand squadron of the Long Range Desert Group in the Western Desert was killed on 17 November 1942 when his column was attacked by Italian aircraft. (Typically, he had been standing up to fire a Bren gun at the attackers.) The award of the MC for his command of the Wollo was gazetted in July 1943. Of many fine characters in this story Mark Pilkington is without doubt one of the more charismatic and he and McLean are remembered with affection by old Ethiopian soldiers to this day.

The visit by Pilkington and McLean happened after Sandford's return from England where he had been representing the Emperor in discussions about the Anglo-Ethiopian agreement, and to look at the origins of this we shall need to go back to Addis Ababa in May 1941 after the Emperor's return. The work of the Occupied Enemy Territories Administration (OETA) in former Italian territories other than Ethiopia was relatively straightforward, involving the setting up of a British administration to replace the Italian administration. In Ethiopia it was quite different. Apart from the fact that the name OETA was offensive to Ethiopians, who never conceded that their country was lawfully occupied by the Italians, there was conflict right from the beginning between an Emperor seeking to re-establish his authority and the British seeking to retain administrative control in areas where operations were continuing. As time went on this opened up into a wider conflict on the future of Ethiopia and what degree of control, if any, Britain should continue to exercise so long as it was providing financial assistance. In this final chapter we will try and follow through these two developments.

The policy of retaining British administrative control, in effect British political officers, in areas where operations were continuing was insisted on by Wavell. As Lush records, 'Haile Selassie did not understand the military policy and Dan Sandford did not fully agree at first, nor did Chapman-Andrews. Wavell told me, *ab initio*, "You have got to make it work." I did!' Making Wavell's policy work cost Lush his good relationship with Haile Selassie and caused many of those surrounding Haile Selassie to be suspicious of British policy. Despite the announcement in the British House of Commons in February 1941 by the Foreign Secretary Anthony Eden that Britain had no territorial ambitions in Ethiopia, the fear that the British intended to impose a protectorate lingered on.

In Addis Ababa difficulties arose between the officers of OETA

275

and the Emperor's officers over transport and housing and the arbitrary arrest by palace officials of Haile Selassie's political opponents. On one occasion Lush records that his British commissioner in charge of the Ethiopian police released 50 political prisoners from the palace compound. 'I had to send the Commissioner out of the country on leave.' The Emperor's staff thought that he should have taken a firmer line with the British and asserted his authority more. Haile Selassie refused to do this. He was a statesman who took a long view. Although he irritated the British authorities in minor matters, he saw clearly that the main objective was to win the war, and did not wish seriously to upset the British to whose military power he was beholden and who he hoped would help him to settle long outstanding Ethiopian problems after the war, for example the Ogaden and Eritrea.

Haile Selassie's first political move did, however, provoke a strong reaction from the British. This was the appointment, without consulting Lush, or indeed Sandford, of seven ministers and of Ras Ababa Aregai as governor of Addis Ababa. The last appointment was a good one and welcomed, but Lush was not happy about at least one of the ministers and considered in any event that the appointments without reference to him were a breach of Haile Selassie's undertaking to cooperate with the British authorities. Mitchell visited Addis Ababa on 23 May and had his first meeting with Haile Selassie to discuss this and other matters. He was on his way to London to discuss Ethiopian affairs and this meeting was the first move in a long process of negotiation, which led to the signing of an Anglo-Ethiopian agreement in January 1942. It is evident that Mitchell expected Haile Selassie to act on the advice of Lush so long as his government was being financed by Britain, and the minute of their discussion recorded by Lush suggests that Mitchell treated Haile Selassie rather as he would have treated the Kabaka of Uganda when governor of Uganda (as he had been), the relationship of a colonial governor to a subordinate native ruler. 'General Mitchell thought that HBM's Government would ask for an undertaking from the Emperor that ... so long as HBM's government were providing funds, he would act according to formal advice tendered to him by the High Commissioner or Chief Political Officer.' The language of this minute hardly depicts Haile

Selassie as an independent sovereign ruler returning to his kingdom, and the mention of a high commissioner, with its connotation of a protectorate, caused the Emperor and his advisers, including Sandford, grave concern. This was a proposition quite inconsistent with the assurances about Ethiopia's future given by Churchill and Eden in London, was never in their contemplation, and indeed was firmly squashed by Eden later.

On this occasion Haile Selassie replied to Mitchell that he had made the ministerial appointments in order to decentralize the work, and that 'his intentions were well known to Brigadiers Sandford and Lush.' He asked Mitchell to obtain decisions from the British government on six matters, the size and equipment of the Ethiopian Army, the provision of financial help, the provision of advisers, the administrative plan for the provinces, the debt due to Great Britain for the campaign, and a draft treaty. Mitchell departed for London to consult with the British Cabinet while the Emperor, assisted by Sandford, continued with his work of establishing his government in the capital and provinces alongside and in tandem with the administration of OETA, the political officers working under Lush. Many of these were former officers of the colonial administrations in East Africa or from the Sudan Political Service, including Charles De Bunsen, formerly of Gideon Force, who took over the important post of Political Officer Tigre.

The Emperor and Sandford also concerned themselves in organizing patriot support for the British forces in areas where operations were continuing, and on occasions the Emperor made expeditions into the operational areas to see things for himself. On one such occasion, on 20 May 1941, the Emperor visited Lechemti (where Kabada Tesemma was now in charge of the Patriots) to view operations, escorted by a platoon of D company 2nd Ethiopian Battalion under Luyt, in motor transport. Luyt, having marched on foot from the Sudan border, perhaps had too much faith in motor transport and took no kit, not even a greatcoat, expecting to return to Addis Ababa the same day. On their return from Lechemti, where they had come under shell fire, the transport broke down and it rained heavily. Luyt found shelter for his platoon and the Emperor's party in an Ethiopian village, and feeling responsible for the Emperor's safety, sent his men under cover and mounted guard himself outside the Emperor's hut, standing all night in the rain without a greatcoat. Next day the party returned to Addis Ababa safely, but not surprisingly a few days later Luyt was in hospital with rheumatic fever, where he joined Tutton who was recovering from dysentery. Both saw Rowe before he died.

During the next few months, while fighting continued in southwest Ethiopia and at Gondar, negotiations for an Anglo-Ethiopian agreement went on in Addis Ababa and in London. The participants were on the one side Mitchell and Lush representing HMG and on the other side the Emperor and his advisers, Ato Teffera Worq, his secretary, Sandford, and Lieutenant-Colonel Charles Mathew (legal adviser). Mitchell and Lush acted under the authority of the general officer commanding the East Africa Command, Cunningham until August 1941, then Wetherall until December, and then Platt. In Cairo the commander-in-chief, General Auchinleck, and the Minister of State, Oliver Lyttleton, were kept informed, and in London Churchill and Eden and a Cabinet committee were directly concerned. Thus the future of Ethiopia had the attention of the highest in the land. There is a current belief that Mitchell and the local military commanders sought to impose a protectorate and this was only prevented by the intervention of Churchill and Eden. That there was an element of truth in this will be seen, and Mitchell and Lush have been criticized for trying to impose excessive controls on Ethiopia, but their critics do not appreciate the military necessity of the time. In the second half of 1941 Britain had suffered a series of reverses in North Africa and the Mediterranean and was fighting for her life. Russia had been an ally since June 1941 but her armies were in retreat. America only came into the war after the Japanese attack on Pearl Harbor on 7 December 1941. Britain could not afford, as Wavell had always insisted, to have the recently liberated country of Ethiopia in a state of disorder on her lines of communication, and this military necessity had a vital effect on the negotiations. Between June and December 1941 no one could be sure of the future, and it was not inconceivable that the Axis forces could have defeated the Allies decisively in North Africa and advanced down the Nile and into Palestine. Mussolini's promises to Nasi at Gondar had not been wholly fanciful. It was more important that the Axis powers should be defeated and Ethiopia's new-won freedom, which depended on this, should be secured, than that they should quibble over the degree of control Britain retained. These at least were the military commanders' views, which Mitchell and Lush tried to put into effect. In London Churchill and Eden took a longer and in the end wiser view, although militarily more risky. Britain went to war in defence of freedom, and, in Wingate's words, 'the right of the individual to liberty of conscience and of the small nation to a just decision at the tribunal of nations'. Ethiopia was the first to be freed, and any annexation of territory by Britain, or even the appearance of temporary annexation, was wholly against the principles for which she was fighting. There was never any intention on the part of the British government to annex Ethiopia or any part of it. When it appeared though that the measures of control proposed by Mitchell 'were steadily developing into something indistinguishable from a Protectorate', Eden intervened decisively, as he had done in Khartoum in October 1940.

After discussing the six points raised by Haile Selassie with the British Cabinet, Mitchell returned to Addis Ababa for further meetings on 1 July and 26 July. At the meeting on 1 July he passed on a personal message from Churchill, 'Go back to Addis Ababa as quickly as possible and see if you can secure HIM's willing agreement on the lines of our discussion in order that we can give help in restoring his government.' In between and after the meetings there was lengthy correspondence between the parties on the matters in dispute, Mitchell writing proposals and Sandford drafting the Emperor's replies, and it seems that Mitchell did some deliberate stalling.

> It is obvious that the conditions in which a treaty can be negotiated do not now exist, but I advise that Haile Selassie should be invited to make proposals. It will take him a long time to produce these and I will comment without improper haste and send them by seamail. It will be improbable that agreement will be reached much before Xmas.

The matters in dispute were five, the appointment of a high commissioner, the degree of financial control, the control of foreign

279

policy, the status and responsibility of political officers, and the reservation to British military administration of certain frontier areas (the reserved areas). The areas proposed to be so reserved for reasons of military necessity for the duration of hostilities were the Ogaden (in dispute between Ethiopia and Somalia), the line of the Addis Ababa–Jibuti railway, and a strip of territory adjoining French Somaliland. The idea of a high commissioner, with its suggestion of a British protectorate, was dropped after strong protests from the Emperor and Sandford, but there is no doubt that it was put forward seriously by Mitchell who saw this as the tidy solution to the problems of administering the former AOI — a high commissioner in Nairobi with deputy chief political officers in the three territories of Eritrea, Ethiopia and Somalia controlling political officers in the provinces, guaranteeing security in this important area. Lush recalls that he was personally much attracted by the idea of getting his family out from England to live in the beautiful Legation compound in a healthy climate, with plenty of horses to ride, and an interesting job — and who would not be!

Even after the idea of a high commissioner was abandoned the status of political officers in the provinces remained a strong bone of contention. Mitchell wanted these as advisers reporting to the deputy chief political officer, Lush, effectively retaining a control over the administration. Sandford, on behalf of the Emperor, opposed this, proposing that the deputy chief political officer should be replaced by a British minister, a diplomatic representative, with no responsibility for the administration as soon as possible, and that British advisers in the provinces should be responsible to the Emperor. This issue was debated and decided by a Cabinet committee in London, which Sandford was invited to attend in order to give evidence. The committee decided in favour of the Emperor and Sandford so his brother-in-law's dream of remaining in Addis Ababa faded. There was nothing personal in this. Sandford and Lush continued to remain friends, although totally opposed in policy. Christine Sandford managed to rejoin her husband in Addis Ababa after an adventurous journey in 1942 and had been as strongly opposed to the policies of Mitchell and Lush as her husband, referring to Lush as 'my younger brother', and not liking much what he was doing.

This was still ahead and in September 1941 Sandford left for England to represent the Emperor and Ethiopia and to give evidence before a Cabinet committee that would be considering the final draft of the Anglo-Ethiopian agreement. No Ethiopian leader accompanied him. Evidently the Emperor trusted Sandford to present the case for Ethiopia. It was at this point that Eden intervened decisively, supporting very largely the views put forward by Sandford. In a letter to David Margesson, Secretary of State for War in Churchill's Cabinet, he said that his conviction was growing that 'the fulfilment of the Cabinet's policy of restoring independence to Ethiopia has been steadily developing into something indistinguishable from a Protectorate', largely because of the strict financial control exercised by the War Office. He proposed instead that the Emperor should receive financial help from the Foreign Office vote. 'We need not concern ourselves with how he spends this nor with how the country is governed.' As a corollary to this looser form of control the advisers should be responsible to the Emperor and not to the deputy chief political officer, who should be replaced by a diplomatic representative. 'If this were so we think that we should find the Emperor more amenable and his chiefs less suspicious.' An agreement on these lines 'will disarm the criticism of our friends and our enemies will not be furnished with a tool for their propaganda.' The military mission in Addis Ababa should continue to be under the general officer commanding East Africa Command and Eritrea and Somalia continue as a War Office charge until peace. He asked for Margesson's support in putting up an agreed paper to the Cabinet on these lines, which 'he understood to be in conformity with Oliver Lyttleton's views'. Eden's letter contains three points of general interest, first that despite Churchill's great authority there was government by Cabinet consensus in the Second World War, secondly that Eden was very conscious that even the appearance of exercising a protectorate over Ethiopia would provoke strong criticism from Britain's friends, namely America, and thirdly that the controls, which had been imposed were more financial than political because of the strict Treasury control of War Office expenditure. Eden's proposals are like a breath of fresh air in comparison with the rigidity of control previously insisted on.

Sandford arrived near Plymouth by air, came up to London by train where he was met by Christine (whom he had not seen since July 1939), and travelled down to Ewhurst, to be greeted by a 'jubilant family and decorated cat!' He was asked to go to the War Ofice to scrutinize the proposed agreement, and for the next two months was almost daily in London attending meetings of the Cabinet committee on policy in Ethiopia, chaired by Sir John Anderson, Lord President of the Council, and often attended by Eden. We have a record of one such meeting on 4 November 1941 at which evidence was heard from Mitchell, Platt, Chapman-Andrews and Sandford separately, each being allocated 20 minutes. Both Sandford and Platt submitted written evidence. Platt, the soldier, favoured the retention of War Office control. 'Troubles ... requiring some form of military intervention are likely to occur ... at times on British lines of communication. Divided control breeds delay. I can only view the division of control between the Foreign Office and the War Office with misgiving.' Sandford started by making it clear that he was the Emperor's principal military and political adviser and should not be identified with OETA in Ethiopia nor with any government department in London. In answer to Platt's fears about security he described in detail the state of law and order in Ethiopia, province by province, including this generous comment on his old colleague and critic in Mission 101, Kabada Tesemma; '*Wallega* [province] The Governor, Fitaurari Kabada, is intensely loyal to the Emperor and an enlightened man. No dangerous situation is likely to arise,' and concluded that no disturbance was likely to arise with which the Emperor, through his own leaders, would not be able to cope. A diplomatic representative should be appointed forthwith, 'this is what the Emperor desires and anything short of this will spell "protectorate" and lead to the continuance of the present friction.' British advisers must be responsible to the Emperor and his ministers and should resign if there was a conflict of loyalties between the interests of Ethiopia and those of the British govern-ment. He opposed Mitchell's proposals for political missions in the provinces, which would make the Emperor's task of re-establishing his authority even more difficult.

After the Cabinet committee of 4 November Sandford signalled to Addis Ababa his hopes of an early return and Haile Selassie responded with pleasure to the news, 'Delay has caused me much anxiety.' Lush in Addis Ababa recorded that the Emperor had been 'desperately worried ... at the danger of British advice taking the form of British control', and he had signalled his worries to Eden who had replied that they were working out with all speed details of means whereby 'my country will assist Your Majesty to restore your own government.' In the end the views of Eden, and of Sandford, prevailed and among the terms agreed by the Cabinet were that a diplomatic representative should be appointed forthwith and that Britain should provide advisers who would be the Emperor's servants, help in raising and training his army, and financial help until the peace settlement at the end of the war. Sandford returned to Addis Ababa early in December 1941 with Mitchell, taking a draft of the agreement containing these terms, which was presented to the Emperor on 20 December. It took another six weeks for the agreement to be signed, much of the time taken up with new points raised by the British government. One point on which agreement was not reached was the question of the reserved areas. The Emperor objected to the retention by Britain of military administration in these areas but Mitchell, on the instructions of the British government, insisted, and the Emperor had to give way. The Anglo-Ethiopian agreement of 1942 is criticized today as unfair, an agreement reached between unequal parties, forced on the weaker by the stronger party. It is true that Britain then occupied the position in the free world America does today and was in a position to dictate terms to a small nation. The only term dictated, however, related to the reserved areas, lines of communication (the Jibuti railway), or areas of potential conflict (the Ogaden), where Britain insisted for reasons of military necessity in the anxious days of 1941 in retaining control. In all other respects the agreement was highly satisfactory for Ethiopia granting the Emperor, in Margery Perham's words, 'the help of British advisers, troops and finance without a vestige of British control'. Mitchell records that he came to have a very high respect for Haile Selassie and of Sandford he wrote, 'I sometimes wondered if Brigadier Sandford, in his devotion to the Emperor's interests, was really going to break off relations with Great Britain.'

283

The agreement was formally signed by the Emperor and by Mitchell on behalf of the British government on 31 January 1942. Railton's C company of the 3rd Ethiopian Battalion was honoured by being asked to provide the guard of honour at the ceremony. The reading of the agreement was 'greeted with applause by the *Rases* and Notables present', as Mitchell recorded in his diary, 'There can be no doubt that it is genuinely welcomed. I found the Emperor, Empress, Princes and *Rases* all beaming smiles.' Sandford's reaction was more measured, 'It is a sound document taken as a whole and the two responsible parties — the Emperor and PEM [Mitchell] deserve credit.' Sandford gave a dinner next evening at the Imperial Hotel for the ministers to meet Mitchell. 'Lorenzo [Foreign Affairs] made a neat little speech. Philip [Mitchell] replied more lengthily. Wolde Giorgis who had never set foot inside the Legation sat next to Philip and they both thawed. W. G. was quite emotional. He had been *"bien touché".*' On the night of the signing the Emperor gave a stand-up supper for 200 at the palace, 'and they danced. Princess Tshai took the floor and several young Ethiopians of both sexes — but not the Princes!'[2]

After the signing of the agreement Lush was replaced by the first post-liberation British minister, Robert Howe, and went off as Civil Affairs Officer Madagascar. Sandford took on the onerous task of adviser to the Ministry of the Interior. Lush was associated with an unpopular policy, the maintenance of control with the attendant suspicion of a protectorate, whereas all he had tried to do was honestly carry out the policy of the military commanders. For many years after the war he was *persona non grata* with Haile Selassie until a reconciliation was brought about with the help of Ras Asrate Kassa. Sandford gives the credit for the agreement to Haile Selassie and Mitchell, but he himself played a big part in making the agreement possible and consistently put forward proposals, which, thanks to Eden's intervention, were in the main accepted. For two months in London he bore the burden alone on behalf of Ethiopia. There can be no clearer evidence of his total independence from any British control than his submission to the Cabinet committee, Mitchell's comment, and indeed his entire conduct during the negotiations.

Sandford's Role Assessed

Haile Selassie's empire lasted until 1974 and he died in 1975, murdered, it is said, by the communist dictator, Mengistu, who ruled until 1991. Many other leading Ethiopians were murdered by Mengistu, including Asrate Kassa. One survivor of the old regime was Kabada Tesemma, in whose household Mengistu was brought up, who died in 1986. One day Ethiopians must acknowledge Haile Selassie's place in their history; in this book it is hoped that the picture has emerged of a patient, courageous, far-sighted ruler, proud and very much on his dignity, with failings like all men but genuinely believing that what he was doing was for the benefit of his Ethiopian people. What happened after he returned to power and why his empire failed must await the verdict of history.

Sandford, made CBE for Mission 101, continued to work for the Emperor's government until his retirement in 1950, first as adviser to the Ministry of the Interior, then as personal adviser to the Emperor, and finally as director-general of Addis Ababa municipality. By this time Kabada Tesemma was mayor (or *kantiba*) of Addis Ababa and it is pleasing to record that the two men worked well together, spent weekends at each other's farms and, according to Kassa, Kebede, Kabada's son, discussed their differences in Mission 101. It is surprising that Kabada still recorded these differences in his book, published in 1969. After retirement Sandford lived with his family on the farm at Mulu and died there in 1972 in his ninetieth year. He therefore never knew of the revolution and deposal of Haile Selassie in 1974. Christine Sandford, also made CBE, died in 1975 and did know of this and the Emperor's fate was the source of great sadness to her. Sandford's death was treated with great honour. In Addis Ababa the funeral was postponed at the Emperor's request to enable him to attend (he was abroad when Sandford died), and 'Ethiopian soldiers lined the route to the Cemetery where six Ethiopian Colonels bore Dan to his last resting place in the presence of the Emperor Haile Selassie and members of the Imperial family.' In the two days of mourning, which followed hundreds of Galla horsemen assembled at Mulu, their leaders galloping up in turn to 'Dan's portrait in the mourning tent to lament their father and friend'. In London a memorial service was held in Westminster Abbey at which the funeral address given by a former British ambassador in Addis Ababa described Sandford as 'this great and valiant Englishman — God-fearing and visionary, brave and wise, warm-hearted, modest and lovable — whose lasting memorial will be the shining example he has set for us all.'

Making allowances for the fact that this was a funeral eulogy, this is a fair description of Sandford's qualities and is the view the British and leading Ethiopians took of him at the time. His vision was a free Ethiopia, which he helped to achieve and the vision was not clouded in his lifetime. Unfortunately this is not the view of Sandford taken by many in Ethiopia today, where he is compared unfavourably with Wingate in any consideration of the events of 1940/1. Wingate was the open straightforward soldier who brought the Emperor in, the man with the single objective to defeat the Italians and secure the freedom of Ethiopia. The case against Sandford is that he was a politician, not a soldier, and that, having learned the secrets of the Ethiopians by living among them, he betrayed them by working for the English as an instrument of a devious British policy whereby the British pretended to be fighting for Ethiopia's freedom but in fact were seeking to annex the country or impose a protectorate. The current view of Wingate is fair and correct. The view of Sandford is unfair and unsupported by any evidence; it is sad also that the belief in the deviousness of British government policy persists, again without any evidence to support it. When OETA was making moves towards a protectorate, Sandford was the first to object. It is true that Sandford had a political role as the Emperor's adviser. He had to look beyond the winning of the campaign to the form of the post-liberation government. Even so he had proved himself as a competent soldier by the actions at Engiabara and Dangila before Wingate took command. The serious charge against Sandford is that he betrayed Ethiopia's trust; this is referred to in Kabada's book in which Kabada either gave a personal view or expressed a current belief. Earlier Kabada had spoken of his shock when Sandford told him on entering Gojjam that he was no longer the Emperor's adviser but was now under the British commander-in-chief. In a later passage he described how Sandford had lived in Ethiopia for many years and had learned the country's secrets. It was as if he had changed sides (changed the colour of his skin) by going over to the British. Therefore he had betrayed Ethiopia's trust.

For the sake of historical accuracy and for the benefit of Sandford's family, which is still serving Ethiopia, it is important to clear Sandford's name from this accusation and from the associated one that he was the instrument of a devious British policy. To do this it is only necessary to refer to the evidence in this book. Sandford, like Wingate, had a single objective, to defeat the Italians and secure the freedom of Ethiopia, but he had held to this for much longer than Wingate, ever since leaving Maji in 1936. Until August 1939 he was able to do little to help Ethiopia except to make representations to the Foreign Office, but from his arrival in Cairo on 1 September 1939 he worked tirelessly to further the patriotic revolt and to prepare for Italy's entry into the war, insisting, against total opposition from the authorities, that Haile Selassie must come out to lead the revolt and thereafter take his rightful place as ruler of Ethiopia. In August 1940 he led Mission 101 into Gojjam to coordinate the revolt with significant results, consistently urging the early entry of the Emperor, and in January 1941 initiated attacks on the Italian forts before Wingate and Gideon Force took over the military operations. When Wingate brought the Emperor into Gojjam (his entry having been deferred for strategic reasons over which Sandford had no control), Sandford accompanied him as adviser, organizing patriot support for the regulars and acting as a bridge between the Emperor and OETA over the demands for the control of the liberated territories. After the entry of the Emperor into Addis Ababa on 5 May 1941 (an event both Sandford and Wingate advised should have taken place earlier), Sandford continued to organize the patriot forces, assisted the Emperor to set up his government, and played a major role in the negotiations leading to the Anglo-Ethiopian agreement. In these he represented Ethiopian, not British, interests, and he made his position quite clear in his evidence to the Cabinet committee. The successful conclusion of the agreement, favourable to Ethiopia and embodying most of the points insisted on by the Emperor, was largely Sandford's doing. On the evidence the allegations that Sandford betrayed Ethiopia's trust and was a tool of the British are baseless and ridiculous. Wingate and Sandford were both great Englishmen who served Ethiopia well. It is sad that while Wingate's contribution is fully acknowledged today, Sandford's reputation is tarnished by misconceptions. It is hoped that this book, by setting out the evidence of what Sandford did, will do something to put this right.

Notes
1. When peace was restored in Tigre, with British help, the Emperor offered the Ethiopian Expeditionary Force for service in the Far East. The GOC East Africa Command (General Platt) replied that he did not think the climatic and other conditions there would be suitable but would consider the suggestion. Nothing further was heard — a pity as Somali and East African troops did well in Burma and the Ethiopians could have made a contribution. The Emperor was reported to have been very disappointed. The author is grateful to Tim Parsons of Johns Hopkins University, Baltimore, for this interesting research. PRO reference is WO/106/4500– cipher telegram of 20 October 1943 from Minister Howe to Foreign Secretary.
2. Princess Tshai, Haile Selassie's youngest daughter. Trained as a nurse in England. By all accounts an exceptionally lively and attractive girl. Died in childbirth soon after the restoration.

Epilogue

E thiopia, 'the first to be freed', owed her freedom in 1941 to British help and the efforts of her own people, the bare-footed and bandoliered Patriots who had kept the flame of revolt going since 1937 and helped the British and Commonwealth forces defeat the Italians. It is an event in which both British and Ethiopians can take pride.

What has this liberation led to? Imperial rule came to an end in 1974 in discontent and revolution, followed by 17 years of the brutal Marxist dictatorship of Mengistu, years of civil war in which thousands died of war and famine. Then Eritrean and Tigrean rebels put an end to Mengistu's rule in May 1991, the Eritreans fighting for independence, which they now have, and the Tigreans seeking to overthrow the Addis Ababa government, which they replaced; there is now a Tigrean president, the first Tigrean ruler since the Emperor Johannes. At least the fighting has stopped and there are moves towards democracy, but much of the country is an ecological disaster and the threat of famine is never far away.

Cynics might say that it would have been better if the Italians had stayed but the rule by one nation of another against the will of the governed can never be justified, and freeing Ethiopia from Mussolini's government in 1941 was as worthy an objective as the freeing of Europe from domination by Hitler's Germany in 1945. Ethiopia must be left to work out her own future and all her friends must hope that the freedom won in 1941 will in the end result in peace and prosperity for all the inhabitants of that beautiful country.

Historical Personalities

British, Commonwealth and Allied

ALLENBY, Field Marshal Lord. C-in-C Palestine 1917–18

ATTLEE, Rt Hon. Clement. Leader Labour Party, Deputy Prime Minister

AUCHINLECK, General Sir Claude. WAVELL's successor July 1941

CHURCHILL, Rt Hon. Winston. Prime Minister of Great Britain 1940–45

EDEN, Rt Hon. Anthony. Secretary of State for War, then Foreign Secretary

LAWRENCE, Colonel T. E. Guerrilla commander in Arab Revolt 1917–18

LEGENTILHOMME, General. Governor French Somaliland 1939–40, then Free French commander in North Africa

LYTTLETON, Rt Hon. Oliver. Minister of State Cairo

SMUTS, General. Prime Minister South Africa

WAVELL, General Sir Archibald. C-in-C Middle East Command

WEYGAND, General. French General C-in-C May 1940

WINGATE, General Sir Reginald. Governor-General Sudan, then *Sirdar*

Others

BEN-GURION, David. Zionist leader. First Prime Minister of Israel

HITLER, Adolf. Chancellor of Germany 1933–45

MUSSOLINI, Benito. Italian Fascist dictator 1925–43

ROMMEL, Erwin. German Field Marshal Commander in North Africa

YASU, Lij. Grandson of Emperor MENELIK, son of Negus MIKAEL successor of Menelik until deposed in 1916. Held in confinement by Haile Selassie. Escaped in 1932, recaptured and remained in confinement until death in 1935. Ras HAILU was implicated in escape and dismissed from governorship of Gojjam.

Biographical Index

ABABA AREGAI, Ras. Police chief Addis Ababa at Italian invasion, then important Patriot leader in Shoa. Governor of Addis Ababa and prominent figure in post-liberation Ethiopia. Gunned down by revolutionaries in failed coup of 1960.

ACLAND, P. B. E. (Peter). *Bimbashi* later brigadier, OBE MC TD. Sudan Political Service 1924. Commissioner Gezira 1940. Released February 1940 then aged 40 to help Boustead form Frontier Battalion SDF. Commanded No 4 patrol company. Wounded at Gulit March 1941 (MC). Later served in SOE organizing operations in Dodecanese and then Brigadier Civil Affairs in North Africa (OBE). d. 1993.

AKAVIA, Abram. b. Haifa 1916. Graduated in civil engineering Haifa Technological Institute. Became involved with Haganah (Jewish secret army), met WINGATE and acted as his interpreter. Clerk to WINGATE in Gideon Force, serving without rank and often as unofficial staff officer. Later joined British Army (Palestine battalion of Buffs), commissioned, finished war as major. Post war trained as accountant, practises in Haifa.

ALESSANDRII, Aldo Tenente in BRACA's 1st Gruppo Bande. Distinguished himself in relief of Kwara (January/February 1941). Killed defending non-combatant column on march out. Awarded *Medaglia d'Oro al VM* posthumously having been awarded *Croce di guerra al VM* twice previously.

ALLEN W. E. D. (Bill) b. 1900. Lieutenant Life Guards. Writer, traveller and one time Conservative MP. Volunteered for operational centres from the 1st Cavalry Division in Palestine with McLEAN, PILKINGTON and RINGROSE. Supernumerary officer in No 5 Centre (VAN DER POST) and then animal transport officer Frontier Battalion. Wrote excellent account of campaign, *Guerrilla War in Abyssinia*.

AOSTA, Amedeo di Savoia, Duke of. Fighter pilot and Air Force general. Cousin of the King of Italy, Victor Emmanuel. Viceroy AOI 1937–41. d. in Kenya of tuberculosis 1942.

ASFAW WOSSEN, Crown Prince. Eldest son of HIM HAILE SELASSIE. Attended Sobat Military Academy (Sudan) 1940/1. Commanded Patriots at end of Gondar operations. Governor of Wollo after liberation. Exile after revolution 1974. Died in London.

ASRATE KASSA. b. 1918, youngest and only surviving son of Ras KASSA. Trained with Crown Prince at Sobat Military Academy. Joined father in Gojjam, made colonel and took part in pursuit of Maraventano. Later succeeded father as *ras*, very important noble in postwar Ethiopia. Murdered by Dergue in 1974.

AYALEWU BIRRU, Dejasmatch. Important figure in feudal hierarchy. Nephew of Empress Taitu (Menelik's queen) and married to Ras KASSA's daughter. Governor of Gondar under HAILE SELASSIE, discontented because he was not made *ras*. Corresponded before Italian war with Italian senator Gasperini. Did not then defect but put up poor performance and submitted as soon as Italians reached Addis Ababa. Then collaborated fully, even offering to capture Ras IMRU. Appointed '*Ras*' by Aosta in 1939 and given large grant of arms in effort to stem revolt in Gondar region. Reverted to Anglo-Ethiopian side in April 1941 in Wolchefit operations until captured. Wounded in raid in June 1941. Never made peace with HAILE SELASSIE.

BADOGLIO, Pietro. Marshal b. 1871. Governor Libya 1928–33. Replaced De Bono in north Ethiopia November 1935. Viceroy briefly and created Duke of Addis Ababa. Chief of General Staff. Prime Minister 1943/4 after fall of Mussolini.

BASTIANI, Sante Angelo. Sergeant major later general. b. 1913. Enlisted Italian regular army 1933 as volunteer private. Served in Libya and Eritrea. Corporal major and Sergeant in Eritrean battalion in Ethiopian war 1935/6. Formed his own irregular *banda* group as sergeant major in 1937. Five times wounded in actions against 'rebels'. Took part in defence of Wolchefit. Commissioned in the field by General NASI in June 1941 for raid in which AYALEWU was captured. Awarded *Medaglia d'Oro al VM* in 1949. Served post war in regular army, retiring as Lt Col. Now General and President of Medaglia d'Oro Association.

BEARD, A. S. Lieutenant later captain. From Northern Rhodesia. Aged about 48 in 1940. Previously held regular commission in

Connaught Rangers and served in 1914–18 war. Commanded B company 2nd Ethiopian Battalion and took over battalion when Boyle was sacked. From April 1941 commanded bodyguard battalion.

BELAI ZELLEKA. Effective and much feared Gojjam patriot leader 1937–40, of peasant origin. Ineffective in 1941 campaign, suborned by Ras HAILU. In 1945 raised rebellion in Gojjam against HAILE SELASSIE with MAMU MIKAEL. Arrested, escaped from custody and in doing so murdered prison warder. Re-arrested, tried and executed for murder of warder, not rebellion. Even so execution of patriotic hero caused much discontent against HAILE SELASSIE. Today Belai Zelleka is the great hero of the patriotic war and since the 1974 revolution the Gojjam road from Addis Ababa has been named after him.

BELL, Mervyn. *Bimbashi* Sudan Political Service 1936–43. Defended Kurmuk with police against Italian advance in July 1940 and later in action against Banda Rolle. Postwar secretary Countryside Commission and chairman Suffolk Wildlife Trust.

BENSON, Geoffrey. Lt Col. OBE. Commissioned Royal Irish Rifles 1916, served in France and Mesopotamia. Then Royal Ulster Rifles Mesopotamia and Egypt 1920–27, SDF 1927–32, Palestine 1936–39 (OBE). Commanded the 2nd Ethiopian Battalion from April 1941 and later an SDF battalion. Mentioned in dispatches for Gianda.

BENTINCK, Count Arthur. Major Coldstream Guards. Aged about 62 in 1940. KAR 1913, wounded and sent home. Rejoined regiment in August 1914, badly wounded on the Aisne. ADC and vice-consul under THESIGER's father in Addis Ababa. Served in Egyptian Army, Arabian Army and International Police on the Saar. With Red Cross mission in Italo-Ethiopian war. Spoke Amharic. Commanded Mission 101 North August 1940–February 1941. Later (1942) in Bush Warfare School under Michael Calvert in Maymyo Burma. Declined to serve under WINGATE though they never met in Ethiopia.

BIGGS, M. W. (Michael). Lt Col. Royal Engineers, later brigadier CBE. Divisional intelligence officer 12 (A) Division at Gondar. Wrote (and preserved!) excellent intelligence reports on Gondar operations, now in National Army Museum, London.

BIRRU WOLDE GABRIEL, Imperial *fitaurari*. Reputed illegitimate son of Menelik. Fought at Mai Ceu. In Palestine during Italian occupation. Commanded Patriots with Beghemder Force and later at Gondar. Governor of Beghemder after liberation, created *ras*.

BLUNDELL, Michael. Lt Col., later Sir Michael KBE. Kenya farmer. Commanded 1st Battalion EA Pioneers at Kulkaber and Gondar, a unit he took over in a state of mutiny. Spoke fluent Kiswahili and Dholuo, the languages of most of his pioneers, and brought the battalion up to a high state of efficiency. MBE for Gondar. Later prominent liberal politician in Kenya, Member Legislative Council and Minister for Agriculture. d. in Kenya 1993. (For mutiny see note below.)

BODY, E. M. (Ted) Sergeant 2nd/1st Field Regiment 6th Australian Division No 1 Operational Centre. Served with Mission 101 and Gideon Force. Commissioned in infantry battalion on return to Australian division. Post war returned to sheep and cattle ranch in New South Wales.

BOUSTEAD, Lt Col. Hugh OBE MC, later Col. Sir Hugh KBE CMG DSO MC. Aged 46 in 1940. As Royal Navy midshipman deserted ship at Simonstown South Africa in 1915 to fight in France, enlisting in South African Scottish. Commissioned, awarded MC and pardoned by King George V for desertion. Regular commission Gordon Highlanders post war, served with Denikin in Russia. Took part in 1924 Everest expedition. Left army to join Sudan Political Service. DC Darfur. Released 1940 to form Frontier Battalion, which he commanded in Gojjam. DSO for Debra Markos. Post war returned as DC Darfur then Resident Trucial States. On retirement looked after Sultan of Abu Dhabi's stud. d. 1972.

BOYLE, E. M. (Ted). Major aged about 40 in 1940. East African Intelligence Corps. Had worked for liquor importing company in Nairobi. Experience on hunting safaris. Commanded 2nd Ethiopian Battalion from August 1940 until sacked by WINGATE in April 1941. Afterwards commanded Somali Scout Battalion. d. 1953.

BRACA, Giovanni. Captain later general. b. Lari 1899. Commissioned 1918. Served in Monte Grappa campaign, wounded and decorated with *Medaglia d'Argento al VM*. In AOI served in Servizio Geografico Militare until June 1940 when obtained viceroy's permission to return to combat duty. Commanded 1st Gruppo Bande di Confine at Metemma, Kwara and Gondar, winning two more *Medaglie d'Argento al VM*. Post Second World War in regular army until retirement as general.

BROCKLEHURST, Lt Col. Courtney. Retired game warden. Proposed encouraging Galla to rebel against Amhara. Stopped on application of WINGATE and HAILE SELASSIE. Later in Bush Warfare School at Maymyo under Calvert. Like BENTINCK declined to serve under WINGATE. Killed in retreat from Burma 1942.

BROWN, Alan. Lieutenant 2nd/1st Field Regiment 6th Australian Division, later major. Pre war bank official and militia officer in New South Wales. Met Ethiopian Coptic priest in Palestine and conceived idea of assisting Patriots. Commanded No 1 Operational Centre in Gojjam. Later commanded his battery in Australian division.

BURKE, J. R. Sergeant 2nd/1st Field Regiment 6th Australian Division. Served in No 1 Operational Centre in Gojjam. Commissioned on return to division. Pre war played full back for Waratah (New South Wales) against New Zealand All Blacks.

CAMPBELL, Guy. *Bimbashi* later Col. Sir Guy Bart OBE MC 60th Rifles. Commanded No 5 patrol company Frontier Battalion. Later joined Composite Battalion SDF. Served in both attacks on Chilga, wounded, MC. Post war commanded Kenya Regiment in Mau Mau emergency in Kenya (1952–56) (OBE) d. 1993.

CHAPMAN-ANDREWS, Andrew. HM Diplomatic Service later Sir Edwin. Vice-consul Harrar 1935/6 during Italian war and much praised for his work then. First secretary British Embassy Cairo 1940. Commissioned major Royal Sussex Regiment and appointed political adviser to HAILE SELASSIE. Entered Gojjam with the Emperor, then adviser to the Duke of Harrar. Post war diplomatic career ending as HM ambassador Egypt.

CHEESMAN, Robert. British consul Dangila for several years before Italian invasion. Ornithologist and botanist. Formed intelligence bureau in Khartoum in 1940 where his knowledge of country and people of Gojjam of great value.

CLARKE, Geoffrey. South African farming in Northern Rhodesia (Zambia). Sergeant 2nd Ethiopian Battalion, commissioned in the field, later captain commanding C company. Returned to farming in Zambia post war.

CRITCHLEY, R. A. (Ronnie) Lt Col. DSO MC. Commissioned 1925 13th/18th Hussars. Served in India 1931–38 making several adventurous expeditions into Himalayas and Afghanistan. Decided in 1938 he was too tall for a tank (6' 6") so learned Serbo-Croat and was in command of Balkan section in Middle

East intelligence in 1940. Invited by SANDFORD to join Mission 101. Entered Gojjam with mission. Immediate MC for reconnaisances of Kwara and Belaiya. Later served in Far East and with TURRALL parachuted into Burma to join Force 136 and commanded column of Karen irregulars on flank of Fourteenth Army (DSO). Post war farmed in Zimbabwe. Now lives in Western Australia.

CUNNINGHAM, Lt Gen. Sir Alan KCB DSO MC GOC East Africa Command 1940/1. Commanded force advancing into Ethiopia from Kenya. Appointed to command the Eighth Army in Western Desert August 1941 where he was not a success. High Commissioner Palestine 1945.

DE BONO, Marshal Emilio. One of the original Fascist quadrumvirate. Governor of Tripolitania 1925–29, then Minister for the Colonies. Commanded northern armies in invasion of Ethiopia 1935 until superseded by BADOGLIO. Executed for alleged treason by Fascist Grand Council in 1944. Author of *Anno XIIII*, an account of the Abyssinian war.

DE BUNSEN, Bimbashi Charles. Sudan Political Service. In charge of frontier post at Bikori. Saw action against Banda Rolle, then joined Frontier Battalion (No 4 patrol company). Took part in march to Belaiya, then ordered back to civil duty. Later Political Officer Tigre.

DODDS-PARKER, Captain Douglas later Col. Sir Arthur KCB Sudan Political Service 1930. Coldstream Guards 1939. Staff captain GHQ Khartoum. Praised for helpful attitude. Later SOE. Post war Conservative MP and parliamentary under-secretary.

DOUGLAS, Major Dougal. Highland Light Infantry and 4th KAR. Commanded Patriots at Debra Tabor, Kulkaber and Gondar (Dougforce). Removed from command before final assault.

DOWNEY, 2nd Lieut. Sydney, later captain 2nd Ethiopian Battalion. Commanded A company. Captured at Charaka river March 1941. Kenya white hunter, after war started safari firm of Ker & Downey with Donald Ker.

DREW, Clifford (Pansy). Sudan Medical Service, captain Royal Army Medical Corps. Medical officer Mission 101 and Gideon Force and much praised for his skill. After campaign returned to Sudan Medical Service.

FOLEY, Lieut. Tim. Royal Engineers (MC). Engineer officer Mission 101. Good sabotage work with Mission 101 North (MC) and Gideon Force. Later served with SOE.

FOWKES, C. C. ('Fluffy'). South Wales Borderers, major general CBE DSO MC. Commanded 22nd (East African) Brigade in Cunningham's advance and then 12 (A) Division at Gondar. Commanded 11th (East African) Division in Burma.

FRUSCI, General Luigi. Commanded Italian forces at Keren and later at Dessie and Amba Alagi where he surrendered with the viceroy.

GETAHUN TESEMMA, Gojjam Patriot. Formed Gojjam Patriots Committee. Entered Gojjam with Mission 101, later served with SIMONDS in Beghemder Force where he was much praised.

GONELLA, Lt Col. Mario. Regular officer of the Alpini. Commanded Wolchefit garrison with courage and determination.

GRAZIANI, Marshal Rodolfo. In Italian war commanded armies advancing from the south. Viceroy 1935–37. Wounded in assassination attempt. Commanded in Libya 1940, defeated by Wavell. Commanded troops in Mussolini's Fascist republic 1943/4.

GREY, G. S. (George) CSM. Later Lt Col. MBE. Aged 27 in 1940. Royal Corps of Signals. Prepared and took out to SANDFORD six suitcase wireless telegraphy sets for Mission 101. Served with Mission 101 and Gideon Force in Gojjam. Commissioned in the field, MBE and mentioned in dispatches. After liberation set up and commanded signals training school for Ethiopian Army under British military mission as Lt Col. Retired to Lincolnshire.

HAILE SELASSIE, HIM Haile Selassie I. b.1891 near Harrar as Tafari Makonnen, son of Ras Makonnen, cousin of Menelik and governor of Harrar. Educated in French (by Catholic priest), Amharic and Ge'ez, the ancient classical language. Succeeded father as governor of Harrar 1910, appointed Crown Prince and regent 1916 on deposal of Lij Yasu under Empress Zauditu. *Negus* 1928 and *Negus Negusti* (Emperor) under title HAILE SELASSIE I 1930. After restoration became post war much respected African elder statesman presiding over the Organization of African Unity in Addis Ababa. Deposed by communist coup in 1974 and believed murdered on orders of communist dictator MENGISTU on 27 August 1975.

HAILE YUSUS, Fitaurari. Gojjam patriot leader Dambacha area.

HAILU BELAO. Gojjam patriot leader Mota area. Nephew of Ras HAILU.

HAILU TEKLE-HAIMANOT, Ras. Reputed b. 1868 illegitimate son of

297

Negus Tekle-Haimanot. Ruler of Gojjam. Succeeded as governor of Gojjam 1907–32 when dismissed by HAILE SELASSIE for implication in escape of Lij Yasu, his son-in-law. Collaborated with Italians who tried to stem revolt in Gojjam by restoring him as ruler in December 1940. On fall of Debra Markos submitted to the Emperor who again treated him with clemency. d. Addis Ababa 1953.

HARRIS, W. A. B. (Bill). *Bimbashi* later Lt Col. MC. Aged 28 in 1940. Educated Rugby and RMC Sandhurst. Commissioned Royal Fusiliers 1931. Western Arab Corps SDF from 1938. Trained No 3 patrol company Frontier Battalion, then commanded No 2 in Gideon Force. Wounded near Dambacha March 1941. On recovery in UK trained as parachutist, dropped at Pegasus Bridge in Normandy in June 1944 as second in command of 13th Parachute Battalion then took over command of another battalion when the commanding officer was killed. Again wounded. Post war commanded his regiment, served in Kenya and retired to farm in Kenya.

HAUPTE SELASSIE, Fitaurari. Shoan patriot leader of Ababa Aregai's army. Commanded Shoans in Dougforce at Debra Tabor, Kulkaber and Gondar.

HAYES, Peter Bimbashi Inspector Plantation Syndicate in Sudan. Second in command No 1 Patrol Company Frontier Battalion. Served in Gideon Force. Post war teacher, learned Amharic, taught air force cadets in Addis Ababa until revolution.

HOLCOMBE, J. C. (John) TD. Solicitor. Middlesex Regiment Territorial major, later Lt Col. Volunteered for operational centres and joined No 3 patrol company Frontier Battalion. Served with Beghemder Force at Bahr Dar and Debra Tabor. Later commanded SDF Battalion. Returned to solicitor's practice in Isle of Wight post war.

HOWELL, W. F. Sergeant 2nd/1st Field Regiment 6th Australian Division. Pre war overseer sheep property Queensland. No 1 Operational Centre in Gojjam and with Safforce. Later commissioned in infantry battalion and killed in New Guinea 1942.

IMRU, Ras. b.1894. Cousin of HAILE SELASSIE and brought up with him. Governor of Gojjam 1932–35. Succesful commander in Italian war and continued resistance until November 1936. Exiled to Ponza. Released on Italian armistice 1943. Post war ambassador to India and USA. Son Michael Imru was prime minister 1974. d. 1980.

JARVIS, Alec. *Bimbashi*. Employee of Gelattley Hankey in Khartoum. Commanded No 3 patrol company Frontier Battalion in Beghemder Force.

JOHNSON, T. C. ('Henry'). *Bimbashi*. Educated Charterhouse and Cambridge. Association Football blue. Aged about 28 in 1940. Inspector Plantation Syndicate in Sudan (the forerunner of the Gezira cotton scheme, which released all inspectors under the age of 30 to the SDF). Commanded No 1 patrol company Frontier Battalion in Gideon Force and later Safforce. DSO for Jibuti ambush and second DSO for Safforce. Later served with SOE in Greece. Post war returned to Sudan and then farmed in West Country. d. 1986.

KABADA TESEMMA, Azaj. Court chamberlain under HAILE SELASSIE. Spent years of exile in Palestine. HAILE SELASSIE's representative on Mission 101 and worked well with SANDFORD though later criticized him. Saw action with his *banda* in Gideon Force. Later commanded Patriots at Lechemti and governor of Wollega. Post war important bureaucrat. Survived both coups. d. 1986. MENGISTU HAILE MARIAM, communist dictator 1974–91 was brought up in his household. Author of *Recollections of History*, an account of the campaign published in 1969.

KASSA, Ras. b. 1881. Elder cousin of HAILE SELASSIE. Ruler of Salale. The most important and respected Shoan noble. Fought at Adowa, mustered Shoans to help Ras Tafari defeat Negus Mikael at Sagale in 1916, commanded northern armies in Italian war. In exile with Emperor, mostly in Palestine, and returned with him and Gideon Force. Commanded Patriots in WINGATE's final battle at Uogghidi. Crown counsellor after the war. Died full of honours in 1956. The KASSA line survives with the children of ASRATE KASSA.

LE BLANC, *Bimbashi*. French-Canadian RAF 1918, squadron leader. Many expeditions in Africa between wars. Transport officer Frontier Battalion.

LORENZO TAEZAZ. Tigrean lawyer. Member of Anglo-Ethiopian Boundary Commission 1934. In exile with Emperor. Acted as liaison with Patriots and visited Gojjam three times. Entered Gojjam with Gideon Force. Post liberation Foreign Minister.

LUSH, M. S. (Maurice). Brigadier CB CBE MC. b. 1896. Educated Tonbridge and RMA Woolwich. Commissioned Royal Artillery 1915 and joined SANDFORD's siege battery in France 1915–18. MC and bar. Egyptian Army 1919. Vice-consul Addis Ababa

1919–20, then Sudan Political Service. Governor Ed Damer Province 1939–40. Deputy chief political officer of Ethiopia 1941–42 and of Madagascar 1942, then senior civil affairs posts in North Africa and Italy. d. 1993. Elder sister Christine married Daniel SANDFORD in 1918.

LUYT, R. E. (Dick) Sergeant, later Lt Col. later Sir Richard GCMG KCVO DCM. Aged 24 in 1940. South African from Cape Town. Educated Cape Town University and Trinity College Oxford (Rhodes Scholar and Rugby football blue). Appointed Colonial Administrative Service Northern Rhodesia 1940. Joined Kenya Regiment, then the 2nd Ethiopian Battalion, D company. Served in Gojjam campaign, DCM for Charaka river. Commissioned in the field, commanded D company. Afterwards adjutant, then CO 4th Ethiopian Battalion in Tigre, then commandant at Ethiopian Officers Training School. Learned Amharic. Post war returned to Colonial Service in Northern Rhodesia, Kenya and finally as governor-general of Guyana. Vice-chancellor Cape Town University. d. 1993.

MacDONALD, Colin. *Bimbashi* Sudan Political Service adjutant Frontier Battalion. Killed at Gulit March 1941.

MacDONALD, Sergeant Thornton. 13th/18th Hussars No 5 Operation Centre. Served in Beghemder Force and at Gondar.

McLEAN, Neil (Billy). Lieutenant Royal Scots Greys, later Lt Col. DSO. b. 1918. Educated Eton and RMC Sandhurst. Commissioned 1938. Volunteered from 1st Cavalry Division in Palestine. Commanded first No 10 and then No 2 Centre, replacing Mackay, at Debra Tabor and Gondar. Also commanded 79th (McLean's) Foot, formerly the 79th Colonial Battalion. Later served with SOE, parachuted into Albania (DSO). Post war Conservative MP for Aberdeen. Saw action with Royalists in North Yemen. d. 1986.

MAKONNEN DESTA, b. 1910. Gojjami leader. Educated at Alexandria and Harvard. Joined Mission 101 in Gojjam and Gideon Force. Liaison officer Frontier Battalion. Postwar minister. d. 1966.

MAMU MIKAEL, Dejasmatch. Great nephew of Ras HAILU. Important pro-Italian *banda* leader at Burye until Burye fell. In 1945 joined BELAI ZELLEKA in rebellion against HAILE SELASSIE and suffered the same fate.

MANGASHA JEMBERIE, Dejasmatch. Important Gojjam Patriot leader from 1937. Aged 47 in 1940. Effective organizer of resistance though himself no soldier. Fought TORELLI at Piccolo Abbai in March 1940 and again in retreat from Dangila February 1941. Welcomed and cooperated with Mission 101.

MARAVENTANO, Saverio. Colonel later General. b. Sicily 1893. Trained as violinist. Enlisted 1913. Austrian front 1915–18, decorated and taken prisoner. Ethiopia 1937 (Lt Col.) then colonel and deputy commissario Gojjam 1940. Replaced NATALE March 1941. Defended Debra Markos and then led column, which eventually surrendered to WINGATE. Conduct of column approved by Italian High Command, promoted brigadier general on merit, retired as lieutenant general. d. Siena 1974. Corresponded with WINGATE's widow Lorna who sent him an Airedale puppy, which gave him enormous pleasure, particularly when it tackled German shepherd dogs!

MARTINI, General. Commanded at Metemma and Gondar and then deputy to General NASI.

MAXWELL, J. R. (Jock). El Kaimaquan (major and second in command) Frontier Battalion, later colonel (DSO OBE). Commissioned Royal Scots Fusiliers. After Gojjam returned to his regiment, which he commanded in Anzio landing (DSO).

MENGISTU HAILE MARIAM, Colonel. Reputed illegitimate grandson of KABADA TESEMMA. Seized power from HAILE SELASSIE in 1974 in communist coup with Dergue (a committee of the armed services). Disposed of opponents (including HAILE SELASSIE) ruthlessly until 1991 when he was turned out by Tigrean rebels. Believed to be in Zimbabwe. His uncle Kassa Kebede, eldest son of KABADA TESEMMA, was a power behind the throne and fled with him.

MESFIN MAKONNEN, Duke of Harrar. Second son of HAILE SELASSIE. Governor of Harrar after liberation. Died in accident 1957.

MILLARD, J. F. (John). Captain OBE. b. South Africa. Colonial Administrative Service Basutoland and Tanganyika. KAR Reserve gunner 1938. Served with 22nd Indian Mountain Battery in Cunningham's advance and then commanded irregulars (Millard's Scouts). Wounded. Sent by SANDFORD to investigate complaints against DOUGLAS at Gondar. Took over Dougforce at Kulkaber and Gondar. Later saw service in Europe. Post war returned to Tanganyika (provincial commissioner). Lives in retirement near Nairobi.

MITCHELL, Major General Sir Philip GCMG MC. b. 1890. Colonial Administrative Service Nyasaland 1912. KAR 1914–18 against von Lettow Vorbeck. MC. Then Colonial Service Nyasaland, Tanganyika (chief secretary), and Uganda (governor) 1935–40. Deputy chairman East African Governors' Conference 1940. Chief Political Officer Middle East Command 1941. Governor Fiji, then governor Kenya retiring 1952. d. 1964.

MOHAMED EFFENDI. Inspector Sudan police. Ethiopian mother. Spoke fluent Amharic. Effective and enterprising guerrilla leader in Mission 101 North.

MOLLOY, P. G. (Peter) Lt Col. OBE MC. Commissioned Somerset Light Infantry 1934, 4th KAR 1938–41, then staff captain operations force HQ. Took command of part of Dougforce November 1941 and fought at Kulkaber and Gondar. Later second in command of 22nd KAR in 11th (East African) Division in Burma (MC).

NAGASH BEZAHBU, Dejasmatch. Aged 32 in 1940. Nephew of Ras HAILU TEKLE-HAIMANOT. Important but not very effective Gojjam patriot leader. Not strong enough to control subchiefs. Persuaded by SANDFORD and KABADA to cooperate with MANGASHA.

NASI, General Guglielmo. Commander Libyan division in GRAZIANI's invasion of Ethiopia from the south. Governor of Harrar. Commanded troops invading British Somaliland August 1940, then deputy to viceroy. Commander Gojjam sector October 1940 to February 1941, then Gondar sector until surrender. The best of the Italian generals. In 1950 proposed as first High Commissioner of Somalia, due to be handed over to Italian trusteeship. Acceptable to Somalis and HAILE SELASSIE but objected to by communist deputies in Italian Parliament on grounds that he was a 'Colonial butcher'. NASI withdrew, not wishing to be involved in controversy.

NATALE, Colonel Leopoldo. Commander in central and southern Gojjam and *commissario*; 35 years' service and long colonial experiences. Respected by his officers. Dismissed by General NASI and replaced by MARAVENTANO for retreating from Burye too far and too fast.

NAYLOR, Lieut. Gordon. 1st Battalion Beds & Herts Regiment later captain. Commanded No 3 Operational Centre in Safforce. Later adjutant of 2nd Ethiopian Battalion. Present at Gianda.

NOTT, Major Donald MC, later brigadier DSO OBE MC.

Educated Marlborough and RMC Sandhurst. Commissioned Worcestershire Regiment 1928. Active service in Palestine 1932–39 (MC). GSO III Intelligence Middle East Command Cairo 1939/40. Jumped at chance of joining SANDFORD's 'scallywag show' as DAA&QMG. In charge rear HQ Mission 101 and accompanied Emperor until April 1941 (dispatches) when sent to command Safforce. Commanded effectively at Deraa until WINGATE took over (DSO). Returned to regiment as company commander. Highly praised at Battle of the Box near Tobruk. Captured when Tobruk fell, POW in Italy for 18 months. Escaped September 1943 at Italian armistice and at liberty in Italy for five months until betrayed. POW in Germany until end of war. Post war commanded 4th KAR in Mau Mau emergency in Kenya (OBE). Later brigadier Territorial Brigade, Colonel Worcestershire Regiment. Artist and naturalist. Kept meticulous diary of campaign as intelligence record. Lives in Worcester.

NURK, Captain Karl MC. b. Latvia 1903. Served in White Russian army 1919 aged 16. White hunter in Kenya. With 3rd Ethiopian Irregulars in southern Ethiopia (immediate MC). Commanded Shoan Patriots at Kulkaber and Gondar. Later served in Greece with SOE.

PILKINGTON, Lieut. M. L. (Mark). Life Guards, later captain. b. 1914. Educated Eton and Christchurch Oxford, then Stock Exchange. Prospective parliamentary candidate. Supplementary reserve of officers 1938. Called up 1939 to 1st Cavalry Division in Palestine. Commanded combined 5th/10th Operational Centre and Wollo *banda* at Debra Tabor, Kulkaber and Gondar. After campaign joined Glubb's Arab Legion in Jordan. Killed in action November 1942 when on detachment to New Zealand squadron LRDG near El Alamein. MC for command of Wollo gazetted February 1943. Letters to wife and parents both entertaining and important.

PLATT, Major General later Lt Gen Sir William. b. 1885. Commissioned 1905. *Kaid* 1939–41. Commanded advance into Eritrea and at Keren. GOC East Africa Command 1941–45.

RAILTON, A. S. (Andrew) MC. b. 1920. Second lieutenant later major. Volunteered from 1st South Staffs in Western Desert. Commanded C company 3rd Ethiopian Battalion in Wolchefit operations (dispatches). Returned to 1st South Staffs, first in Western Desert, then in Arakan in Burma. When they became part of WINGATE's special force Railton, with one platoon, joined Dah Force operating near Chinese border (MC). Post war set up business with his wife.

RINGROSE, Major later Lt Col. B. H. (Basil) DSO. b. 1904. Territorial Commission Notts Yeomanry 1927. Volunteered for Ethiopia from 1st Cavalry Division Palestine (Sherwood Rangers). Commanded Patriots Wolchefit (DSO). Later SOE Palestine to set up Jewish sabotage in event of German occupation. Served with regiment in northwest Europe (second in command).

ROLLE, Lt Col. Veteran of Libyan and Ethiopian campaigns. Commanded Banda Rolle of 1500 Shoans in advance into Sudan October 1940. His *banda* was sent to man the Awash crossing in April 1941 but its morale had collapsed and it surrendered *en masse* to South African Engineers working on the road.

ROSSINI, Gastone. *Tenente* later major. Served in pack battery in NATALE column and later in MARAVENTANO column. Has written on colonial troops and WINGATE (see bibliography).

ROWE, Ken S. Rhodesian. Worked for oil company in Nairobi. KAR Reserve. Lieutenant later captain 2nd Ethiopian Battalion, commanded C company and served with Safforce. Fatally wounded at Uogghidi 20 May 1941. d. Addis Ababa 31 May 1941. Nicknamed 'Jiggsa' (Galla — the strong one who makes his enemies bite the dust) and remembered under that name to this day.

SANDFORD, Brigadier Daniel Arthur (Dan). Royal Artillery CBE DSO Légion d'honneur. b. 1882, fourth son of Revd E. G. Sandford later Archdeacon of Exeter. Educated St Pauls and RMA Woolwich. Commissioned Royal Garrison Artillery 1900. Served in India and Aden 1900–8. Crossed Ethiopia on mule in 1907 from Dire Dawa to Roseires and resolved to return. Egyptian Army 1908, ADC Sudan till 1913 then vice-consul Addis Ababa 1913–14 under Captain THESIGER, British minister. Rejoined regiment 1914, commanded siege battery in France (DSO and bar, Légion d'honneur, dispatches, wounded). Married Christine Lush 1918. Ethiopia 1920. General manager Abyssinian Corporation. Then resigned commission and farmed at Mulu, north of Addis Ababa. Became friend and counsellor of Ras Tafari, later Emperor. Adviser to governor of Maji 1935. In England during Italian occupation.

August 1939 recalled to colours as Colonel Middle East intelligence in Cairo under Wavell. Planned, formed and commanded Mission 101 to help Ethiopian Patriots until succeeded by WINGATE in February 1941. Then military and political adviser to HAILE SELASSIE as brigadier (CBE). Important role in Anglo-Ethiopian agreement in 1942. After liberation served Ethiopian government as adviser to the Ministry of the Interior, adviser to HAILE SELASSIE, and director-general of Addis Ababa municipality. Retired 1950 and lived at Mulu till death in 1972.

SANDFORD, Christine née Lush CBE, elder sister of MAURICE LUSH. Classics degree Girton Cambridge and taught classics at Newcastle Grammar School. m. DAN SANDFORD 1918 and moved to Ethiopia with him in 1920. Like her husband became friend and counsellor to imperial family and supported HAILE SELASSIE in exile. Returned to Addis Ababa 1942 with two younger children and started school, which became SANDFORD English Community School still existing today with 700 children of 50 nationalities. After seven years handed over to son-in-law, Leslie Casbon, who was succeeded until 1994 by her daughter-in-law Pippa Sandford, whose husband Stephen is agricultural economist working in Ethiopia. CBE 1966. d. 1975.

SEYUM, Ras. b. 1887. Grandson of Emperor Johannes. Governor of Western Tigre 1910–35. Fought in Italian war then submitted and collaborated. Rejoined allies before Amba Alagi. Reappointed governor of Tigre after liberation. Gunned down in 1960 coup.

SHEPPARD, L. F. Bimbashi later Lt Col. DSO. Aged 36 in 1940. Lecturer in English poetry Cairo University. Joined NOTT at Mission 101 rear HQ and then replaced BENTINCK in Mission 101 North. Served with Patriots in Gondar region until fall of Gondar (DSO). Later joined SOE in Greece where he was killed in 1944.

SILVI, Captain Luigi. Reserve officer of engineers. Served in 1915–18 war. Civil engineeer between wars. Recalled June 1940 and commanded pontoon company on Abbai. Joined MARA-VENTANO column. POW in Kenya and on Italian armistice in 1943 built excellent tarmac road Nairobi-Nakuru with POW labour. Post war resumed civil engineering career and in his seventies was still working on Igwassu dam project in Brazil. Left '*diario*' of march of column. His daughter Rita, now Signora Rita Dinale, recently professor of Italian poetry Boston

State University, has written an entertaining account of life as a young girl in Addis Ababa (see bibliography).

SIMONDS, Major MBE now Lt Col. A. C. (Tony) OBE. Territorial commission 6th Devons then regular commission Royal Berkshire Regiment 1931. Army boxing champion. Served in intelligence Palestine 1936–39 (MBE, dispatches three times). GSO2 Middle East Command Cairo 1940. Joined Mission 101 as GSO2 1941. Commanded Mission 101 temporarily, then commanded Beghemder Force at Bahr Dar and Debra Tabor (dispatches). Joined MI9 in September 1941 and set up organization for escape of Allied POWs (OBE). Retired to Cyprus.

SLIM, W. J. (Bill). Brigadier later Field Marshal Viscount Slim GCB GCMG GBE DSO MC. Commanded 10th Indian Brigade in attack on Gallabat in November 1940 and later in advance into Eritrea when he was wounded. Later commander Fourteenth Army in Burma, CIGS, and governor-general Australia.

SMITH, Captain later Lt Col. Allen. b. 1910 Waharua New Zealand. Missionary Sudan Interior Mission Galla country 1933–35. Spoke Galla. Norwegian-Swedish Red Cross in Italian war. Awarded Swedish decoration. Taught Ethiopian refugees' children in Isiolo camp 1936–39. Adjutant 2nd Ethiopian Battalion August 1940. Sacked by WINGATE with BOYLE April 1941. Later military administration Somalia, Lt Col. Returned to New Zealand 1949 and trained as doctor intending to return to missionary work in Ethiopia but died of heart attack 1952.

STEER, G. L. (George) *The Times* correspondent in Addis Ababa at time of Italian war. In UK took part in discussions leading to HAILE SELASSIE's return and returned to Khartoum with him in July 1940 as staff officer. Formed propaganda unit, himself serving with PLATT's forces in Eritrea, his deputy, Sultan Effendi, with Gideon Force. Killed in Burma 1942. Author of *Sealed and Delivered*.

SYMES, Sir Stewart. Governor-General Sudan 1940, succeeded by General Huddleston.

THESIGER, W. P. (Wilfred). *Bimbashi* CBE DSO. b. Addis Ababa 1910. Son of British Minister Captain W. G. Thesiger DSO and grandson of Colonel Thesiger, chief of staff to General Napier and later Lord Chelmsford, commander British forces in Zulu war. Educated Eton and Oxford (boxing blue). Invited to HAILE SELASSIE's coronation 1930 and attended on Duke of Gloucester's staff. Expedition to Danakil country 1933–34. Sudán

Political Service 1935. *Bimbashi* Eastern Arab Corps SDF 1939. Served at Gallabat, then replaced Critchley in Mission 101. Served with Gideon Force and Safforce (DSO). Afterwards saw action with LRDG in Western Desert until asked for by HAILE SELASSIE to go as adviser to Crown Prince in Dessie. Found job impossible because of intrigue and joined Locust Control in Arabia. Then in Empty Quarter 1945–50 travelling journeys recorded in *Arabian Sands*. There followed seven years in Iraq recorded in *The Marsh Arabs*. Has published autobiography, *The Life of my Choice*. CBE for distinction in travel and writing.

TORELLI, Colonel Adriano. Aged about 53 in 1940. Thirty years' service, in 1914–18 war, Libya and Ethiopia. Commander 22nd Colonial Brigade in north Gojjam based on Dangila. Fought MANGASHA at Piccolo Abbai March 1940, wounded, recommended for *Medaglia d'Oro al VM*, which he was later awarded. Fought MANGASHA again in retreat from Dangila February 1941, defended Bahr Dar (again wounded). Reserve brigade at Gondar, twice went to help of Chilga garrison and ran successful convoy through to Kulkaber. An energetic, courageous and much respected commander.

TURRALL, Lieut. Guy. Royal Engineers later major DSO MC. Joined Gideon Force at Dambacha, fought at Gulit and commanded mortars at Mota and Debra Tabor (MC). In 1945 parachuted into Burma with CRITCHLEY to join Force 136 and commanded column of Karen irregulars advancing on flank of the Fourteenth Army (DSO).

TUTTON, M. W. L. (Michael). Aged 27 in 1940. 2nd lieutenant, later captain. Educated Eton (Kings Scholar) and Exeter College Oxford. Colonial Administrative Service Tanganyika. Joined 2nd Ethiopian Battalion from Intelligence Corps August 1940, commanded D company in Gojjam campaign, later adjutant. Commanded D company again in Gondar operations. d. 12 November 1941 of wounds received in attack on Gianda on 11 November 1941. A much loved officer, remembered like ROWE to this day. Fluent in Kiswahili and Italian. Among his many interests was entomology. His 1931 natural history diary dealing particularly with bumble bees is now in the Cambridge University library.

UGOLINI, Lt Col. Augusto. An infantry officer of the regular army. Commanded garrison at Kulkaber. Awarded *Medaglia d'Oro al*

VM for successful defence on 13 November 1941 and gallant but unsuccessful resistance on 21 November.

VAN DER POST, Laurens later Sir Laurens. South African. Father fought against British in Boer War. Captain Rifle Brigade. Commanded No 5 Operational Centre, the only centre not to lose any camels on the march to Belaiya. Evacuated sick from Burye.

WANDAFRASH FALAKA. Corporal 2nd Ethiopian Battalion, C company. Knocked out two armoured cars at Charaka river 6 March 1941. Served with ROWE in Safforce. Killed at Uogghidi 20 May 1941.

WERKU, Fitaurari. Gojjam patriot leader Kwara area. Much feared by Italians. Besieged Kwara and took Matabia. Killed in action 20 December 1940.

WETHERALL, H. E., Major Gen. later Lt Gen. Sir Harry. Gloucestershire Regiment. Commanded llth (African) Division in Cunningham's advance from the south. Later acting GOC East African Command August–December 1941. In command during Gondar operations.

WIENHOLT, Arnold. Second Lieutenant DSO MC. Australian cattle rancher from Queensland. b. about 1880. Mounted Scouts Boer War. Lion hunting in German South West Africa pre-1914, badly mauled. Scout in German East Africa campaign 1914–18 (DSO MC and bar). With Red Cross in Italian war and fought with rearguard. Killed near Matabia September 1940.

WINGATE, Orde Charles. Major Royal Artillery later major general DSO. b. Naini Tal India 3 March 1903 son of Colonel Wingate Indian Army. General Sir Reginald Wingate (Cousin Rex) was father's first cousin. Both parents Plymouth Brethren. Strict upbringing with intensive Bible study. Educated Charterhouse and RMA Woolwich. Service in UK then SDF 1928–33 — operations against Ethiopian poachers. Palestine 1936–38 where he commanded special night squads (DSO and wounded). Became Zionist and learned Hebrew. In UK 1939/40. Brigade major in anti-aircraft brigade, revolutionized anti-aircraft tactics, served in anti-aircraft ship during Dunkirk evacuation, produced scheme for resistance if England invaded. Sent for by Wavell in 1940, arrived Khartoum 7 November 1940. GSO2 GHQ Khartoum. Commanded Gideon Force and Mission 101 in Gojjam and Safforce in Wollo (second DSO). On return to Cairo attempted suicide July 1941. Convalesced in

UK, summoned again by Wavell in 1942 to organize guerrillas in Burma, commanded first long range penetration column (Chindit I) in 1943 (brigadier, third DSO) and Special Force (Chindit II) in 1944 (major general). Killed in aircrash 24 March 1944.

WOLDE GIORGIS. Ethiopian bureaucrat. Sent with BENTINCK as Emperor's representative on Mission 101 North but proved useless. After liberation Minister of the Pen under HAILE SELASSIE 1941–55, wielding enormous power. The British found him very difficult.

Biographical Sketch of Two Typical Patriot Soldiers

AYANA BIRE, Shambul. Aged 23 in 1940. From Armachaho. Heard of arrival of HAILE SELASSIE in Khartoum. Walked to Gedaref to see SANDFORD who sent him back with a letter to Ras Wubneh, a local leader who was some help to BENTINCK. Returned to Gedaref and enlisted in Mission 101 as bodyguard and served throughout campaign, in Gideon Force as one of KABADA's *banda*. Fought at Mankusa, Dambacha, Debra Markos and the Jibuti ambush. Fought alongside WINGATE at Mankusa and admired him enormously ('WINGATE would never run away'). Letter from under-secretary War Office confirms award to Lieut. Ayana Bire of Mission 101 of Africa Star and 1939–45 Star. Later served in HAILE SELASSIE's army.

ZAUDI HUNEGNAW, Colonel. b. Gojjam 1920. Fought aged 15 with father under Dejasmatch Wolde Mariam Bedada in Ankober in Italian war. Escaped to Kenya and was *dubas* (tribal policeman) at Isiolo camp. Enlisted in the 1st Ethiopian Battalion on abortive march to Maji, then No 2 Operational Centre and served first under Mackay and then under McLEAN at Bahr Dar, Debra Tabor, Kulkaber, Fercaber and Gondar, fighting in all actions having been on active service without leave from January to end November 1941. Helped, with several others, by McLEAN to get into officers training school and joined HAILE SELASSIE's army retiring as colonel.

Note on 1st Battalion East African Pioneers' Mutiny

The Pioneers mutinied, they said, because they had joined the army to fight for King George, not to work as labourers on airfields in the Northern Frontier District (of Kenya). When the ring leaders were tried at a court martial in Nairobi presided over by Robin Wainwright, district officer Nairobi (later Chief Commissioner Kenya), Wainwright listened to what the men had to say, dismissed all charges against them and sent them back to their unit — a sensible act of clemency, which did no harm and probably a great deal of good.

Bibliography and References

Author's Note: In the original script references were numbered in the text and there were 99 pages of chapter notes. On editorial advice there are now no references to authorities in the text and very few chapter notes. Most quotations are identified but some are not. If any reader would like an authority or quotation identified the author will be pleased to do this.

Books

English

Allen, W. E. D., *Guerrilla War in Abyssinia*, Penguin, 1943

Bates, Darrell, *The Abyssinian Difficulty*, Oxford University Press, 1979

Boustead, Col. Sir Hugh, *The Wind of the Morning*, Chatto and Windus, 1971

Casbon, Eleanor, *The Incurable Optimists: Chris and Dan Sandford of Ethiopia*, United Writers, 1993

Cheesman, Robert, *Lake Tana and the Blue Nile*, MacMillan, 1926

Churchill, Winston S., *The Second World War*, vol. 2, Cassell, 1948

Clapham, Christopher, *Transformation and Continuity in Revolutionary Ethiopia*, Cambridge University Press, 1988

Coffey, T. M., *A Lion by the Tail*, Hodder and Stoughton

Crosskill, W. E., *The Two Thousand Mile War*, Robert Hale, 1980

De Bono, Marshal Emilio, *Anno XIIII*, translated by Bernard Miall, Preface by Benito Mussolini, Cresset Press, 1937

Gilbert, Martin, *Second World War*, Wiedenfeld and Nicholson, 1989

Glover, Michael, *An Improvised War*, Leo Cooper, 1987

311

Haile Selassie, *My Life and Ethiopia's Progress 1892–1937*, translated by Professor Edward Ullendorff, Oxford University Press, 1976

Hamilton, Nigel Monty, *The Making of a General*, Hamish Hamilton, 1981

Henze, Paul B., *Ethiopian Journey*, 1976

Hodson, Arnold, *Seven Years in Southern Abyssinia*, Fisher Unwin, 1927

Lewin, Ronald, *The Chief*, Hutchison, 1980

Lush, Maurice, *A Life of Service: The Memoirs of Maurice Lush 1896–1990*, privately printed by A. J. M. Lush, London, 1992

Mansfield, Peter, *The British in Egypt*, Weidenfeld and Nicolson, 1971

Mitchell, Sir Philip, *African Afterthoughts*, Hutchison, 1954

Mockler, Anthony, *Haile Selassie's War*, Oxford University Press, 1984

Moorehead, Alan, *The Blue Nile*, Hamish Hamilton, 1962

Mosley, Leonard, *Gideon Goes to War*, A. Barker, 1955

Moyse-Bartlett, Lt Col. H., *The King's African Rifles*, Gale and Polden, 1956

Orlebar, John, *Tales of the Sudan Defence Force*, privately printed, 1986

Orpen, Neil, *Salute the Sappers: Official History of the South African Engineer Corps*, vol. VIII, *South African Forces World War II*, Sappers Association, Johannesburg

Pankhurst, Richard, *Travellers in Ethiopia*, Oxford University Press, 1965

Perham, Margery, *The Government of Ethiopia*, Faber, 1969

Pilkington, Mark, *Letters*, privately printed

Piranho, The Duke of (Dr Alberto Denti), *A Cure for Serpents*, Eland Books, 1985

Rolo, Charles, *Wingate's Raiders*, Introduction by Gen. Sir Archibald Wavell, Viking, 1944

Rooney, David, *Wingate and the Chindits: Redeeming the Balance*, Arms and Armour Press, 1994

Sabaachi, Alberto, *Ethiopia under Mussolini*

Sandford, Christine, *Ethiopia under Haile Selassie*, Dent, 1946

Schlee, Ann, *The Guns of Darkness*, MacMillan, 1973

Slatin, Rudolf C. (translated by Colonel F. R. Wingate), *Fire and Sword in the Sudan*, Arnold, 1898

Steer, G. L., *Sealed and Delivered*, Hodder and Stoughton, 1942

Sykes, Christopher, *Orde Wingate*, Collins, 1959
Thesiger, Wilfred, *Arabian Sands*, Longman, 1959
— *The Life of my Choice*, Collins, 1987
Warner, Philip, *Dervish*, Macdonald James, 1973
Welby, Captain M. S., *Twixt Sirdar and Menelik Harpers*, 1901

Amharic
Kabada Tesemma (translated in part from Amharic by Diana Spencer), *Recollections of History*, Addis Ababa, 1969

Italian
Del Boca, Angelo, *Gli Italiani in Africa Orientale: La Caduta dell'Impero*, Laterza, 1982
Dinale, Rita, *Una Ragazza Svagata e Allegra*, Galleria Pegaso Editore, Pisa, 1993
Giacchi, Antonio, *Truppe Coloniale Italiane*, private publication, Firenze, 1977
L'Italia Storica, *Conosci l'Italia*, vol 5, published by Touring Club Italiano, Milan, 1961
Ministero della Difesa Stato Maggiore Esercito, *La Guerra in Africa Orientale*, Ufficio Storico, Rome, 1952 (New edition under title *Le Operazioni in Africa Orientale*, Rome, Edit. Alberto Rovigli, 1988)

Articles and Other Documents

English
Akavia, Abram 'War Diary' WO 217/37, Public Records Office, Kew
Barton, Col. J. E. B., 'The East Africa Campaign', Public Records Office, Kew. Chapter A, 'Sudan Border', CAB 44/76, Chapter F, 'Subsidiary Operations Northern and Western Sectors', CAB 44/80, Chapter G, 'The Patriot Movement: Mission 101 Gideon Force', CAB 44/81, Chapter O, 'Final Operations Gondar', CAB 44/86
Bell, Mervyn, 'Sudan Papers', with Mervyn Bell
Bentinck, Major Count Arthur, 'Mission 101 North Despatches', WO 169/2858, Public Records Office, Kew
Biggs, Brigadier M. W. CBE, 'Gondar Papers' including 12 (A) Division Intelligence Reports, National Army Museum, London
British Medical Journal, 'Obituary F. B. Buttle' includes reference

to Wingate — Akavia Papers, *British Medical Journal*, vol. 287, 9 July 1983, held by Abram Akavia

Cheesman, Robert, 'Intelligence Reports', CAB 106/952, Public Records Office, Kew

Critchley, Capt. R. A., 'Gojjam Itinerary', also D. A. Sandford's comments on Barton history, CAB 106/935, Public Records Office, Kew

Cunningham, Lt Gen. Sir Alan, 'Official Despatch Operations in East Africa', Imperial War Museum, London

De Bunsen, Charles, 'Operations on Sudan Border', held by De Bunsen family

Downey, Syd, 'Memoirs', held by Cynthia Downey

Ethiopian Herald, Letter from Major Johannes Abdu about Wingate, 1973

Ethiopian Observer, 'The Ethiopian Patriots', vol. III, no. 5, 1959; Article by Salome Gabre Egziabu, vol. XII, 1969; 'The Ethiopian Patriots, 1936–1941', vol. XII, no. 2, 1969, British Library

Grey, Lt Col. G. S. MBE, 'Sound Recording', Imperial War Museum, London

Harris, Major W. A. B. MC, 'Guerrilla Warfare in Gojjam', WO 201/308, Public Records Office, Kew

Humphreys, Major L. F. MC, 'Account of the Battle of Chelga', Imperial War Museum, London, ref. 84/25/1

Johnson, Major T. C. DSO, 'Sound Recording', Imperial War Museum, London

Lush, Brigadier M. S.CB CBE MC Report on the Operations of OETA Mardon Papers, held by V. R. Mardon

Luyt, Sir Richard GCMG KCVO DCM, 'Gojjam Diary', held by Lady Luyt

Mardon, V. R., 'Abyssinian Papers', held by V. R. Mardon

Maxwell, Col J. L. DSO OBE, 'Journal and Letters', National Army Museum, London

Millard, J. F. OBE, 'Memoirs', held by John Millard

Molloy, Lt Col. P. G. OBE MC, 'Personal Account of the Battles of Kulkaber and Gondar', held by Peter Molloy

Nott, Brigadier D. H. DSO OBE MC, 'Diary', held by Donald Nott

Pawluk, Veronica, 'Diary and Papers of her Brother Michael Tutton', housed in Imperial War Museum, London

Platt, Lt Gen. Sir William, 'Official Despatch — Operations of East Africa Command 12 July 1941 to 8 January 1943. Supplement to *Official Gazette*, 16 July 1946'. From the private papers of Lt Col. A. W. J. Turnbull MC

Railton, Major A. S. MC, 'Report of Operations round Wolchefit and Amba Giorgis, 1948', held by Major A. S. Railton

— 'Sound Recording', Imperial War Museum, London

Sandford, Brigadier D. A. CBE DSO, 'Despatches Mission 101', WO 201/278, Public Records Office, Kew, held by Philippa Langdon

Sandford, Brigadier D. A. CBE DSO, Sandford papers in England with Philippa Langdon and in Addis Ababa with Stephen and Pippa Sandford

Sandford, Christine CBE, 'Tape recordings of D. A. Sandford's Letters to her 1939–1942', (Sandford tapes)

Shores, Christopher F. and Corrado Ricci, 'The Air War in East Africa', *Air Pictorial*, vol. 45 (1983) and vol. 46 (1984), Imperial War Museum, London

Simonds, Lt Col A. C. OBE, 'Appendix to Wingate Despatch', CAB 106/648, Public Records Office, Kew

— 'Memoirs: Pieces of War', Imperial War Museum, London

The Times, Letter from Mrs Mary Coughlan about camels, January 1988

Thesiger, W. P. CBE DSO, 'Report to OC Mission 101 on the Operations at Dangila, Piccolo Abbai and Meschenti: February 1941 by Captain W. P. Thesiger' (Sandford papers Addis Ababa)

Tutton, Captain M. W. L., 'Diary', Imperial War Museum, London

— Pawluk papers, held by Mrs Pawluk

War Diaries, Public Records Office Kew. WO 169/173 'First Ethiopian Battalion'; WO 169/2860 'Second Ethiopian Battalion'; WO 169/2861 'Third Ethiopian Battalion'; WO 169/3045 'Fourth Ethiopian Battalion; WO 169/3030 'First Battalion Nigeria Regiment'; WO 169/3072 'Second Battalion Nigeria Regiment'; WO 169/2845 'Third/Fourteenth Punjabi Regiment'

War Journal, 'Fifth (Kenya) Battalion KAR', author's copy

Wetherall, Lt Gen. Sir Harry, 'Official Despatch on Operations', East Africa Imperial War Museum, London

Wingate, Major Gen. Orde DSO, 'Despatch on Gojjam Operations of Gideon Force', CAB 106/648, Public Records Office, Kew

Yohannes Berhane, Ato, 'A Review of the Gojjam Patriots', Institute of Ethiopian Studies, Addis Ababa University

Italian

Bauer, Col., 'Guido Indice dei Diarii Storici', Ufficio Storico, Rome Cap 1528/41. Report of Col. Guido Bauer, 'Commissario del Gojjam Meridionale', Naples, 1953

Braca, Gen. Giovanni. Estratto di Studii Storici Militari, 1986, Roma, 1987, 'Il Gruppo Bande di Confine nell "Operazioni dell" Amara', Gen. Giovanni Braca

— Report to Col. Rossi on relief of Kwara 23 February 1941, 'Diarii Storici', Ufficio Storico, Rome, Cap 1524/26

Celi, Capit. Giovanni, 'Relazione del Capitano Giovanni Celi del 1 Gruppo CCNN sulle resistenza del presidio di Culcuaber', Diarii Storici, Ufficio Storico, Rome, Cap 1529/13

Goglia, Prof. Luigi, 'Un Aspetto dell'azione politica Italiana durante la campagna d'Etiopia 1935–36: La missione del Senatore Jacobo Gasperini nell'Amhara', Estratto da 'Storie contemporanee anno 1977', Societa editorica il Mulino Bologna

Maraventano, Gen. Saverio, 'Diario della Colonna Maraventano AOI, 1941', Domodosola, 1963

— 'Relazione della Colonna Diarii Storici', Ufficio Storico, Rome, Cap 1529/7 and 8

Martini, Gen. 'La Guerra nel Amara Diarii Storici', Ufficio Storico, Rome, Cap 1529

Medaglie d'Oro al VM, Citations Prof. Luigi Goglia

Nasi, Guglielmo Gen., 'Intelligence reports', Cap 1529, Diarii Storici, Ufficio Storico, Rome

— 'Lecture to British officers at Combined School of Infantry Nakuru Kenya August 1944', English copy, Biggs papers, National Army Museum, London. Italian version, 'Diarii Storici', Ufficio Storico, Rome, Cap 1529

— 'Report on Gojjam operations', Cap 1529, Diarii Storici, Ufficio Storico, Rome

— 'Report on surrender of Debra Tabor', Cap 1529, Diarii Storici, Ufficio Storico, Rome

— 'Report on Wolchefit operations', Cap 1529, Diarii Storici, Ufficio Storico, Rome

Rossini, Gastone, 'I nostri ascari 1885–1941'

— 'Il Lawrence d'Etiopia — Orde Wingate', Verona, 1971

Silvi, Capit. Luigi, 'Diario', from personal papers of Signora (Professoressa) Rita Dinale – nata Silvi

Ugolini, Col. Augusto, 'Relazione sulla caduta del caposaldo di

Culquaber', Mombasa, 21 February 1942, Diarii Storici, Ufficio Storico, Rome, Cap 1529/9
Verbali di Interrogazioni di militari fugiti – Debra Tabor, 'Diarii Storici', Ufficio Storico, Rome, Cap 1529/9

French
Houerou, Fabienne le, 'Une tentative d'interpretation de l'administration coloniale fasciste en Ethiopie (1936–1941) à travers la politique du marechal Graziani avec les dignitaires de l'Empire ethiopien', Eleventh Conference of Ethiopian Studies, Addis Ababa, 1991

Personal Interviews and/or Correspondence

British and Commonwealth
Acland, Brig. P. B. E. OBE MC
Akavia, Abram
Bell, Mervyn
Biggs, Brig. M. W. CBE,
Blundell, Sir Michael KBE
Body, E. M.
Burke, Mrs Grace
Campbell, Col. Sir Guy Bart
OBE MC
Critchley, Lt Col. R. A. DSO MC
Dillon, Major Brian MBE
Dodds-Parker, Col. Sir Arthur
KCB
Downey, Mrs Cynthia
Grey, Lt Col. G. S. MBE
Harris, Lt Col. W. A. B. MC
Hayes, Peter
Holcombe, John C. TD
Johnson, T. C. DSO
Lush, Brig. M. S. CB CBE MC
Luyt, Sir Richard GCMG KCVO
DCM
McLean, Lt Col. Neil DSO
Millard, J. F. OBE
Molloy, Lt Col. P. G. OBE MC

Nott, Brig. D. H. DSO OBE MC
Pankhurst, Dr Richard
Railton, A. S. MC
Riley, J. C.
Ringrose, Lt Col. B. H. DSO
Stockden, Lt Col W. J. OBE
Swynnerton, Sir Roger CMG
OBE MC
Thesiger, Wilfred CBE DSO
Turnbull, Lt Col. A. W. J. MC
Turnbull, Sir Richard KCMG
Wainwright, R. E. CMG

Ethiopian
Alemaiyu Hailu, Shalaka
Asefa Saifu, Commander
Ayana Bire, Shambul
Desta, Col. T. M.
Enko Haile Mariam, Col.
Gitacho Kassa Gaaga
Jemmere Wolde Admassu
Kassa Kebede
Nega Selassie, Lt Gen.
Skhael Alemaiyu, Kenyasmatch
Tsehai Berhane Selassie Dr
Wudineh Lodi
Zaudi Hunegnaw, Col.

Italian

Barberis, Gen. Raimondo
Bastiani, Gen. Sante Angelo
Braca, Gen. Giovanni
Butera Prof. Michele
Camorani, Col. Augusto
Casto, Brig Gen. Alberto
Chiarini, Giuseppe
Cicolella, Gen. Vittorio
Dinale, Professoressa Rita (nata
  Silvi)
Druetto, Giuseppe

Gallia, Capit. Giuseppe
Gonella-Pacchiotti, Gen. Enrico
Guillet, Col. Barone Amedeo
Malara, Gen. Giovanni
Malfredini, Bortolo
Maraventano, Dr Vanni
Raho, Salvatore
Rossini, Magg. Gastone
Valeri, Rolando
Vallisneri, Gen. Giovanni
  Battista

Index